R37/5

CA

Urban development and urban renewal

An edited selection of papers presented at the
Fifth World Congress of Engineers and Architects in Israel,
convened by the International Technical Cooperation Centre
(ITCC) and the Association of Engineers and Architects
in Israel in December 1979

Editor: Dan Soen, PhD
Associate Professor, School of Social Work
Bar Ilan University

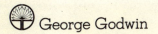 George Godwin

© Conference Associates, 1981

First published 1981 by
George Godwin Limited
The book publishing subsidiary
of The Builder Group
1–3 Pemberton Row
Red Lion Court
Fleet Street
London EC4P 4HL

British Library Cataloguing in Publication Data

World Congress of Engineers and Architects in Israel
(*5th: 1979: Israel*)

Urban development and urban renewal.
  (International forum series)
  1. Urban renewal – Congresses
  I. Title   II. Soen, Dan   III. International Technical
  Cooperation Centre IV.   Association of Engineers
  and Architects in Israel
  307.76   HT170

ISBN 0-7114-5728-X

Printed and bound in Great Britain at
The Pitman Press, Bath

Contents

The Contributors

□ Professor Alexander Berler is on the staff of the Settlement Study Centre, Rehovot and Haifa University, Israel.

□ Enrique Browne is an author on housing matters and a former consultant to the United Nations and the Organisation of American States.

□ Dr Naomi Carmon is a member of the Faculty of Social Sciences, Tel Aviv University, Israel.

□ Louis A. Dernoi is a consulting urbanologist in Ottawa, Canada.

□ Professor Elisha Efrat is Head of the Department of Geography, Tel Aviv University, Israel.

□ Dr Hans Esping is with the Secretariat for Futures Studies, Stockholm, Sweden.

□ M. Gluskinos is on the staff of the Institute of Urban Studies, Ramat Gan, Israel.

□ David Guggenheim , co-author of Paper 24, is a Jerusalem architect.

□ Jean-Elie Hamesse is a Belgian architect and planner and Assistant Professor in the Department of Architecture at the University of Braunsehweig, Germany.

□ Dr Gerd Hennings is on the staff of the Institute of Urban and Regional Planning, University of Dortmund, Germany.

□ Dr Dilys M. Hill is a senior lecturer at the University of Southampton, England.

□ Professor Moshe Hill is in the Faculty of Architecture and Town Planning at the Technion, Haifa, Israel.

□ Professor Michael Hugo-Brunt is Head of the School of Architecture, University of Western Australia.

□ Bernd Jenssen, co-author of Paper 6, is on the staff of the Institute of Urban and Regional Planning, University of Dortmund, Germany.

□ Desmond Kaplan is a lecturer at the Institute for Urban Studies, Rand Afrikaans University, Johannesburg, South Africa.

□ Louis Karol is an architect in private practice in Cape Town, South Africa, and chairman of the editorial board of Architecture SA.

□ Michael Kuhn is on the staff of the San Luis Obispo School of Architecture and Environmental Design, California Polytechnic State University, United States of America.

□ Leon Kumove is President of Leon Kumove Social Planning Ltd, Don Mills, Ontario, Canada.

□ Alexander B. Leman is President of the Leman Group Ltd, Toronto, Canada.

□ Herbert S. Levinson is on the staff of Jake University and is a Fellow of the Institute of Transportation Engineers, United States of America.

□ Professor Klaus R. Lunzman, co-author of Paper 6, is Director of the Institute of Urban and Regional Planning, University of Dortmund, Germany.

□ John McNamara is with Bather Ringrose Wolshield Jarvis Gardner Inc, Minneapolis, United States of America.

□ A. Mazor is on the staff of the Institute of Urban Studies, Ramat Gan, Israel.

□ Dr Jacob O. Maos is on the staff of the Department of Geography, University of Haifa, Israel.

□ Dr P.A. Oluwande is a senior lecturer in the Department of Preventive and Social Medicine, University of Ibadan, Nigeria.

□ Rita Pasqualini is Associate Social Affairs Officer, United Nation's Centre for Human Settlements, Nairobi, Kenya.

□ J. Prushansky is a Senior Lecturer Emeritus at Jerusalem University.

□ Arie Rahamimoff is a Jerusalem architect.

□ Professor Edgar A. Rose is Head of the Department of Planning, University of Aston in Birmingham, England.

□ Professor Daniel Shefer is Chairman of the Graduate Programme in Urban and Regional Planning, Technion, Haifa, Israel.

□ Professor Dan Soen is a faculty member of the School of Social Work, Bar Ilan University, Israel.

□ Eliahu Stern is on the staff of the Ben Gurion University of the Negev, Israel.

□ E. Tollman is a senior lecturer in the School of Architecture, University of Natal, Durban, South Africa.

□ Alfred A. Wood is County Planner/Architect of the West Midlands County Council, England.

□ Gil Yaniv, co-author of Paper 24, is a Jerusalem planner.

Introduction and review paper 1

J. Prushansky   Israel

PRESENTATION SEQUENCE

The contributions in this volume are edited versions of papers presented at a session of the Fifth World Congress of Engineers and Architects held in Tel Aviv in December 1979.

They represent a wide selection of current views on one of mankind's major pursuits - that of providing and operating adequate settlements for the world's ever-growing population. The form of communal living preferred by our gregarious race is that of towns where, according to the ancient Greeks, the "good life" is to be found. The ways of attaining this desirable goal in our ever-changing world are discussed by urbanists and scientists from different parts of the world. The various aspects of this broad subject are sure to provide practitioners and enlightened readers with ample material for thought on the pressing problems of urban development and renewal.

In the following review, the contributions contained in this collection are referred to in the order of their appearance, their groupings having been determined, as far as possible, by the affinity of their main contents.

APPROACHES TO URBAN DEVELOPMENT

Some fundamental definitions and approaches to urban planning are discussed in four papers. The first, by Alexander B. Leman of Canada, points out the need to develop a generally accepted definition of the phenomenom known as "human settlements". The author proposes an expanded version of the definition given by Doxiadis which reads: "Human settlements are the territorial arrangements made by Anthropos for himself." In his fuller version, the author introduces what he calls the four-dimensional concept to replace the two-dimensional territorial one, and proposes a definition stating that "human settlements are spatial/operational arrangements made by humans within certain scales in order to support life and to pursue their operations, goals and targets". The paper discusses the various elements of the proposed broader definition, explaining why certain concepts have been selected in preference to others.

The second paper in this category is by L.A. Dernoi of Canada and proposes adding to the three-dimensional concept of planning space a fourth dimension - time. In the author's opinion, this additional dimension may produce a remedy for the worsening problems of big cities. So far, our activities have crowded us together in one mass and at the same time. Many of the resulting problems can be relieved by the adequate distribution of our activities over the time dimension. Continuous peakless exploitation is an effective answer to any type of scarcity. Time-space use intensity maps could be drawn for urban areas to show how many people use a certain area or structure and at what frequency and duration. The result should help to plan the best investments for a community, measured in terms of benefits for the maximum number of people in a given period. Innovations in time management may include staggered working times, compressed or reduce working weeks and job sharing.

The third paper, by Enrique Browne of Buenos Aires, also advocates the introduction of the time dimension in city planning. In recent times, urban development has had a basically spatial character. The persistent synchronisation of work in modern societies has increased the simultaneity of their inhabitants' activities. This has led to peaks in demand curves which, in time, have resulted in greater tendencies towards congestion. Present practices are causing increasing disuse of urban availabilities and investment returns diminish as congestion worsens. Two alternatives in temporal solutions for this problem are discussed in this paper. The first scales the "de-simultaneousisation" of urban activities. The other seeks changes in city-use modalities, leaving aside as far as possible the modality of specialised use which has characterised the planning, design and regulations in cities for the past half century.

The fourth paper under the same general heading is by Dr Rita Pasqualini of Kenya and deals with indicators in human settlement planning. The author submits that in order to reconcile environmental requirements with social, economic and functional efficiency, the performance of human settlements has to be monitored and evaluated. This requires indicators that are different from basic statistics in that they are synthetic, organised in sets and directed towards policy action. Also needed are standards which reflect society's goals and means in respect of acceptable or desirable conditions in the present or in the future. The interrelation between indicators and standards is twofold. The former point out what the present situation is, either in relation to an established standard, or as a basis for the formulation or revision of a standard. In the case of unrealistically high standards, appropriate indicators can provide a basis for more suitable standards. A methodology is set forth for the application of human settlement indicators to the formulation of standards.

PLANNING STRATEGIES

The first paper under this heading proposes planning strategies to relieve internal pressures in overgrown urban areas and to reduce the imbalance between the metropolis and the nearby rural areas. Professor Klaus R. Kunzmann of the University of Dortmund underlines the immense growth of metropolitan areas to the disadvantage of rural areas, which suffer from the lack of social and physical infrastructure that is indispensable for economic development. To remedy the situation, the author recommends two integrated strategies that may help to develop the necessary urban settlements in rural areas. The first strategy is to channel the ongoing development process in metropolitan areas to select "relief poles" in the hinterland of the metropolis. The second strategy consists of creating urban nuclei in rural areas. Such nuclei should be bound to basic need concepts, should use existing physical and human resources and should help to decrease migration into the great urban centre. The paper describes these strategies in detail and illustrates them by case studies of development areas.

Dr Dilys M. Hill of the University of Southampton argues that to be successful, development projects need both efficient administrative skills and the participation of local people. In developing countries such participation is in fact flourishing, but in underdeveloped countries the city planner is faced with numerous difficulties. These include low income levels, rapid population growth, immigration and an inadequate urban structure. In the face of these problems, participation may be regarded as irrelevant, but it will nevertheless appear in its own particular form, based on individual and group demands for concrete help and services rather than an awareness of community as such. On the contrary, development plans will fail if grass-roots support and practical involvement are not forthcoming. In the long run, administration can only achieve success through some form of local government representative institutions.

HOUSING

The constant concern of city planners with housing is reflected in the papers included in this section. The first, by Desmond Kaplan of the University of the Witwatersrand, notes that a housing market can go a long way towards achieving dweller satisfaction. The usual attitude surveys undertaken to establish people's preferences in housing do not get close to the "real world" where people make decisions on their housing. Even after having made the choice, people tend to make changes in their dwellings over time in response to changing needs. A conclusion reached by the author is that a house is not by any means an architectural one-time solution, but rather a function of many complex interactions constantly changing and adjusting. He concludes that there is a clear distinction between housing products (architectural, decorative and furnishing) and housing processes, the very life-blood of living and home making.

The factors influencing housing are also taken up in the paper by Professor Jean-Elie Hamesse, of Braunschweig, West Germany. He discusses in a generalised way the reciprocal influences of urban and rural areas. As migrations are not a one-way traffic, some influences turn back to the area of origin and some bear marks of the area of reception of the first migration system. Influences are movements of ideas and their pressures on the zone of reception. Assimilation without adaptation of external influences gives rise to local tensions, as is the case with some urban influences on village housing in rural settlements. In the usual planned development there is hardly enough flexibility for adaptation to concurrent influences. An exception, however, is the "rolling plan" which is already in use in some countries. This is a five-year plan that is revised every year for the following five years. It is thus adapted annually to the new situation. In order to arrive at a conceptual framework, factors such as the roots of the actual development, its future trends and the flexibility of its planning have to be taken into consideration.

The paper by E. Tollman of the University of Natal deals with future trends in urban housing, and refers specifically to the city of Durban. The author's aim is to identify the growth and change in the demand for urban housing. The paper comprises an analysis of the emerging trends in providing urban housing for the full spectrum of socio-economic subgroups in respect to population growth, changing aspirations, mobility patterns, land availability and legislative restraints. Durban, a city poised between the First and Third Worlds, applies a full range of housing strategies to accommodate the rapidly increasing urban population. In conclusion, the author proposes policy indicators to accommodate the emerging trends.

TRANSPORTATION

Transportation facilities and their effect on urban development are a major concern of town planners throughout the world. This is reflected in the papers included in this section.

In his paper on land use and transportation perspective, Herbert S. Levinson of Jake University looks at the twenty-first century American city in the context of current trends and public policy options. The paper also shows how various land development strategies, social programmes, transportation technologies and energy supplies will effect urban forms, lifestyles and mobility. It describes the steps needed to bring about major changes in existing development patterns and trends, and takes a look at the city twenty-five, fifty and seventy-five years from now.

In his study on public attitudes to an innovative transit system, Dr Eliahu Stern of Ben Gurion University examines the set of preferences and degree of satisfaction of consumers in respect of inter-urban bus services in the sparsely populated area of the Northern Negev. Next, the author examines public response to the characteristics of the suggested improvement plan. Preference and satisfaction profiles were built by the "paired comparison technique", based on Thurnstone's law of comparative judgment. It was found that the urban population of the Northen Negev showed preferences that differed greatly from those of the rural population. Their attitudes were influenced by the existing level of service and a negative correlation was therefore found between preference and satisfaction. Higher service frequency, shorter walking distances and higher reliability were found to be the most important factors, and this led to the notion of a regional transit system supplemented by local feeder lines.

URBAN DEVELOPMENT IN ISRAEL

Since the congress was held in Israel, particular attention was given to the host country's urban development problems. Michael Kuhn, an architect, attempts to look anew at well-known phenomena in order to arrive at new hypotheses, conceptions and goals. This attempt is based on the assumption that all the settlements, open spaces and general services in the coastal plain of Israel constitute a unified and continuous sytem with a holistic character, while the towns and cities on the mountain watershed remain discrete and specialised. This evalution of the actual situation runs counter to the currently accepted policy of population dispersal over the entire territory of the state. It also leads to a new evaluation of the existing rural settlements as urbanised communities. They are not towns in the accepted sense, because they have completely different physical forms and ways of life. They present a kaleidoscope of communities with decreasing personal autonomy and increasing collective autonomy.

A more comprehensive approach to Israel's planning needs is proposed by Professor Elisha Efrat in his paper on the country's future development. In envisaging the long-term physical planning of state territory, the author examines the effects of political and technological assumptions and evaluates current forecasts for Israel's development. The purpose of the study is to outline the state's possible development towards the twenty-first century in four main areas, territory, population, settlements and communication in the light of developments of the past thirty years. Each of these aspects is subjected to a thorough examination and, in conclusion, the author proposes a set of development priorities for the twenty-first century. These priorities take account of the country's limited natural resources and measures are suggested to cope with the constraints of these limited resources.

The paper by Jacob M. Maos, of the University of Haifa, deals with a single though important region of the country - the upland part of Galilee, whose development has been somewhat retarded, compared with the rest of the country. In addition to its difficult topography, the region faces a social and political problem in that there are only a few Jewish settlements in the area and these lack territorial continuity between them. The stated national aims of repopulating Galilee with Jewish rural and urban settlers will require considerable efforts by the country's various institutions. The prerequisites for the advancement of this beautiful but neglected mountainous region include a physical infrastructure, including easy and rapid access, industrial parks for new plants, land preparation for urban and rural housing, and the development of tourist facilities and recreational resorts.

A specific subject relating to town development in Israel is taken up in the next paper by A. Berler of the Settlement Study Centre, Rehovot. In the growth of a new town, the author states, a critical period is reached when it no longer depends on external incentives for continuous development. This transition he terms the "take-off" stage. The concept was tested on the town of Beersheba. The study included surveys of manpower and population, real estate, land uses, industry and commerce and inter-urban public transport. The surveys produced about fifty series of variables for all spheres of urban activity. The "take-off" process in Beersheba received considerable stimulus in the mid-1960s, when external incentives were halted. At that time the transition began in Beersheba from rapid to more moderate growth, and a stable urban structure evolved. In this sense Beersheba differs from many development towns suffering from demographic and economic stagnation.

□ The remaining contributions in this volume deal with urban renewal as a remedy for the deterioration of neighbourhoods and formerly adequate urban centres. In these papers the problems involved are considered from various viewpoints, including historical, social, economic and architectural.

NEIGHBOURHOOD DETERIORATION AND REVITALISATION

In diagnosing the widespread affliction of neighbourhood deterioration, Professor D. Shefer of the Technion finds that such decline begins at a stage when a mature stable neighbourhood is no longer capable of generating the capital investment needed for the operation and replacement of existing assets. The physical appearance of structures begins to show signs of obsolescence and deterioration, soon reflected in socio-economic characteristics. As new residential suburbs develop owing to the locational preference of resident, the competitive qualities of older neighbourhoods are further diminished and their deterioration accelerates. Remedies for the deterioration process must be adapted to the unique circumstances of a particular neighbourhood and its relation to the urban structure in general. When this target neighbourhood is surrounded by well-kept urban areas, the externalities generated by them could contribute to the success of the programme.

In their systematic study of the same subject, Morris Hill and Naomi Carmon present a well-organised statement of the major aspects in their joint paper. They see the causes of neighbourhood decline in the influx of immigrants from underdeveloped countries in the large stock of minimal standard temporary housing and the general rise in the country's standard of living that renders previously acceptable accommodation substandard. Another cause is neglect by the public authorities of the older towns and their preferential treatment of new towns. Among the social aspects of neighbourhood deterioration is the inevitable negative selection of residents in less attractive locations. The purposes of current rehabilitation projects are seen as social - decreasing the gap between the have's and the have-not's; political - paying the debt owed by the government to its supporters; and national - providing a common goal for Jewish communities abroad. The guiding principle of urban renewal is stated by the authors to be rehabilitation rather than relocation. Development should encompass both the social and physical aspects of each neighbourhood and the inhabitants should be involved in the programme.

Such involvement is discussed in detail by Professor Dan Soen in his paper on citizen participation in urban renewal projects, illustrated by the case study of a residential quarter in Israel. Though newly constructed, the quarter began to show signs of physical and social deterioration, owing to lack of maintenance, individual alienation, appearance of street gangs and other evils. The remedy involved the planning of a community centre in which active participation of the residents was systematically enlisted, with manifestly good results. The community workers adopted the so-called Charette technique for involving the residents. A group of twenty-five persons was elected from among the residents to serve as steering committee for the project. The result was an adequately designed community centre, planned by specialists in consultation with the residents. Since its completion, the centre has become the main focus of local community life and has stimulated participation by the quarter's residents in local community life in general.

INSTITUTIONAL RENEWAL

Another aspect of revitalising the inner areas of towns is discussed by Professor Edgar A. Rose of the University of Aston in Birmingham, who considered the efforts of local authorities in Britain to increase employment opportunities in the older parts of urban areas. Policies and proposals are not easily translated into practical programmes. The author explores the conceptual and practical difficulties, with special reference to the findings of two research projects on local employment initiatives sponsored by the Social Science Research Council and the Department of the Environment and co-directed by the author. He concludes that there may be generic processes of change and choice that are valid across national boundaries and therefore deserve the attention of researchers and practitioners in planning and related fields.

A more specific subject involved in urban renewal is discussed by P.A. Oluwande of the University of Ibadan, Nigeria. His paper relates to the sanitary problems of some developing countries in Asia and Africa, arising from a lack of adequate drinking water, insanitary methods for the disposal of human waste, and poor housing. These problems are particularly acute in slum areas where the majority of urban dwellers in developing countries are found. Some such slums are located in the old cores of cities. The removal of slum dwellers in groups to new areas provided with the necessary amenities will succeed only if commercial firms taking up the vacated land can be made to participate and cover the resettlement costs. In this regard, the elimination of open drains and their replacement by sewers is a vital necessity. Where no flush toilets are possible owing to a lack of water, the aqua privy is recommended.

OVERALL CITY REJUVENATION

The renewal and revitalisation of the city of Tel Aviv is taken up in the paper by A. Mazor and M. Gluskinos who state that the city has been affected by processes common to many metropolitan centres. Tel Aviv has experienced an invasion of its residential areas by business and commercial activities, together with a decline in environmental quality, out-migration, and deterioration of public services, housing stock and the socio-demographic composition of its population. This paper describes the methodologies developed in the preparation of a master plan for the renewal of the city. By their application it was possible to identify for each zone of the city the major areas where change would increase residential attraction and improve the migration balance. The findings provide a framework for all planning and renewal activities in Tel Aviv.

A more general and historical view of city decay and revival is given by Alfred A. Wood, a British town planner, in his comprehensive paper on city renaissance. The peripheral spread of cities following the industrial revolution has led to the neglect of the inner core of cities, strikingly exemplified in the city of Detroit. Generally, suburbs sprang up in surrounding areas, complete with shopping centres, office blocks, hospitals and universities - all to the detriment of the cities. Not least, this caused a substantial increase in motor traffic choking old city streets. According to the author, one of the remedies is permitting car access no further than the periphery of central areas and turning streets into pedestrian-ways complete with recreational facilites. The paper discusses various public projects now being undertaken in Britain and elsewhere to improve the economy, environment and transport infrastructure of the central areas of the old cities. In these projects, personal social services are particularly important since the greatest single problem to be tackled is low incomes.

[A late contribution to this section comes from architects and planners Arie Rahamimoff, David Guggenheim and Gil Yaniv and discusses planning considerations in the renewal of Ramla Old City, which dates from the eighth century.]

SMALL-SCALE RENEWAL PROJECTS

The effectiveness of public projects is considered in greater detail by John McNamara in his paper relating to the United States where a shift is now experienced from the large-scale urban renewal efforts of the 1950s and 1960s to smaller neighbourhood-based revitalisation projects. Opposed to total demolition and redevelopment, the author stresses the efficacy of neighbourhood planning and development in which the neighbourhood association exercises control over the project and budget while the public agencies serve as instruments of implementation. The purpose of neighbourhood revitalisation is defined by the author as the design of a functional and secure urban environment which provides convenient goods and services to its residents and promotes healthy interaction among its members, building a strong sense of "community".

The preservation of old buildings, now often found desirable in the renewal of city cores, is discussed by Louis Karol in his paper on the adaptive use of buildings. Though often costly, adaptation can even be done in such a way that some of the existing tenants remain in the building while the alterations are proceeding. Mass demolition is no longer favoured and the new tendency of in-town living, prompted by the energy crisis, promotes the adaptation of structurally sound old buildings to new uses. In embarking on an adaptive use project special emphasis should be placed on technical and economic evaluation by an adequate professional team. The architectural and historical value of the building to be adapted should be thoroughly researched.

In Australia, urban renewal is less pronounced than in other countries, as argued by Professor Hugo-Brunt in his paper, which is mainly concerned with Perth. Renewal activities are aimed at the introduction of new types of structures and the development of city centres, rather than improving or replacing older buildings. In Perth, the development of the city centre and the construction of major shopping areas and institutional complexes are representative examples of urban renewal, though rehabilitation of existing housing is also pursued. In order to revitalise the central area that "dies" over the weekend, some planners want residential accommodation reintroduced in the core, particularly for pensioners and young people.

SOCIAL PLANNING

The social aspects of planning are taken up by Leon Kumove, who considers in broad theoretical terms what he terms "social impact planning" to meet the future. The author submits that such planning provides the objectives, policies and programmes which enable a social unit to cope with the effects of major social, economic, technological and physical change upon its structures and functions. Social impact planning is designed to use the opportunities that development offers, to avoid unbalanced social change and to deal with problems resulting from development. The effectiveness of such planning will depend on the manner in which the social unit deals with the impacts while it continues to identify with the central institutions and symbols of society.

In another paper on social planning, Dr Hans Esping points to the insufficiency of available resources in most industrialised countries to meet public ambitions. The need for reallocation of priorities has aroused much interest and has found expression in some reform in the government system of "social programmes". Through the analysis of a specific social programme in Sweden, the programme for the care of the elderly, the author arrives at the conclusion that it is possible to identify a number of situations where informed analytical judgments could improve the programme or even resolve the current deadlock. A simple pilot scheme can be devised.

I: APPROACHES TO URBAN DEVELOPMENT

Human settlements: the second definition

2

Alexander B. Leman   Canada

There is an urgent need to develop a generally if not universally accepted definition of the term human settlements in order to avoid an increasingly dangerous confusion of major proportions. The term human settlements has come to denote a very complex, all-inclusive concept which until recently has been referred to by such partial and marginally useful terms as cities, urbanisation, housing, cities and towns; and which is being studied in a number of new disciplines such as planning, urban and regional science and urban sociology, to mention but a few.

When looked into more carefully, the most commonly used term, city, denotes different things to different people, depending on their field of interest or what affects them most in a given situation. When asked to define "city" using one key word and to identify its major problem and solution, architects reply "the city is buildings"; the problem is "bad buildings"; the solution is "beautiful buildings". Similarly, a transportation expert will respond with "traffic"; "traffic tie-ups"; "new expressways" (or "public transit", as of late). A sociologist tells of "poverty"; "low income"; and "higher welfare assistance"; and a politician of "municipal government"; "inadequate tax base" and "more money from the central government". The city is, of course, all those things, but all those things do not make a city. Nor is "city" an adequate term to define human settlements, because it leaves out such settlements as towns, villages, neighbourhoods and hamlets, as well as metropolises, conurbations and others.

It seems clear, therefore, that there is a need for a definition of the term human settlements that will represent a general and a wide consensus among the many disciplines concerned with the various aspects of human settlements and human settlements as a whole. There has been far too much confusion in this area ever since humans realised that within the natural environment they have evolved a new recognisable phenomenon, a certain man-made environment, the shape, immensity, complexity and impact of which are just being recognised. Yet, the phenomenon itself is still neither defined nor understood. This confusion mounted during the past few decades in the course of which increasing stresses caused new imbalances, leading to partial responses. In turn, this produced further imbalances, thus compounding the confusion that has lately led to a state of apathy and helplessness.

Eventually, concerned govenments convened a world gathering to face up to the problems and consider some of the issues. Fortunately, the United Nations Conference on Human Settlements, held in Vancouver in 1976, by its very name gave global recognition to the holistic concept of human settlements which up to that point - except in the works of C.A. Doxiadis and those who collaborated with him - was being thoroughly confused with the partial and marginally useful concepts discussed in the opening paragraphs. Doxiadis published the first definition in 1976 in his book entitled Action for human settlements, one of four volumes prepared specifically for the UN conference. Yet, the United Nations held this conference, in which 132 governmental delegations participated, without a definition of the term which was the subject of the gathering itself.

It is difficult to see how, in order to follow up the recommendations of the United Nations conference in Vancouver, the various governments can now proceed with the development of national policies on human settlements, or engage in international cooperation programmes without a clear, widely accepted definition, and without a consensus on what human settlements are in the first place. If every national government or concerned institution were to evolve its own definition of human settlements, confusion akin to building the Tower of Babel would ensue. In order to avoid such waste and bring about a certain degree of international consensus on the meaning of the term human settlements, the following definition and discussion are offered.

Let us first look at Doxiadis's definition, stated as follows: "Human settlements are the territorial arrangements made by Anthropos for himself."[1] The advantage of first definitions is that, in what until then was an amorphous, dimensionless and concept-less area, a line is suddenly drawn, a water-mark appears, denoting the current level of understanding of a given phenomenon which can be effectively considered by a wide number of persons only from that point on. Moreover, first definitions offer the first opportunity for testing and evaluating the appropriateness of the "inclusions" and "exclusions" effected in developing the definition.

Having subjected the first definition of Doxiadis to such a test and evaluation, I propose the following second definition: Human settlements are spatial/operational arrangements made by humans within certain scales in order to support life and to pursue their aspirations, goals and targets.

SPATIAL/OPERATIONAL ARRANGEMENTS

When Doxiadis states that "human settlements are territorial arrangements", this is of course correct; they are. But human settlements are not only territorial arrangements; they are also spatial/operational. "Territorial arrangements" tends to limit the definition in several ways, while "spatial/operational" includes all aspects pertinent to human settlements.

"Territorial" is two-dimensional; it is a geographic concept which essentially refers to surface rather than space, and may have been borrowed from the work developed by zoologists in studying territorial claims made by birds and animals. While concern with territoriality may be in order in analysing the geographic distribution of "ground" animals, it is neither precise nor useful in dealing with humans whose nesting and movements - somewhat like those of birds - are spatial rather than surface arrangements.

"Territorial" also tends to refer to the surface, to which the spatial/operational arrangements are usually projected and from which they arise into the four-dimensional domain. The surface itself may not necessarily be flat and purely two-dimensional. In the case of larger settlements it may undulate over the hills and even mountains. Nevertheless, a term such as "territorial" limits the reference to surface rather than space. Because it is difficult to draw lines in space, spatial/operational arrangements have been delineated on the ground surface by fences, walls, rivers and fortifications, but claims were rigorously maintained on a spatial basis.

While certainly territorial, human arrangements have from the earliest times also been spatial, i.e. moving beyond a two-dimensional surface distribution. To this the caves on the islands of Crete and Sicily in the Mediterranean, the Göreme caves and the two and three-storeyed buildings of Pompeii all bear witness. Spatial concern (i.e. four rather than two-dimensional) in making such arrangements is evident in claims made by individuals, institutions and even nations which extend into space well above their territory.

Individuals and corporations accept others in spaces below and above them, but only on clearly defined terms such as "leased space" arrangements in a multi-storey building, or through a rather complex condominium agreement, in which case the agreements give both sides the practically uncontested control of their own space. Institutions such as the New York Central Railway Company and the Toronto Transit Commission lease the air rights above the territory controlled by them for their rail lines precisely because there is a general assumption implied in legisliation that arrangements for the control of the surface are merely expressions of spatial/operational arrangements. It is because the spatial arrangement was violated that the USSR shot down the American U-2 plane flying over Soviet territory. Transgressions into sovereign space are often charged by neighbouring but unfriendly states. The USA and the USSR are tolerating each other's space satellites in "their space" only because they cannot yet destroy them, not because they are abandoning claims to spatial arrangements.

The term "territorial arrangements" also seems to limit the definition to static and physical concern with things, with parts, as the science of anatomy is concerned with physical parts of the human body. In fact, whether territorial or spatial arrangement concepts are used in the definition, the problem inevitably arises that one seems concerned with the physical, to the exclusion of all else. This possibly stems from the earliest notions of planning which were based solely on physical planning, which is concerned with things and parts rather than the interactions between things and parts, i.e. the functions and operations (as is the science of physiology).

That humans have spatial/operational perceptions of themselves is shown in the work of Edward T. Hall[2] who observed human behaviour and movements and analysed them in the light of the individual's attitude toward personal space, i.e. the "human bubble".

Still, when one speaks of spatiality, not only does one not refer to a two-dimensional defined area, but one is not confined to a three-dimensional order either. We often speak of "space" in terms of a space in time between events and, significantly here, it is precisely the four-dimensional space/time order which is that "primordial reality which has no qualities beyond the spatial and temporal and from which further qualities and higher levels of existence eventually emerge".[3]

Moreover, the term spatial also points to an essential "spatialising activity of man", basic to the two-dimensional concept of territory or physical, geographic space. An example may be useful here - a comparison between one's closeness to a friend approaching on the sidewalk, and the sidewalk itself. Physically speaking, the sidewalk is closer than the friend, yet one feels no closeness to or awareness of the sidewalk itself. The point is that the "spaces" established in our everyday dealings and concerns are often primordial to the abstract space of physical objects; and that man as a "spatialising being" himself assigns meanings to objects of concern in the world about him, thereby establishing what is near or far, what is significant and what is not. This brings us to the operational component of our definition.

The term operational is an essential component of the interlocking and integrative concept because it denotes the practical, non-static, continuously changing aspects of the spatial arrangements made by humans which, importantly, are not nonsensical, however wrong they may seem or may in fact be at times, but purposeful operational arrangements made to accomplish and attain something. In this definition, quite deliberately, the term spatial and operational are interlocked into one integrative concept, as they are mutually supportive. The term "functional" was deliberately not used as it implies primarily the efficient and the utilitarian. Similarly, the term "activities" was rejected as it tends to relate primarily to physical actions and movements.

The practical necessity of the terms spatial and operation being combined into one integrative concept is best demonstrated by considering the purely three-dimensional spatial arrangements that do not take into account such aspects as the sense of security, the noise, the visual exposure or the privacy, the smells and odours among separate spaces. In such cases, concern with three-dimensional spatial arrangements only is quite clearly inadequate, as demonstrated by the high-rise apartment buildings and the typical suburban housing development.

MADE BY HUMANS

This part of the definition has many important ramifications, particularly in relation to our responsibilities towards human settlements and our programmes of action to solve their problems. Because human settlements are made by humans, it is clear that there can be no settlement unless there are humans to make them. This causal relationship between humans and their settlements has provided the platform for various critics of "urbanisation" who have denied the right to make their settlements to those who, in their view, are not acting in the best interests of all. Thus, in some societies, governments have reacted against squatters' shanty towns and favellas with some vigour, including forceful and wholesale demolition, while in others activists have brought vast building programmes of governments and industry to a virtual standstill. In both cases, the motives are the same: one group of humans does not accept the spatial/operational arrangements made by other humans.

While critical of the blunders made by humans, Margaret Mead in her 1975 keynote address to North American planners in Vancouver defends the right of humans to act and build their settlements: "We must stop this nonsense of admiring the bees building their beehives, the birds building their nests or the beavers building their dams - as a perfectly natural activity, yet blaming and criticising humans at every step in their attempts to do what is perfectly natural for them - build for themselves. What we must criticise is what humans do and how they do it, not the fact that they do it."[4] This natural tendency of humans to build for themselves is sometimes confused with a notion that settlements are therefore a biological phenomenon. Except in the broadest possible sense, where it could be argued that anything that happens in the universe is natural, human settlements are not a natural phenomenon because they only come into being when made by humans, through actions willed by Anthropos, rather than through the evolution of natural systems.

Two important qualifications must be stressed here: human settlements do have many similarities with natural biological entities; and human settlements do interact with the natural systems (ecosystems) within which they are made and within whose constraints they must operate. C.A. Doxiadis has often enough made the point of similarites. Settlements, like biological entities, can be born, can grow, can have personalities and character - like a Spanish village, a New England town or the Bombay metropolis - can become sick and, if neglected, can wither and die. But the distinction between similarities and substantive sameness is profound. C.H. Waddington[5] and Jonas Salk have on numerous occasions discussed the similarities and analogies between human settlements and biological organisms but, like Doxiadis, have frequently warned against carrying the analogies too far and have, of course, never equated the two.

That does not permit us, however, to treat human settlements as independent of nature and natural systems. Every settlement, as it is being made by humans, represents an intervention in natural systems. In recent years we have come to realise that we are intervening on a scale and at an order of magnitude that calls for much more understanding of the consequences of our actions and a great deal of care in what we do, what we do not do, and what we undo.

This bring us to some quite important ramifications arising from the "made by humans" part of the definition. From the foregoing, it should be clear that the responsibility for what is made with and within human settlements (made including what is decided and what is acted upon, what is not made as well as what is unmade) does not rest with some mystical laws of the inevitability of the evolution of settlements as a biological entity, but with humans. This point has yet to penetrate the human consciousness, particularly in times such as the present where alienation between groups of people and remoteness from the decision-making process by vast numbers of people blur this line of responsibility.

Finally, this part of the definition explains some of the very important traits of human settlements. First, "made by humans" means that settlements are never and can never be perfect or ideal because humans are neither perfect nor ideal. This should help us understand why none of the "ideal" cities ever turned out that way. Second, settlements are made by humans not by a human. Without belittling the important contributions made by thousands of individuals, it must be remembered that human settlements are never made by an individual, even if his name is Haussmann, le Corbusier or Lucio da Costa, but always by a vast number of humans whose efforts and contributions span generations.

Little wonder then that recent urban history is full of instances where the "masterplanning" of human settlements, the daydreams of one, turned into the nightmares of the multitudes, for some time at least.

WITHIN CERTAIN SCALES

There is no phenomenon that can be fully understood unless it is properly defined in terms of its scales. Accordingly, human settlements must also be defined in terms of time/space scales. No settlement is made in or for an instant, but over and for a period of time. That this is so is considered to be axiomatic but time as a factor in the evolution of human settlements is not always understood. A great deal of conceptual research has yet to be done in relating time and human settlements, much of it well beyond the simplistic conservation of the past heritage or devising the master plans for the future. This is particularly important in order better to understand the spatial/operational arrangements portion of this definition.

Similarly, the space scales of human settlements must be defined and understood if settlements are to be understood. In this area, too, there is considerable confusion because it is not generally understood that a city is smaller than a metropolis but larger than a town, yet this type of distinction is quite important. Space scales can best be determined by first bracketing the lower and the upper limits and then finding a reliable and meaningful system of progression from one end to the other. Human settlements evolved from smaller ones to the larger ones we have today, and it is useful first to examine the lower end of the scale with which we are more familiar.

At first, village, hamlet and house appear to be the smallest-scale settlements, but on closer examination it appears that the smallest identifiable human settlement is the "personal space" occupied by one person,[6] be that a tent, a log cabin or a Bedouin's tent-like robe which also serves as his shelter. For the purposes of defining human settlements, anything smaller, anything that would not accommodate a human is irrelevant. Of course, there are still smaller spaces, objects and artifacts vital to human settlements' existence and operations, but they do not, as such, constitute a settlement.

At the other end of the scale, at the conceptual and the theoretical level, the largest human settlement so far is C.A. Doxiadis's and John Pappaioannou's Ecumenopolis[7] the global system of interrelated settlements woven into one recognisable spatial/operational arrangement. While many still find it difficult to perceive or accept this scale, there are a number of signs that such ecumenopolitan systems are very much in the making.[8] The two world wars were consequences of friction arising between two or three near-global spatial/operational arrangements dating back to fifteenth and sixteenth century concepts and to the systems spurred by such concepts. On a more positive side, the global (ecumenopolitan) network of air carriers connecting all nations in the world for the movement of goods, people, and ideas is another manifestation of concepts and forces which are building Ecumenopolis despite differences in race, colour, religion or politics and despite setbacks from time to time.

An American Express credit card is the first ecumenic/economic "citizenship certificate" for those who live and work at the international scale. With such a certificate an individual can maintain his existence and provide for his basic needs or even luxuries. Multinational corporations, socialist international Third World countries and the World Bank are other types of building blocks of ecumenopolitan systems. Going beyond the ecumenopolitan scale at present is not very useful. Although man has set foot on the moon, has lived and operated in a space capsule for prolonged periods of time, and "space colonies" are being seriously discussed, efforts are so marginal that they can be ignored for the time being.

It should be pointed out that at both ends of the scale there are vastly smaller and vastly larger systems without which no human settlement could exist. The solar system and the hydrogen atom system are but two examples. There are no human settlements at those scales, however. Internally, between the lower and the upper limits of the scale within which we find human settlements, C.A. Doxiadis has developed a useful and not yet successfully challenged system of logarithimic scales, covering fifteen ekistic units of human settlements (Figure 1).[7]

IN ORDER TO SUPPORT LIFE

This part of the definition bring us to the question: why human settlements? What is their purpose, and why do humans so feverishly endeavour to rebuild them after a disaster strikes? It is useful to examine how it was at the beginning so that we can better understand the nature of our actions today.

The first human act in making a settlement was of a rather basic order. When the first tree branch was broken off and placed so as to provide a form of shelter against the cold wind during the night's rest, or when that branch was placed across the cave opening, or a boulder was rolled into such a position in order to protect the occupants against wild animals, the first conscious act of building, of making a shelter, of making the primitive settlement occurred. It occurred because the humans who so acted sought shelter, i.e. protection against the elements and the enemy, both of which could bring an end to human life. Led by the primordial instinct for self-preservation and continuation of the kind, humans have been making certain spatial/operational arrangements throughout "urban" history in order to maintain and support the continuity of life. Roofs against the hot sun or cold rain; walls and doors against the cold winds or deadly animals; fences and fortifications against maurading enemies - all were made in such a way that they not only protected against elements and enemies, but also supported the continuance of life which is a primeval responsibility of all living organisms, humans included.

This brings us to the final concept which addresses the continuity of life. It not only reinforces the need for the support of life, but goes beyond and tends to explain why spatial/operational arrangements have been continuously made by humans over such long periods of history, with such devotion, persistence and single-mindedness and in the face of all adversities.

AND TO PURSUE THEIR ASPIRATIONS, GOALS AND TARGETS

Soon after they had made a few settlements of even the most primitive type, humans learned that life in settlements was safer and easier and offered more opportunities for attaining what they wanted than the life outside them. Significantly, once humans started building settlements they never abandoned the idea of building or improving them, although they did abandon a few settlements here and there.

The link between building human settlements, meaning spatial/operational arrangements, and pursuing life's aspirations, goals and targets, becomes much easier to perceive once we understand what human settlements are and why they are made. It all starts with the human instinct to support life and man's need to pursue his aspirations, goals and targets, from which arises the need to make certain spatial/operational arrangements. In part, and only to a certain degree, such spatial/operational arrangements are physically visible in the form of buildings (shells) and networks. Even today, many recognise and are concerned with only the physical manifestations of the arrangements. Some others, more alert, perceive at least partially the non-physical and address themselves to the social aspects or the socio-economic aspects, if they consider themselves really perceptive. Very few, as yet, see and understand the whole which we call human settlements.

If human settlements are what this definition says they are, it becomes easier to understand why humans have endured such continuous efforts over such long periods to make the spatial/operational arrangements required to support life and pursue their aspirations, goals and targets. It becomes easier to understand why a man will spend a lifetime building his home, why a family will desperately hold on to the "estate" or the "homestead" (often perhaps as a symbol of goals and aspirations lost) or why a civilisation will produce Oxford, or a Greek village, or New York City.

It also becomes easier to understand why, after killing most of the people, the next most effective way for a conqueror to disable the conquered is to destroy and burn to the ground their cities, towns and villages - their settlements as their total system of life. Life support and the pursuit of life's aspirations, goals and targets are so much more difficult without the properly functioning framework we now call human settlements.

I deliberately include terms such as aspirations, goals and targets in the definition. I assume that terms and concepts such as needs, wants, purposes and the like are considered to be components and, perhaps, determinants of the aspirations, goals and targets. It may be useful, however, to explain the hierarchy and the impact which the aspirations, goals and targets have upon human settlements. Aspirations are taken to mean that which is desirable, perhaps even ideal but subject to mutation and evolution through time. Most importantly, aspirations are thus usually out of reach. In fact, in the view of some, the only aspirations worth having are those that are out of reach but without which life is not worth much. Furthermore, aspirations need not be clearly defined, seen or understood. Often, they are only vaguely sensed, but nevertheless provide a powerful stimulus for action over long periods of time and over vast distances. It could be said that justice for all, the preservation of human dignity, and safety under all circumstances are some examples of such aspirations.

Goals, on the other hand, are often attainable with some work and the necessary skills and technology. A certain high rate of literacy, level of income, level of artistic achievement and, perhaps, public health or housing standards are examples of goals.

Targets, finally, are readily and frequently attainable through a combination of work, skills and technology. The number of housing starts, tons of wheat produced or numbers of public transit passengers are examples of targets.

The priority order in which various societies place their aspirations, goals and targets (versus, for example, targets, goals and aspirations) strongly determines the major characteristics of the resulting settlements, as do the contents and specifics of the aspirations, goals and targets themselves. There is one other characteristic of aspirations, goals and targets that is of great significance to the settlements: their relationship with time. Targets span a rather short time, often only a few months, seasons or a few years; goals may take decades or generations; aspirations, on the other hand, may take generations and centuries of strife to reach - and then, they change!

This brings us to the point where the second definition of human settlements can be restated as follows: Human settlements are spatial/operational arrangements made by humans within certain scales in order to support life and to pursue their aspirations, goals and targets.

There is, however, an important qualification. When it comes to definitions of such phenomena as human settlements, it is important to realise that even the term definition might be somewhat misleading. It implies a definitive, final statement of what human settlements are; yet humans are just beginning to learn and to understand what the phenomenon is all about. It is safe to assume that it will be some time yet before we can say with a reasonable degree of certainty what human settlements really are.

This definition is therefore offered not as a final statement of what human settlements are, but as one based on our current knowledge and understanding. As time goes on and better insights are gained, we might reasonably expect to develop a better understanding and a more accurate definition.

REFERENCES
[1] Doxiadis, C.A., Action for human settlements, Athens Centre for Ekistics. Also W.W. Norton, New York (forthcoming).
[2] Hall, E.T., The hidden dimension (1966), Doubleday.
[3] Webster's Third New International Dictionary, page 2180.
[4] Mead, Margaret, Keynote address to the joint meeting of American Association of Planning Officials, Community Planning Association of Canada and the Canadian Institute of Planners, Vancouver, 1975.
[5] Waddington, C.H., "Space for development", Ekistics (1971), Vol 32, No 191.
[6] Hall, E.T., The hidden dimension (1966), Doubleday.
[7] Doxiadis, C.A., and Papiouannou, J.G., Ecumenopolis (1974), Athens Centre for Ekistics. Also W.W. Norton, New York (forthcoming).
[8] Leman, A.B., and Leman, I., (eds) Great lakes megalopolis: from civilisation to ecumenisation (1976), Ministry of State for Urban Affairs, Ottawa, Canada.

Figure 1

Ekistic logarithmic scales and grid for population and area

Ekistic unit	1	2	3	4	5	6	7	8	9	10	11	12	13	14	15
Community class				I	II	III	IV	V	VI	VII	VIII	IX	X	XI	XII
Kinetic field	a	b	c	d	e	f	g	A	B	C	D	E	F	G	H
Name of unit	Anthropos	Room	House	House-group	Small neighbourhood	Neighbourhood	Small polis	Polis	Small metropolis	Metropolis	Small megalopolis	Megalopolis	Small eperopolis	Eperopolis	Ecumenopolis
Population	1	2	4	40	250	1,500	9,000	50,000	300,000	2M	14M	100M	700M	5,000M	30,000M

Dimensions   3

Louis A. Dernoi   Canada

TIME AND SPACE

As planners we are likely to agree that urbanisation occupies an eminent position in the
"ascent of man", a concept popularised by Bronowsky's TV series, shown on both sides
of the Atlantic in the mid-1970s. In a sense, the concepts of urbanisation and the ascent
of man have been inextricably tied together throughout history.

The permanent occupation and organisation of the three dimensions of space began in
primeval times. Of the one-dimensional, street-oriented string settlement we have traces
from prehistoric Egypt (Fayum Oasis, Lower Egypt, about 5000-6000 BC).[1] The principle
still surfaces in today's uncontrolled roadside development - an old format which now
causes much headache to planners and public administrators. Linear new towns such as
Ciudad Lineal, Spain, designed by Soria y Matas in 1882, did not prove much of a
success, either.

The occupation of the second spatial dimension followed the linear settlement. Remains
of towns and villages from as early as the 5000 BC have been unearthed in the Near
East revealing street systems which added depth to the primitive roadside development
e.g. the early settlements of Sumer: Ur, Uruk and Kish. Survival - some would say
degeneration - of this pattern is best demonstrated by our early suburbs composed of
spread-out subdivisions.

When cities were running short of centrally located land as a result of pressure from
centrally needed activities, invasion of the third dimension took place. Although
multi-storey structures sprang up in abundance in most ancient centres, high-rises in
today's sense (and for the same reason) appeared only in about the time of Imperial
Rome and Byzantium.[2] After that they emerged here and there throughout history,
reaching their present heights and densities as well as general diffusion in our century.
And here is "where the buck stops". Our ever-increasing space needs have pushed us
from prehistory's single street to the present highly concentrated three-dimensional
settlement. And while problems subsided temporarily with each new spatial occupation,
undesirable fall-outs (pollution, crowding, etc) became obvious limitations.

Recent peaking of three-dimensional concentrations triggered a natural space-biased
remedy worldwide: decentralisation. Regional development policies, such as the New Town
movement, the French "pôles d'équilibre", the Italian mezzogiorno, to quote a few, tried
it on a macro scale, while spontaneous suburbanisation followed by "megalopolisation" was
the answer at the micro level. Did all this help? Yes, it did, to a certain extent. Our
world cities would have been much worse off today had it not been for these efforts in
spatial decentralisation. The chief complaint about this solution is like the old adage: too
little, too late.

Present "problématique". As things now stand, we have far too many million-plus cities, either existing or about to be, together with captive urban functions within them - constituents of the emerging Ecumenopolis. Big city problems worsen and multiply fast, so that a short-term remedy is needed, and quickly. Costly and long-range spatial solutions are just that: expensive, far in the future and space-demanding, and space is a highly unrenewable resource. In view of the fact that there will be six billion Earthmen by 2000 or so, those solutions should nevertheless also be relentlessly pursued, planned and implemented. Still, the immediate practical answer lies in the next dimension ahead, time.

Western man has shown great ingenuity and organisation ability in transforming the physical environment for his needs, but up to now has failed to "manipulate" time for the same purpose. We do most of our things when crowded together, in one mass and at the same time. We work during the same hours in the same overpopulated urban niche. We take our meals in the same eateries at the same time. We all take the same weekends, mostly the same yearly vacations and crowd the same spots, arriving there by the same route and means. To service these wasteful whims, public transport agencies in Europe, for instance, have to keep valuable rolling stock in dusty depots for a whole year, to be rolled out eight times a year only - when the uniform long weekend exodus occurs or summer holidays begin - totalitarian "Gleichschaltung" (full synchronisation).

One may ask: what is the use of excelling in sterile spatial/physical planning if we are unable to follow it up with time design? The latter should by now be inseparable from land planning or, better still, precede it. The rational use of public and private investment through proper time management seems an imperative in a resource-conscious world. Continuous, peakless exploitation of capital investment and energy production is an effective and the least expensive answer to any type of scarcity. It is time to plead for a more reasonable usage of this fatally unrenewable resource in order to stop further waste of things and humans.

Man has created a valuable spatial container: the built environment, the infrastructure of human existence. The question is: how do we fill it with our activities? Its role is that of luggage - we just keep on throwing things in carelessly while we may need only two or three of them and while, with proper organisation, even the weather-beaten old piece may do the work. Today, we seem to have neither the money nor the time to get additional containers for our travel equipment. Let us organise our things (= human activities) so that they will fit on the only luggage containers we have (= our present built environment), at least for the voyage that lies immediately ahead of us (= the next decade). If we turn to this "new" dimension, time, we may find ways to pack our luggage adequately, instantly and at minimal cost.

But there is another aspect to this proposition, the human one. As the French say, "On perd sa vie à la gagner", i.e. while making a living one is losing one's life. To carry the above allegory further, today's problems go even beyond the luggage or its contents. Numerous difficulties seem to besiege the "packer". When we think of planning, designing, rearranging activities in the fourth dimension with investment or resource savings in mind, we should not forget the human price we have been and still are paying for doing so little in time management. To organise time should mean creating our freedom. Because, beyond the material/financial considerations, man's freedom as well as his opportunities, choices and energies, nerves and dignity are at stake. These, too, are valuable and costly resources and should not be mindlessly wasted as they are today. Why should life be sliced like a salami into educational, professionally active and then retirement periods? Social transfer payments from the middle part of life to the edges are pretty costly both in financial and human terms. The monotony of the daily trilogy "métro-boulot-dodo" (commute, work and sleep), and the life scale "formation-profession-démission" (education, work, abdication) should give place to fuller living. A better integration is needed in all human endeavours, instead of military-style regimentation and the boxing in of activities in sterile space-time niches.[3]

Let us open up one of the vistas of time management. Figure 1 may recapitulate the above statements and designate some eventual tasks.

Time-space use intensity maps could be drawn for urban areas in order to recognise possible areas where time management, or at least proper time and space utilisation, is actually at work or where improvements may be effected. These would show how many people use a certain are or structure, and at what frequency and duration . Maps such as these will illustrate the use of space in daily, weekly and yearly time cycles. The result will reflect the "best" investments of a community measured as benefits for the maximum number of people in a given period (or by frequency). If land and investment funds are limited, the findings of such maps could determine priorities, real estate assessment and taxes. Or, simply, they could conveniently guide planning of future/alternative use of areas, plots or structures.

The explicitly non-conventional purposeful intervention in the time dimension is relatively new. Of necessity it happened in the activity field which still is the most important time block of man's life in industrial societies - work. When we look at a daily, weekly, yearly or the life-long time scale of man, we find work-related activities occupying the largest single block in the waking part of our life pattern: about ten hours daily, five days a week, i.e. well over 200 of the year's 365 days and approximately 40-50 of the 70-75 years of total life expectation. Having acknowledged this, one may further speculate on the factors that chiefly influence man's conditions within the work activity. The first which come to mind are technology, position in the work hierarchy, management's attitude towards subordinates and particularly the personal dispensability in space and time. These have always been main determinants of employees' time schedule and their life style with it.[4]

The diagrams in Figure 2 illustrate, along these lines, workers' space and time conditions in various types of societies: feudal, high industrial and, eventually, post-industrial.

WAYS OF TIME MANAGEMENT

The distinction present-future is actually not entirely correct. Western societies are already engaged on the road leading from the "high industrial" to the "post industrial". Time management, in its radical versions, began during the 1960s, on both sides of the Atlantic. Let us briefly review what variations can be detected in "l'aménagement du temps".

Quantitative steps	Changes along traditional patterns	Innovations in time management (radical stances)
I	(Spatial decentralisation)	Staggered working time
II	Reduced working time,	Compressed or reduced work week,
	Part-time work	Job-sharing
III	Shift work type of arrangements non-seven-day work cycle	Flex-time or flexi-time
IV	Self-employment	Open work time and manner
Qualitative additions	Facilitating new time management are such work-related innovations as job enrichment, the Volvo experiment in Sweden, "Mitbestimmung" in Germany, all applicable to both patterns.	

Various combinations of the above are obviously also possible. Some are already being applied. Since these concepts and practices have become part of our daily vocabulary, no more than a few brief notes on the four main types of temporal innovations are required.

Staggered working hours. While keeping the usual eight-hour work day more or less, this system permits employees some individual choice of blocks in working time. Early start and early finish, or late start and late finish alternatives are open, with a defined obligatory core-time attendance at the work place in the middle. This system obviously helps to reduce traffic congestion and other peaks in public or other facilities. At the same time, people's life-habit preferences or needs are also catered for. Effects can be seen in the daily routine.

Compressed, reduced working week. This is a more intensive work-leisure split in the days per week dimension. The rearrangement of the basic forty or so weekly hours of work from its spread across five days to four or three, may or many not carry reduced working time with it. The 5 x 8 routine gives way to 4 x 10 or 3 x 13 hours or, more "humanely", to 4 x 9 and 3 x 12. This generalised long-weekend effect throughout the year may bring radical changes in all aspects of public and private life.

Flexible working time. This provides a wide variety of working time distributions, from daily to life-long time banking. Under this system the employee has almost complete control over his time: when he works and for how long. It may also vary from day to day, or by any other time cycle. This method permits the employee status to reach the highest levels of individualisation while retaining a distinct work place, and a greater "porosity" of life activities. This means a better integration of activities than the 8-8-8 hours regime, although the blur in content between work, leisure, education, etc may not necessarily be there. People are allowed to plan and dispose of their time budget with much the same freedom they now have in disposing of their financial and space budgets, i.e. choice in spending and land-use options. Free time may thus accumulate and be in a time bank for later use in any of the time cycles - from daily and weekly levels to sabbatical years in the life-time budget.

Open-time use. This means a maximum of self-disposal in time and location, restricted only by the nature of the activity. To a large extent, this "futuristic" state has been the prerogative of some freelance workers in some professions. Many artists, scientists, professionals and craftsmen enjoy this complete porosity in their life activities, mainly due to the individualistic nature of their engagements. Collective work, leisure or educational practices show more resistance to open-time scheduling. However, the emerging trend towards the "small is beautiful" state will greatly facilitate decentralisation of time and space.[5]

IMPACTS

The spread of more varied time schedules in western societies now seems quasi-imperative. Apart from people's desire for more autonomy in the management of their lives, the overburdening of our material stock and social institutions by present mass-society peaks, energy problems, the general crowding and congestion in urban (or resort) centres will necessitate a massive move away from "Gleichschaltung".

While the timetable and intensity of the fourth-dimensional transformation will be hard to predict, it seems likely that the planner's time of twenty to thirty years for action will from now on also have to take account of these changes and their consequences. Figures 3-5 represent some likely effects-in-principle of new time-use patterns by time-cycle. If projected directly in the physical environment, the introduction of four major new time schedules could produce different effects of varied intensity. An intuitive visual matrix (Figure 4) may reflect the consequences. (The darker the shading, the larger the foreseeable impact in that particular field.) However thoroughly and comprehensively the physical impact matrix may be applied, results will be achieved in a relatively static environment. It is rather unlikely that, while temporal innovations take place, other features of human activity (technological or social) will remain unchanged. Only complex forecasting with multiple cross-impact analysis will cope with the need and yield reliable data for planning. A sample cross-impact matrix (Figure 5) has been drawn up to stimulate discussion.

Figure 6 gives another example of possible radical changes in man's time budgeting, whether produced by abundance as viewed in the 1960s or by the scarcity projections of the 1970s. This exercise may induce us as planners to review our past assumptions and future projections about man and the environment he will need and seek in the coming decades. The first diagram of the figure represents the life perspective of the average mid-twentieth century working person in his/her activity mirror of 24 hours. The second diagram represents a radical detour, reflecting the scenario below.

SCENARIO:
ONE OF THE MANY ALTERNATIVE LIFE-CYCLES THE FUTURE MIGHT OFFER
The life of John Smith: 1985-2070
Place of birth: Chicago
Status of mother: single, aged 27

Age 1-8 years	Attended elementary school
Age 8	Travelled with a class of 15 students; visited a number of countries around the world; learned several languages and cultures
Age 10	Returned to the US and resumed formal studies
Age 15	Entered a rotating work-study programme, electing to serve as an apprentice in three fields: architecture, social research, and communications science

Age 18	Went back to formal studies in the liberal arts, and took advanced courses in architecture
Age 19	Spent three years abroad, studying comparative architecture
Age 22	Returned to the US and was employed as a draftsman. Lived for two years in an urban commune with nine other young professionals
Age 24	Moved into an apartment with three friends - two female and one male. The were all "married" to one another and all income and properties were pooled
Age 27	Divorced himself from his living arrangements and married a woman who was also divorced. She had one child, aged six. Took and passed his architectural exams
Age 35	He and his wife took two years leave from their jobs, took their fourteen-year old son and went to live on Nantucket. There, the three of them jointly developed their interests in the arts: painting, sketching and sculpting
Age 38	Divorced his wife and lived by himself
Age 50	Set up house with two career women in their mid-forties. The relationship was economic and sexual, but not exclusive. He dated other women and they dated other men
Age 60	Left his job and residence, and went to teach communications science to students in a developing country
Age 65	Returned to the US and resumed work part-time. Also went back to school part-time to update his formal education
Age 67	Remarried. His new wife had two children, both grown with children of their own
Age 72	Took two years' leave and he, his wife and one of their grandchildren travelled around the world. The sixteen-year old grandchild remained with a family in London. He and his wife returned home
Age 74	Resumed work and school. Became interested in photography. Developed it as a full-time hobby and part-time income
Age 80	Took on a teaching position at a nearby university. His students ranged in age from twelve to eighty-seven. His subject was comparative architecture
Age 85	Died of sudden lung failure

Approximately nineteen transitional periods are noted in the course of John Smith's lifetime. These make his life-cycle significantly difference from the present conventional patterns. However, many of these transitions are already reality for some segments of our population who have broken out of the traditional life-cycle model. The question now is how many people, at how many stages in their lives, will vary significantly from current norms.

Finally, this being an idea paper, it was not the intention of the author to go into detail or present an overview of eventual outcomes for the planning practice that these tables and diagrams may have hinted at. This is being left to the creative imagination of all those interested in this problem, at least until scientific, trade or government agencies assume the required forecasting role.

REFERENCES

[1] Dernia, L.A., History of domestic architecture (1954), Vol 1, Ancient Egypt.
[2] Habitat (1961), CMHC, Ottawa
[3] Lamour, P., and de Chalendar, J., Prendre le temps de vivre (1974), Editions du Seuil.

[4] Dernoi, L.A., "Prospectives 2000 - Travail, loisir, mode de vie" (1977), doctoral thesis, Université d'Aix Marseille, France.
[5] Schumacher, E.F., Small is beautiful (1974), Abacus.

Figure 1   Primary field to consider in time planning

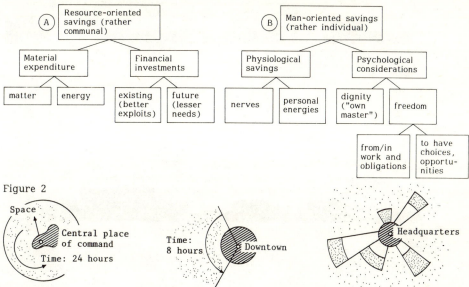

Figure 2

PAST
Slave-keeper or
feudal society.
"Manager" has free
choice of manpower
at his disposal, any
time, any place. Quasi-
total space and time
control of workers.

PRESENT
High industrial society.
Availability of manpower
to management restricted
in space (place of work)
and in time (eight hours).
Limited control over space
and time of employees.

FUTURE
Pluralistic, electronic, post-
industrial society. Availability of
manpower to management. Partly at
defined places (at work) and in small
blocks of time, partly dispersed in
space and time. Occasional guidance
rather than control over some time
and space segments of employees.

Figure 3

Time scale	Effects concerning			
	Physical material resources		Man	
Daily	More intensive use of both production and service establishments /continuous operation/	better exploitation of leisure and information oriented invest- ments/recreation, resort, etc/	Family chores and recreation opportunities facilitated	good off-peak use oppor- nity of services /commercial, recreational, health, cultural, etc/
Weekly				
Seasonal	Fully balanced use of educational and other facilities/also: adult education/		Cyclic recuperation periods through short-run holidays	
Yearly				
Life cycle	Saving manpower resources through non-obligatory retirement; less need for transfer payments and for old-age homes, etc		Permanent/adult education exchange programmes, long travels	Retraining; teen-age work opportunity; extended middle-age leisure, etc
Life			Financially and spiritually useful engagement in active life; integration with society	

Figure 4

PHYSICAL IMPACT MATRIX

CHANGES IN WORKING TIME	PLACES OF HUMAN ACTIVITIES					NETWORKS/DELIVERIES			
	WORK	HOUSING	SERVICE, PROTECTION	LEISURE	EDUCATION, INFORMATION CULTURE	URBAN PLUMBING	MOVEMENTS OF		
							PERSONS	GOODS	INFO.
STAGGERED									
COMPRESSED OR REDUCED									
FLEXTIME									
OPEN									

LITTLE OR NO IMPACT
IMPACT OF MEDIUM WEIGHT
STRONG IMPACT

Figure 5

CROSS IMPACT MATRIX

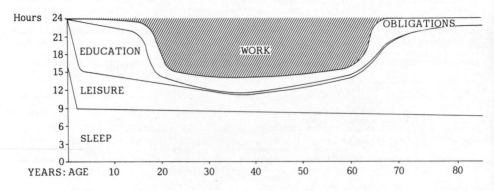

CHANGES IN WORKING TIME	TECHNOLOGICAL INNOVATIONS						SOCIAL INNOVATIONS				
	PRODUCTION	ENERGY	MOVEMENTS	HABITAT	COMMUNICA-TION	URBAN PLUMBING	UNITS: FAMILY COMM'S	LIFESTYLE	SERVICES	TRANSFER PAYMENTS	PARTICIPA-TION IN GOVERNMENT
STAGGERED											
COMPRESSED OR REDUCED											
FLEXTIME											
OPEN											

Figure 6

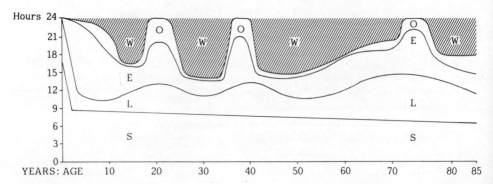

Temporal actions in cities 4

Enrique Browne   Argentina

USE OF SPACE

The "functional city", elevated to an international statement of principles for the planning, design and regulations for cities in the Charter of Athens (1933), has become the urban paradigm of our century. Its central trait is its search for a solution to urban problems through a set of measures, preferably of space order. Man, society and its activities on the one hand; the distribution in space, on the other. This would be the key to problems and, therefore, to their solutions. The temporal aspects involved are barely considered.

Nevertheless, use demands of city dwellers are time-spatial. In fact, all activities are located in space and in time. They occur "here and now". Traffic congestion illustrates this point well: were it not for the simultaneous concentration of people in space and time there would be no problem.[1] In turn, people require certain amounts of time and space in order to carry out their activities. For these reasons, all use demands may be expressed as curves fluctuating between both coordinates of daily human occupations (see Figure 1). The levels of the curves at a given moment depend on the number of people involved in their respective activities and on density coefficients which translate the number of people into space demands. Urban availabilities may be expressed in a similar manner. The difference between use demands and urban availabilities lies in the fact that the latter remain constant for short periods of time; for example, one day. In any case, the area below the demand curves expresses time-space use (measurable in m^2 per hour, etc). The area above the demand curves and below the constant level of availabilities expresses time-space disuse. In turn, if the demand area tends to exceed the level of space available, time-space congestion occurs.

This was not included in the models which were the forerunners of the modern city. Their unilateral emphasis on the space-society relationship also led them to propose the modality of specialised use as the only alternative for the internal reordering of cities. Although the Athens Charter does not specifically say so, there are in fact three great use modalities: superimposed, specialised and alternative use. These are demand distribution patterns in time and space for the purpose of fitting user needs to their real availabilities. In superimposed use, the same space is used at the same time for two or more activities. In specialised use, each space is dedicated to only one activity at any given time. In alternative use, one space is used for two or more activities at different times in a relatively cyclic fashion. The first is an indiscriminate use modality, the second discriminates use in space, the third discriminates use in time (see Figure 2).

Each modality's occurrence is related to the spatial and temporal coming into being of the existing division of labour and the insertion of the users into this division of labour. All this determines the location and duration of the users' activities and, therefore, the synchronisation of their use demands. On the other hand, the occurrence of the various modalities is related to the users' availabilities. Thus, superimposed use normally corresponds to a pattern of disorganised activities, together with a scarcity of resources. Specialised use tends to occur with more synchronised activity patterns, together with a higher resource level. Alternative use usually appears with a synchronised pattern of activities and scarce resources.

After the Industrial Revolution, the urban population not only grew but the number of different activities multiplied, owing to the greater specialisation produced by the division of labour. In turn, demand acquired greater fluctuations owing to the greater simultaneity of social activities. Violent discrepancies then appeared between greater, diversified and fluctuating demands on the one hand, and availabilities lacking in both size and quality, on the other, giving rise to a phenomenon in cities which was now on so large a scale. A new kind of superimposed use arose, generated not by the desynchronised characteristics of the demands but by availability restrictions. This led to confusion, conflict and inefficiency. According to contemporary prototypes, the solution was to segregate activities in space according to their specific requirements. The CIAM was emphatic in encouraging the advantages of specialised use, separating spatial demands as much as possible. It also proposed that they be legally ratified and programmed through zoning laws. The Athens Charter states in Point 15 of the commentaries that zoning is "the division of a city plan for the purpose of giving each function and each individual their proper place". According to the charter, this is "based on a necessary discrimination between the diverse human activities which each claim their own particular space". Specialised use is presented as the only possible solution, even though it is the most expensive in terms of the space necessary to satisfy any particular set of demands. On the other hand, the emphasis on specialised use can be noted also in the unwillingness to re-use physical availabilities in the cities. In fact, Le Corbusier's Voisin Plan was to have practically demolished all of one central zone in Paris which was then to be rebuilt according to the new needs. He himself used to say in a derogatory manner that the area consisted of houses which had been converted into offices. In any case, measures for population decentralisation, the reduction of distances between homes and work sites, the introduction of parks and green areas, the remodelling of cities and zoning laws have become the most constantly repeated slogans in policies for contemporary urban improvement. They are clearly all measures of a spatial nature.

Within these measures there is a radical change in the manner in which cities are used: specialised use becomes the modality which illustrates the programming, design, construction and the regulation of contemporary cities. This use modality is also applied to housing.

THE PRESENT OUTLOOK

Today, several decades after spatial measures were first accepted and executed, the functional city does not function. If there is any one characteristic of the city today it is its progressive inefficiency in responding to its inhabitants' demands.

A comprehensive look at cities today is disheartening. Habitat, the United Nations Conference on Human Settlements, said in 1976: "Human settlements are in crisis. Neither rich nor poor countries satisfy people's needs. Symptoms of crisis may be observed everywhere: poverty and unemployment, massive exodus from rural zones, shanty towns and spontaneous settlements, pollution, world-wide housing scarcity, inability of governments to provide for such basic needs as water, sanitation and electricity. The nature and gravity of these problems vary, but no country is free of them."

The urbanisation process has grown. In 1975, 40 per cent of the world population lived in urban zones. Conservative projections estimate that this figure will reach 50 per cent before the end of the century, which means that there will be 600 million more people living in cities in the next ten years. This is of particular significance for the Third World. In 1950, only 70 cities in the world had more than one million inhabitants. At present there are 84 such cities in developed countries and 74 in the Third World. Toward the end of the century there will be 276 in underdeveloped countries alone.

These increments in urban population imply unprecedented increases in the size and diversity of inhabitable space use demands. Furthermore, division of labour becomes subtler and more differentiated every day, while its coordination in time increases in precision and expands in space. Clearly, there are differences between industrialised and underdeveloped nations in this respect, owing to, among other reasons, varying access to contemporary technology. In any case, these changes have led to an increase in the simultaneity of use demands or, what amounts to the same thing, these demands have shifted from the time toward the space axis. Increasingly, these use demands tend not only to be greater in size and more differentiated in quality but to produce greater fluctuations between peaks and valleys.

The resources necessary for greater inhabitable space availabilities are obviously limited for both developed and underdeveloped countries, although these are differentially affected. The United States, Europe, the Soviet Union and Japan, together constituting only one-fourth of the world's population, possess 70 per cent of the planet's wealth.[2] Problems of unemployment and unequal distribution of internal income in Third World countries lend increased gravity to the problem of limited resources.

More and more urban residents are living in conditions of extreme poverty. A study based on five important cities in underdeveloped countries - Bogotá, Nairobi, Ahmadabad, Seoul and Madras - showed that the percentages of urban families whose monthly income was less than 125 dollars fluctuated from 60 in Seoul to 90 in Madras.[3] These levels drastically limit the possibility of obtaining even a minimum amount of habitable space. For example, the same study estimated that the percentage of familites lacking money for the cheapest available dwelling fluctuated bsween 42 in Bototá and 66 in Nairobi.

The clearest evidence of urban poverty is the "squatter settlements" which abound in the big cities of the Third World. Nine per cent of Lima's inhabitants lived in squatter settlements in 1957, and by 1969 this had increased to 36 per cent. The percentage in Mexico City went from 14 in 1952 to 46 in 1966. About 35 per cent of big-city inhabitants in Latin America are estimated to live in "favelas", "callampas" "barriadas", etc.[4] In other regions of the globe these percentages are sometimes higher. Sixty-seven per cent of Calcutta's population (two million people) live in squatter settlements. In Addis Ababa the figure is 90 per cent. We can therefore conclude that if urban growth in underdeveloped countries is high - 3 to 5 per cent a year - the growth of squatter settlements is still higher. In fact, it is estimated at between 6 and 12 per cent a year.

The problem of lack of habitable space also appears when we consider the overall economic potential of these countries. Cost of habilitation of these spaces is not less than 1000 dollars per new urban resident and may be as much as 10,000 dollars. It has been estimated that if the poorer countries spent all their net savings on space habilitation, less than 800 dollars per additional person would be available. Although these figures are higher in other Third World countries, nevertheless, and more specifically, urban administration everywhere suffers from a lack of funds. Bombay's municipal income is 84 million dollars, i.e. 330 dollars per new resident. Far more prosperous Caracas has a municipal income of 120 million dollars, i.e. 1000 dollars per additional inhabitant a year. However, for the most part this income is spent on the upkeep of services for the established population.[5]

It is therefore evident that Third World resources for the construction of habitable space are radically scarce. In this situation, the indiscriminate application of the specialised use modality as the conceptual axis for the planning and construction of cities and housing is an error with serious consequences. In fact, the adoption of this modality presents problems even to countries with plentiful resources. I have pointed out that demands tend to increase progressively in extent, diversity and the sharpness of the periodic fluctuations. In industrialised nations, the increment of growth of demand curves is low owing to a lower rate of urban population growth. Nevertheless, there is a remarkable increment in diversity and above all in fluctuations because of the incessant specialisation of the division of labour and the coincidence of these specialisations in time and space. In this way great qualitative changes in the curves occur, resulting in an accelerating number of demands and a tendency toward peaking in the curves. Adequate response to these tendencies within the modality of specialised use requires an increase in both the number and the size of the habitable spaces, in order at least to reach the level of the curve's highest peaks. Thus, even though the population level to be served remains constant, total and per capita spatial requirements increase notably.

Jean Gottman is referring to this phenomena when he says that urban growth tendencies cannot be easily grasped from available population statistics. He says that increasing economic development requires greater spatial consumption of land for construction and transportation. This "causes the growth of many urban characteristics even if the number of inhabitants does not vary".[6] Consequently, cities voraciously devour their surrounding space and total population density tends to diminish. The habitable space needs per person increase. It is estimated that the total habitable space available in England is at present 100 m^2 per person. In Milton Keynes, a new city, this figure will be 355 m^2 per person.[7]

Vienna is a case in point. In 1940 its population stood at 1,870,000, a figure which by 1960 had diminished to 1,747,000. During the same time the per capita average income in the metropolitan area increased from 580 to 1120 dollars and the built-up area from 344 to 559 m^2, i.e. gross population density decreased from 54 to 26 per hectare. This phenomenon is repeated in other cities of the industrialised world. Doxiadis and Papatoannou[8] have compiled a series of statistical tables for fifteen cities, including Paris, London, New York, Tokyo and Stockholm for the years 1940 to 1960. These tables show that in those cities in which per capita income had increased, gross population density in the built up areas decreased. This only serves to underline the fact that diversification of use demands and their growing tendency towards peaks caused by increased simultaneity imply a notable increment in total spatial needs per person when specialised use is in force.

The above pheonomenon is accompanied by growing disuse of the availabilities of habitable spaces. As I have stated above, when the simultaneity in the development of an activity increases, internal displacements from the time axis toward the space axis occur on the demand curves, incrementing the peaks even when the total volume of time-space demands remains constant. In this case, the increase in spatial requirements at a given time is compensated for by a decrease at other moments during the time period considered. If the increase in the maximum demand peaks is greater than the spatial availabilities, there is congestion. The only possible solution to this while specialised usage is applied is to increase space quantities until their level is at least equal to the highest point on the curve. If this is accomplished (while keeping the volume of time-space demands constant), the percentage of use of the availabilities decreases. Demand diversification produces similar effects.

My empirical studies on the use of housing point out this increase of disuse which accompanies progressive diversification and simultaneity in the development of activities.[9] I investigated the use made of housing by two types of families: extremely poor families and well-off families that were well integrated in their countries' societies. The former had relatively disorderly activity patterns in time which were reflected in the use they made of their housing. In the latter group, individual family members had a greater number of different activities which tended to take place according to pre-established schedules and in a more simultaneous manner. For example, all family members had breakfast and other meals together at the same time. In order to find out how these phenomena influenced housing space demand, I calculated what the minimum space required would be for each activity in the daily life of each family, according to specialised use. To avoid distortions, I used a density coefficient per person which remaind constant for all activities and families. In this way I obtained the total and per capita spatial requirements per family. Owing to differences in diversity and simultaneity, wealthy families had 80 per cent more per capita spatial demands than poor ones. On the other hand, the average duration of activity was 31 per cent less in wealthy than in poor families. Next, I calculated the percentage of use which the lodgings would have according to the observed demand pattern in each case. On average, the poor families' lodgings had a use index of 21 per cent while the middle class families' index was only 12 per cent. This was true even when the per capita time spent in the lodgings was slightly higher for well-off families. If the amount of disuse which accompanies greater diversification and synchronisation of activities when the specialised use modality is adopted is important when housing is considered, the phenomenon is even more relevant to the general urban case. In this respect, the relative weight which "sleep" as an activity has within total domestic activities must be considered, for it acts as a leveller of differences produced by other family activities.

Increases in the quantity of habitable spaces imply the investment of enormous economic resources. It also happens that indiscriminate application of the specialised use modality in the planning and construction of cities increments availabilities at the same time that their disuse increases. Paradoxically, investment and waste go hand in hand. Thus, cities become bottomless pits. On the othern hand, since resources are always limited, problems snowball. Resources used to satisfy some demands with diminishing returns are substracted from those required for the solution of other problems. In this manner, housing scarcity, traffic congestion, lack of services and equipment and many other problems appear ever more frequently, even in the cities of economically properous nations.

On the other hand, construction of habitable spaces presupposing future specialised use tends to make the re-use of these more difficult. This also has implications for the best use of resources. Obsolescence periods for spatial structures are independent of variation produced by demands. The former are caused by physical deterioration which is related to the quality of materials and construction and level of maintenance. Variations produced by demands are related to economic, social and technological changes which affect groups of users. On the whole, obsolescence periods tend to be relatively constant through the years while changes in demands accelerate progressively.

The planning, design and construction of habitable spaces complying as closely as possible with the characteristics of each demand, according to the formula "form follows function", makes the transformation of these spaces difficult for other uses in future. All this tends to accelerate the construction-demolition-construction cycles affecting contemporary cities and this in turn implies inefficient waste. In the past 20 years new buildings have been built and old buildings torn down at a faster rate than in any other similar period of history. For example, the old section of downtown Paris, well known for its stability, its fine historical monuments and its severe conservation policies, witnessed the demolition and reconstruction of one-fourth of its entire area between 1954 and 1974.

If the progressive waste of resources inherent in the general adoption of specialised use patterns in cities is considerable in economically developed countries, it is even more pernicious in the Third World. In the latter, the quantity of demands has increased much more owing to the rate of urbanisation, while the diversification and greater fluctuation of demands may be discerned above all in the sectors directly involved in the modern economy of these countries. Growing disuse, congestion and other problems which appear in the cities of industrial countries are repeated in these parts of the urban structures.

At the same time, the resources allocated to attempts to solve (inefficiently) the problems of these sectors are substracted from those needed to satisfy the requirements of the growing number of poor. Superimposed use rather than specialised use predominates in the "squatter settlements" founded on the initiative of those directly interested in spite of the fact that these are against established norms. For example, recent studies of the International Labour Organisation have shown that the "non-official sectors" of those shanty towns absorb a large part of the Third World's excess labour force. This sector consists of illegal small industries or retail commercial activities which, for the most part, take place in the home. By way of illustration, this "non-official sector" provided employment for about 50 per cent of Djakarta's total work force in recent years. Similar cases have been discovered in Abidjan in the Ivory Coast, in Nairobi, Kenya and elsewhere. A study of the shanty towns of Howrah in Calcutta showed that 63 per cent of these enterprises were conducted within the family dwellings.[10]

Furthermore, superimposed use prevails in these domestic activities. A short while ago I had first-hand experience of this in Cochambamba, Bolivia. One of the poor districts there is called "El Solterito" ("the little bachelor") and for the most part is composed of rural migrants who have an unstable monthly income of less than 50 dollars per family. On average, there were 5.1 persons per bedroom and three per bed. Also, a bedroom was used for the preparation of food in 32 per cent of the dwellings.

The source of superimposed use in these settlements is twofold. On the one hand, it is related to an extreme lack of construction resources and, on the other, to use demands which for the most part follow a pattern which is disorderly in both space and time, a product of the same defective placement of these families in their respective social environments.

In any case, the official search for solutions to the problems of squatter settlements on the basis of specialised use is both illusory and counter-productive. In housing policies this, along with the high standards laid down for materials and construction, places the "minimal solutions" beyond the reach of the very families that should be assisted.

Half a century has elapsed since the planning and execution of measures of a spatial nature began as a solution to the chaos, congestion and overcrowding inherited from the first industrial cities. As a decisive element among these measures, specialised use became the conceptual and practical axis for the reordering of urban structures. It was to be one of the ways by which order, efficiency and collective welfare would be achieved in the cities. Today these cities are characterised by the very opposite of these virtues. Specialised use, if applied indiscriminately in cities, places scanty resources in a broken bag together with our best hopes.

TEMPORAL MEASURES

The problem is that urban functions are not solely spatial. Alfred North Whitehead (1861-1947), the English mathematician and philosopher who in collaboration with Bertrand Russell wrote the Principia mathematica, a fundamental work of mathematical logic, said in 1925 that by localisation he meant "a principal characteristic which refers equally to space and time...what is material can be said to be here in space and here in time, or here in space-time".

The postulates propitiated through the "functional city" at more or less the same period in which Whitehead was speaking of the meaning of localisation consisted basically of measures with a spatial character which almost completely ignored the temporal aspects inherent in the use of urban structures. This unilateral vision doubtless constitutes one of the main causes of its own failure.

The measures of a temporal order which may be applied in the search for solutions to the problems afflicting cities have an importance at least similar to those of the spatial order. In any case, it is essential that urban development policies contain, in a simultaneous and complementary manner, measures for both temporal and spatial order. For the sake of clarity only, on the remaining pages I shall refer to actions in a temporal dimension on their own.

Temporal measures for urban improvement may be classified principally in two categories. One comprises those actions which tend to diminish the growing peaks of demand curves by altering the distribution of activities in time. The purpose of these "desimultaneousising" measures is to reduce the maximum requirements for habitable space, diminish the tendencies toward congestion and increase the levels of use of what is available - all this without questioning the specialised use of cities. The second category involves changes in the established use modalities of habitable spaces, taking advantage of the strong fluctuations in demands. A decrease in the total need for space, a mitigation in the tendency towards congestion and an increase in the use of availabilities may also be achieved through these actions. It must be made clear, however, that these two types of measures are generally mutually exclusive in any particular case: while some actions attempt to reduce the fluctuations in demands, others rightly take advantage of them in order to diversify the use of availabilities. This notwithstanding, both categories of actions may be applied to problems not closely related to each other. At times they may be compatible under special circumstances which I shall describe later.

THE "DESIMULTANEOUSISING" OF URBAN ACTIVITIES

These measures may be applied in the distribution of activities in any period of time, whether it be a day, a week, a month or a year. Although these modifications may be introduced for any regular period, the week is one of the favourite proposals because, unlike other periods of time, it is not determined by physical pheonomena. Its arbitrary nature allows possible variations in length and composition.

At least two attempts at altering the week are known. The first was when the Romans changed from an eight-day to a seven-day week after the adoption of Christianity. The second was when the French National Convention decided on 5 October 1793 to adopt a new calendar making the first day of the Republic (22 September 1972) the beginning of a new era. It was decided to divide the year into twelve months of 30 days, plus five or six additional days. Each month was in turn divided into three weeks of ten days, with each 10th day a holiday. Clearly, the main interest in making these modifications was not the better use of urban facilities. The cause was religious - in the first case, Christianity; in the second, its exact opposite. After abolishing the monarchy and executing the king, the French revolutionary government went on to attach the Roman Catholic Church. As part of this offensive it decided to change the long weekend and replace religious holidays with civic holidays.[11] More recently, in 1929, the Soviet Union instituted an "ongoing week" of five days. During the week each individual worker had one day off. The working masses were divided into five fifths. The free day of each fifth fell on a different day of the week, so that on any given day one-fifth of the work force was absent from its job site. Nevertheless, the industrial complex functioned without interruptions. The purpose was to increase the use of installations and thus production. The application of these measures brought about organisational problems both at a domestic level and on the job. In 1931 the country changed to a six-day week and in 1940 returned to a seven-day week with Sunday as a holiday.[12]

Changing the week has also been examined on a theoretical level with greater emphasis being placed on the problems of city use. H.G. Wells (1866-1946), the noted author of War of the worlds and The invisible man, once expressed his discontent with the current week. He said that a longer working week of ten or eleven days placed between three or four-day weekends would have beneficial effects both for labour and rest.[13] Although this fourteen-day week would not by itself diminish the degree of synchronisation of activities, nor the tendency toward peaks in demand curves, it might achieve these ends if the worker could choose between this option and the one currently in force. As long as everyone did not make the same choice there would be some persons at work while others were resting and vice versa. In practice, some Japanese and German firms have begun to try out the "double week". Robert Sergen, industrial psychologist of the University of Sheffield, and Donald MacGregor have been studying the effects of this system for some time. Both agree that industrial productivity increases and absenteeism decreases. Again, the four-day weekend offers better opportunities for rest, since the worker can leave the city with greater liberty and ease. Nevertheless, both admit that this method could not be applied in high-risk or efficiency industries because it would be too tiring for the workers. Furthermore there would be problems in coordinating the workers' and employees' schedules with those of their families.

Yona Friedman proposed another kind of change in the week. He maintained that in ancient times, until the end of the eighteenth century, the family was the predominant social group in charge of the children's education, cooperation in production, etc. Towards the end of that century public education appeared on the scene and groups were formed on the basis of common school age. At the beginning of the nineteenth century industry redistributed men in groups on the basis of their work. At the beginning of this century the liberation of women began, redistributing them also in terms of their work. A transition has therefore taken place from the biological family group to groups constituted on the basis of determinants. Thus, it is possible to vary days of rest according to persons' work; this would have been impossible while the family group predominated. The purpose was to free cities from congestion. Friedman then proposed to keep the seven-day week but to vary the rest days according to the different areas in the social division of labour. For example, office workers would rest on Mondays and Tuesdays, industrial workers on Tuesday and Wednesdays, professionals on Wednesdays and Thursdays and so on.[14]

Another proposal on the week was made between 1975 and 1977 by an Argentinian professor, C.M. Varsavsky.[15] He acknowledged that man must alternate work and rest but rejected the system of simultaneity according to which all men must interrupt their routine activities on the same day of the week. According to him, this was necessary in pre-industrial societies but there was no longer any justification for it, all the more so if it was in fact being violated by an important fraction of the work force, at considerable economic and social cost. He proposed an "ongoing nine-day week" in which all days would be equal, and different persons would have free time on different days. He suggested dividing the population into three thirds, and keeping two-thirds at work while one-third rested. A nine-day week would have numerous advantages, beginning with a better use of capital inversions. "If, for example, we consider buildings - and the thousands of millions of dollars invested in private and state offices as well as classrooms at all levels of education - we see that these are paralysed for two of the seven weekdays." The ongoing week would increase their use by 40 per cent without modifying the number of daily working hours.

Something similar would happen to recreational, industrial and service installations. Other benefits would accrue from greater speed in commercial transactions. Banks and public offices would be open every day and there would be an increase in the productivity of firms and a decrease in absenteeism since employees would not need free days to accomplish tasks which cannot be undertaken over weekends. Furthermore, there would be greater flexibility in the number of working days, since housewives, students or elderly persons could choose to work for three days only. To this would be added a positive impact on the use of free time owing to the increase of this period to three days and the possibility of taking part in any unpaid activities during this time. Lastly, "the ongoing week would minimise the peaks and valleys of so many activities. Traffic jams usual on weekends would disappear and rush-hour traffic would decrease by a third".

Varsavsky lists the problems which the acceptance of his proposals would entail. They are those of a religious and social nature, planning for different sectors of the population and their activities, problems relating to the replacement of positions of greater hierarchy, etc. On the other hand, Varsavsky states that the application of his proposal depends on context. "Given that many of the arguments in favour of the ongoing week are based on the evils of the big city and the optimum use of industrial equipment, it is immediately obvious that the ongoing week is appropriate in a big metropolis but not in wide open spaces. In other words, in spite of the six thousand years of history, in fact, in many parts of the world, conditions are not much different from what they were when the week was introduced, particularly with reference to social life." He therefore suggests that it is necessary to carry out a careful simulation during the period of transition from one system to the other, and to experiment on a progressive scale.

Kevin Lynch, author of the Image of the city, has also considered the distribution of urban time. His book, What time is that place?,[16] is a study of the temporal image of the city; a logical complement of his first work. The adjustments of interior time (how our bodies and minds are subject to time) to exterior time is, he says, the central theme of his book. He considers a great variety of themes in a balanced manner. One of these is the distribution of urban time. He states that time is structured in various dimensions and holds that we believe that the "natural" combination - disagreeable but inevitable - is a structure of fine-grained time, with a short period and great amplitude that is quick, synchronised, regular and oriented to a coming future. Nevertheless, other structures which have considerable advantages over this one are possible. Within this range he proposes altering the current week. He warns that a change in our week would present difficulties even if only on account of the great number of activities coordinated within it, but that it would be interesting to know if a different work-rest system, or even a non-cyclical system, would be preferable for certain persons.

Lynch is very much interested in the problem of synchronisation within any period. He says the imposition of exterior time is oppressive. To eat, wake and rest at the same time does not always fit in with our immediate preferences. Western society has always tended to be far more temporally rigid than is necessary. It has uncritically carried the requirements of its production system into other areas of its existence. But the synchronisation required in production does not need to be transplanted into other spheres and, in fact, production itself may be changed. In practice, nocturnal production and special night services or service on holidays have become more common. The time is past when all vacations were taken at the same time. Now they may be enjoyed throughout the year. In any case the structure of time must be sufficiently flexible to tolerate a wide diversity of temporal group structures. This requires widely known events which are to be the milestones of important changes and the symbols of social cohesion. Many imposed rigid factors and unnecessary synchronisms may be eliminated. In practice, several activities are ripe for an experimental temporal modification, such as eating and school schedules. Certain office jobs may be carried out at unconventional hours and firms could sometimes allow their workers to fix their working hours as they please. If enough people prefer to do their shopping on Sundays or late at night and shop-owners are willing to serve them, there is no reason why this should not be done.

Essential services, such as transportation, food stores, cleaning establishments, medical care and communications, should be available at all times, in the same way as firemen and policemen are always available. The volume of shops and services in big cities permits certain schedule differences and even twenty-four-hour-a-day availability. Certain statistics could be used to predict the loads. There is a group of people in each personal preference which is sufficiently large for anyone to synchronise his or her conduct with them. This "desynchronisation" would not only offer advantages in that it would make exterior time fit the interior time of urban inhabitants,"...it furthermore offers the parallel advantage of making loads lighter and of using installations in a more efficient manner". The author also discusses the problems of setting these plans in motion and suggests rehearsals on a reduced scale.

Jacques de Chalendar is another supporter of the "desimultaneousising" of urban activities. His book L'aménagement du temps,[17] published in 1971, contains numerous statistics, especially on Paris and public opinion soundings. He says that in rush hours "there is not enough room for everybody". This happens daily, weekly and yearly. He gives examples of congestion in the Paris transportation system and calculates the cost of solving the problems of rush-hour traffic by increased construction and equipment. "It is in order to face peak hours during the season that the SNCF has been obliged to keep old model coaches for a longer time than normal: 1500 out of a total of 7600 are used only temporarily; 400 alone are used for the exceptional peaks such as Christmas, Easter or the longer vacations...Peak-hour traffic has made it necessary to triple and quadruple tracks, to build intermediate terminals, to transform existing stations...Once a certain level has been exceeded, the necessary investments add up to hundreds of millions...the same thing happens to the roads."

He confirms that trying to deal with peaks by increasing space and equipment would lead to disproportionate investments: no degree of supply can be completely guaranteed, since its costs would be infinite. For the same reason, the reduction of peaks must be attempted. In this respect, everything depends on the duration of these activities. Preference must be given to housing and work, since the activities related to the former take up twelve hours a day and those related to the latter about eight hours daily. However, activities pertaining to circulation and free time have more pronounced peaks and occur in a shorter length of time. Therefore, action must be taken by desynchronising persons' activities. In fact, many people already live in this matter, e.g. those who have nocturnal work schedules in public services. In any event, de Chalender enquires: "Should desynchronisation be authoritarian and rigid or flexible and elective?" He chooses the latter and applies it to different periods. In this fashion, he arrives at the concept of daily, weekly or annual "stretches of time" whose dimensions (and what de Chalendar calls the position on the axes of time), though remaining relatively stable in each social-cultural context, may vary in respect of climate, traditions, inadequacy in transportation and free-time facilities, and the prevailing congestion.

With respect to the daily distribution of activities, he emphasises the success of some "obligatory scaling" measures in work schedules, but he also points out this method's problems and failures. For example, the city of Strasbourg, on the initiative of the National Committee for Planning of Work Time, decided that the midday break for public employees should begin at 11.45 a.m. and that for school-children at 12.15 p.m. This permitted mothers to collect their children and prepare lunch without rushing. The results were excellent: there was no more traffic congestion and public transport not only became more accessible but also increased its passenger load by 37 per cent, thereby causing a decrease in the use of private cars.

Similar measures introduced in Paris reduced transit by 13.5 per cent during rush hours on some Metro lines. Other examples may serve to illustrate these measures but problems arise owing to families and their habits. Therefore, the author points to the convenience of installing systems with flexible and personalised schedules. In this system, workers would be free to choose their schedules within a certain space of time as long as they spent a certain number of predetermined hours at their jobs. Only some fraction of this time would be common and obligatory for all persons in one firm. This system has been tried out in Germany in several firms - with great success and enthusiasm on the part of the workers.

De Chalendar proposes something similar in respect of the week. He suggests changing the seven-day week to a fifteen-day week. Sundays would be retained and workers allowed to take three consecutive days off at the end of one week and only Sunday at the end of the following week. People would choose the distribution of their long and short rest periods at their convenience and, in the first case, would choose between Friday to Sunday, Saturday to Monday, and Sunday to Tuesday. This work system would have to be coordinated with the school system. As for the year, the author underlines the problem that common and obligatory scaling down of vacations brings, owing, among other reasons, to the complementary nature of commerce and industry. He therefore suggests dividing the year into two parts: a period of "full activity" lasting seven months around winter, during which schools, societies, firms and services would function at top capacity, and a period of less activity lasting five monehs around summer-time, during which the main employers would permit a variable fraction of their personnel - not more than 30 per cent - to be absent on vacation at times chosen by those involved. Furthermore, de Chalendar proposes to extend his concept of "stretches of time" to the lives of people in such a manner that principal activities, study, work and play, which at present are rigidly related to age, may alternate in a more flexible and convenient manner for the development and welfare of the population. In this, de Chalendar comes fairly close to the "recurring education" proposed by Olaf Palme in 1969 at the European Conference of Ministers of Education.[18]

The proposals for temporal change in the distribution of activities which I have mentioned could be expanded with concrete examples of applications with similar objectives and on a small scale in various cities around the globe. In any case, all these proposals, in one way or another, are designed to reduce the peaks of demand and, by doing so, to reduce congestion and the need to increase habitable spaces. Curves showing a more even distribution of points go hand in hand with a greater use of what is already available and a decrease in the misuse of investment resources - all to the benefit of the urban population.

Some of the proposed measures may seem somewhat utopian in their scale and nature. Such a measure is the "ongoing nine-day week". But if we consider the possible reduction of the working week to four days in certain industrial nations, the ongoing week does not seem so illusory. In any case Lynch's and de Chalendar's flexible proposals seem more attractive and feasible.

CHANGES IN THE USE MODALITIES OF CITIES

The purpose of the preceding measures was to try to decrease simultaneity in use demands in such a way as to diminish their tendency to accumulate in peaks, and consequently to reduce growing congestion and disuse of availabilities. It is clear that the tendencies toward congestion and disuse are produced by the combination of actual demands with the specialised use modality. It should therefore be possible to eliminate these problems in another way - by discarding specialised use as a central axis for the planning, design and construction of cities.

Measures of this sort imply a shift toward a new generalisation of use of cities. Unlike the preceding measures, these do not seek to alter the distribution of activities in time. Peaks are accepted but they are used to introduce congestion and efficiency in the functioning of urban structures. This is very feasible. The progressive diversification and synchronisation of activities produce two parallel phenomena. On the one hand, the number of different demands increases and internal transferals take place on the curves from the time axis to the space axis. This results in a considerable increment in the maximum peaks. On the other hand, the various demands tend to have a lesser duration and to overlap less in time. Demands tend to be either more simultaneous or more clearly sequential in their arrangement in time. These characteristics appeared in my empirical studies on the use of housing which I have mentioned before. In the case of poor and well-to-do families respectively, on average 8.66 and 11 different activities took place at home. Desynchronisation of activities would make poor families require on average 3.20 units of space per capita, whereas well-to-do families demanded 5.78 units. The various domestic activities lasted on average 6.34 hours in the case of poor families, and only 4.36 hours in the case of well-to-do families. Furthermore, average overlap time taken up by the various activities was 1.65 hours for poor families and only 0.62 hours a day for well-to-do families.

When specialised use is adopted in the needs of the well-to-do families, it leads to congestion and disuse, but those needs offer an ever greater potential for using space to satisfy the requirements of two or more activities at different times. In the daily, weekly or annual periods in which availabilities are partially or totally in disuse, they may be used to satisfy the demands of other activities. For this to be achieved, both a spatial and temporal requirement must be fulfilled. The spatial demands of the two or more activities must be qualitatively similar and the curves of these demands must have asymmetrical peak axes in time.

If historical tendencies toward a greater synchronisation of the division of labour are taken into account, a shift toward the generalisation of use of cities would have alternative use as its principal goal. Nevertheless, this does not mean there is an inflexible option. On the contrary, the aim is greater use of the whole range of use patterns in accordance with the possibilities and restructions of each specific case.

Within this flexible content, specialised use would be limited to cases in which it was very necessary, for example those activities with implications which are dangerous or irritating to people - gas emanations, noises, etc. It also occurs in those activities in which spatial requirements are unique and much equipment and many installations are involved, such as those concerned with laboratories, public bathrooms, subterranean transportation, airports and others. This also applies to indispensable activities which are of short duration but occur with unpredictable frequency, such as those involved in fires or other emergency services. Specialised use is necessary in its own right when activities produce relatively even and continuous demands in time, as do those concerned with hospitals and other services. It is clear that the occupants of housing units must have unrestricted liberty to choose combinations of use modalities which best fit their habits and limitations. Nevertheless, generalised use of their interior spaces may be encouraged.

Superimposed use predominates in the shanty towns of the Third World, owing to the scarcity of construction resources and "desimultaneousised" demands. Both causes are, in turn, the result of the defective infusion of the corresponding social groups in the modern sectors of their respective economics. But at the same time, for these social groups, superimposed use becomes an efficient way to survive in their difficult situation, for it permits a precarious balance between their demands and their spatial availabilities. In my studies, this use pattern showed a decrease of about 38 per cent on average in the poor family's spatial requirements, compared with what it would have needed to satisfy the same demands with specialised use. All in all, obstacles should not be put in the way of superimposed use in the cities and housing of the Third World. But if the very causes of extreme poverty are tackled successfully, demands will diversify and become synchronised, increasing their level of fluctuation. If this happens, a large part of the origin and convenience of superimposed use disappears for these special groups. If congestion and disuse are to be avoided, the emphasis must shift to alternate use.

In spite of this, there are cases in which the application of superimposed use in integrated groups and developed societies is useful. If any city adopts on a large scale the measures of temporal change in activities discussed in the preceding section, we will have an example of just such a case. These measures desynchronise demands and for the same reason permit this pattern in the development of activities which are not mutually exclusive. In this situation, the advantages and savings of both types of measures come together, but even in situations where these measures are not applied, superimposed use is valid on a reduced scale. An example would be where the development of the desired activities implies a high degree of social interaction, such as those related to community centres, public squares and others.

But the central destiny of a possible generalisation in the use of cities is alternative use. This modality is the usual answer to the diversifying and fluctuating tendencies of demands when the resources are limited. It specialises use in time instead of use in space. To do this, advantage is taken of the fact that greater synchronisation of activities implies more simultaneity in some and great chronological differentiation in others. Considerable spatial necessities are saved. For example, this modality applied to a Japanese house I studied meant a 40 per cent reduction in the spatial requirements necessary to satisfy the same group of activities with specialised use. It implied, by the same token, a considerable decrease in the tendencies toward congestion and disuse.

Experiments with this modality have begun in many cities of the world. The "pedestrian's paradise" every Sunday in Ginza, Tokyo's main commercial avenue, is well known. Fifth Avenue, Lexington Avenue and Madison Avenue in New York were made into pedestrian promenades at about the same time. During the summer, autumn and Christmas season of 1970, those streets were closed to traffic at night and on weekends, so that they could be exclusively used by pedestrians. The streets were decorated with toy trains and there were street musicians and fashion show. One Saturday there was a tennis match at an intersection that is normally congested, and on another Saturday an artificial ice-rink was placed outside Tiffany's.

The applications of alternative use are extremely varied. In 1969 the Catholic University of Chile founded DUOC which is dedicated to the specialised training of adults. A few years after the inauguration there were 103 branches of DUOC throughout the country with a student body of 60,000. There were no proper classrooms, however, and classes were held in union halls, parish halls and other venues when these were not being used. Thousands of square metres of space and other resources were saved in this manner.

The advantages of alternative use are not limited to the reduction of spatial needs to satisfy the demands of any one group of activities. In practice, these reductions have the positive effect of increasing total population density. This produces savings in transportation and in other urban services. Furthermore, the variations in uses in time introduce variety and diversity into urban life.

The costs involved in these changes of use are usually small. A project on a large scale which I undertook with my students some years ago demonstrated this. Recreation areas were to be offered to the large settlements of poor on the outskirts of Santiago, Chile. Their demands were extremely great on weekends. The area best equipped in every way for the purpose was the civic and commercial centre of the city which was highly congested during work days but practically empty on Saturday afternoons and Sundays. The demand curves for public transportation, cars and pedestrians in the various public areas of the centre were carefully measured during weekdays and weekends. It appeared that the streets, covered walkways, squares and other places offered thousands of square metres suitable for recreational pursuits. The reduced weekend traffic could be diverted down a few streets without creating problems, leaving the rest of the centre free for pedestrian use. The students proposed attractive options for temporary occupations in the spaces available. Throughout, the cost was very low. However, at the same time this study emphasised the need to perfect planning techniques and control over alternative use on a large scale.

The generalisation of use of cities and alternative use in particular require a drastic change in legislation and zoning applicable to land use. It is necessary to replace the functionalist conceptual axis which fosters specialised use in cities, bringing all the disadvantages which I have commented upon. Some initiatives have been taken in this regard. For example, in 1967 the first school-housing complex was set up in New York in the shape of a three-storey school with twenty-five cooperative buidings with 400 apartments. Modifications were proposed in the zoning to permit the school and the apartments to share the open spaces. The playgrounds and other facilities would be used by the residents when school was not in session.[19]

The generalisation of use of cities also expedites the permanent use changes which take place in then: if one of the availabilities is used for two or more activities for short periods of time, it is easier for the space to be used for one or more other activities on a permanent basis. In this way, frictions are lessened between the constant periods in which physical structures become obsolete and the ever more rapidly changing variations in demands. Cities thus adjust better to the economic and social changes affecting them. This means that resources are saved since the cycle of construction-demolition-construction so common today is halted. It also implies better preservation of a collective memory. The physical structures of these cities, however modest, bear witness to their own history. When in 1975 in Perth, Scotland, an old waterworks was restored and transformed into an exhibition and tourist information centre, its usefulness was preserved, together with the memory of the very first example of hydraulic engineering in the area.

However, I reiterate that it is not only the conservation of isolated buildings that is at stake. Out of context, whatever it may be, the best of buildings has a touch of falseness. The decision to save a monument because of its importance almost invariably means the condemnation of the "uninteresting" urban area surrounding it. This has not happened in Rome. The entire city is the scene of a permanent process of use readjustments and this has been the main factor in preserving the living city which has been given a charm not found in mummified historical monuments. In fact, the conversion of ancient buildings gives them a contagious energy, because a change in use breaks our routine blindness and makes explicit the formal characteristics of spaces.[20]

In any case, these permanent changes in the use of habitable spaces may occur within one use modality or they may produce a change of use modality. The permanent change, in turn, may introduce interior variations within each modality in relation to its common or private character. Years ago, when the private park of a family in Concepción, Chile, was made the Lota Park there was a change from private specialised use to public specialised use. The patios and corridors of the old Latin American "haciendas" were used simultaneously for circulation, resting, socialising and other activities. Some of these houses have been converted into hotels and the spaces mentioned have continued to be used in a superimposed fashion but with a public character. Something similar occurs when a Japanese house is transformed to make it suitable for public use: its "tatami" rooms keep their alternative use, but in public, not privately.

Neither measures tending to change the distribution of activities in time nor those tending to change use modalities cancel out actions of a spatial character in the cities. On the contrary, they are complementary to them: urban development is time-spatial. But there can be no doubt of the urgent need to adopt measures in time so that efforts at urban development do not fall into empty space.

REFERENCES

[1] Anderson, J., Time budgets and human geography: notes and references, Discussion paper 36, Graduate School of Geography, London School of Econonics, January 1970.
[2] Ward, Barbara, "The home of man: what nations and the international community must do", Habitat, Vol 1, No 2, pages 125-32.
[3] A study of the World Bank, citied in the United Nations: "Tugurios y asentamientos de ocupantes sin títulos en las ciudades del Tercer Mundo", Habitat, A/Conf, 70/RPC/9, 1 May 1975.

[4] Van der Rest, J., and Browne, E., "La conferencia de Caracas sobre ssentamientos humanos", Mensaje No 243, October 1975, pages 450-543.

[5] World Bank, "Urbanisation", A document of work on the sector (1972), pages 20-4.

[6] Gottman, J., "The present renewal of mankind's habitat: an overview of present trends of urbanisation around the world", Habitat Vol 2, pages 159-61.

[7] Milton Keynes Development Corporation, The plan for Milton Keynes; Vol 1, Figure 7, page 22. (If parks and areas held in reserve are discounted the figure is 295 m^2/person.)

[8] Doxiadis, C.A., and Papatoannou, J.P., Ecumenopolis: the inevitable city of the future (1974), Table 8, pages 409-11, Athens Publishing Centre.

[9] Browne, E., El uso de las ciudades y las viviendas, Parte III (1978), SIAP-CLACSO Editions, Buenos Aires.

[10] Studies of the ILO quoted by the United Nations: "Tugurios y asentamientos de ocupantes sin títulos en las ciudades del Tercer Mundo", Habitat, A/Conf, 70/RPC/9, 1 May 1975.

[11] Varsavsky, C.M., Why seven days in a week? (1977), Department of Economics, New York University, page 14.

[12] Moore, W.E., Man, time and society (1963), New York.

[13] Quoted by J.B. Priestley in Man and time (1968), pages 27-31, Dell Publishing Company.

[14] Cook, P., Arquitectura planeamiento y acción (1971), Ediciones Nueva Visión, Buenos Aires.

[15] Varsavsky, C.M., Propuesta para el estudio de alternativas sobre la actual semana de 7 días, (1975), Harvard University; and Why seven days in a week? (1977), Department of Economics, New York University.

[16] Lynch, K., What time is that place? (1972), MIT Press.

[17] De Chalendar, J., L'aménagement du temps (1971), Desclée de Brower.

[18] Palme, O., "Are young people getting too much education?", The Futurist, June 1970.

[19] The American Society of Planning Officials, ASPO Newsletters 25 July 1975.

[20] Schneider, P., "Converting the past", Arquitectural Plus, March-April 1974.

Figure 1
Use demands and availabilities

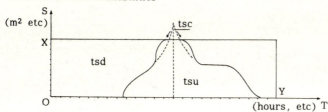

S = space
T = time
X = area of inhabitable space
Y = time-period considered
XY = time space available
TSU = time-space use
TSD = time-space disuse
TSC = time space congestion

Figure 2
Use modalities

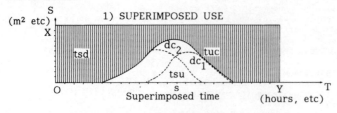

1) SUPERIMPOSED USE

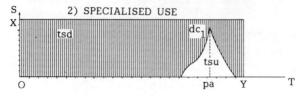

2) SPECIALISED USE

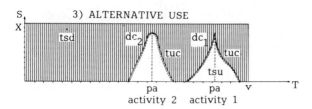

3) ALTERNATIVE USE

S = space
T = time
X = area of inhabitable space
Y = time period considered
pa = peak axis
dc1 = demand curve activity 1
dc2 = demand curve activity 2
tuc = total use curve
tsu = time space use
tsd = time space disuse

Monitoring change 5

Rita Pasqualini   Kenya

INTRODUCTION

Future trends in the development of human settlements seem to imply continuing growth and concentration of population. Most studies or speeches on the subject repeat highly impressive figures for the twenty-first century, if not sooner, and predict future situations where additional needs deriving from change will be on a scale comparable with the total provision of shelter, infrastructure and services available in settlements today.

While scenarios for the future may include possible innovations, the new realities to be expected do not promise improvement for the majority of the world's population as far as quality of life in settlements is concerned. Human settlement managers will probably have to run faster and faster to avoid losing ground in the face of accelerated change, and they will need help in keeping track not only of actions that are needed and carried out, but also of their effects within the complex system of human settlements.

Throughout the world, most actions on human settlement development tend to occur outside or ahead of plans, and sometimes even against them. Growing awareness of this reality has changed the character of human settlement planning in the direction of more flexible and open proposals, depending on the variations of circumstances, actions and events such as migration and employment, natural disasters, balance of payments and availability of resources, in addition to the usual consideration of smaller-scale human settlement components, such as infrastructural needs, population composition and land-use distribution

In order to reconcile social, economic and functional efficiency with physical and environmental constraints and requirements, the performance of human settlements has to be monitored and evaluated, so that changes required to improve the quality of life in them can be recognised and encouraged through the appropriate measures. The key factors of change, including the nature and the impact of their interrelationship, need to be identified. To a great extent, the planning process then becomes a control exercise in which all these forces are described in several alternative situations for the purpose of meeting specific goals in time and space. Because the behaviour of these forces cannot always be predicted, feedback information is necessary to re-evaluate initial goals and objectives.

It is usually acknowledged that urban development strategies should be part of a comprehensive plan. Yet, too often, even where a plan exists, there are disorganised development actions, mostly due to the lack of reality of the stated goals, the lack of coordination between planning and financing agencies or the lack of trained personnel. In most cases, however, the failure of development plans is related to the inadequate assessment or monitoring of the problems to be tackled, the resources available and the mechanisms that might maximise the effectiveness of those resources.

The dynamics of the urban environment must be evaluated carefully and closely monitored if rational decisions, appropriately and coherently adapted to the overall requirements of development, are to be made. Such considerations have prompted the search for indicators of the quality of the urban environment, or other measures providing a sufficiently accurate understanding of movement towards or away from goals or standards, observable over a period of time and providing time series data on specific geographic areas.

The present study on urban indicators reflects an intersectoral approach to the challenge of development. It attempts to convey the multiple dimensions of monitoring urban changes and to serve as a basic tool in the formulation of goals and standards for the planning and management of human settlements.

The areas of concern for urban analysis and planning have to include each of the constituent elements of the urban ecosystem: population, spatial structure, social and cultural organisation and economic premises. In the choice of indicators for physical planning, primary emphasis will be placed on factors most closely related to physical elements.

Because of their complexity, urbanisation problems have to be analysed in a way that allows an adequate understanding of the linkages within and between sectors. Among the technical characteristics recommended for indicators are that they be quantifiable, readable and based on a conceptual framework.

Within the broad range of identifiable urban indicators, attention should be given to "spatial indicators". In assessing the quality of urban environments, attributes of specific parcels of land, small areas or sections of the urban area (site characteristics) may be important but they mask some of the significant spatial relationships which define the quality of urban development in terms of access to required services (situation characteristics). Any attempt to assess urban quality should, therefore, incorporate indicators which measure the differential access to public facilities, services, employment, etc. In some instances, spatial indicators of access may provide a more accurate picture of urban quality than other indicators.

The first step in the formation of standards is the specification of goals and this involves a judicious use of indicators. The goals of development for human settlements must be clearly stated, to compare what is expected with what is available, and to choose a feasible way from the present reality to the desired future.

As for services provided in human settlements, the goal is adequate services at acceptable costs and equitably distributed. The need for service is mostly related to the population structure, its spatial distribution and the pattern of land use. Education, recreation, health and welfare are services directed towards population groups, while transport and communication, water supply and sanitation services are directed toward land use and structures. In other services, such as fire and police protection, both factors appear equally important.

Appropriate measures are required for the level of service, including the cost of providing it; the accessibility in space and time, including the cost of using it; the density, or number of users per unit, related to the average cost per user. The population or locational need can be established and the level, access and density of the services can be described by means of suitable indicators. The Appendix provides a list of indicators of this type.

DEFINITIONS OF URBAN INDICATORS

A set of indicators should describe the quality of the urban environment and be organised to provide useful information to those responsible for making decisions on the quality of that environment. Indicators are synthetic in nature, are organised in a set and have a function within policies. These three characteristics distinguish indicators from statistics.

Concerns define what to measure (e.g. indoor space), indicators define how to measure it (e.g. m^2 per person) and the actual measure or value of the indicator (e.g. 9.6 at a given time for a given area) is the result. Concerns are important aspects of human settlements and refer to the values expressed by the population groups and decision makers. Indicators should also be distinguished from the notion of criteria, which has several meanings according to context, e.g. plans or programmes may be evaluated in terms of several criteria. Standards differ from indicators because they have a compelling force while indicators simply convey information.

Urban indicators can be defined as measures of well-being or the quality of life within urban areas, along social, economic, cultural, environmental and other related dimensions. They are not ordinary data or statistics but measure quantitatively how well off the city is. Indicators can show how much or how well a particular goal or objective has been achieved. If a specific standard of achievement has been set, they can indicate whether the standard has been met.

Basic statistics on population and land use in human settlements provide information on occupancy and use that is necessary to construct meaningful indicators of the quality of development. For example, if land previously occupied by a few luxury residences is converted to mixed residential/commercial use with a higher density of structures and population, we can expect that the quality of life in the area will change. From the environmental point of view, there may be more traffic congestion, more solid waste, more noise and perhaps pollution, but from the point of view of access to services, there may be a marked improvement in that new structures are built and non-residential uses are added. In some cases the abandonment of luxury residences may reduce extreme differences in residential space available to the various population groups.

As previously stressed, indicators differ from statistics because they are synthetic, that is they combine in a simple formulation various aspects of complex information. For example, the "percentage of people with access to a given service within a given time distance" combines data on population distribution, land use and transportation that could be derived from separate sources of statistical information. Alternatively, indicators may be obtained through special surveys, where such synthetic information is measured with the methods of social research.

The second feature that differentiates indicators from statistics is their integrated character, i.e. their organisation in a set. A set of urban indicators provides quantitative information in terms of several units of measurement and indicators instead of a single index. It is useful to present the information in a way that is not excessively aggregated, to avoid the risk of allocating to various aspects a precise "weight" from the start. That means that the relative importance of various effects, e.g. those of transport on safety, noise and pollution, should be left open for decision rather than built into the single indicator of "noxiousness". To evaluate development of human settlements we need to look at the interrelationships of the various aspects involved. The more we know about factual conditions and relationships, the narrower will be the scope for disagreement on how to evaluate the set of facts that we consider "development".

The danger of biased indicators is reduced by constructing a set of measures aimed at the same concern, to illuminate different aspects of a complex condition. For example, a simple figure on m^2 per person should be associated with the distribution of qualitative elements or amenities, such as water supply for residences, pupils per class for schools, type of equipment for recreation areas, etc.

It is also inappropriate to use a single index whenever a satisfactory common unit of measurement is not available. For example, it is neither possible nor advisable to rely solely on monetary expressions, because many aspects of human settlements cannot be measured in that way.

Although statistical information also comes in sets, it is not structured in terms of causal relations and functional links. Organising information in this way constitutes the role of social research, and a combination of statistics oriented towards the discovery or confirmation of such relations is part of the work required in formulating indicators. A conceptual framework must underlie each choice of indicators. For example, the importance of sanitary provisions (water supply, flush toilets, etc) derives from the consideration that these are not mere amenities that make life more pleasant but necessities for survival, especially where population density is such that contaminated water and open sewers would create health hazards.

The third and perhaps most important feature of indicators is their function within policies. Whereas statistics can be considerd "raw" quantitative information, indicators are "processed" information that is adapted to policy formulation, implementation and evaluation.

Proper identification of goals and plans or programmes is of basic importance, and it poses practical difficulties. In this regard we may note the various levels of scale at which indicators may be required to be consistent with the range of plans and programmes. More detailed indicators may deal with various population groups and geographic areas, even within a single settlement, while general indicators may be area-wide at the settlement, regional or even national level.

Indicators can be used to control the discrepancy between reality and a given reference situation, so that corrective action can be taken. The time involved in these "early warning systems" may be very short, as in the case of alert and prevention measures for air pollution, based on given reference levels (thresholds or standards). At the opposite extreme, a long time may be involved when the difference between reality and a desirable situation requires the definition and implementation of new programmes and plans, especially long-range ones affecting large areas and covering several decades.

In the case of physical planning for human settlements, the role of indicators with regard to policies is related to that of goals and standards, and is most notable at the beginning of each planning cycle. To formulate policies it is important to go beyond general statements of "improved conditions" and "better distribution". A clear relationship with the existing situation and its specific aspects has to be stated in terms of indicators and standards. For example, "improved housing conditions" and "reduced disparity in standards of accommodation" could be expressed in terms of increased surface area per person and provision of amenities for the less privileged, and a possible maximum limit on space or "luxury".

At the start of physical planning operations, it is necessary to know what is there as well as what is wanted. A set of indicators can give a picture of the existing situation, its evolution in the past, its present trends; it also shows relationships between various elements, and points to the areas of concern that have to be acted upon. Knowledge of "what is" guides the formulation of steps to be taken towards improvement. If policies are stated in the same form as indicators, for example as percentage changes from the existing situation, goals take the form of standards, that is desired levels for indicator measures. Conversely, if goals or standards are set, policies must relate to changes in indicator values. The amount of change feasible may sometimes not be the amount of change desirable. It is important to focus expectation on realistic goals, to formulate policies that can be implemented, especially in the shorter term, if physical plans are to become a reality and affect the quality of life in the desired direction.

Once indicators are established as benchmarks to describe an existing situation, they can be measured at intervals to monitor the implementation of policies and evaluate their effects. The evaluation of variables observed through indicators, such as housing condition and adequacy of services, becomes an input for policy measures and goals for the future. Standards can be adjusted if levels reached in reality do not correspond to what was planned, or policies can be modified or strengthened, depending on priorities and resources.

THE INTEGRATED APPROACH

Indicators should literally point out relevant aspects of reality, to assist in the understanding of complex phonomena, the comparison of different situations and the monitoring of change.

In the field of human settlements, indicators of the quality of development are needed to represent the situation at various points in time and space. The complexity of human settlements makes the choice of indicators crucial. To be useful, indicators have to be synthetic and not too numerous, but must also reflect all relevant aspects of development.

The main issues should be defined in relation to each other. For example, access to employment and environmental quality cannot be pursued independently because types of productive activity and modes of transportation affect the environment.

In formulating meaningful physical planning policies related to the overall quality of human settlements, it is important to choose indicators not only for immediate physical aspects, but also for social and economic aspects that are closely linked with the development. For example, when planning for productive activities and industrial areas, the need for employment and income data is as important as that for measures of energy supply. If existing economic development plans did not specifically consider the physical aspects connected with human settlements, such as the land needed to house the employees of new factories, it is essential to compare the indicators used in the formulation of economic plans with those applied to the planning of settlement development.

Therefore, indicators recommended for physical planning represent useful tools for comprehensive or integrated planning. Integration should mean a common framework applied to physical, economic and social plans, as well as plans for various areas within a larger unit, and plans for various sectors of human settlements, such as water supply, education, commerce, transport and housing. To achieve integrated development, the location and distribution of different land uses, infrastructures and services must be related to the various elements of settlement. For example, residential areas should have adequate access to areas of employment and recreation, be supplied with water, sewers, electricity, telephone lines and other infrastructure, and include services such as schools, shops and playgrounds.

To provide a reference framework summarising links between various elements, this section will look at human settlements and indicators, pointing out the main relationships that affect the formulation of physical planning standards.

We consider two basic groups: aspects of human settlements for which physical plans are made, and concerns for urban indicators, for which measures of "what is" are devised. "What should be", corresponding to the goals of physical planning and specified through standards, can be defined only after considering the main interrelationships between elements of the two groups.

For each group, the suggested methodology advances from a simplified list of main headings to a detailed enumeration of specific types. For example, transport is an aspect of human settlements that can be subdivided at first in two main categories: intra-urban or city traffic, and inter-urban or long-distance transport. Each of these can be further specified by mode (land, air, water), means (train, car, truck), built elements (roads, rail lines, bridges, ports, stations) and other possible factors, such as speed, number and type of passengers, pollution etc. It should be noted that transport and the various ways to look at it also appear among the concerns for indicators, and the subdivisions listed above could apply to the formulation of detailed indicators.

Although the various categories listed above attempt to cover the entire field, it is conceivable that a new or unusual type of transport (or something else) may be found in human settlements which does not fit in the existing categories. The purpose of the more general categories would be, in such a case, to provide broad guidelines on the relevance and applicability of indicators for the formulation of standards. An example could be aerial tramways: they can be considered intra-settlement transport (as they are usually of short range); whether the mode should be land rather than air (as their structures may need a base on the soil at frequent intervals) depends on the specific instance, and they can therefore be included under the broad category of intra-settlement passenger transport.

The main pupose of the general headings, however, is to present some principles in a simplified form, as a first step from which further details can be elaborated with a common reference point. The tables in this section are examples, and alternative formulations are possible according to specific circumstances.

In Table 1 a tentative presentation is made of the direction in which the main elements affect one another. This corresponds to the general experience of physical planning in most countries, and special cases where different relationships could apply are not considered, in order to keep the table as simple, clear and useful as possible. In this, as in other schematic presentations, the spirit (or methodological approach) counts for more than the letter (or the specific examples presented). Users should not feel limited to what is presented, but include along similar lines what applies in their case.

The most general subdivision that we propose considers six main aspects of human settlements: industry, services, shelter, recreation, transport, utilities. This sequence does not imply any hierarchy, but has the advantage of allowing more than one way of regrouping the headings. For example, industry, services, shelter, and in part, recreation may be called "structures", while transport and utilities are mainly "infrastructures". Also, industry and services are the main places of employment, while residence and recreation are the places for rest and leisures. Transport and utilities usually do not represent places but rather movement of people, goods, energy, water, waste.

Concerns for indicators of the quality of urban development may be grouped under the following headings:

□ Natural environment: geography, climate, disasters and environmental nuisances (the latter, although man-made, affect mostly air and water).

□ Economic factors: income, employment, industrial activity, and building activity as a special case.

□ Social (or service) factors: health, education, welfare, safety and recreation.

□ Spatial structure and other "settlement" factors: housing, transport, urban development (as a synthesis of access factors), land tenure and costs, slums and squatter settlements.

Table 1 should be used as a model for establishing the main cause and effect relations between elements. The chosen symbols represent one-way causal links between concern and aspect (→) or between aspect and concern (←); mutual effects (↔); and effects in two different directions(↑→), as in the case of utilities and natural environment: climate and geography affect mostly the supply, while disposal affects the environment. A "general" category has been added to include broader implications, so that only the most important links between concerns and specific aspects appear in the table.

It may be useful to provide a short explanation of Table 1, with direct reference to physical planning processes. In view of the goals of improving the quality of life in human settlements, plans are formulated to orient action for better conditions. Existing conditions, as reflected by indicators, provide a starting point and a constraint; in time, the same indicators will show what improvements have been made. To formulate and draw up plans for residences and transport, one should consider their impact on settlement conditions and their feasibility under existing circumstances. Location plans for industry should take into account the effects on the environment, mainly to avoid the creation of nuisances; they should aim at improving the economic picture but, at the same time, are clearly conditioned by the existing economic situation. In general terms, natural and economic factors tend to act as constraints on various aspects of human settlements, limiting the quality levels that can be attained in them. Conversely, social concerns and settlement-related indicators will be mostly affected by changes in various aspects of human settlements.

A further step in orienting the user of indicators for the formulation of physical plans could be a list of concerns, including all those named in the groups above, combined with a similar broad division in the aspects of human settlements. Choosing the two most relevant components for each aspect, we propose a model where residences could be conventional, or slums and squatter settlements; transport could be inter-urban or intra-urban; utilities could be in terms of provision (water, gas, electricity) or disposal (sewerage, solid waste); and the general category could be subdivided between structures (buildings) and infrastructures. Such divisions should be used only where marked differences appear in the relationships between concerns for urban indicators and each of the two secondary aspects.

These two preliminary stages should have alerted users to the importance of relating and integrating various types of goals and actions. To prepare an operational set of guidelines for physical planning, the extensive list of functional aspects of human settlements proposed in the Appendix as land-use information should be used as model, with all the required adjustments for specific situations. Each land use under the relevant headings would be considered in respect of an equally extensive list of indicators, compiled with the help of the examples listed in the Appendix. If an indicator or measure is chosen for air pollution, guidelines in respect of land uses that can affect that measure should be formulated with a view to their impact on the indicator.

Table 2 is presented as an example of the proposed second stage. It relates more specific aspects of human settlements to the more detailed concerns listed above. A new symbol, $\cong$, indicates similarity between concerns and aspects.

Note that housing, transport, recreation and industry appear both as concerns and as aspects of human settlements. This reflects the basic role of these elements, both as land users and as determinants of the quality of life and development. In particular, services such as health, education, welfare and safety appear in detail among the concerns, because of the variety of indicators representing them. Detailed lists of services as land uses should be related to another type of information, the demographic composition.

Indicators are synthetic information well adapted to policy formulation, implementation and evaluation. Indicators of the quality of development in human settlements should clearly focus on the need for, and the provision of, services and other elements of development.

For population-specific services, such as health, education and welfare, indicators should be related to the population segments that need the service most. An essential component of such indicators is the demographic structure, as well as the distribution of population over the area. However, population structure is not an immediate indicator of existing conditions or the quality of human settlement development. Demographic statistics represent a very important component or input of more complex formulations on the quality of life. To illustrate the difference, the following section will describe in detail the use of data on population in devising indicators that are useful for human settlements.

POPULATION

Although not in themselves indicators of urban development, demographic data such as size, structure density and changes in population by age, sex, ethnic group, area of residence and other specific variables are basic inputs for indicators of need and provision of population-related services, as well as those for employment/income and shelter.

The growth in population (natural and migratory) is the basis for forecasts and planning provisions. If great differences over time, space and population groups are found in such demographic elements as births, deaths, migration, density and age-sex composition, they probably reflect extreme conditions and socio-economic imbalances. Changes in such factors may be the result of policy action, especially in the long term. As demographic data are collected in censuses and other official surveys, they may be the starting point for a system of indicators.

However, the relative ease with which demographic statistics are collected, compared with other measures proposed for indicators, should not bias the choice of indices and data, especially in their application in planning. Of particular importance is the distribution of variables. In demographic terms, this can mean distribution of the population over different areas (for example, in certain places density may reach values far above the acknowledged averages), and distribution of characteristics among social groups and geographic areas. Age compositions may differ widely between sections of a settlement and clearly affect standards for education or welfare provisions. It is therefore advisable that survey research methods be considered in addition to administrative record-keeping systems for human settlements, especially in less developed countries.

The Appendix proposes some important types of demographic data to be used in physical planning operations. More detailed formulations may be used for specific purposes.

LAND

Another basic element of human settlements is land. In establishing guidelines for physical planning, land-use allocation is probably the main concern: information on existing land use is an important basis for evaluating human settlement development, but it would be incorrect to call such data "indicators". Land tenure and costs, however, have been listed among detailed concerns for indicators, as they represent the interplay between socio-economic factors and the physical element of land. Indicators on tenure and cost should be associated with land uses, to give a clearer picture of development.

For planning purposes information on existing land use should be gathered with the degree of detail that is feasible and appropriate. If there are plans for future land uses, information on them should also be collected and compared with the existing situation. As suggested in the Appendix, categories can be more or less general and the information presented in maps showing locations and surfaces or in tables indicating the area or the percentage of total surface area allocated to each use. The concentration or dispersion of land uses should be noted, along with the adequacy or inadequacy of land allocation for various uses.

On the basis of the existing situation and plans, especially with data on changes in land use over time, standards for land use can be formulated which will take into account need, feasibility and equity in distribution. For example, public parks and accessible open spaces may at first glance provide enough surface area per inhabitant, either in the existing or in the planned allocation of land use. However, the nature, size and location of public open spaces may not cover the needs of some population groups (by area, age or other characteristic), or may be too costly to maintain, especially in relation to the actual users.

Information on land use should be used together with population data in the formulation of indicators and standards for services and recreation. To ensure access for the population groups concerned, a specific concern for indicators has been called "urban development" and is a synthesis of access factors.

GENERAL GUIDELINES

Too much information may be as misleading as too little. In establishing a set of indicators for physical planning, the practical choice should focus on the quality and quantity of data, so that useful synthetic measures are derived from reliable sources of information. A survey of available and potential sources is a necessary step at the beginning. This will avoid the choice of indicators that are unavilable and will set up in advance means to gather crucial information that may be missing.

The period and areas for which data are available should be compared with those for which indicators are required. Within limits, extrapolations can be made by assuming some trends over time or some homogeneity over space. It is better, however, to obtain at least sample information to check these estimates. Comparisons between areas and periods should be made carefully; the data base should not be incompatible. A mistake to be avoided is the waste of time and money on elaborate calculations with data that are not accurate or adequate. Rather than sophisticated models, a simple commonsense approach is recommended which is in direct contact with reality as far as possible. For example, data on land ownership and costs may come from sources related to taxation, and it is legally possible for different names to appear for parcels owned by one individual or family, and it is also possible that prices of transactions are not correctly recorded. Knowledge of the local economic scene or information from various sources may correct this type of bias in the official sources. This is particularly important if standards have to be derived in relation to the existing situation, because an incorrect picture may cause targets to be set beyond the range where they are useful and relevant.

INDICATORS AND STANDARDS FOR PHYSICAL PLANNING

It is important that the information of "what is" - indicators, statistical data and survey results - should not only reflect the economic, social and environmental aspects of human settlements, but be related in a functional and comprehensive way to the existing situation and the desired path for change and development. For example, the importance of the informal sector should be recognised through indicators of its role in the economy and society, in particular regarding slums and squatter settlements. If policy goals for such settlements involve an upgrading in the quality of life, inherent limitations such as land requirements, demographic patterns and cost of materials should be considered. A comprehensive view of the various elements involved and of their causes and effects is necessary to devise decisions, plans and physical standards feasible in a reasonable period of time.

It has been noted that, in almost all developing countries, the total capital requirements for services and amenities at existing standards exceed the available resources. In addition, given the prevailing power structure and the strong pressures from the minority whose standard of living calls for the monopolisation of most of the nation's savings, virtually no resources can be diverted to the needs of the lower strata of the population.

There is a need to identify the expected demand for services and infrastructure of a large segment of the population whose needs and aspirations are constantly evolving. Intimately related is the need to formulate priorities based on minimum standards that will benefit the majority and not continue to fulfil the aspirations of the few as is at present the case. Basic "trade-offs" attitudes should regulate the delicate balance between the levels of service, the cost involved within the basic constraints of an endemic shortage of funds, and the proportion of the population served.

The choice of reference values for indicators is the formulation of standards and norms. Norms and standards are the expression of the relative priorities set by governments and therefore the representation of a political process. Most standards related to the control of human settlement growth and development set targets for actual policies. This situation, given the peculiarity of each contextual situation, precludes any attempt to define standards applicable to all developing countries.

Social science can attempt to provide some basis for assessing performance standards (once they have been formulated by the political authority), to measure the actual process, compare it with these norms and standards, and to recommend measures which may help narrow the gap between the ideal and actual situations. Public policy makers should be cautioned against excessive optimism: urban indicators are no substitute for a clear concept of the process to be controlled, nor for the type of thorough administrative process necessary when hypothetical figures are to be translated into real changes which affect the life of people in urban areas.

The purpose of indicators in development planning is to determine the relevant entity to be observed, so that an adequate level can be identified for the crucial factors and efforts focused on reaching that level. For example, the needs of people in human settlements include elements of vital importance for health and survival, especially clean and safe water, clean air and food. Clean and safe water has to be defined in terms of the presence of extraneous elements: their level and frequency represent one aspect of the indicator to be observed at different points in time and space to establish trends and evaluate progress in the provision of safe water for human beings. Another aspect of the indicator is the number of people and the times they are provided with water of a certain quality. A standard for quality and provision has to be established in relation to the desired goal. For clean water it may be a "safe" level of extraneous elements for an established proportion of users. Such a standard can be evolved over time.

The relation of standards to indicators is twofold. Not only are indicators needed to establish what is a feasible and desirable standard; a standard or fixed measure is often needed to develop indicators such as the previously mentioned safe water supply. The following discussion of indicators and standards should be read in its more general methodological implications: the word "standard" is interchangeable with "target" or "goal" and therefore can apply to broader processes of human settlement planning.

As the value of indicators changes, so should the target. For example, the required number of parking spaces per dwelling has to increase with car ownership. This may be achieved through gradual (discontinuous) rises in standard level or through a functional (continuous) evolution related to indicators. It is therefore important to obtain information at different points over a period of time so that indicators will give a clear picture of "what is" in respect to "what was before". Any forecast of "what will be" can thus be compared with evolution in the recent past, and be periodically verified with actual data. In the example of car ownership (indicator) and provision of parking spaces (standard), the two approaches to changes in time can be presented as follows.

Figure 1 illustrates a hypothetical curve of car ownership per y people , e.g. 10, 100, 1000, according to circumstances. In the recent past, the number of cars per y people has increased more or less continuously, and it can be expected to increase at the same rate. On the basis of this projection, standards for adequate parking space can be set in different ways. One is to choose the expected car ownership in twenty years and set a standard that will be adequate then. During this period, a physical plan is expected to be gradually implemented and therefore gradual additions to parking space will be made according to the new standard. The graph reflecting the provision of parking space could be like that of Figure 2.

There is, however, the possibility that future developments in car ownership will not correspond to expectations. If car ownership grows faster than expected, the standard will soon be inadequate. Conversely, if the increase in car ownership does not reach the expected level, the chosen standard may involve more expense than necessary or be disregarded.

Another approach is to set standards in gradual increments, following the expected rise in car ownership, but allowing for periodic adjustments, as in Figure 3. If intermediate standards are set according to the expected figure for car ownership after five, ten and fifteen years, they can be compared with the values actually recorded for the indicator at the same intervals. This procedure would involve a trial-and-error approach. As Figure 1 shows, in case (a) actual values are higher than expected, and after five years (Figure 3) a higher standard than before would be chosen for the next interval. After ten years, a slight downward adjustment can be made by comparison with the actual value of indicators, and so on. In case (b), actual values are lower than expected, and the standard is adjusted accordingly. The hypotheses presented in Figures 1 and 3 are chosen to show the effect of two opposite situations. Comparing the two figures, we note that adjustments in the standards are delayed by one period (in this example, five years) but still present a pattern closer to actual data than the original forecast.

The danger of recognising a trend when it is about to change is inherent in measurements of phenomena subject to cycles. Periodic adjustments will avoid the most serious mistakes, especially where plans are made for a relatively distant future (twenty to thirty years or more) and their implementation depends on relatively scarce resources. Flexible standards tied to indicators could also be formulated as a continuous function of indicator values for phenomena measured at intervals more frequent than the revisions of plans and regulations in which standards are embodied.

As an example of a functional relationship between standards and corresponding indicators, when the value of the indicator varies continuously, we suggest a case where accurate projections can be made for a reasonable period (five to fifteen years). The population of school age can be used in this instance, because within the range of time indicated the annual enrolment in compulsory educational programmes can be precisely forecast on the basis of the population that will be of school age in the near future, combined with normal rates of school attendance. The size and distribution of schools should closely match that of the student population, and it is possible to express a standard for provision of classrooms in relation to the number of potential users, based on current demographic data and projections rather than on an abstract estimate. Therefore, instead of a ratio between classrooms and total inhabitants, assuming a hypothetical or "average" distribution of schoolchildren, a ratio could be expressed with direct reference to the school-age population living in the area to be served. We suggest, for example, a standard such as "one classroom (for a given school level) for every X children attending that school". This implies a definite age range for the students, as well as an appropriate distance range between the school and the homes of students. On this basis, it is possible to adjust and plan the provision of individual schools in two otherwise identical areas, in terms of the demographic structure of each, rather than impose a set formula on population groups that vary in their composition. Clearly, this approach is also very valuable in providing for changes over time: plans for schools to be built in five to fifteen years will match the expected need at the established standard level. The "optimal" number X of children per classroom should not be rigid in its application. While a single figures is used to compute the number of classrooms for a given student population, it practice classes will cover a range for which X could be the middle point. Where large-scale migration occurs, the method proposed can still be useful although there will be a certain time lag.

Standards and indicators are important elements in efforts to improve the quality of life in human settlements and in general. They should also be used to achieve a more equitable distribution of benefits, with priority given to the needs of the most disadvantaged people. Indicators of distribution beyond the "average" figure are needed to ensure that improvements occur where the situation is inadequate, and that standards are met everywhere. For example, a variable such as m^2 per person (dwelling space per resident, office space per worker, classroom area per pupil) can be measured as an average but should be seen in its actual distribution. If we plot the percentages of people (p) having at least (s) m^2 each, we may find that the various patterns do not automatically correspond to average values. If the distribution is like this, the average is 4.7 m^2 (Figure 4). If the standard of space were five m^2 per person, 60 per cent of the population would have reached it; but only 30 per cent have six m^2 or more and 40 per cent have two or fewer m^2 per person.

If the situation changed to that of Figure 5, where the average is 5.3 m^2 per person, 40 per cent of the population would still have two or fewer m^2 per person. The hypothetical standard of five m^2 would still be met by 60 per cent of the population, and the only improvement would be that 50 per cent would have six or more m^2, 40 per cent eight or more, and 20 per cent the hypothetical maximum of ten m^2 per person. If equitable distribution and the needs of the disadvantages are important goals, a more appreciable improvement could be realised with the distribution shown in Figure 6. The average is again 4.7 m^2, as in Figure 4, but the proportion of people with two or fewer m^2 is reduced to 10 per cent, and the standard of five m^2 is reached by 70 per cent. Those with six m^2 or more still account for 30 per cent, but their surface area per capita is now within more reasonable limits. On the assumption that five m^2 is an accepted standard, the indicator for space availability could be "percentage of people with 4-6 m^2 per person", i.e. within a margin of one-fifth, or one square metre above or below the standard value. This indicator, unlike the average surface area, would differentiate between the situations of Figures 4 and 6, respectively 30 per cent and 70 per cent, while the average was 4.7 m^2 in both cases. For the situation of Figure 5, which gave an average of 5.3 m², the new indicator would be 20 per cent, pointing to an inequality in distribution and the importance of extreme values.

In the preceding examples, the figure chosen for the hypothetical standard was both the mid-point of the range (assumed from 0 to 10) and the full figure nearest to the existing average. In Figures 4 and 6, five m² is also the modal value, i.e. the value at which the highest number of cases is found. Figure 5 would have three modes: at ten, eight and two m² per person, since all three values apply to 20 per cent of the population. In the choice of indicators and standards, a variety of tools can be used, such as statistical measures and mathematical operations. However, the criteria for selecting the appropriate tools depend on the criteria applied in the selection of indicators and standards.

Feasibility is an important aspect, and concerns the availablity both of information for indicators and the means to implement standards. Another example on m² per person could illustrate this point.

In Figure 7, the range of m² per person goes from "two or fewer" to "ten and more", and it is not possible to derive an exact average value from the information available. As "two or fewer" is the mode, we cannot consider it as a suitable standard; a mid-point for the range could be five or six or anything above that.

The only statistical tool suitable in this case could be the median (four m² in this case). It could be justified as the level reached by 60 per cent of the population, and as the level to which the remaining 40 per cent should be adjusted to bring the largest disadvantaged group on a level with the majority. If the costs should be too high, a minimum standard could first be set at three m² per person, to be raised later as the situation improves. The ideal is to have no one below the established minimum standard, so that a desirable higher standard can be reached. This concept corresponds to the ideal of progressive minimum standards.

METHODOLOGY AND APPLICATION

An example of the use of indicators in relation to goals and strategies can be provided by some observations on the following proposals made by the United Nations in 1971. Items of particular relevance to physical planning were selected.

Strategy elements	Proposed indicators
Improvement of levels of health	a) Crude death rate
	b) Infant mortality rate
	c) Expectation of life at birth
Provision of health facilities	a) Doctors per 1000 of population
	b) Nurses per 1000 of population
	c) Hospital beds per 1000 of population
	d) Dentists per 1000 of population
Improvements of housing	a) Average number of occupants per room
	b) Proportion of dwellings with three or more occupants per room
	c) Proportion of dwellings with two or fewer rooms

  d) Proportion of dwellings with piped
      water
  e) Proportion of dwellings with
      electricity

The indicators proposed above also illustrate some differences between possible types
of data. The first two indicators of health distinguish only between the rate of mortality
of the entire population and that of one age group. Both rates could be specified by
main causes, especially where some types of illness are predominant and can be clearly
related to environmental conditions. For example, mortality caused by gastro-enteric
diseases is related to poor sanitary conditions, especially water supply, and its
improvement should reflect a better access to pure water. Further breakdowns of
mortality rates by social groups may be useful in special cases: for example, a higher
rate for women may reflect maternal mortality and therefore lack of medical assistance
during and after pregnancy and childbirth.

Frequently this problem can be detected through perinatal mortality (i.e. infant deaths
occurring shortly before or after birth). The most useful indicators of health for
physical planning, however, should be those related to areas, showing how death rates
(by cause and victim) vary between different types or sections of human settlements.
Unlike the third proposed indicator (expectation of life at birth), mortality rates can be
computed easily and updated frequently, and often the information is collected on the
basis of relatively small areas.

In the provision of health facilities, the proposed indicators focus on the number of
professionals or equipment in relation to the number of people. This may apply to an
entire country or a large region, and it is not an adequate indicator for physical
planning since it does not consider the distribution of services provided in relation to
the distirbution of the population they serve. The example of health can be generalised
to education and other services.

Indicators of services provided or at least services readily available in human
settlements should focus on the population served. The proportion of people living within
an acceptable distance from the service, or the average number of people per service
found within such a distance, should give a better idea of the accessibility of health,
education or other facilities. On maps and plans, the density of population and that of
services could be compared visually by geographic areas, highlighting deficiencies as
well as areas where standards are exceeded. It should be noted that facilities for health,
education or other services should be differentiated in their specialisation and scope.
There are neighbourhood clinics and regional hospitals, elementary schools and
universities, and the number of people to be served and the acceptable distance will
vary in each case.

Improvement of housing is certainly a common goal in human settlements, and the
proposed indicators are probably the most clearly related to physical planning. The first
(average number of occupants per room) is easily calculated, and should be readily
available for small areas. In extreme cases, however, some occupants may not be
enumerated, especially if their presence is illegal, and some rooms may be very different
from others, even within a rather limited context. The next two indicators,
complementary in nature, look at the crowding of housing stock (proportion of dwelling

with three or more occupants per room) and at its composition by size, focusing on the smaller dwellings (proportion with two or fewer rooms). The latter may be useful in some cases, but could be misleading if the context is not specified. For example, single people may live more than adequately in apartments counted as "two rooms" (or fewer). Local customs may encourage very large communal spaces in dwellings, still counted as "one room" but not comparable with other "rooms" even in the same area. Second houses or guest cottages may have one or two rooms but no regular occupants. If crowding and inadequate size of dwellings are a concern, more appropriate indicators could focus on the proportion of inhabitants sharing a room with two or more others, or living in a dwelling with no separate kitchen or sleeping space. By area, this information should be easily obtainable, supplementing central data with surveys when the former is not adequate or up to date. 'It can provide guidelines for standards and their implementation, concentrating efforts on the most needy groups. A more precisely measurable and comparable indicator is m^2 per person, but such information is not as frequently or easily collected as that on rooms per dwelling.

Similarly, the proportion of dwellings with specific amenities such as electricity, flush toilets and piped water, should be supplemented or even supplanted as an indicator by the proportion of inhabitants with or without such amenities by area, and other relevant characteristics, such as age, family size, income level and occupation.

In the brief review of these examples, various types of indicators have been discussed: general versus specific (death rates: overall, by victims, by cause, by area); provision versus use (existing units per total population versus population within range of service); average values versus extremes (occupants per room or proportion in overcrowded conditions); and the existence of selected amenities (piped water, electricity). The choice among the various types and their combinations should be guided by availability of information, and the reliability and relevance to the condition investigated.

By availability we mean the existence of sources and time series of data; reliable data are consistent and sound in quality; and information is relevant when it relates to what we want to know. For example, if we want to know about population access to services, data on public transportation routes and schedules and length of roads and streets leading to services are more easily available than reports on the time used and the distance covered by actual and potential users of the services. The time required by a bus to cover a given distance does not always correspond to what appears on the schedule; repeated measures will show the extent of variation that can be found. The smaller this variation, the better the reliability of the source of information. If it is known through obwervation, or if it can be reasonably assumed that the majority of users of the service reach it by means of public transportation, the relevance of bus schedule information to accessibility will be much greater that if most users reach it on foot, by bicycle or by car.

The above criteria are similar to those of "feasibility" and "validity" proposed by the Organisation for Economic Cooperation and Development (OECD) in 1975 for classifying indicators according to the following scale:

(1) Denotes an indicator for which data, whether administrative or obtained from surveys, exist, are regularly published and correspond closely to the specifications of indicators for the majority of OECD member countries.

(2) Denotes an indicator for which data collecting methods exist, which could be applied to the indicator in the short term (say, within two years). This could be done by modifying existing statistical programmes, e.g. by adding questions to a survey, or by designing new surveys.

(3) Denotes an indicator for which the problems of specification and definition have not yet been resolved, or for which data collection would imply a large-scale statistical effort. Data for such an indicator could only be obtained in the long term.

Two criteria are used in classifying the indicators according to their validity: whether an indicator measures all or only part of the social concern it is intended to measure; and whether an indicator measures only the social concern it is intended to measure, or whether it is influenced by factors independent of that concern, i.e. it is systematically biased by such factors.

Thus, the validity of an indicator depends on how well it matches the corresponding concern or sub-concern. The three points on the scale of validity are therefore the following:

(a) Denotes an indicator which corresponds exactly to a social concern, and which is not biased by independent factors.

(b) Denotes an indicator which is not biased by independent factors, but which corresponds to only part of a social concern.

(c) Denotes an indicator which is biased.

In some cases, however, where a number of indicators complement one another in such a way that together they correspond to the social concern they are designed to measure, they are grouped together and assigned the same degree of validity. As a preliminary step in the establishment of feasible and valid indicators, the Appendix to this paper will propose for different concerns the main types of indicators that appear useful for human settlement planning purposes. Specific examples are also given, mainly to suggest the practical application of the general principles, not necessarily to direct (much less to limit) the choice of indicators to be used in particular contexts.

It should be observed once again that data on population and land, while of basic importance in the formulation of indicators, seldom provide the kind of information that could be classified as an indicator of urban development. The Appendix therefore lists demographic and land-use information first, followed by indicators and examples of measures for the concerns listed in this paper.

Table 1.

Concerns for Indicators	ASPECTS OF HUMAN SETTLEMENTS						
	Industry	Services	Shelter	Recreation	Transport	Utilities	General
Natural environment	←			↔		↑→	→
Economic	↔						→
Socio-cultural		←		←			←
Settlement factors			←		←		←

Table 2 Specific aspects of human settlements related to detailed "concerns"

CONCERNS FOR INDICATORS	GENERAL RELEVANCE	SPECIFIC ASPECTS OF HUMAN SETTLEMENTS												
		STRUCTURE					SERVICE		RECREATIONAL		INFRASTRUCTURE			
		INDUSTRIAL			RESIDENTIAL						TRANSPORT		COMMUNICATION	UTILITIES
	Structure	Infra-structure	Capital-intensive	Labour-intensive	Convent-ional	Slums & Squatter Settlements	Public	Private	Covered	Open space	Inter-space	Intra-urban	Provision urban	Disposal
ENVIRONMENT														
Geography	↑	↑								↑	↑		↑	
Climate	↑	↑								↑			↑	
Disasters	↑	↑			↑						↓			↓
Nuisances	↓		↓											
ECONOMIC														
Income	↑	↑		↓	↑		↓				↑	↑	↑	
Employment			≈ll	↕				↓					↓	
Industrial activity	↕			↕	↕						↓			
Building activity	↑													↓
CULTURAL														
Health	↓		↓	↕		↓	↓	↓				↓	↓	↓
Education				↑			↓		↓					
Welfare							↓		↓					↑
Safety			↓	↓		↓		↓						
Recreation	↓								≈ll	≈ll	↓	↓	↓	
SETTLEMENT														
Housing	↓		↓		≈ll	≈ll	↑				≈ll	≈ll	↑	↑
Transport	↑			↓						↓				
Urban development	↓											↓	↓	
Land tenure and costs	↑				↑	↑	↑	↑		↑				
Slums and squatter settlements	↓		↓			≈ll	↓					↕	↕	↑

Figure 1
car ownership
per y people

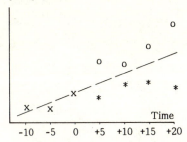

x = actual data up to the present
o = possible data in future (case a)
* = possible data in future (case b)

Figure 2
Parking space
per y people

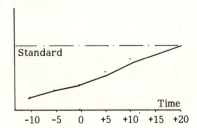

Figure 3
Parking space
per y people

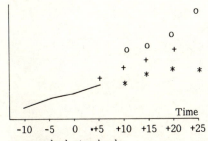

++ gradual standards
oo adjusted standards (case a)
** adjusted standards (case b)

Figure 4

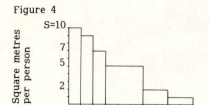

Figure 5

Percentage of people
with at least (s) m²

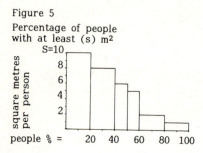

Figure 6

Percentage of people
with at least (s) m²

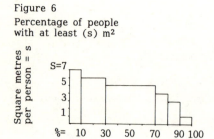

Figure 7

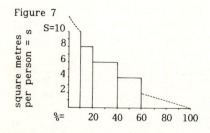

APPENDIX: PROPOSED TYPES OF INDICATORS

DEMOGRAPHIC INFORMATION

Indicators

Size, structure, density and changes in population by age, sex, ethnic group, area of residence, and specific variables relevant in each case.

Examples

□ Live births per 1000 females of child-bearing age, related to the age/sex structure and mortality rates, represent natural population growth over a certain period.

□ Net rate of rural/urban migration per 1000 population, related to existing rural/urban composition, represent population change due to migration.

□ Density of population, in relation to area of residence and age/sex structure, shows the extent of depopulation or overcrowding, when compared with overall averages or with a standard considered the acceptable level in the area.

□ Number, percentage and average size of families in rural and urban areas show the extent of family needs, e.g. in housing, and in specific sub-areas can be compared with average size of households in the entire area.

□ Other examples of demographic information showing the need for population-related services are school-age population (for education), infant and overall mortality (for health), retirement-age population (for welfare).

LAND USE

Indicators

Location, distribution, surface area or percentage of total rural urban or other land at the national, regional or local level used or planned for specified purposes.

Examples

□ General categories: human settlements, urban or non-urban uses, residential or non-residential, accessible or not to the public, vacant.

□ Specific categories

- agricultural (arable, irrigated, cultivated, pasture, forest, specific cultures)
- mining and quarrying (underground, above ground, adjacent facilites)
- manufacturing (light, heavy, noisy, hazardous, polluting)
- energy production (by mode, scale of area served, type of installation)
- transport (intra-urban, inter-urban, type of facility)
- storage and warehousing (related to transport, industry, commerce)
- commerce (gross, retail, import/export, local)
- offices (related to industry, commerce, transport)
- government (by level and types of facilities, including military)
- services (by type, level: health, education, etc)
- housing (by type, scale of area served)
- recreation (by type, scale of area served)

- open space (by type, scale of area served)
- other, according to specific circumstances, e.g. religious uses; major construction
  sites; redevelopment areas.

CLIMATE

Indicators
Number or percentage of days, people or surface area associated with specified clamatic
conditions: average values, distribution in time and space, extreme levels, effects in
relation to area and people exposed over the statistically available period.

Examples (macro-climate and micro-climate)
□ Normal temperatures and number of cooling or heating degree days per year, persons
  and surfaces affected.
□ Maximum and minimum temperatures and percentages above maximum and below minimum
  established as acceptable.
□ Monthly precipitation, hours of sunshine, ventilation (speed of air movement, rate of
  air change).

NATURAL DISASTERS

Indicators
Population, structures and services affected by natural disasters over statistically
relevant period.

Examples
□ Annual average over X years of population, structures and services affected by
  earthquakes, floods, landslides, subsidences, high winds or hurricanes, etc.
□ Total effect of latest disaster.
□ Total effect of worst disaster in the past Y years.

ENVIRONMENTAL NUISANCES

Indicators
Level of relevant or disturbing factors, their distribution in time and space, and the
number or percentage of people affected at certain levels.

Examples
□ Air pollution: population in areas with outdoor concentrations or specific pollutants in
  excess of defined levels on average, or with a percentage of observations above
  defined levels for shorter periods.
□ Drinking water: population multiplied by number of days when water supplied is not
  safe for drinking, according to defined levels of safety for specific pollutants.
□ Recreational waters: percentage of total shore line and shore length per 1000
  inhabitants where water quality allows swimming, boating, fishing, other water sports
  and visual amenities.

□ Noise: population exposed to specified levels by day and by night.
□ Solid waste: amount of waste produced in relation to inhabitants, area for disposal, collection, recycling.

DISTRIBUTION OF INCOME

Indicators
Absolute and relative amounts of income available to households and individuals, consumption of goods and government consumption expenditure per household or individual affected (mainly by residence, ethnic group, age, sex; mean or other statistical value, and percentages of total represented by the highest and lowest fractile groups).

Examples
□ Income data: household and per capita disposable income, its sources and composition (earned or unearned, money or other).
□ Consumption data: household and per capital total consumption, its composition (percentage of food, clothing, shelter), government consumption expenditure assigned to households.

EMPLOYMENT

Indicators
Number and percentages of people employed or not, over the total, and the working age population, by sex, ethnic group, area of residence, age range, education level, occupational sector and other specific variables relevant in each case. The relation of the above to physical structures, economic factors and time.

Examples
□ Labour force data: rates of participation, composition of labour force and population outside labour force.
□ Industry data: average number of employees per establishment (in manufacturing and other economic sectors); average space per establishment and employee; and days worked, paid holidays, hours lost for accidents or labour disputes.

INDUSTRY

Indicators
Level and composition of output in mining and manufacturing, in relation to GNP import/export, local resources, needs and population. Quantity, quality and growth of industrial plant and equipment, by area and period of time.

Examples
□ Production: average yearly output, and its percentage of GNP, share of inputs from local resources, share of final output for local use, origin and destination of intermediate products.

□ Development: new investment relative to existing stock and GNP; age composition of plant and machines; production increases relative to cost increases; and changes in productivity and their components.

CONSTRUCTION

Indicators
Amount and type of construction by area, in relation to economic and social factors, inputs and outputs.

Examples
□ Economic data: total construction as percentage of fixed capital formation and GNP; value added by construction sector to GDP; and building materials in relation to imports, local production and requirements.
□ Social data: percentage and characteristics of active population employed in construction; and relation between local construction activity, resident and employed population; and between new construction and immigration.
□ Physical data: composition and distribution of construction by types (buildings, roads, other; residential, commercial, public buildings; high or low rise, cost, density; local or imported materials, etc).

HEALTH
Indicators
Health condition of population by area and groups. Health services provided and received. Access to health services. Sanitary conditions in areas of residence and work.

Examples
□ Mortality: rates by age, sex, cause; maternal, perinatal and infant mortality; life expectancy by sex and age group.
□ Disease: number and incidence of selected communicable diseases of public health importance; ratio of physically handicapped from birth, disease or accident; and rate of prevalence of illness (people too ill to pursue normal activities).
□ Nutrition: percentage of population with adequate nutritional intake (energy, protein) by age group and sex, in particular pregnant and nursing mothers; malnutrition in children (percentage by age group); and access of population to safe drinking water (see also environmental nuisances).
□ Services available: number and characteristics of available conventional health service buildings and hospital beds, by area and population served within a given radius; and number and speciality of practising medical personnel by area and population served within a given radius.
□ Services received: proportion of births attended by doctors or trained auxiliary personnel; proportion of population in relevant age groups immunised and vaccinated; proportion of population visiting primary health service posts; average frequency of visits; average duration of stay in hospitals; average delay between occurrence of an emergency event and appropriate treatment; and average delay between awareness of functional disturbance (non-emergency) and appropriate treatment.

□ Health costs: total annual expenditure on health services as percentage of GNP;
average annual expenditure on health per household or individial; and share of costs
paid by users or financed from other sources.

□ Sanitary conditions (by area and population affected): types of sanitation available:
water supply, sewers, waste removal and disposal; and hazards: presence of
health-damaging factors near places of residence or employment.

EDUCATION

Indicators
Level and cost of education obtained and available by sex, age and ethnic group, area of
residence, income and occupation.

Examples
□ Education obtained: literacy rates, years of school completed, types of formal and
informal training.

□ Education available: yearly enrolment by type of education or training, full or
part-time; ratio of teachers to full-time students; number and type of conventional
educational buildings in relation to population served within adequate range; and
percentage of population living within a reasonable distance from the various types of
institutions.

□ Cost of education: total consumption expenditure on education as a percentage of GNP;
sources of expenditure; cost to individual students; and gross fixed capital formation
in education (by level) as percentage of total.

WELFARE

Indicators
Level and type of assistance provided, in relation to population served; structures for
assistance, cost of services.

Examples (mainly by area, sex, age and social group)
□ Eligible population in relation to total population and recipients of benefits.

□ Number and type of conventional buildings for welfare services, in relation to
population served (eligible, recipients, resident in area).

□ Type and total cost of welfare assistance in relation to population served (eligible,
recipients, resident in area).

□ Share of welfare payments in total available income and government spending.

SAFETY (POLICE AND FIRE PROTECTION)

Indicators
Number and type of incidents by area, people affected, action by public services.
Number of protective facilities and services by area and population affected; results of
action.

Examples (mainly by area and social group)

☐ Incidents: loss of life and property caused by fires or crimes, in relation to total population in group; and number and incidence of offences known to the police, and fires reported.

☐ Action: number and rate of intervention in fires or crimes; rate of dentention; length of terms in prison actually served.

☐ Facilities: number of fire and police stations and employees on duty by area and population served; and number of places of detention or correctional institutions in relation to inmates, crime rate or load of judicial system.

LEISURE

Indicators

On the basis of time allocation to various activities, the role of leisure in relation to human settlements: demand for space and equipment for leisure and recreation. Available facilities and their use; presence and importance of other factors (such as associations or consumer durables).

Examples (mainly by area and social group)

☐ Demand: number and proportion of people and time devoted to leisure activities requiring open space, open air or indoor sports facilities, specialised or generic buildings for cultural activities.

☐ Availability: number, capacity and actual use of various facilities (concern halls, theatres, museums, libraries, playing fields, stadiums, swimming pools, etc), in relation to area and population served, and to present and future demand; and surface of open public space, with and without special equipment, in relation to area, population, demand and actual use.

☐ Other factors: number and membership of recreational, sports and cultural associations, in relation to area, activity, total and relevant population; number and circulation of books in public libraries, newspapers and magazines, in relation to population and area served; and number and distribution among households and individuals of major durables related to leisure and recreation, e.g. cars, caravans, radio and television sets, etc.

HOUSING

Indicators

Number and percentage of houses and residents in particular conditions; need and availability, cost and expenditure, amenities and other characteristics in relation to total housing, population and area.

Examples (mainly by area and social group)

☐ Need: land required per dwelling unit; number of persons per room; proportion of existing housing stock that requires upgrading; and proportion of homeless in total population.

□ Availability: conventional residential buildings and their characteristics (location, type, floor area) in relation to total housing stock and population; proportion occupied and vacant; and additions to housing stock in relation to existing house, total population and increase in population.

□ Production: residential construction as percentage of total construction and fixed capital formation; and new residential units per 1000 inhabitants, by income level.

□ Cost: components of housing development costs; cost of land; price increases in land and housing.

□ Expenditure: expenditure on housing services; share of total personal or household expenditure; and total cost of housing services.

□ Amenities: housing units and residents supplied with specified levels of sanitation and electricity.

□ Density: living quarters with one room only, and percentage of residents in them; living quarters occupied at or above a specified level of density; and number of people per given floor area by area and income group.

TRANSPORT

Indicators
Type, cost, extent, capacity and frequency of services in relation to population and areas of residence and employment.

Examples
□ Percentage of population with access to a public transport stop or an all-weather road within a given distance.

□ Number of passengers multiplied by distance by mode of transport and area; cost of different modes.

□ Passenger capacity multiplied by distance travelled by public transport per year in relation to population served within the area.

LAND TENURE AND COSTS

Indicators
Location, distribution, surface area or percentage of land under consideration in public, private or other forms of ownership at various price levels, in relation to other prices and cost of development.

Examples
□ Land values, prices, rents, taxes by use and area, over time.

□ Concentration or dispersion of land tenure and uses related to it.

□ Land costs as percentage of total costs for housing or other uses.

□ Land price indices compared to consumer price indices.

URBAN DEVELOPMENT

Indicators

Spatial and functional relations between population distribution and land use in human settlements, such as access to employment and services.

Examples

□ Number and percentage of people with access to a food store, a post office or other representative services within distance X (in time and space).

□ Number and percentage of employed people living beyond a given time/space distance from their place of work.

SLUMS AND SQUATTER SETTLEMENTS

Indicators

Characteristics of slums and squatter settlements and their population, in relation to total area and population, in particular regarding housing stock and services. Need for or feasibility of their provision or upgrading. Role of slums and squatter settlements in the spatial, demographic and economic development of the area.

Examples

□ Area and population of slums and squatter settlements, in relation to total and conventional housing, by income group or other socially relevant characteristics.

□ Location and access to employment and other urban services.

□ Forms of self-help housing, their share of total slums and squatter settlements, and total housing in relevant area.

□ Existing programmes and plans for slums and squatter settlements, their stated goals and actual results.

□ Demographic, social and economic characteristics of population in slums and squatter settlements, compared with total population and residents of other ares or types of dwelling.

□ Spatial, structural and service characteristics of slums and squatter settlements, in relation to their residents and other areas or types of dwelling.

II: PLANNING STRATEGIES

Deconcentration by the promotion of relief poles

6

Gerd Hennings and others   Germany

INTRODUCTION

The growth of metropolitan areas in developing countries has reached a stage where it can hardly be controlled or managed. Warning examples are reported from throughout the Third World: Calcutta, Mexico City, Lima, Bangkok and Lagos. All these reports emphasise the importance of the problems and the hopeless efforts to solve them. The uncontrolled influx of rural migrants to the metropolitan centres and high natural birth-rates have caused extensive urban unemployment, rapidly growing slums and squatter settlements, increasing environmental pollution, water shortages, traffic congestion and considerable deterioration in public services.

The financial resources available are not even sufficient to cope with the most urgent and visible social and physical consequences of the situation described. In order to reduce the agglomeration diseconomies, a considerable proportion of the national budget is poured into the metropolitan areas. In this way the urbanisation process will only be accelerated, rural out-migration encouraged and the development of rural regions slowed down.

This gloomy picture may be valid tomorrow even for those urban centres which today are functioning and manageable, unless political action is taken. The Habitat Conference in Vancouver (1977) stressed the issue and brought it to political attention worldwide. But mere attention will not be sufficient. What is needed above all is strong political commitment to remove the social and economic causes.

Planners have emphasised the importance of urban decentralisation or deconcentration in national development for years, but no major achievements can be reported. External dependencies and internal, dualistic socio-political and economic structures may be the major reasons for the apparent disregard of worldwide warnings. There is evidence that policy statements in national economic plans have not stopped the influx from the rural areas to the big urban centres.

Taking into consideration the political conditions, economic potential, administrative capacity and the social values which differ slightly in most developing countries, we have to find or combine strategies to reduce the most serious problems.

An attempt to develop the principles of such a strategy was made during the past year at the Institute of Urban and Regional Planning at the University of Dortmund on behalf of the German Ministry for Economic Cooperation. The final report of the project contains three main sections. In the first, the extent of the problem is stated after an analysis of six metropolitan areas: Cairo, Bangkok, Lima, Algiers, Tehran and Dar Es Salaam. Local consequences of cumulatively and circularly caused urbanisation processes were traced and the respective strategies for the solution of the problems scrutinised. The second section is devoted to a description of the proposed strategy. The elements of the strategy are described on the basis of the findings and the conclusion of the analysis. In the third section an attempt is made to adapt the strategy to local conditions. Two case studies for the metropolitan areas of Bangkok and Cairo were undertaken. They demonstrate an approach to the evaluation of possible locations for future growth poles in the metropolitan region.

THE DECONCENTRATION OF METROPOLITAN REGIONAL DEVELOPMENT

The strategy for the deconcentration of metropolitan regional development is based on the fact that hitherto in most countries all national planning efforts to decentralise and deconcentrate urbanisation processes have failed. Regional policy strategies, generally, need a rather long period before they show physical, economic and social effects. They need a relatively sophisticated system of guiding instruments and are dependent on functioning administrative structures. Many of these necessary preconditions hardly exist or are poorly developed. Thus, concepts of growth poles and central places, policies to strengthen the role of small and medium-sized urban centres outside the agglomerations, combined with more or less appropriate agricultural development strategies, have not yet brought the expected immediate relief to the metropolitan areas.

The western-orientated capital city has always been stronger. The pull effect on rural job-seeking migrants is widely known. Public and private economic investment is still concentrated in the agglomeration because of a number of locational advantages.

These considerations have led to the assumption that short and medium-term success can only be achieved by filling in the obvious gap between the necessary long-term urbanisation strategies for national deconcentration and metropolitan development concepts in actual practice. This implies that the metropolitan region, defined as the catchment area of the metropolis (about one hundred kilometres), should be given special attention. Although the proposed strategy is concerned with the metropolitan region so defined, it concentrates on the outer ring which represents an area between about fifty and one hundred kilometres from the metropolis. This is referred to below as the study area.

On the assumption that the dualistic nature of the economy has to be accepted as fact in many developing countries and that it can hardly be changed within a short time, the economic development of the potential relief pole has to be based on both the modern sector and the informal sector of the economy.

Whereas the development of the modern (formal) sector plays a significant role in the creation of the economic base, the hitherto unused development potential of the dynamic parts of the informal sector has to be regarded as an equally decisive factor. In general, it is essential to channel and coordinate the national, regional and local measures for promoting economic development. Appropriate enterprises have to be installed at the potential relief pole, in order to secure sufficient job and income opportunities for the growing population. The total economic pattern comprises newly created potential, transferable potential, and existing local potential.

New potential includes all new enterprises of the secondary and tertiary economic sector. They are to be built up according to the overall national economic development strategy. Appropriate locations must be sought for them. The selected relief pole would be a suitable location for those firms which depend on access to the metropolitan agglomeration and therefore could not be installed in other more distant regions. Besides the enterprises of the formal sector, any establishments and firms which could be encouraged to develop out of the informal sector are also part of the newly created potential. The types of enterprise depend on the policy and priorities of the national development strategy. Agro-based and basic goods industries could be appropriate; so could finishing industries using local materials and products. Final recommendations can only be drawn up after a careful analysis of national economic development goals. Special attention has to be paid to the time factor, as it will determine the development of the necessary physical and social infrastructures.

If private foreign investments are admitted and encouraged, a careful selection of branches has to be made in order to ensure the necessary backward and forward linkages within the economy. In the first phase the location conditions have to be synchronised with the location demands of the selected branches. Promotion of the informal sector (local domestic industries, small firms, artisans and other local businesses of the traditional semi-modern type) is necessary. Generally this is a very labour-intensive sector which uses adapted technologies but lacks long-term orders and security. Strategies for the development of the informal sector have to be found and implemented. Since the public tertiary sector also plays an important role in the economic development of the relief pole, the possibility of building up new administrative and service units (governmental sub-agencies, development corporations, scientific institutions, banks, insurance companies, scientific institutions, etc) should be investigated. Observation in many metropolitan areas shows that even now this kind of institution is forced to locate at the periphery of the metropolis.

Transfer potential strengthens the economic base of the potential relief pole and possibly contributes to decongestion of the metropolis. Potentially transferable are primarily those enterprises which suffer from increasing costs owing to the negative agglomeration effects; those which want to expand and need cheap land for expansion; those driven from the inner city by more profitable land use and are subcontractors to newly installed enterprises. In addition, those with transfer potential include polluting industry which has to be removed from the metropolis. This also applies to institutions which do not necessarily have to be based in the agglomeration. It is obvious that considerable incentives are necessary to encourage the dislocation of these enterprises.

Development of the existing local potential is indispensable for a balanced social and economic structure of the relief pole. To preserve this essential economic sector, it is important to select the branches of new industries and enterprises carefully, otherwise competition will certainly destroy parts of this informal sector after a short period.

Promotion of the informal sector by adequate incentives, e.g. credit facilities or loans, has to be planned carefully. Administrative regulations and restrictions should be minimised as far as possible. Adequate organisational structures (joint ventures, cooperatives, etc) could improve productivity and open up access to a larger market.

Technical and social infrastructure. Small and medium sized urban centres in developing countries generally have a considerable lack of developed infrastructure. This, in turn, is one of the principal restrictions on autonomous growth in the population and local economy.

The proposed strategy can only be successful if the existing infrastructure (social as well as physical) is systematically improved. As a rule, the investment necessary for the qualitative and quantitative adaptation of existing infrastructure to user demand is not available. Instead of launching special programmes which would consume scarce capital, existing regional development plans should first be scrutinised. It might be possible to concentrate regional investments in a few selected relief poles.

The infrastructure is important because it creates the necessary preconditions (locational conditions) for industrial development, while contributing to the development of the immediate hinterland of the relief pole and improving the living conditions of the local population and future rural migrants. Physical or technical infrastructure comprises, above all, energy and water supplies, telecommunications, rail and road connections and sewage and garbage disposal. Possibilities of using alternative local technologies should be investigated. Incrementalism should be encouraged. There is absolutely no need to plan and implement an infrastructure of a very high standard from the outset. The standard can be improved step by step in accordance with economic development. Instead of constructing highly sophisticated systems, which demand much foreign currency and are too sensitive to external interference, small locally manageable systems should be developed, using local material and know-how as far as possible.

Industrial estates or parks should be planned to accommodate industrial enterprises. Various organisational models are well known. Publicly owned industrial estates have proved the profitability of public investments.

Social infrastructure comprises the housing sector, education, health and social and recreational facilities. The dualistic structure of the population will impede the quality and quantity of the social infrastructure. Therefore, efforts have to be made to reach a somewhat balanced system. Local characteristics will decisively influence the standards and location. Self-help activities should be encouraged and used as often as possible, above all in the housing sector. Carefully designed and organised site and services schemes may be one form of solving the housing problem. All housing schemes should be combined with job-creating measures in the informal sector.

The development of the education system is essential for the future economic and social structure of the relief pole. The primary and secondary education system is sufficiently well developed in many countries but in most of them professional education has to be strengthened. Technical schools should be founded to train students for local industry. This will ensure the availability of qualified local personnel for existing and future firms.

Appropriate physical urban structures. The physical structure of the relief pole has to be built up in accordance with economic development. The internal physical structure flows from the economic development, but in turn also initiates or stimulates the development process. This can be achieved by designing adequate low-priced settlement structures together with their infrastructure, and by using labour-intensive technologies and self-help activities. Thus, local resources can be widely used to create jobs and a considerable part of the local population can be involved in the production and development process.

In order to avoid a situation where current planning demands determine future development possibilities, physical structures have to be laid out in such a way that they can be adapted step by step to future socio-economic development. This implies that settlement patterns should not be static but changeable with time.

The internal physical structure of the relief pole will also be characterised by its dualistic economic structure and the visible consequences of this. Thus, from a pragmatic point of view, dualistic settlement patterns have to be accepted. Modern industrial parks and service facilities have to be designed to attract potential investors, but the demands of the local informal sector and the marginal population also have to be satisfied. The design of dualistic settlement patterns does not imply the acceptance of dualistic structures in general. This will help to overcome the dualism in the long run. The concerted approach to the problem is, however, important.

Low-priced settlement structures. These can be achieved in various ways. The first is to activate, encourage and involve self-help groups. Self-reliance as essential for development. This is known and accepted all over the world, but unfortunately not exploited enough everywhere. These structures can also be achieved by a reduction in standards or the formulation of appropriate standards. Imported standards for low-cost housing schemes and infrastructure facilities are inappropriate for low-priced settlement structures. Besides consuming considerable amounts of financial resources, they cause considerable social and economic problems for the users. Adequate technologies and coordinated programmes have to be developed for local conditions and different population groups. The third method is to use multi-purpose public facilities. Schools and kindergartens, sports facilities and other social and cultural facilities could be designed for multiple use. There is no reason why classrooms should not be used by different classes in the mornings and afternoons and for vocational or political instruction in the evening.

Spatial organisation. The spatial organisation of the relief pole will primarily depend on the physical and ecological conditions of the location, which should be carefully analysed. Many future difficulties can be avoided if nature and environment are allowed to determine the directions and limits of future expansion. For a number of reasons linear structures are preferable. They are capable of expansion, avoid traffic problems, allow an even distribution of public facilities, encourage the formation of neighbourhood centres, facilitate the economic operation of public transport and make the linkage of urban and agricultural land use possible.

Further planning principles are the design of functional and spatial units which can be filled in accordance with different dual demands; the utmost functional mix of different land uses, avoiding a mono-functional traffic generating the separation of different land uses; the dispersal of working places in the modern sector in order to reduce journey-to-work distances; the creation of a polycentric structure, where the various single centres have different functions; and the dispersal of spatial reserves where intermediate uses may be allowed.

All planning proposals and measures are to be discussed with the population concerned to encourage self-help activities. The neighbourhood should form the basic design unit, not for aesthetic but for social reasons. The neighbourhood unit will represent the spatial component of self-help activities and will facilitate social integration of immigrants and marginal groups. Various types of neighbourhoods will arise from the different social demands of local groups but these neighbourhood units are bound together within a hierarchically organised urban fabric.

The possibility of adapting the physical structure of the relief pole to future development has to be taken into consideration in order to reduce investment to a minimum. The solution of this problem, which is aggravated by the uncertainty of future development, lack of control and incomplete information, is not an easy matter. A possible approach is to overlay short-term minimal demand structures with conceivable physical long-term settlement patterns. The synchronised transformation of the original structure into an expected future pattern will produce different structures at different time periods. Thus, various stages of development can be defined and the infrastructure standards needed for each stage can be determined. It is obvious that such a dynamic approach to physical planning requires considerably more planning and monitoring efforts than the usual master-plan and zoning approach, but it is much more appropriate to conditions and development problems in developing countries. Moreover, it serves to a much greater extent the overall goal of balanced national social and economic development.

Improving administrative capacity. Local administrative and political conditions will determine the success of the deconcentration strategy and the social and economic development of the relief pole. Development planning cannot be successfully applied from geographically distant headquarters. The initiative and political support have to come from the central government, but the development plans and controls have to be executed by local administrative and political bodies. Coordination and feedback processes with central government agencies will still be indispensable.

The obstacles to the implementation of these administrative structures and the devolution of political responsibility in the relief pole are immense. Efforts can be made on two levels to remove these obstacles. In anticipation of long-term policies of administrative deconcentration or decentralisation, the selected relief pole should receive a specific political status, possibly through a presidential decree or Act of Parliament. (Similar decisions have been made in a few countries with regard to a new national capital.) The planning and administrative capacity required for the establishment of a policially controlled development corporation can be built up. Historical or social and political roots in the potential relief pole should be identified and strengthened since they could considerably hinder or promote future economic and social development.

The relief pole has to be given planning and administrative capabilities by the central government. Since implementation will depend very much on active participation of the present and future population, additional strategies have to be developed to foster local self-determination and self-help activities. Both measures need to be concerted and coordinated. The mechanisms of decision making have to be institutionalised.

It has already been pointed out that the proposed strategy demands the utmost use of local resources. This also implies that planning and administrative personnel have to be located in the relief pole. Experts from the central government can be consulted, but the basic and essential work has to be done by local experts. Continuity, identification with the socio-cultural environment, proximity to the population and the local decisions makers are prerequisites for a continuing development process. Local training programmes for technicians, administrators and secretaries have to be initiated. Initially, the local administration should consist of seven departments, which will be responsible for housing, technical infrastructure, social infrastructure and welfare, promotion of industry and business, general administration, finances, and policy and planning.

How the administration is to be controlled by local political bodies has to be decided in accordance with regional circumstances. Local political power should include the right to issue regulations and set up investment plans.

Self-help activities. Experience in a few countries has shown that self-reliance campaigns and the introduction of self-help activities are preconditions for evolutionary and innovative social development. Self-reliance and self-help activities, however, should not be considered only as a substitute for personal and financial resources; they are equally a strategy for the evolutionary creation of political awareness and responsibility among those population groups which have not yet been able to articulate their demands or defend their individual rights.

Social control, communication capabilities and further development of manual skills are but a few positive features of self-help activities. Self-help activities can be promoted by a number of measures, such as the development of local organisational structures, above all in the housing sector; the delegation of responsibilities and decision-making powers to local neighbourhood groups; the establishment of self-help promotion centres for the personal, financial and material support of self-help groups; and the introduction of adult education programmes to prepare future decision makers for active and competent cooperation.

Adequate planning, guidance and control instruments. It is essential to install adequate planning, guidance and control instruments and devices in order to guide the development potential to the relief pole, which is the prime objective of the proposed strategy. It is obvious, however, that the nature of control devices and guidance systems will depend on the political and ideological system of a country. In capitalist societies the government intervenes to ensure the achievement of social goals agreed beforehand. This is necessary if not indispensable in most developing and developed countries where the market mechanism does not adequately meet the needs of social goals. In socialist societies, where central planning can determine development in its entirety, concerted economic and social development is much easier. This implies that the control and guidance potential of capitalist systems is smaller than that of socialist societies.

Adequate guidance instruments and control devices have to be developed to suit the various development stages of administrative structures, and available access to information. If not, the goals cannot realised, because control and guidance devices can overload the system as such. In general, existing instruments and devices will have to be identified, evaluated and further developed. Instruments and devices should be simple, flexible and adaptable to future demands. The necessary personnel needed for the application have to be trained to ensure the proper use of existing instruments and devices.

The following examples illustrate the types of guidance instruments and control devices that can influence the planned development of the selected relief pole. They are very much generalised to show the wide range of possibilities from which a selection can be made locally.

☐ The strategy of metropolitan deconcentration has to be introduced into and linked with the overall economic and social development policy at both the national and regional level and with sectoral national and regional policies. A mere statement of policy would be insufficient, however, unless specific commitments are made, e.g. the reservation of a certain percentage of the budget for the development of the selected relief poles. At the national level a new planning unit should be attached to the central planning agency, and this should be charged with the coordination and control of all measures.

☐ The urban development in the relief pole should be planned and controlled by a policy and planning section within the development corporation. Coordinated sectoral plans have to be designed in terms of overall local goals. Urban land policy is a key element in future urban development. If possible, the development corporation should be in a position to acquire cheap land in time to avoid land speculation. Some urban land policy devices and instruments have proved effective in developed countries. Their transferability to developing countries should be carefully scrutinised.

☐ Certain tax devices have been successfully applied. These include a tax on land, tax penalties for construction counter to public policy, a tax on unused land, and tax benefits for socially desirable activities. Other instruments are land reserves, land registers and land banks, expropriation and pre-emption and purchase of development rights.

☐ Land-use plans and zoning regulations can be enforced by zoning controls, subdivision regulations, construction and location permits and land consolidation and pooling. In general, minimal planning principles, rather than inflexible and rigid detailed requirements, should guide planning and design. Planning and construction permits should only be granted if the required social facilities are assured, if ecological impacts have been taken into account and if consequences for the capacity of the technical infrastructure have been examined and provided for.

☐ The dualistic settlement pattern and the uncertainty of future physical and economic development of the relief pole are additional factors which should guide the development of adequate devices and instruments.

There are some essential policy requirements for the economic development of the relief pole. In generalised form, these include the following.

☐ Active information and advisory policies are important for the attraction and promotion of enterprises. Adequate organisational structures ensure that both the formal and informal sector gain access to information.

☐ A contract policy should, for example, lay down that a certain percentage of public contracts will be allocated to investments in the selected growth pole or to firms operating in the relief pole.

☐ The instrument of tax policy is widely known and hardly needs any elaboration. Tax rebates, tax exemptions, capital and interest subsidies are but a few of the possible devices.

☐ Finally, national and local tariff structures should be re-examined. Transport, energy and communications in the relief pole could possibly be subsidised by reduced tariffs, or additional "congestion" charges could be added to the tariffs in the metropolis.

This long list of factors to be considered in the implemenetation of the strategy of deconcentration may give the impression of an over-sophisticated planning approach. It must be stressed, however, that the proposed strategy combines well-known concepts, strategies, instruments and devices. It does not pretend to be a new strategy. The essential basic idea may be that known economic and spatial concepts and ideas are coordinated and channelled into a few selected towns on the periphery of the metropolis. To a certain extent, the strategy respects the economic and social dualism, and positively blends the advantages of advanced technologies with those of the informal sectors. Thus, the selected relief poles could become model towns.

A FIRST CASE STUDY

So far, the stragegy whose essential features are presented here has been developed as a theoretical concept, but it is about to be applied in practice in two case studies: Cairo and Bangkok, where sites suitable for potential growth poles have already been selected.

Both agglomerations suffer from uncontrollable growth and from the impact of that growth on the environment, the economy and social life. In both countries, Egypt and Thailand, there is hardly any prospect of short-term solutions. In Thailand, no real efforts have been made to stop migration to the metropolis; in Egypt, a concept of new satellite towns has been proposed, but the required funds exceed by far the available resources. Thus, both countries have the required conditions to demonstrate the feasibility or otherwise of the proposed strategy.

The site selection process consists of the following steps: delineation of the study area, analysis of land-use and settlement structures, analysis of the technical infrastructure, analysis of social and economic conditions, and a comparative evaluation of potential relief poles.

This approach has been conceptualised in a few maps, but detailed analysis is indispensable before final decisions are taken.

People, planning and development   7

Dilys M. Hill   United Kingdom

DEVELOPMENT

The argument over development and how to achieve it involves two sets of issues. First, there is the question of the amount of resources available, and the way in which these are allocated on a sectoral or spatial basis. In the past, there has been a tendency to concentrate on the former. Now, however, most governments are concerned with the spatial dimension - the location of plant and services, the need to consider alternatives to urban over-concentration - and they have increasingly tried to incorporate physical and social planning into the overall economic strategy.

The second set of issues concerns the degree to which development requires the participation and active commitment of ordinary people and the expression of grass-roots opinion. Again, this has been controversial. The need for national policy, coupled with the scarcity of resources, has led many countries to stress the need for overall planning and allocation of resources in view of technical requirements and the need to achieve as rapid a rate of growth as possible. On the other hand, there has been a growing recognition that without the active involvement of ordinary people, planning and its implementation might in fact suffer even further delays and shortcomings.

But how, and in what ways, participation should be part of the planning development system, still remains a matter of debate. In recent years the stress has been on self-help, on mobilising peasant communities to improve agricultural techniques and production and to involve people in the direction of their own lives. Currently much interest is being shown in the different approaches and achievements of the Kibbutz, the Ujamaa experiment in Tanzania and the Harambee movement in Kenya. This paper explores some of the problems involved in the concept of participation in economic development, the conflicts between national and local levels of government, and between government policy and attempts to encourage local and individual involvement.

There is another controversial issue in the debate on development. As Ayres has suggested, there is now an urgent need to discuss the problems of distribution as well as of production, and to consider the possibility of "livable" and "workable" societies rather than "developed" ones of the Western kind.[1] Ayres, writing in the context of Latin American development, says that the goal of such a policy would be "livable" societies as viable alternatives to hyper-urbanised, semi-industrialised, permanently underdeveloped, permanently inequitable societies. This demands that greater emphasis be given to the short as opposed to the long term, and to the distribution of income and resources as opposed to capital concentration, growth and the relative depression of consumer demands.

Allied to these arguments are debates about the need for labour-intensive as opposed to capital-intensive industrial and agricultural projects. Gunner Myrdal has also argued that development policy must produce changes in the living and working conditions of the mass of the people, changes which must bring about both increased productivity and greater equality.[2] In the agricultural sphere, this must imply fundamental reforms in land ownership, without which community development will be ineffective). But, he says, development is more than economic advance: it is the whole upward movement of the entire social system. In the words of this paper, people, planning and development are inextricably intertwined.

This is demonstrated, for example, by the problem of implementation of plans. Labour-intensive development as an alternative strategy to capital-intensive projects, for example, raises the question of how it is to be administered and organised. Ilchman and Uphoff have made some very interesting suggestions.[3] They show that such projects need both efficient administrative skills and the participation of local people. For example, they argue that land development activities (irrigation and drainage) are more actively participated in than larger public works and community development projects, that programmes are enhanced when the persons affected by them shape their ends, and that it is possible to appoint local leaders to supervise projects in the place of civil service personnel.

Apart from the debate on participation and labour-intensive projects, there is also a lively controversy about the efficacy of decentralisation of plans, programmes and resources in improving development strategy. There are two approaches.

One stresses that, to be effective, economic and social strategy must be determined at the centre. In addition, it is said, the main programmes should be contralised (in the cities and existing large industrial sites) in order to benefit from large-scale enterprise, from economies of scale (including the availability of related services and a skilled or trainable work force), and so on.

The opposite approach is to argue for more decentralisation, both of planning to the regional level (in order to integrate economic planning with physical and social planning) and of the projects themselves (to use spare capacity in the small towns and to deconcentrate the adverse effects of over-urbanisation in the large cities). Common to both approaches, however, is the increased recognition of the need to look to the regional level and integrated social and economic planning in order to make the best use of resources. But decentralisation as such needs to be carefully weighed against available resources. Many observers agree, nevertheless, that urban policy must emphasise the building up of secondary centres, satellite towns, and the "selective concentration" of existing or new industries in the sub-areas and the hinterlands of large cities.[4]

URBANISATION AND URBANISM

This paper will consider four aspects of urbanisation and urbanism. First, there is the nature of urbanisation itself and the extent to which it has been seen as a "problem" of development. Secondly, there is the debate on the ways in which urban living affects the attitudes and behaviour of successive waves of migrants to the city, and how people are resocialised into new lifestyles and values. Thirdly, there is the question of participation in the city. This depends both on the existence of old styles of self-help and familial and ethnic relationships and on the emergence of voluntary associations and class groups which establish new avenues of involvement and political participation. Fourthly, there is a recent re-evaluation of the question of shanty towns or squatter settlements around major cities.

Urbanisation has been considered a problem of development because of the continued migration of rural populations to the large cities and the high degree of unemployment and underemployment this level of urbanisation has produced. Though the city remains the centre of productive and other skills and the most advantageous educational and social services, it also gives rise to problems of employment and housing opportunities which have led many observers to advocate alternative strategies of deconcentration and decentralisation. Urbanisation, it is well known, does not necessarily result from the growth of manufacturing industry or even the increase in non-agricultural opportunities. Mookherjee and Morrill show, for example, that in India the degree of urbanisation in the various states is related to the level of commercialisation of the cities and employment in the tertiary sector. The urban population increases faster than employment in the secondary sector, despite government's industrial planning efforts, and is self-generating. The basic urbanisation problem, therefore is not where new opportunities are created but the creation of more opportunities per se.[4]

The second issue - the way in which urban life alters the attitudes and behaviour of successive waves of immigrants - stresses the importance of ethnic clustering in the cities, the continued link with the countryside among new migrants and the stabilising effect that this may have, and the network of self-help voluntary associations.

This leads to the third area of interest: these associations are adaptive mechanisms of change and they encourage help among family and ethnic members (credit, jobs, housing), but they are also influenced by new forms of association. In the city, class divisions and interest groups based on work and political parties and government institutions increasingly play a dominant role.

The fourth issue is the changing approach to the problems of illegal settlements around cities. It is pointed out that these are not usually the home of recently arrived migrants (who go rather to the inner-city slums and family members to be near job opportunities), but result from the invasion of groups of people from inner city areas who take over public or private land on the town periphery where they try to establish squatter communities and eventual title to the land. In the past the common approach to this problem has been for governments to try to discourage such settlements, and periodically to clear them in the hope of eliminating them. Now, however, they may be more favourably viewed as potential self-help projects in which the efforts of the people themselves can in time produce viable communities.

It must be recognised, however, that problems remain: site and service housing development is still needed, as is help with credit, building materials, and basic planning. And there is also the danger that participation and self-help in the illegal settlements may be welcomed by governments for the wrong reasons - governments may decide that this relieves them of the necessity to produce strategies of improvement and to reallocate resources. Where this happens, there is also the danger that there will be little or no redistribution between the rich and the poor areas of the city and the affluent, articulate suburbs will continue to be the most effective participants whose demands for improved services are met (see below).

PLANNING

In the Western world there has been a wide-ranging debate in the past decade on the goals of planning, the procedures which will produce the most effective and the most democratic plans, and the part which ordinary people should play in both policy and its implementation.

In discussing planning in the context of development in Third World countries, there is a danger that both too much and too little may be made of these recent developments in Western countries. Two points, however, now appear to command general consent. The first is that planning must take the integrative approach, that is, it must include economic and social planning in physical plans, and vice versa. Secondly, planning must also include a strong regional dimension. Such decentralisation is seen as essential to provide channels of local and district support for successful implementation. The regional unit must be taken into account as the optimum level for integration of economic and social resource planning, and must also be seen as the effective level of administration.

In addition, there is also a debate on allegations that planning is too general and too remote from the actual needs of the people and that more basic, intermediate plans are needed which take into account self-help, slow development over time (for example, housing sites in illegal peripheral settlements) rather than large-scale redevelopment, and mobilisation of local leadership into plan making and plan implementation.

In the past decade and a half, six main areas of concern have emerged from the deliberations of United Nations experts and others. These are: the need for development planning which integrates local and regional plans into an overall national policy; the need for basic research; the importance of city and regional planning; problems of public administration (both in terms of the structures through which decisions are made and implemented, and in the need for more and adequately trained staff); the need to organise or expand community services; and the importance of civic participation if plans are to be effective.

The stress on the region in planning has two aspects. From the point of view of the centre, the region can act as a unit of implementation for national plans, and as the basis on which resources are allocated to both locations and the various sectors of the economy. The region may be viewed differently by people at the local level, however. For them, the region may be the main channel of political and administrative contact with the centre. At the region, they may find themselves faced with the district office or other central government officer, who exercises control over the activities of the district and localities in his region. There has been a growing recognition of the need to strengthen intermediate communities in the region. These intermediate communities could be stressed in development policies as the strategic points in modernising rural areas and in regulating or reducing the flow of migrants to the cities, and in acting as a communication link in the rural-urban migration.[5]

But the same United Nations review stresses that while most countries have adopted national economic and social planning as a major instrument of development, few have until very recently concerned themselves with the locational and spatial aspects of planning. This problem has become urgent because, in spite of the advances which have been made in recent years, there is still a divorce in the eyes of many experts between the economic and physical planners. For example, housing planning and policy is often embarked upon under severe pressure without reference to economic or physical planning criteria (especially the relation of housing projects to local and regional employment opportunities), with the result that public action is piecemeal and in the end families have to fend for themselves to obtain a livelihood and shelter.

There is also the negative side of planning to be recognised. Where urban planning relates to the overall development of the city but ignores the behaviour of families, especially poor families and the new migrants, then what actually happens in the city may ignore "planning" entirely. For example, in many developing countries the overall strategy for cities ignores the patterns of behaviour of migrants and their families: illegal peripheral settlements are ignored or dismissed as aberrations. But the wave of settlers from the inner slums to the outer settlements continues and, in defiance of building regulations and laws on the title to land, families continue to settle the land and build squatter settlements. Much of the subsequent construction is thus clandestine, not subject to legal protection, and the end result is corruption, sharp practice and wholly ineffecting "planning".

As the United Nations report already quoted observed, many cities have adopted regulative plans but these concentrate on the spatial aspects of city growth and are dominated by architectural and aesthetic considerations and therefore tend to ignore the income levels and social characteristics of the families seeking jobs and shelter, as well as the actual current ownership and prices of urban land, and the structure of political power.[5] As a result, such "plans" are quite ineffective in controlling the expansion that takes place. Not only do the peripheral settlements continue to develop despite the "plans", but they learn how to make participative demands in defence of their continued existence (see below). In this respect, human development and urban settlement proceed in spite of, rather than as a result of, "planning" by the experts. According to the United Nations report, many developing nations are thus faced with an intractable dilemma which goes to the heart of the relation between economic development and physical urban planning. Every attempt to strengthen the city, its industry and industrial entrepreneurship, including the development of economic infrastructure and public services, such as housing, will widen the gap between this modern sector and the rest of the country - and, it may be added, between this modern sector and the compromise solutions to the burgeoning squatter settlement demands.[5]

Planning in any abstract sense must also come to terms with political reality. In many developing countries this will mean that while planners may see the need for regionalisation, decentralisation, and the development of intermediate settlements, political authorities may stress the need to concentrate resources and development in the primate cities and stress national planning as against decentralisation and local involvement. Planning must also come to terms with the gap between the standards set by society and government and the ordinary people's demand for housing. Whereas orthodox planning and building standards seek to determine the location of housing and urban building by which government controls the standards of people's lives, the people themselves see these as inappropriate and unattainable. Housing regulations imply fixed standards, but poor people need flexible standards which will allow them to start from minimal beginnings and evolve standards over a period of time. The concept of "progressive development" in terms of which people progress from relatively primitive beginnings to more permanent dwellings according to their means, is not a new idea, but still one which planners and decision makers dismiss as unsuitable and offensive to good planning. This is short-sighted.

In advanced societies, planning theory and practice have become sophisticated and eclectic. In the past decade, three areas have received particular attention. First, there is the need to see planning in the wider framework of social and economic planning and bring together a number of specialists in the social science disciplines to ensure an integrated approach to the problems of the city, including underprivileged areas, the cycle of poverty and the crucial role of transportation policy. Secondly, planners have devoted much time and discussion to their own professional status and the need for more interdisciplinary training, including information on the political and administrative processes in society on which the success of their planning ultimately depends. And finally, the planning profession has taken a new look at the relationship between the planner and the citizen and between the role of planning in a democratic society and the demands of ordinary people, and at the claims of planners to be experts in the face of uninformed lay opinion. Two trends have emerged in this long debate. On one hand there is the tendency to take the overall approach, to be sympathetic towards corporate planning and other innovative management techniques and use a sophisticated range of computer and other techniques. On the other hand, some planners believe that this sophisticated, technical approach is not enough, and that the planner can no longer claim to be the purely disinterested expert. He must be positively committed to society and to change. As such he must not hide behind professional neutrality but become an advocate for the restructuring of urban life. In this he has a particular responsibility for the views of ordinary people, including the poorest sections of society. Many of his plans will affect the housing opportunities and lifestyles of working class people who have little choice but to accept the designs and plans which the experts decide upon. They have little chance to reject these for some other alternative. Therefore, the planner must be an advocate not only of "good design", but also of the wants and demands of large numbers of citizens forced to live in the areas and houses the planners produce.

The experience of planning in advanced societies may be applicable to the modernising sectors of less developed countries but generally the overall problems will be very different. The range of resources available will limit the use which can be made of sophisticated techniques, and more time and effort must be put into basic questions such as the feasibility of the implementation of plans and the relation of administration to policy. Plans must be implementable by existing levels of civil service and other staff, and they will have to be carried out through existing governmental and administrative structures. Because of these constraints, the overwhelming demand is that the plans be simple, flexible and adaptable. The need is not so much for "master plans" but for intermediate infrastructure plans which will recognise that the planning of cities will necessarily be piecemeal and evolutionary and moreover that economic development must play a major role in setting the framework for physical planning. At the same time, while the increasing range of participatory devices now being incorporated with planning in Western societies may not be relevant for development strategies, the general principle of popular involvement is vital.

PARTICIPATION

The city planner in underdeveloped countries is faced with grave problems: low income levels, rapid population growth, immigration and an inadequate urban infrastructure. In the face of these problems, participation may be regarded as irrelevant and positively harmful. What is needed, it could be argued, is more technical expertise, better administrative structures through which improved services can be implemented, and a more coherent and comprehensive national policy of development. Participation can only be disruptive: people are short-sighted and demand immediate remedies instead of seeing the need for overall plans and long-term solutions. People are selfish: without leadership and guidance their participation amounts to little more than demands by vested interests with little regard for the good of the community as a whole. Finally, national leaders trying to improve the conditions of the society as a whole may argue that such participation would be harmful because it would be sectional and divisive. The rich elite or the tribal or ethnic groups are too prone to force their demands on society, and this makes the pursuit of an overall strategy, including the redistribution of resources on technical and equitable criteria, almost impossible to achieve.

From the perspective of the individual citizen, too, participation is different in many ways from the processes in advanced societies. People in developing countries respond primarily to employment opportunities: they need jobs, shelter near these jobs, transportation to work, education for their children and basic health care. For many years to come the main thrust of participation will therefore be instrumental, that is, it will be based on individual and group demands for concrete help and services, rather than an awareness of community as such or even the efficacy of involvement in the political system of their society.

These imperatives may contrast sharply with the theoretical outlook of Western observers. The tradition of advanced industrial societies is firmly grounded in the tradition of John Stuart Mill and subsequent advances in democratic theory. In this theoretical framework, three main themes predominate. First, there is the belief in popular rule based on periodic elections contested by two or more political parties. The people as a whole are thought to have a right to participate in these structures and are encouraged to take part in all stages of the process - in voting, standing for election, contributing to parties and voluntary associations, making demands of leaders, and so on. Secondly, the theory of a democratic, participant society stresses the rights of minorities and the safeguards for these rights which are built into the structure. In addition, the system guarantees a spectrum of freedom of association and expression and stresses the role which communication (including the mass media) plays in the democratic policy and the development of true participation. Participation, it is argued, cannot be effective unless there is a wide-spread dissemination of information, unless people know what their governments are planning and can comment on these plans. Finally, advanced societies based on this heritage stress the need for a pluralistic system: that is, may groups have the right to take part in making decisions through a vast and complicated network of advisory bodies, interest-group bargaining and multiple levels of decision making (national and local government, and the self-regulation of the professions, the universities, and so on).

But this tripartite model may be alien to both the history and present condition of many developing societies. The competition of political parties may be denied as inappropriate; local government and other centres of decision making may have only a very minor role to play; and the main emphasis may be on national policy and planning and the local mobilisation of values and effort in support of national plans. In addition, the flow of communication may be severely limited.

This does not mean that participation does not have a vital role. On the contrary, the implementation of plans will be ineffective if grass-roots support and active involvement are not forthcoming. In this regard, however, we must distinguish a number of areas and issued. First we must recognise that in developing societies participation has been encouraged, and institutions for its manifestation have been provided, at national rather than local level. Political participation has been associated with the growth of central authority rather than local institutions There has also been a conflict between the demands of citizens for the right to take part in political life and the decision making processes, on the one hand, and the need for a professional and independent bureaucracy based on criteria of merit, impartiality and technical expertise, on the other. These dilemmas have not been resolved. There is still tension between national aspirations and the degree to which local government and grass-roots participation can be accommodated or allowed, and there is still conflict between the need for technical administration and that for a responsive bureaucracy.

Within this overall framework, however, certain trends can be discerned. As we suggested earlier, participation in developing societies, far from being non-existent, is actually flourishing. In the cities, the migrants, shanty-dwellers and the urban poor may be involved in instrumental participation on a large scale. That is, people are effective in making demands of the system and of officials to obtain certain specific remedies for immediate short-term problems. Evidence from research done in certain Latin American cities shows that this does not necessarily mean that the individual feels more confident of his own ability to affect what officials do or to obtain remedies. Nor does it mean that he will take an interest in some abstract concept of the community, have any knowledge of local affairs or look to the future development of his city. What it does mean is that he can see the practical usefulness of joining with his neighbours in making certain demands of officialdom in return for some effort on his own part. That is, he demands basic services or legal rights in return for making his own site habitable, building his own home, getting credit and employment help from family, neighbours and associations rather than from public funds. His demands for instrumental participation help in the general recognition that much of what happens will depend on his own contribution and effort. There have been extensive examinations of the family and group networks through which this instrumental participation takes place. Demands of officials and local government for services by voluntary associations are usually highest when individuals are trying to establish their right to stay in illegal settlements and they are in need of basic services. Later, this degree of involvement may diminish. At the same time, participation in a network of self-help is basic to the individual's life in the city, his leisure and educational needs as well as his need for a job and shelter. These groups act as a bridgehead between the old and the new cultures. Where they are based on ethnic, village and family ties they serve to integrate the new arrival into city life, give material help and transmit values and skills. At the same time, however, the city is also an arena for different groups and associations based on workplace and political ties. The city is also the setting for employment diversification, the growth of middle class and professional groups and a wider range of values and attitudes. New bases of stratification emerge, and political parties encourage the individual to participate in the political structure of society, acknowledge and support national goals and become development oriented in a wider and more universal sense.

The main issue is thus how this energy and potential involvement may be harnessed for planning and development. It still needs to be stressed that the success of this will depend on local leaders and their active values and orientations towards change. Such leadership can evolve from self-help movements and traditional leaders in the urban setting (we have already pointed out that such people can be recruited to supervise self-help projects in the place of civil service personnel). Usually, involvement of ordinary people in planning will be by groups and neighbourhoods rather than individuals. It will depend very much on the ability of the planners and decision makers to show the immediate relevance and benefits of plans to local people and offer them a step-by-step approach which corresponds with their demands and their perceptions. From this point of view, planning is likely to be more successful if planners are accessible to local gorups and leaders, live in the area rather than in the national capital, provide information and understandable data (preferably through simple visual aids) and are willing to alter plans in the light of experience gained in progress.

This does not disguise the fact that the main participants in the political and planning systems are the middle class (both individually and through professional groups, voluntary associations and residential defence groupings), the administrators and other official decision makers, and the political parties and official institutions of government. Participation may have a distorting effect if the demands of one group - the middle class suburb which knows how to articulate its needs and how to approach government bodies - is dominant. The government's policy for development and its plans for establishing priorities for the allocation of resources can be undermined by vigorous participation by those motivated primarily by self-interest. It is as true in developing countries as it is in developed societies that those taking part in political and community affairs are more likely to be middle class than working class. Participation is strongly associated with social status. For this reason, as well as for reasons of democratic self-government, it is often suggested that local government institutions offer additional avenues for a wider range of working class involvement in community life so that they may mitigate if not entirely remove the predominance of middle class participation.

It is easier, it is argued, for ordinary people to take part in local government institutions, both by voting and by standing for election, and to make demands of local councillors. In many developing countries, local government has been viewed with disfavour as inefficient, corrupt, undermining of national aspirations and goals, and too weak to implement development programmes. But this view must be counteracted by the fact that local institutions are vital to harness the active cooperation and work of local people. Future trends seem likely to be towards the strengthening of city administration and those at the regional level, where administrative and government structures must take account of public opinion and can only do so effectively in the long run through some form of local representative institutions.

REFERENCES

[1] Ayres, R.L., "Development policy and the possibility of a livable future for Latin America". American Political Science Review (1975), Vol LXIX, No 2, pages 507-25

[2] Myrdal, G., "What is development?", Ekistics (1975), Vol 40, No 237, pages 84-7.

[3] Ilchman, W.F., and Uphoff, N.T., "Beyond the economics of labour-intensive development: politics and administration", Ekistics (1975), Vol 40, No 237, pages 88-101.

[4] Mookherjee, D., and Morrill, R.L., Urbanisation in a developing economy: Indian perspectives and patterns (1973), Sage Publications.

[5] International Social Development Review No 1, Urbanisation: development policies and planning (1968), United Nations, ST/SOA/Ser X/1, pages 47; 49; 57; 85.

III: HOUSING

Options, choices and responsive housing 8

Desmond Kaplan   South Africa

If one accepts that there is a basic drive in every person to optimise his or her well-being or "quality of life" in response to the specific context and time in which he finds himself,[1] and that each individual has different preferences and priorities, then access to a wide range of options for achieving well-being and an understanding of the implications of the options must help each individual to optimise his well-being by choosing that option that he can identify as offering the best "deal" in the circumstances prevailing at the time.

Choice from a variety of options can be seen as a self-regulating process which allows individuals to respond to their own situations, preferences and priorities; and the wider the range of options the better.

This process is akin to that of a market place offering a wide range of goods and services, each having certain advantages and disadvantages for the individual concerned. Not everyone can afford to have everything that he or she would like to have. If, however, people can decide for themselves which sacrifices to trade off against which advantages, or which priority to satisfy in place of another, according to their individual circumstances, they will usually be more ready to accept the lesser satisfaction of other demands because they selected the trade-off themselves.

These trade-offs are constantly being made by individuals and groups in all areas of human activity. Housing is no exception. For example, a family may decide to live in rather poor but inexpensive accommodation in order to send a child to university. They will then be giving a higher priority to the child's education than to housing. In other words, they will trade off quality of housing for the child's education. Their psychological well-being may well be quite high in the poorer accommodation because it has been their own choice and they perceive the cost benefit. Physical discomfort from, for example, poor heating will then be tolerated or solved by wearing extra clothes in the cold season.

The lower tolerance levels or limits in housing conditions are flexible and open to change over time, particularly when discomforts or disamenities are seen to be temporary or when they are exchanged for other benefits. In other words, people's tolerance is dependent on their perceptions of their condition. If, as in the example above, housing quality is of lesser importance than education, once the child's university education is completed and paid for, the family can afford to acquire better housing and may well do so, if no other priorities emerge.

The parameters of tolerance of discomfort or disamenity and changing priorities over time cannot readily be included in conventional attitude surveys. Well-meaning researchers often fall into a trap when they try to establish housing preferences and priorities with conventional survey techniques. There is little doubt that they cannot hope to get really useful results. This is simply because survey questions and answers are subject to time-specific conditions on the part of respondents as well as the relationship between the interviewer and the person being interviewed. No matter how good the training of the interviewer, there will always be a degree of misleading subjectivity in eliciting and recording responses.

A particularly glaring example of the folly that can be encountered in surveys of this kind is a recent South African case. In a survey conducted in low-income single-storey residential neighbourhoods, people were asked whether they would prefer living in a single-storey detached house or in a flat ten floors from ground level. It is hardly surprising that there was an overwhelming response in favour of the former. Nevertheless, this response was presented by the researchers as evidence of the preference of the community and as a guide for policy making. Not only did the question exclude any reference to the cost benefits associated with the options, but in most cases the respondent's experience of living in a flat on the tenth floor of a building would have been either non-existent or at least minimal. In other words, there was no basis for expressing a valid preference. Furthermore, the respondents could perceive no real advantage in answering the question in any way other than what they thought the interviewer most wanted to hear. The survey was undertaken for a government department by a reputable research group. At this stage the questionnaire and preliminary results are still confidential.

People's choices among options are meaningful only when they are actually in a situation where they make and act on a choice, because that is the time when they seriously take into account the complexities in their own situation. This fact was amply demonstrated in a South African National Building Research Institute project. In collaboration with the Human Sciences Research Council, peoples' preferences in a variety of housing options over a period of time were monitored.[2] The group of participating families were all "in the market" for housing and all finally made specific choices of houses and moved into them. Before making their final choices, participants were separately inteviewed on a number of occasions. It was found that during the series of interviews the majority changed their minds on the most preferable situation to be in. Models, drawings and cost parameters were used to explain the options during these interviews, whereas final choices were made after the options were seen on the ground. In the event, no fewer than half the participants finally selected houses other than those selected during the last interview where drawings and models were used. What makes the outcome particularly significant, is the fact that the participants certainly had a far better briefing on the options than any survey interviewer can usually give.

Another aspect highlighted by this project is how difficult people find it to understand situations with which they are unfamiliar. For example, all participants were familiar with and could readily relate to the standard layout and house types conventionally used in low-income housing developments. In this project, however, a range of new house types was provided and a new kind of layout used. It comprised groups of houses sharing semi-private forecourts connected to a road serving the neighbourhood.[3] (In a conventional layout houses are on separate sites served by a conventional road grid.)

The innovations were fully explained with models and drawings, but it was found that many participants fully understood the new house types and the forecourt concept only after they had seen and experienced the reality.

Another example of participants' lack of perception owing to inexperience was produced when a group of employees of one company had to decide whether they wished to live together, with other employees of the same company, or quite separate, i.e. scattered among strangers in the neighbourhood. Of the thirty employees, ten chose to live together, sharing one of the forecourts. After a while it was found that some of those who had chosen to live apart regretted that they had done so once they fully appreciated the benefits enjoyed by the group who stayed together - even though these had been discussed at length with them before they made their choice. These benefits included the cooperation enjoyed by neighbours in the group at an early stage of occupation, because they knew each other fairly well before moving in, and the greater security of well-known neighbours living in close proximity. The forecourt concept and the benefits of sharing with known neighbours later influenced the employees of another company who moved into the area. When they were able to see the realities of the situation all opted to live together in groups.

This project succeeded in simulating a "market place" situation by providing a wide range of options based on a combination of intuition and fairly straightforward studies of existing development in the area. Demand for the new options was then monitored and further development geared according to previous responses, in an ongoing reiterative cycle.

The "market place" concept is a self-regulating one but it must be emphasised that it cannot operate well unless the people who make the choices are in a position to undersand the implications of their decisions. Nevertheless, errors of judgment or understanding do occur, as shown in the example above. Furthermore, people's circumstances and priorities change over time. They can be accommodated, however, if the disamenity flowing from the "mistaken" decision is readily tolerated because those affected realise that it was their own decision; or the situation is open to adaptation or change, e.g. if a house can be adapted to alter its image, or a room can be added or the house can be otherwise improved; of if there is housing mobility whereby the family can move elsewhere. All these possibilities usually exist in a healthy "market place". This is what gives it flexibility.

In the project mentioned above, the various house-types offered were all designed for easy adaptation and extension. Thus, houses were not only provided at a reasonable initial cost but they could extended as and when the occupants wished and could afford to do so. Nevertheless, a degree of short-term adaptation was facilitated by building the houses to a very basic level of finish. This meant that they were built at a cost less than the available budget and each family was then given the opportunity to decide how the balance should be spent. In some cases this balance was sufficient for the construction of a small extra room. The people themselves could then decide whether to spend the money on extra accommodation or on upgrading the finish of the house.

Local decision-making control may be regarded as fundamental to people's psychological well-being: "When dwellers control the major decisions and are free to make their own contribution to the design, construction or management of their own housing, both this process and the environment produced stimulate individual and social well-being. When people have no control over, nor responsibility for, key decisions in the housing process, on the other hand, dwelling environments may instead become a barrier to personal fulfilment and a burden on the economy."[4]

For this reason, it can be argued that it is better to allow "mistakes" to be made than to improve situations. A choice from among options that are adaptable and therefore open to change gives people the opportunity to exercise individual decision-making control and cope with "mistakes" and changed circumstances.

Architects and planners very often think in terms of dwellings and their immediate environment as wholly completed products or commodities which must be provided in full, down to the last detail. Those who think this way fail to recognise that home-making and the very actions of living are so much of a dynamic process of ongoing transitions that dwelling-places cannot but be affected by them. The nature of the effects depends on the control that people have over their environment and the housing processes affecting them. For example, in the much publicised Pruitt Igoe project in St Louis in the United States vandalism and environmental degredation assumed such proportions that local administrators concluded that there was no option left but to demolish the buildings. This was done and the development was labelled an "architectural failure", even though it received architectural awards when first built. Later, many fingers were pointed at the architectural profession for creating the "monster".

Less well known, however, is another project in the same area, not too dissimilar in the physical and architectural sense to the demolished scheme which suffered from vandalism and environmental decay. In this case the "problem" was identified somewhat differently. The administrators were able to turn the development into a success by handing over to the residents much of the responsibility for decision-making on administration and management. In other words, similar environments were, respectively, failures and successes because the housing processes were different. As a result, the perception of these environments by the residents was different.[5]

These examples are not quoted to absolve the architectural profession from all blame for the problems in Pruitt Igoe. There were certain architectural shortcomings in the development, but they were not the only issue. It is the non-physical side of the experience that reinforces the argument for dweller control in decision-making. Furthermore, one's attention is drawn to the need to differentiate between housing products and services, on the one hand, and housing processes on the other.

As mentioned earlier, people's actions in home-making are ongoing, whether they are manifested in actual physical changes to the building, in furniture and fittings, or in the administrative or legal context. These actions, which include the ongoing management and maintenance associated with the actions, may be called the housing process. John F.C. Turner summed it up when he said that housing was "...a verb that describes people doing things".

Housing products, on the other hand, are the components, elements and assemblies (or commodities) which people acquire or make and assemble as part of the housing process. Where they control the processes, but do not (or cannot) physically act themselves, they make use of housing services. Housing products or housing services can therefore be said to be "nouns" and can be identified as options in the "market place".

In wealthier communities, a range of products and services is often already combined as dwellings (and therefore as commodities) when people acquire them. Nevertheless, they are chosen and the decisions are, therefore, individually controlled. In many cases an architect is retained to design the dwelling and a contractor to build it. In these situations, too, decision-making control is largely in the hands of the individual. After occupation, however, people add other products and services such as furnishings and carpets and often make structural changes as part of their ongoing housing activities. After these changes and developments the original products are no longer the same. The housing process will have made them different commodities in the "market place" by the time they are sold.

The additive, and sometimes subtractive, process by which occupants change their dwellings occurs in increments of various kinds and sizes over time. For example, occupants may one year buy paint and hire a contractor to paint the dwelling. The following year they may purchase a carport in kit form and erect it themselves. In this way dwellings mature and evolve over time; the degree and nature of change is determined by the demand for it, the ability of the building to absorb change and the availability and access to products and services with which to affect changes. In addition, a major role is played by the occupants in terms of both their ability and willingness to act.

If one accepts the process of incremental development as healthy and positive in terms of its value as a way in which people can improve their well-being by adapting their environment, then housing should be designed not only in physical but also non-physical terms. Of the non-physical apsects, security of tenure and access to finance have a major effect of people's ability and willingness to contribute towards developing their environment.[6]

Security of tenure implies that one is able to transfer, bequeath or otherwise benefit from investments made in one's environment. Obviously, this does not mean that there should be no rental accommodation. There is always a demand for such accommodation by people who value the mobility that it allows them, but security of tenure is a means of closing the gap often found between people's ability to contribute and their willingness to do so. For example, a family renting a house may undertake only a minimum amount of maintenance, if any at all; and their maximum contributions to their environment will probably end with a bit of painting, besides what they do with their furniture and fittings, even though they may be able to afford more substantial improvements. On the other hand, if they see an opportunity for recouping their investment when they move, they will be inclined to contribute more (as in a situation of secure tenure). Classic examples of this pattern are evident in areas where tenure is insecure, e.g. squatter areas and lower-income rental housing. Residents tend to invest in movable items such as furniture, motor cars and so forth, while the physical environment reflects minimal care and investment. Where tenure has been secured, however, the area takes on a completely different aspect. Maintenance and home improvements become the norm, rather than the exception. There are numerous examples of this.[7]

Finance in the form of savings or loan facilities affects the rate at which development can take place as well as the size of the increment that can be made, where people are willing to invest. While people in wealthy and relatively stable communities can afford to make long-term commitments in respect of repayments on mortgage bonds, and therefore acquire large, highly developed products or increments of development, people in poorer communities usually have difficulty in obtaining long-term loan finance. Even when it is available, they may be reluctant to commit themselves because incomes may be irregular and their situations transitional and therefore relatively unstable. In many developing countries, for example, poor families who have acquired sites on which to build make quite modest increments of development at any one time. Very often a temporary structure is first erected at the back of a site. A permanent structure is then gradually build in front, usually in stages, while materials and components are stockpiled in small batches.[8] The process is not dissimilar to that applied in wealthier communities but the pace of development is somewhat slower. In fact, it is the process which is both valuable and significant. It allows people to develop their homes in a manner and at a pace which suits their individual preferences, priorities and means.

For some time, many architects have been aware of the positive value of "personalisation" of housing by residents. Others regard it as "spoiling the architecture". If it were actually planned for, however, and appreciated as a valuable input which allows people to contribute to their home environment, the "problem" of "spoilt architecture" need never arise.[9] Although "personalisation" has been seen as an expression of identity (usually through applied imagery), insufficient attention has been paid to the wider issues and processes affecting people's perceptions and cognition of their environment. For example, with incrementalism (and the "personalisation" that goes with it), people respond to their own preferences and priorities by controlling the decisions. They automatically take into account issues and complexities that go far beyond "personalisation" in the sense of merely expressing an identity. It goes almost without saying that the better the access people have to supportive networks and technology making it possible for them to have control, the better can be their responses to their environment. Similarly, in both physical and non-physical planning, one needs to facilitate individual and group responses to that which is first provided or acquired, and make sure that they have the means to do so. Individually controlled changes, adaptations and improvements over time, by whatever size of increment, will certainly be more appropriate to the complex diversity of demand over time than anything that could be totally preplanned in detail.

In many parts of the world architects move into existing, often old, houses which they convert for their own use. They have many and varies reasons for doing so, including economic advantages and the character of the building established by the many layers of habitation stamped on it by previous occupants. The houses, therefore, have a degree of attractive maturity. These and similar arguments are important, but a significant factor seldom discussed is the fact that in the housing process decision-making over time is so complex that even architects enjoy having many of the decisions already made for them through the constraints of an existing building. They are then free to concentrate their energies on the finer details that are often more difficult to resolve when designing an entirely new building. When they move into an existing house, they can live with the situation, taking their time to decide how, where and when to make changes and improvements. Often they produce a finer degree of detailed design resolution for themselves than might otherwise be the case. Even building design professionals, trained to achieve the "right" solution, therefore tacitly acknowledge the value of incremental development by seeking out existing situations which can absorb changes well. There is little doubt that one is in a much better position to decide on improvements to a space which one can actually stand it that to one which only exists on paper or in model form.

If one is to take account of the complexities of the housing process and allow for responsiveness in housing architecture, architects need to place themselves in a position to understand them better. By designing housing that facilitates responsiveness in the physical environment, a variety of paths and options can be offered. Individual users can respond to them and enjoy improving their well-being in their own way. Thus, they are able to participate more fully in the housing process than is possible in a totally predetermined environment.

To sum up, healthy housing markets are ways of facilitating individual choice in order to cater for changing individual preferences and priorities over time. They should include the following: a choice from among a variety of options as starting points, which are both physical (housing products and commodities) and non-physical (tenure options, financing alternatives etc), the implications of which are well communicated (possibly through mediating institutions or aid organisations); the potential for a degree of adaptation in each option (i.e. responsive housing); housing mobility (i.e. the opportunity for people who enter the market, make a choice and adapt it as far as possible, to re-enter the market and repeat the process); a wide range of supportive networks, products and services; and ongoing experimentation, monitoring and feedback.

REFERENCES

[1] Marans, R.W., Evaluation research and its uses by housing designers and managers (1979), Paper from the Institute of Social Research, University of Michigan.
[2] Smedley, L.N., Finlayson, K.A., and Kaplan, D.S., Choice in housing (1979), South African Human Sciences Research Council, Research Finding SN158.
[3] National Building Research Institute, Progress report on the kaNyamazane project (1978).
[4] Fichter, R., Turner, J.F.C., and Grenell, P., "The meaning of autonomy" (1972) Freedom to build (ed by Turner and Fichter), Collier-Macmillan.
[5] Kaplan, D.S., Course notes from special programme on: Housing in development (1978), (under the direction of John F.C. Turner), Development Planning Unit, London.
[6] Kaplan, D.S., Housing: a perspective on development (1979), Master's thesis, Faculty of Architecture, University of the Witwatersrand, Johannesburg.
[7] Kaplan, D.S., "Squatter settlements: international experience" (1977), Paper given at the Cape Building Congress, Cape Town.
[8] Finlayson, K.A., and Kaplan, D.S., Urban settlement dynamics (1976), Background document for a National Building Research Institute slide and tape programme prepared for the Commonwealth Association of Architects and screened at the Habitat Conference, Vancouver, 1976.
[9] Allen, E., (ed) The responsive house (1974), MIT Press.

Factors influencing housing and settlement planning 9

Jean-Elie Hamesse   Belgium

Planning areas are identifiable by their contents and their components which are related to the specific intentions and tasks proposed for these areas. From the point of view of development, planning areas, including human settlements, are broadly classified according to rural and urban characteristics.[1]

The rural area, taken as a whole, with its low population density owing to sparsely settled expanses, is characterised by its very strong consciousness of tradition and therefore its abnegation of change, its non-quantitatively measureable components and its natural growth process. The urban area with its high population density, is marked by its rapidly changing values, its capability to absorb new structural and technical dimensions, and its mainly quantitatively measureable components.[2] These areas can be further subdivided according to degrees of urbanity or rurality in heavily centralised and urbanised areas, or, on the other side, in marginal areas. These subdivisions and their characteristics, however, are not yet considered indivisible parts of a whole, but rather separate elements which develop independently of each other. Nevertheless, there are spatial and sectoral interrelations (primarily economic and socio-cultural) between these distinctive areas. They are to be found primarily in the various migration processes and in communications, such as newspapers, advertisements and satellite television.

Spatial interweaving exists in fast developing areas, such as so-called rural-urban fringes. Movement of people and goods also leads to movement of ideas through communications. This bring us to the concept of material, human and spiritual relationships in various areas. These movements create change in the area of reception (or area of impact, if drastic changes occur) and are at the origin of the constant process of evolution guided by external and internal forces. Colby describes this as follows: "This evolution involves both a modification of the long established functions and the addition of new functions...Apparently these developments of functions, form and patterns are governed by a definite although as yet imperfectly recognised set of forces."[3]

As for the influences brought together with migration streams both in the reception area (mostly urban areas) and in the area of origin (mostly rural areas), a mutual relationship cannot be considered here. The dimensions of the components of rural influences, i.e. influences having their origin in rural areas, cannot cope with the dimensions of urban components in the reception areas, as mutual criteria are not synchronised.

As migrations are not one-way affairs,[4] some influences created by them turn back to the area of origin, bearing some marks of the area of reception of the first migration stream. This way a double field of tension is created by a movement and its reaction. In this context I would like to quote Barbara Ward who speaks of a "transmission belt" which does not work.[5]

IDENTIFICATION OF EXTERNAL INFLUENCES

Influences can be defined quite accurately by considering their area of origin, their target (or area of reception) and their internal components, although this definition is purely intuitive and comprises mostly qualitative values. Influences are movements of ideas and their pressures on the zone of reception. These pressures can affect directly or indirectly components of this zone, according to the response that is given to the influences and the situation of change they have caused.

The movements can be defined as centripetal or centrufugal,[6] according to the magnetism or the anti-magnetism of the area of origin. The terms endogenous and exogenous[7] could also be used here, but will be related merely to the components of influences and their impact on development planning.

The most important items to be taken into account in the various sectors of development planning are the factors contained in the influences. These can be classified as follows: factors obstructive to development, dragging factors, impulsive factors, recessive factor, neutral factors and factors leading to dimensional change. Some influences create inertia leading to apathy in decision making; some influences contain potential forces which should be recognised so that they can be used in a development process. At the basis of influences are external factors that can be divided into the following three categories. Spatial factors seldom act alone as they are always connnected with technical, infrastructural, social or economic features. Functional factors are mostly bound to spiritual activities in the socio-economic compound. Sectoral factors can be defined and classified more accurately and include also components which can be used for development. Social factors include mainly qualitative values, for instance, prestige values. Economic factors include mainly quantitative values. Technological factors[8] combine spiritual and material values and contain infrastructural as well as managerial elements for a dynamisation of the sectoral factors to allow them to become operative. To a certain degree this factor could be included among functional factors. Spatial factors, based on regional or local conveniences or inconveniences, make influences capable of moving because of interregional imbalances and local magnetic forces.

A CONCEPTUAL FRAMEWORK

The first step is that the acceptance, integration and guidance of these influences in the planning process will contribute to a relaxation of local tensions, though it has been proved in some cases that assimilation without adaptation of external influences creates local tensions. This applies to some urban influences in village housing and in rural settlement structure.[9] In development planning, a substantial part of the working process is knowledge of the target group of our planning. It can be derived from a consideration of the target group's internal and external structures which may influence the whole planning process. Ignorance, neglect and unwillingness to recognise origins of facts are mostly based on our economic system, which tends to impose universal principles and organisations.[10]

Non-recognition is due to the following sets of circumstances: spiritual unawareness, over- or underestimation, ignorance, lack of information, false information, laziness or apathy, and misinterpretation of facts; deficiencies in implementation, lack of money, lack of time, and lack of technological skill; deliberate spiritual deficiencies, prestige, deliberate under- or overestimation, and inconvenience of tackling such problems.

The first principle for an optimum in an integrative planning process is the willingness to include influences which identify the target group. The search for unused potential forces moves the planning process from the merely curative towards a preventive one, thus preventing some problems from arising.

Another reason for the need to consider influences in a planning process is the constant dynamic situation, i.e. a situation which perpetually is a preparatory stage for the next situation, and to which planning concepts are hardly adapted at present. At the urban level, for example, the image of the city and its dynamic components should be visible in planning strategies. Only in that way can planning and reality be integrated totally in the development process (Forrester speaks of "urban dynamics" when he analyses the life cycle of an urban area.[11]) McLoughlin writes the same: "So, if we see the city as a dynamic system that evolves in response to many influences, it follows that plans for it must be cast in similar forms."[12]

The growing importance of influences is an integrative part of the dynamic aspect of our present-day society and can be found in the new concept of growth. Growth is no longer related to a natural development process, but is submitted to the rule of excess and uses a multiplicity of elements of different dimensions not always synchronised to each other. It is difficult, if not impossible, to adapt the traditional way of planning to these components, "perpetual change" and "growth".

Planning, used in a static form at present, is mostly an implementation of a development programme to reach an assigned goal based on an actual situation. There is hardly enough flexibility for adaptation to further influences during the planned development process. One exception, however, is the so-called "rolling plan" used in some Asian (Japan, China and India) and European (Yugoslavia, Poland) countries. This is a five-year plan but it is revised every year for five years.[13] It is adapted yearly to the new situation.

In order to summarise this attempt at a conceptual framework, the following factors have to be taken into account: the roots of the actual development of the target groups; future trends (recognition of possible impacts of further influences, internal and external); and flexibility in development planning, allowing these factors to be included when necessary and at the right time.

HOUSING

As many external influences have various impacts on housing, the search will be directed towards a classification of components in order to obtain a multi-disciplinary and integrative approach which can be put into practice. In the early 1950s intensive research was started in order to take into account in a scientific manner the influence of climatic conditions on housing. Social and economic aspects, however, are even today not sufficiently included in housing schemes.

An attempt is made to classify socio-economic components that influence housing strategies in Figure 1. The socio-economic components and their implication in the housing sector can be found in all sectoral branches related directly or indirectly to housing strategies. Availability of material is influenced by economic factors, including transport, storage and commerce. Quantitative deficiencies can be related to lack of management or lack of political ingenuity. Tensions in housing are all related to the social sectors: health, education, social welfare and tradition versus modernity. Availability of resources is directly influenced by energy, manpower and know-how, and covers at the same time the important field of self-help strategies which will be developed further on.

The following brief description of some of these sectors takes into account external and internal forces and their influences on the target group of the housing strategy. The labour sector is directly related to housing as it provides the future inhabitants (the target group) with the financial support for the proposed housing scheme. One of the goals of housing strategies should therefore be the financial participation of the future inhabitant himself so that he may feel that the dwelling was built by him and not for him. In accordance with this scheme, a voluntary and interdisciplinary organisation is in fact planning and building houses for the poor and destitute in the state of Gujarat (India). The Ahmedabad Study Action Group (ASAG) tries to involve the target group itself in the design of the houses and the layout of the site. [14]

House construction, especially in slum-relocation programmes and rehabilitation procedures, should always be combined with financial security through labour. A struggle against influences that lead to apathy is of primary importance. Another aspect of labour is the self-help sector in construction: influences are here confined to the recognition and ingenious use of potential capacities of the target group. External influences are those coming from public and private institutions and agencies; internal influences, however, are immediately connected with tradition and the social condition of the individuals forming the target group.

Self-help strategies. Rural housing, being a part of rural development, is concerned with traditional societies, some of which still have feudal economic systems. Self-help has always been utilised in rural societies, in the form of individual skill and know-how. The Western concept of self-help, which we propose and sometimes impose, is different. It is bound to overall preconceived goals and therefore influenced by a cooperative mind which clashes often with the established socio-economic system.

Two types of self-help are thus to be observed here: first, the system which is inherent in the traditional life of peasants who use their own skill to reach their objectives; and, second, the cooperative self-help system used as an instrument for egaliterian development. (This system is, however, also employed in primitive socities for some communal tasks.) D. Rothermund places self-help between self-determination and external determination. [15] The former can be connected with endogenous forces of tradition; the latter can be ruled by exogenous forces imposing a collective goal. The use of self-help strategies should therefore be carefully structured according to the influences of traditional individualism and the forces of collectivism in the development process of housing. The strategies range from the site-and-service system that gives free reign to individual decision-making to the imposed low-cost "boxes" in which the target group participates in collective form.

Health and education. Both these sectoral branches can be integrated in an overall welfare sector divided into spiritual welfare (education) and physical welfare (health). Both are responsible for the somatic welfare of the population. No other sectoral branches have been so deeply influenced by external factors as have health and education. The impact of these influences has been so strong that while well-organised medical and educational structures have long since been set up they are unable to cope with the needs and the chronic deficiencies in the welfare sector of the majority of the population of the Third World.

The remaining traditional values in these sectors cannot cope with values imported and imposed from Western civilisation which have been developed into a leitmotif for universal welfare. The discrepancies in these combined sectors have various impacts on housing. Traditional methods to use the climate or cope with it are replaced by mechanical implements allowing the architect to plan dwellings without considering climatic conditions. The users of these dwellings can therefore rely on technique only in order to satisfy their physical welfare. The traditional value of placing dwellings according to local social systems is constantly destroyed by the influence of imported values, so that the concept of neighbourhood is almost completely lost. When dwellers lose contact with their neighbourhood they no longer consider their physical environment properly. The result is that shelter itself is losing qualitative values. Shelter and neighbourhood are both subject to the same influences.

Some rare schemes, mostly competitions or studies, consider neighbourhood values as essential for the welfare of the population and succeed in resolving these problems, at least on paper. Examples prove that housing programmes sponsored by governments and national or international agencies never consider the possible influences of external and internal forces on the target groups, nor do they try to integrate them in the housing scheme. These large-scale housing programmes are planned and built according to preconceived norms, but not for people. Consideration of the target group's welfare should allow a certain controlled freedom in the planning and implementation process of housing.[16]

The following threefold interrelationship should determine all housing schemes: the shelter itself and the endogenous tensions; the neighbourhood as security valve for communal tensions; and the controlled freedom which can be considered guidance strategy for exogenous factors, These exert influences on the proposed housing scheme and therefore bring individual know-how into play. Our planning efforts for better housing constantly fail to include the structures of the target group and its unused potential forces in the planning process. From the very outset, this leads to misunderstanding and an aversion to forces which could influence the efforts of the planning institutions positively.

INTEGRATIVE HOUSING STRATEGIES
The basic concept of this strategy is shown in Figure 2 and will be completed according to the reaction to different groupings of social and economic components. This diagram shows that exclusion of one or more sectors in setting up objectives for housing strategy will produce incomplete results and therefore unsatisfactory housing construction and conditions. The integrative strategy comprises in a positive form partial reactions and their negative aspects on problems in the housing sector. This strategy is possible only

if the tagret groups participate. External and internal influences can bring about positive or negative apsects in housing.

Mass-production of houses is a necessity if we consider the huge deficiency revealed at the Vancouver Habitat conference. Yet, declarations are not enough; strategies must be developed. Building according to personal need but without system is done only by a minority of upper middle-class people. In many cases the result is a totally built-up landscape. For this reason alone it cannot become a strategy for the masses. To protest is a legitimate democratic step to show up quantitative deficiencies in housing. Most of the time this first step remains the only one. Alternatives to resolve this problem are sporadic. Planning and building without consideration of local circumstances means failing to consider the natural and social environment.

The integration of these four partial reactions in the field of housing strategies demands well-developed managerial talents. A recipe which chould be used for any housing scheme is neither possible nor advisable, because of disparities at regional and local levels. Approaches at these levels should therefore be set up by both planners and target groups, according to the regional and local aspects, their influences and potential forces. According to the diagram, if tensions are to be eliminated, housing strategies should become integrative and multi-disciplinary. These four points will not all have the same weight in the integration process. The weight will depend on the type of needs at the origin of a planning strategy and the resources available.

TOWARDS A RUR-URBAN SYMBIOSIS
The approach to rural influences has to be different from that to urban influences. It is known that urban values are mostly conditioned by growth while rural values are orientated mostly to stability. The disparity between these values prevents influences and their impact on life from being grouped together (an urban poor is totally different from a rural poor, the essence of poverty being different). Rural-urban symbiosis, secotral as well as spatial remains a dream, therefore, unless some values change in future. I personally see hope in the energy-cum-environment crisis which could bring at least some rural and urban values closer together.

This non-realised symbiosis at present has an impact on housing at two levels. The first is the continuous urbanisation of the rural area, especially in housing. The sterile way of life in urban aras and its social tensions find expression at rural level. But this is only an intermediate stage, as the multi-faced but sterile urban life and its influences already reach settlements in the so-called rural-urban fringe. Secondly, the rural way of life of slum-dwellers in the Third World is a contradiction of the rules of urban life. Non-observance of these rules (urban sanitation, traffic, social life, etc) leads to constant tensions which have their most visible impact on shelter.

SYNTHESIS AND WORKING SCHEMES
The following influences should be integrated or at least considered in any small-scale planning strategy: the roots of the actual development (historical values); the roots of the target group (traditional or Western influences); actual values (micro-spatial, macro-spatial and sectoral influences); future values (recognition of future trends and possible potential forces); technological influences (planning tools and their respective values, implementing tools, e.g. laws and by-laws and know-how of planners); and the factor time and its inclusion in the planning process.

A rough integration without detailed specification of all these values and their influences can be represented as they are in Figures 3 and 4.

REFERENCES

[1] In the context of this paper, urban and rural characteristics are taken into account. Others could be industrial/agricultural, built-up areas/free landscape, central/marginal, etc.

[2] Dimension: Measurement of any kind, including also new types of relations between human beings and between human beings and their environment. When Lewis Mumford describes "the crystallisation of the city" as a "purpose beyond mere survival" he introduces in my opinion a new dimension in human life.
Component: This is an attempt to stress a constituent part of a unity which helps to form an entity.
Element: This term conveys the concept of a constituent part of a unity which develops more or less independently inside this unity.

[3] Colby, C.C., "Centrifugal and centripetal forces in urban geography" (1933), Annals of the Association of American Geographers, Vol XXIII, No 1, pages 1-20.

[4] Cox speaks in the context of migration of "feeding back" and "chain migration". See Cox, K.R., Man location and behaviour (1972).

[5] Ward, B., "The poor world's cities" (1969); The Economist, page 62.

[6] Colby, C.C., "Centrifugal and centripetal forces in urban geography" (1933), Annals of the Association of American Geographers, Vol XXIII, No 1, pages 1-20.

[7] Compare a study of "Endogenous dragging development structures in India" in Blenck, J., "Endogene und exogent Entwicklungshemmende Strukturen" (1974), Heidelberger geographische Arbeiten Vol 40, pages 395-418.

[8] In its roots, the word "technology" contains both terms.

[9] Hamesse, J.E., Urban influences on rural housing and living patterns in India (1979), Fort Lauderdale. German edition: Urbane Einflusse auf Wohn- und Dorstrikture in Indien (1979).

[10] Beteille, A., "Closed and open social stratification" (1966), European Journal of Sociology Vol VII, pages 224-46.

[11] Forrester, J.W., Urban dynamics (1969).

[12] McLoughlin, J.B., Urban and regional planning (1973), page 83.

[13] In Yojana, a publication of the Planning Commission in New Delhi, the Rolling Plan is described as follows: "Under the new Rolling Plan scheme there will be a five-year plan in continuous existence, being reviewed and extended year by year...The economic realities will be assessed afresh..." In a fast changing world any rigidity in planning becomes and operative burden. Therefore, new external forces which happen to influence and change the whole socio-economic life in a country should be integrated the same year in the next plan. In the same manner, some internal forces can have an influence on development realities. See Krishna, K.C., "The Rolling Plan, a step in right direction" (1978), Yojana, Vol XXII/16, pages 21-2.

[14] See Shah, K., "Housing for the urban poor in Ahmedabad" (1978), A. de Souza (ed) The Indian city, pages 145-170. See also Hamesse, J.E., "Rehabilitation par participation" (1979), Cooperation-Neuf-Monde No 7, pages 22-6.

[15] Rothemund, D., "Self help, instrument or objective in rural development" (1976), A.A. Bondenstedt (ed) Self-help, instrument or objective in rural development, pages 116-120.

[16] Some well-known authors in various disciplines have demonstrated this in the form of case concepts in Turner, J.F.C., and Fichter, R., Freedom to build (1973).

[17] The same types of diagram were used in the context of working process in which special aspects of development planning are considered. See, Hamesse, J.E., and Stubenvoll, B., Methodische Atsatze zur Entwicklungsplanung im landlichen Raum (1979.

Figure 1

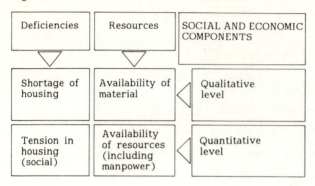

Figure 2

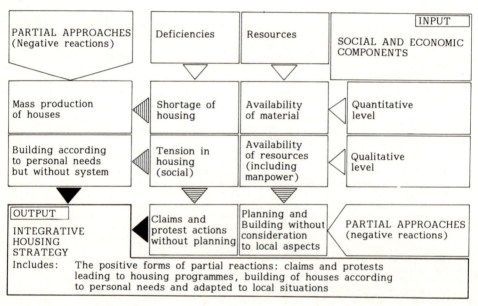

◁ INPUT OF COMPONENT

◁ REACTION

◀ INTEGRATION PROCESS

Figure 3

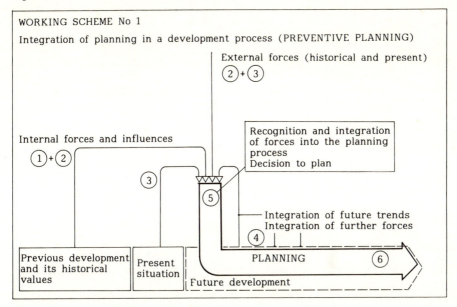

Figure 4

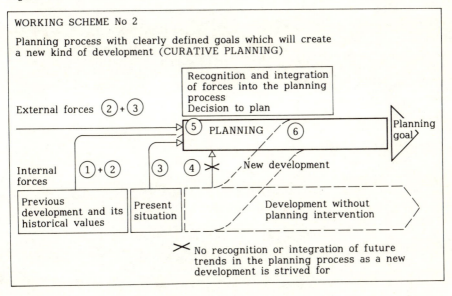

The future of urban housing in metropolitan Durban

10

E. Tollman   South Africa

INTRODUCTION

Urban housing more than any other functional element in the city structure calls for strategies to resolve the environmental degradation of cities of both the developed and developing nations. Housing invariably represents the greatest extent of urban land use; accordingly, the standards of density coupled with unit amenity will (in relation to city structure as a whole) substantially determine the environmental quality of urban life for a city's peoples.

This paper will explore briefly the nature of cities and societies and their consequences for the housing element. South African cities and the case of the Durban metropolitan area in particular will be examined in greater detail. Housing strategies at present employed there will be reviewed and policy alternatives to accommodate the increasing scale of urban growth will be suggested.

COMPARISONS WITH COLONIAL AND WESTERN CITIES

All cities have a unique character that defies rigid categorisation. Nevertheless, there are patterns of spatial organisation that repeat themselves from city to city and show similarities which do not appear to be the result of either their historical development or their specific location. The two prototypical models which provide a base against which to evaluate the contemporary South African city, of which metropolitan Durban is characteristic, are the pre-industrial colonial city and the advanced western industrial city.

Colonial cities developed as a result of the settlement and domination of a technologically advanced group over a technologically backward indigenous population. Because of its political authority, the dominant group is able to control social and economic relationships among the various ethnic groups. Owing to discrimination in trade, industry, property-buying, education and training, the majority of the urban popultation remained in a semi-traditional underdeveloped state, available to serve as a labour force. The urban structure of these colonial cities manifests a pronounced level of spatial segregation, based on race, and enforced by regulation. The dominant colonial group occupied the environmentally desirable sites located conveniently for the centralised functions of the city, while the indigenous population groups were settled on land rejected by the dominant group as undesirable for development and located on the city periphery. In this distributon of race groups, economic and social status declined progressively from the core area of the city to the periphery. Only after the transportation infrastructure had been established did the high-status areas expand in a sectoral form to desirable suburban locations. The urban structure of colonial cities has also been modified by the growth of peripheral slum settlements as a result of large-scale urbanisation.

The advanced Western industrial city, on the other hand, is highly integrated and the product of open competition between the members of its relatively mobile socio-economic groups in a market-exchange economy. Residential location is not enforced by statute but regulated by the balance beween income and the cost of housing and transportation. The spatial distribution of the colonial model is reversed in the advanced industrial city. The residential locations of the affluent are diverted to more distant suburban zones considered to be socially and environmentally desirable. The mobile middle class follows in the wake of the wealthy; for both of them a wide range of alternative residential environments, housing types and life styles is available. The low-amenity inner zones of the city are taken over for high-density housing for the low-income groups who have little choice in the form or location of their housing.

The argument thus far has concerned two theoretical spatial alternatives as reflections of two very different forms of economic and social organisation. The purpose has been to provide a context in which to examine the nature of the spatial organisation of South African cities.

SOUTH AFRICAN CITIES

South African society has its roots in a complex colonial past. Outwardly the economy today is is sophisticated and supported by an advanced technology and a developed infrastructure, but there are many parallels between South African cities and those of underdeveloped nations. The rapidly growing masses remain in a position of economic, social and political underdevelopment, while economic and social initiative rests with a small predominantly white élite. The economy is not wholly dominated by whites, but class privilege has been maintained both by prescribing employment levels to various population groups by law and custom and by differential access to education and training.

The structure of South African cities bears a striking resemblance to that of former colonial territories. Unlike the cities of advanced Western industrial society, the South African city is primarily organised on the basis of race and only secondarily in relation to socio-economic status. Until 1950, segregation in South African cities was determined by the socio-economic forces of the colonial tradition. The promulgation of the Group Areas Act of 1950, however, radically altered and intensified the race-class spatial relationships within the city. Approximately ten years after the enactment of the Group Areas Act, officially approved plans began to appear for all cities and towns throughout the country. These plans featured group areas separated by strong physical or man-made barriers emphasisng the intention to reduce social relationships between race-class groups to a minimum. The major public transportation routes were designed so that, wherever possible, each race group would be given direct access to places of work. This apartheid city, though more complex, maintains the core-periphery relationship of the colonial city. The coloured, Indian and black groups were further decentralised in relation to the city centre, and there have been only marginal improvements in locating these groups near the major industrial zones. The sectoral-spatial structure arising from Group Areas legislation has added substantially to the cost of the transport and effort of the subject classes.

DURBAN

In the case of metropolitan Durban, the plan clearly shows the pronounced sectoral-ethnic pattern as well as a movement system designed to minimise inter-group contact. The core areas of the city have been reserved for white residence while coloured, Indian and black groups occupy peripheral sectors. Thus, Durban, a highly developed industrial harbour city, exhibits the characteristic spatial structure of the colonial city, with the poor houses in peripheral sectors and a more affluent white core extending sectorally to desirable suburban localities. Within the modernistic white areas, socio-economic mobility resembles closely that of advanced industrial societies, but the majority of non-whites have little choice in their location or housing. An aggravating factor has been the growth of peripheral squatter settlements resulting from large-scale migration from the rural areas to the cities. It is doubtful if adequate resources are available to house these people properly, so that many workers in the field hold that squatter settlements, despite their degrading physical environment, contribute positively to the urbanisation process in that they provide a social environment which the immigrant can afford and from where he can make the transition to a more amenable urban existence.

In order to appreciate fully the generating forces for Durban's spatial structure, a basic understanding of the physiographic context is essential. Metropolitan Durban, situated on the south-east coast of Africa, is dominated by the Bay of Natal and the sixty-metre coastal dune, or Bluff, that shelters its entrance. Originally almost twenty square kilometres in extent, the bay projects from the coastline into the semicircular form characteristic of coastal cities. Adjacent to the bay in the north, south and west are extensive alluvial flats which do not exceed fifteen metres in elevation. The coastal plain is flanked on the west by a sandy ridge of hills running parallel to the coastline and rising to a general elevation of 120 metres. West of this ridge lies the inland section of the metropolitan area which is intersected by deep river valleys running eastwards towards the coast. The hills between these valleys rise to an elevation of 360 metres and contain the gently sloping land of the large Pinetown basin. To the west of the basin, the terrain again rises steeply over an escarpment to the Kloof-Hillcrest plateau, which at a general elevation of 600 metres forms the western limit of the metropolitan area.

These physiographic features have largely predicated the location of the region's major elements, the city's core area and its major industrial concentrations. The city centre has developed on the site of the first trading settlement established in 1824 on the northern shore of the bay. The major industrial areas are located on the alluvial flats to the north and south and in the Umgeni valley and the Pinetown basin. The same features have also influenced the design of the city's major transportation routes. These have evolved from the first rough tracks that radiated from the initial settlement northwards and southwards along the foot of the Berea ridge towards Zululand and the Eastern Cape respectively, eastward towards the harbour landing stage at the Point, and westward following the undulating slopes between the valleys of the Umbilo and Umhlatuzana rivers towards the Pinetown basin and the Kloof plateau. The construction of the major route to the interior, Berea Road, was a later development. These corridors still underline the city's major road infrastructure. Similarly, the first railway routes constructed in 1860 established the corridors for the rail network which constitutes the major transportation mode for the city's labouring classes.

The region's physiography, the transportation infrastructure, central government legislation and, finally, a planning philosophy which is colonial, capitalist and élitist and formulated specifically to reinforce socio-economic barriers and entrench the privilege of the dominant ruling class - all these are apparent in the disposition of the city's residential component. The prime locations adjacent to the waterfront and the commanding slopes of the sea-facing Berea ridge are white housing areas, while the black dormitory townships of Umlazi and Kwa Mashu are located at the region's northern and southern extremities on land that is severely broken and steeply sloping. The Indian and coloured settlements at Chatsworth and Phoenix are sandwiched between the white and black housing areas. Beyond the periphery, squatter settlements are on the increase as rural-urban migration and natural population increases mount.

Thus, the pattern of residential settlement of the Durban metropolitan area may be summarised as follows. The desirable locations adjacent to the beach-front and harbour-front respectively have been developed as high-rise high-density areas. They surround the central area and are characteristic of the advanced Western industrial model. The climatically desirable slopes of the hilly ridge extending from north to south parallel with the coast are taken up predominantly by free-standing family dwellings on individual sites. On the central ridge close to the core, fairly extensive pockets of high-rise intermediate-density apartment buildings have been zoned. The residential land to the lee of the coastal ridge contains predominantly single-family dwellings, as well as an enclave of the highest residential density in the metropolitan area.

Because of Durban's sub-tropical climate, the extensive high-rise high-density apartment development near the coast is totally unsuited to the family-type accommodation required. Beyond this area the sprawling low-rise low-density development of the outer suburbs is strung out along the city's western and northern routes to the affluent white suburbs and along its southern route to white working-class areas. Beyond these, both to the north and south, the formal Indian, coloured and black housing areas are located on a seemingly interminable landscape of low-rise low-density low-amenity single-family dwellings with poor accessibility to places of work, especially the core area and all centralised nodes. Beyond the formal black townships, an expanding band of informal squatter housing has taken root, largely in response to the lack of proper accommodation but partially also as a preferred alternative to the leasing of available public housing. The average densities on the ridge lines of the undulating terrain are high, but decline as they advance to the rural-urban fringe.

In terms of city structure the die is now cast - a developed infrastructure of services, utilities and transportation routes is well established. In addition, central government legislation coupled with entrenched land ownership is likely to perpetuate the pattern of distribution of housing areas. Town planning controls intended to preserve environmental amenity are blunt instruments that succeed only in preventing the worst excesses. The major density control is one of a bulk ratio that is a function of the site area, while the so-called controls on environmental quality are site coverage, restrictive building lines, height restriction and elevation control. These controls are well intended but frequently confound their purpose.

In a situation where the location of housing areas has been determined and much of the housing stock is extant and inhabited, any policy alternatives put forward must of necessity be circumspect. There appear to be three areas of manoeuvre: first, the policy on vacant city land, particularly in close proximity to or within easy access of the core area; secondly, the policy on optimum residential densities and their distribution; and finally, the policy on controls on the quality of residential development (which I do not propose to elaborate in this paper).

Taking a long and optimistic view of the situation I would suggest that racial segregation could cease to be the primary criterion for housing location. Nevertheless, both custom and economic forces would tend to perpetuate the status quo even if the race restrictions were to be reversed. Irrespective of this, however, Durban's colonial model could well be modified by using the large tracts of vacant land adjacent to the central city for medium-density housing disposed about landscaped squares for ownership by any population group. This would assist greatly in reasserting the free market system in housing. There is a parallel to this in the free trade area that has been proposed for the CBD of Durban, as well as a precedent in the new government policy of desegregation for city hotels and restaurants. It is argued that this policy, controlled only by the market mechanism, will greatly improve the quality of urban life and the vitality of the core area: the increase in population will stimulate central area activity and reverse the trend that is at present threatening the central area of Durban and those of expanding cities through the world.

In the second area of manoeuvre, a complete rethink on the distribution of housing densities is suggested. The model proposed suggests that housing densities should increase in relation to two factors, namely core proximity and natural environmental quality. The 0-15 minute isochrone from the CBD should be developed at substantially increased densities, of the order of thirty to forty units to the hectare suited to family-type accommodation. The increase in population density resulting from this policy would create a residential environment in which pedestrian access to schools, shopping centres and recreational facilities would be a viable and desirable variant. There would also be decreased dependence on the motor car for access within residential areas, and a new possibility for a viable public transport system between residential area and the urban core would be opened up.

The environmentally deprived Indian and black areas of the city are developed at comparatively low densities and with a minimal infrastructure of services. There are opportunities for a combination of unit infill and upgrading which, through an increase of density, would make possible the provision of adequate community facilities, including a public transport system to reduce the excessive journey-to-work time which is one of the most negative aspects of the present structure.

What then should be our goal for an urban housing policy, as we press on into the twenty-first century? Those trends of need and desirability as perceived by central and local government which are antagonistic to a healthy city structure should be questioned and, where found wanting, replaced by goal-directed policies. In broad terms, it is argued that urban settlements should be more compact and that urban sprawl should be contained by intensifying the existing residential land use. This alternative is seen not as a necessary or regrettable compromise, but as a positive mechanism for improving the quality of life for the city's population as a whole.

Urban migration and natural increase in the population is inevitable. In formulating planning goals to help redress inherent structural weaknesses and stimulate a more healthy urban environment, it is hypothesised that urban residential densities should be as high as architectural ingenuity can permit, without injury to the environmental priorities of family life.

This paper has attempted to identify theoretical models for city spatial structure so as to provide a context for the special case of metropolitan Durban, a city poised between the First and Third Worlds and accordingly an eminent case for critical analysis. In postulating alternative strategies for the housing element as we move towards the twenty-first century, remedies for the dual problems of an anachronistic city spatial structure and the increasing scale of urban growth have been sought.

REFERENCES

Davies, R.J., "The growth of the Durban metropolitan area" (1963), South African Geographical Journal, Vol XLV, pages 15-43.

Davies, R.J., Of cities and societies: a geographer's viewpoint, University of Cape Town, New Series No 38, pages 1-20.

Hallen, H.H., An urban needs and resources study (1977), preliminary studies and statements about functional Durban. Urban Foundation for the Natal Region, pages 1-37.

IV: TRANSPORTATION

The twenty-first century metropolis

11

Herbert S. Levinson   United States

INTRODUCTION

Cities throughout the world continue to grow in size, complexity and importance as economies strengthen and populations expand. Managing this future urban growth to maintain mobile and livable environments will remain an important challenge in the years to come. There is no simple answer. Cities of differing size, culture and economy will have their own specific needs, both in the developed and developing countries. Bangkok and Boston, Jakarta and Jerusalem, Tehran and Toronto, each will have its unique set of land-use and transportation requirements. Relations among nations, the stability of governments, and rates of economic growth will have an important bearing on the future metropolis. Other key factors include population expansion, willingness to renew old cities and build new ones; energy availability; new systems for acquiring, allocating, managing and servicing urban land; energy and resource availability; and continued advances in technology and governmental structure. Predicting how these factors will interact is no easy task. It calls for understanding the past, assessing the present and probing the future to find ways to bring resources, society and technology together. The observations which follow focus on the North American metropolis. They show how space, time and public policy will interact in shaping urban environment. In varying degrees, they may also apply to other cities in the developed world.

A HISTORICAL PERSPECTIVE

One way of viewing the future American metropolis is by "temporal analogy", i.e. looking at changes which have occurred over comparable time spans in the past, to answer the questions: How much different will the next twenty-five years be from the past? Will it change more or less rapidly over the next century than it did over the last? What qualitative differences will take place?

Technology. We are all aware of the effects of technology on urban form, for our cities are largely products of modern industrial society. The roles of the skyscraper, automatic elevator and electric railway in centralising cities are well documented. The motor vehicle, refrigerator, air conditioner and new industrial processes are among the technologies that have played equally significant roles in recent decades. They, too, have influenced the size and form of cities, the internal distribution of population and activities, and the modes of travel. The modern jet aircraft has vastly improved air travel and today the airport is often the second largest urban activity centre. Tables 1 and 2 show some of these interrelationships.

Between 1875 and 1900 the steel-frame skyscraper, vertical elevator and electric railway changed the scale of the city and its centre. The "electric railway city" replaced the "pedestrian city" as the radius of development increased from three to over ten miles. This city reached its peak by about 1925, prior to the great depression.

Between 1925 and 1950 urban change was in many respects less dramatic. The trend towards decentralisation continued, although it was constrained by depression and war.

Between 1950 and 1975 the "automobile city" emerged. There was decentralisation of shops, industry and housing; expansions of suburbs and decline of the central city; and a shift from public to private transport. Problems of central city obsolescence and tax base; urban sprawl and declining transit passenger numbers; environmental intrusion and energy consumption led to accelerated federal programmes with a highly varied urban response.

Between 1975 and 2000 "new technologies" will mainly improve the "efficiency" of existing technologies. (For example, automatic train operation on new rail transit systems, computerised traffic control systems and modular housing developments.) Communication is not likely to reduce the need for transportation or direct personal contact.

Future advances in urban technologies, such as development of viable low-cost personal rapid transit or people-mover systems, data automation and computer advances, new building techniques, and new goods distribution methods, will influence future urban activity patterns. Because new technologies, particularly those concerned with transportation, evolve gradually over many years, no radical changes during the next several decades are expected in current travel modes, movement patterns or urban forms. Moreover, the existing urban environment serves to constrain the rapid introduction of new transport technologies.

Social and economic factors. The second world war triggered a major influx into metropolitan areas of people who previously had lived in rural areas. This last "great wave of immigration" initially was caused by job opportunities in war plants and, subsequently, the attractiveness of urban welfare programmes in major urban centres. In turn, the influx of rural and minority people into the central city caused social unrest and resulted in middle-class whites leaving the central city for the suburbs.

The period after the second world war reflected the preferences of climate, space and privacy. Suburbia was largely a response to the desire for free-standing houses, informality and, in some cases, proximity to outdoor recreational resources. FHA low-cost housing loans and improved construction equipment also contributed to the rapid suburban growth.

Planning initiatives and public improvements. Major urban planning efforts, such as the L'Enfant and McMillan plans for Washington and Burnham's plan for Chicago, have left their mark on many of our major cities. So, too, have many bold public improvements which have become a reality. The impacts of New York City's subway system and its Grand Central and Penn Station terminals are well known. Equally significant are the bridges, beaches, parks, and parkways defined in the First Regional Plan which became a reality some 25 years later. Almost every metropolitan area has public improvements which have influenced urban form and amenity. Examples are Chicago's lake-front development, New Haven's new-town centre, Los Angeles' freeways, and Washington's in-town south-west renewal. Viewed in this context, the 21st century metropolis will reflect those current plans and projects which will become a reality by 2000, for example the Dallas-Fort Worth regional airport.

Past perceptions. Planners and urbanists of the past also provide insight into the future, especially the extent to which their proposals and visions have been realised. Frank Lloyd Wright's Broadacre City, a decentralised community where the distinction between country and city is obliterated, has been achieved, even though not in Wright's organic form.[1] So, too, has Le Corbusier's Radiant City, his blueprint for the future, although in a much less qualitative way.[2] In reality, the urban development process is far too complex to fit any such concept.

GROWTH TRENDS - 1975-2000

In the years to come urban settlement patterns will, of course, be influenced by relationships among countries and the national economy. Barring war, sustained oil embargoes or major economic recession, the following trends are likely within the United States.

□ The nation's population will continue to grow. The dimensions and patterns of this future population growth are well known and documented. There will be fewer young people (at least in the decade ahead) owing to a declining birth rate, and more older people owing to greater longevity. The nation's 1977 population has been estimated at 217 million and 1975 census projections anticipate 245 to 287 million by 2000, compared with 271 to 322 million projected in 1971.

□ Metropolitan areas will continue to grow and continue to absorb most of the national population growth, except perhaps for a few large centres in the north-east. Most of the growth will take place in exurban and suburban areas. "Megalopolis" will have its Great Lakes, Pacific Coast and Gulf of Mexico counterparts. There will be growth in smaller towns and cities because of a better quality of life, more recreational opportunities, and increased job opportunities resulting from communications and aviation improvements.

□ "Sun-belt cities" will continue to grow rapidly while there will be much slower growth in the north-east, owing to the continued regional population shifts from the north and east to south and west.

□ Urban living and travel preferences will reflect continued economic growth. The number of two-wage-earner families will continue to grow as more "working wives bring home a second income". In the future, as in the past, rising incomes will raise per capita space requirements, although probably at a lower rate than in the past decades. Almost every comprehensive urban transportation planning study has found that urban land consumption and travel outpaced population growth over the past several decades. Unless constrained by public policy or a sustained shortage of energy resources, these trends will probably continue.

□ The changing mix of the nation's population will bring new types of housing to the urban scene. "Planned unit developments" combining single and multi-family residential units will become increasingly common in response to changing community needs and values, as well as the increasing costs of residential construction. There will be new developments for specific age groups, such as retirement communities for senior citizens. An increase in leisure time, such as might result from a four-day work week, will accelerate the growth of second homes, vacation, travel and outdoor recreation. Second homes may be as far as three hours' travel time from home, provided there are no travel constraints. Apartment and condomimium living will become more popular as the proportion of elderly in the population continues to increase, and there are more later marriages, childless marriages, unmarried couples and divorces. For some, rising fuel prices and disenchantment with home ownership will also make such a life-style attractive.

☐ Decentralisation of commercial and industrial activities will continue. Despite active downtown building programmes in many cities, and despite concern over air quality and energy, the number of regional shopping centres continues to grow. New industrial developments are mainly keyed to highways and airports outside the built-up cities, and the corporate office park has now emerged as a challenge to the city centre.

☐ The city centre will grow slowly in most urban areas. Growth will take place mainly in government, public facilities, services and finance, but in some large cities there will also be growth in the retail, hotel and residential sectors.

☐ Urban person-travel will continue to outpace population growth. The greatest increases will be in non-work trips. Work trips will probably grow from 0.6 to 0.8 trips per capita per day. By 2000 there will be about sixteen daily person-miles per resident, compared with about twelve today. Trips to the city centre will be longer than today. Most travel growth will take place in suburban rings around the city, often as "circumferential" trips. Automobile travel will continue to grow and there will be some gain in public transport trips.

☐ Public policy will influence urban settlement patterns to the extent that is real, responsive and timely. Evolving federal policies and programmes relating to national urban growth, urban housing, renewal and land-use, transportation funding, energy, and the environment will progressively influence urban growth. Recent years have seen a decline in urban freeway construction and rethinking of public transport strategies in view of limited resources and changing priorities. Urban renewal efforts appear to be accelerated or retarded in accordance with specific federal attitudes. Federal (or state) financial aid to cities and participation in urban welfare programmes will affect impending fiscal crises.

☐ A new federal energy policy will influence urban form and transport, especially in the long term. The shift away from natural gas is already apparent. In the short term, motor vehicle travel may be suppressed, particularly long-distance recreational trips. Eventually an energy-conservant city may emerge, as urban development decisions adapt to energy availability and as compactness replaces spread.

These trends imply several important planning challenges for the urban area and its central city. Improved government arrangements, economic incentives and land-use controls will be needed. Planning for growth implies careful emphasis on regional development patterns, and on establishing those key planning decisions which will affect regional growth, i.e. water supply, utilities, access, open space and employment. Planning for little growth (or "zero population growth", although this is perhaps not realistic) calls for qualitative improvements within the existing urban area, i.e. better housing, community facilities and transportation, and improved social, economic and educational programmes.

We have taken many important steps to preserve or revitalise our city centres. Continued action by government agencies and private developers will be necessary, and can be expected. The improvement opportunities are highly selective, however, especially for retail and residential activities. In-town residential development offers most promise, where amenities can be improved (i.e., Inner Harbor, Baltimore) or where the area is not surrounded by declining residential neighbourhoods. The extent of downtown rebuilding will depend on the specific economy and situation of the city centre, and initiatives of the public and private sectors. There is no magic formula.

There is an urgent need to upgrade the areas surrounding the city centre. This is a far more challenging task, since there are no obvious solutions. Almost every city has such declining wholesaling, warehousing, manufacturing and railroad areas. New modern industrial parks, in-town college or vocational school campuses and, in some cases, "new towns in town" are among the opportunities which should be explored. Finding and implementing the right mix of activities and economic incentives is an important planning challenge.

Within the central city, there is an obvious need progessively to improve housing stock, schools and community services. Over the next several decades, similar renewal efforts will also be required in many of the older suburban areas which surround the central city.

THE TWENTY-FIRST CENTURY METROPOLIS

The preceding trends and needs provide the context for various scenarios for the twenty-first century North American metropolis, for how well we plan for change today will profoundly affect the quality of urban life tomorrow.

One approach is to define metropolitan options in terms of alternative land development strategies for a given time. Such land-use options could include the traditional "trend or sprawl", "multi-centre" and "corridor" development concepts which vary key decisions such as downtown employment, central city renewal, public open space, population distribution, highways and public transport, and public utilities.

A more realistic approach would be to vary the extent of public intervention and technological change through time. This approach leads to the following three views of the twenty-first century metropolis.

Metropolis 2000. This will be one of "minimum change". It will be generally similar to today's metropolitan area, if somewhat larger and more dispersed. The reasons are apparent. Much of this metropolis is "in place" today, and little change is expected in built-up areas. Moreover, there is a time lag between the initiation of public policy and its translation into actual changes in the urban landscape. In many respects, we are looking at this metropolis today.

The city centre will grow as a result of continued renewal efforts, but mainly as an office and government centre. There will be some upgrading of the urban housing stock, but the "rings" around the city centre will continue to decline, with a net loss in central city population. Older suburbs, too, will have problems of form, obsolence and, in some cases, economic survival. Suburban shopping malls, industrial parks and office clusters will continue to proliferate, but at a declining rate.

There will be improvements in the quality of public transport services, and some gains in passenger numbers. Rapid transit, or "LRT" will have become a reality in cities such as Atlanta, Baltimore, Buffalo, Detroit, Los Angeles, Miami and Pittsburgh, and we will be able to assess its impact on urban structure and land use. Selective freeway construction and better traffic management will improve road travel.

Rising petrol prices and potential problems in fuel availability will limit future increases in automobile travel, although the car will remain the primary travel mode for most urban trips. They will first restrain long-distance vacation and weekend recreational trips and then the journey to work as well. Trip sharing (multiple stops per car) will be more common than ride sharing (more persons per car).

We will have learned many lessons by the turn of the century, which will lead to better cities in the years ahead. These are that the proliferation of city and suburban governments may not be in our best interest; that cities are too important to abandon; that increased commitment to renew our cities in a physical and social sense is vital; that land as well as energy is a scarce resource; and that urban transportation system development calls for a creative partnership with urban land development.

We will have learned how to recognise fads and place them in clearer perspective. Examples are the following: first, the focus on long-range planning, and then on short-range planning; that freeways are vital, then that they are in conflict with cities; that rapid transit is essential, then that it is unnecessary; that mobility can be improved only by construction, then only through operational improvements (traffic management). We will have learned how to put the pieces together in a more rational manner.

Metropolis 2025. This will reflect the result of more than a quarter of a century of concerted public action. The models of metropolitan government, found today in Toronto, Miami and Indianapolis, will have many counterparts in other metropolitan areas. We will have found means to encourage the flow of private investment into our metropolitan areas, to finance our urban communities through private capital and through municipal, state and federal funds.

We will have implemented new metropolitan approaches to housing, education and economic development, in addition to land-use and transportation. The city centre will once again have twenty-four-hour life, and the ring around it will contain productive commercial, industrial or residential areas. We will have upgraded our urban housing stock. More importantly, we will have initiated the essential social and economic programmes which will bring improved opportunity to all urban residents.

The revitalisation of our cities; the clustering of people and jobs along transportation corridors; selective increases in urban densities; and the expansion of public open space will improve urban form, increase urban compactness, reduce travel distances, make public transport viable, and conserve energy.

There will be more "off street" rail and bus transit which will be built at minimum capital and social costs, commensurate with demonstrated need. Strategically developed motorways will complement public transport in providing mobility and shaping urban growth. Within the centres of our large cities, selective automobile restraint will become a reality not only through improved public transport and energy constraints, but by the redesign of the centres themselves to a pedestrian scale.

Metropolis 2050. This will reflect the impacts of new technology as well as public policy. National urban growth, brought about by the needs to conserve energy and equalise opportunity, will limit growth in large metropolitan areas and create new communities.

The new cities of the twenty-first century will be built in an environmentally sensitive and energy-conservant manner. They will be compact, yet diverse, and afford a wide range of housing and employment choices. They will cluster development and transport in order to minimise the need for travel. Public transport services, private transport vehicles and pedestrians will each have their own separate rights of way in a full application of the principle of access control.

These new cities will be built around new construction, energy and transport technologies. Personal rapid transit may become a dominant travel mode, and palletised conveyor systems may move urban goods. Nuclear and solar energy may reduce dependence on petroleum-based energy sources.

Existing cities, too, will enjoy the benefits of new technologies, yet they will retain their charm and heritage of the past. They, too, will embody our visions and plans.

THE METROPOLITAN CHALLENGE

These views of tomorrow's metropolis identify some of our future choices in the United States. The challenge is for increased commitment in the years to come to anticipatory rather than reactive planning. It is time to plan now for tomorrow's metropolis, to take the necessary bold actions to improve the quality of urban life. In this way, our cities will continue to be the centres of our culture and society.

REFERENCES
[1] Wright, F.L., The living city (1963), Mentor Books.
[2] Le Corbusier, The radiant city, first published in 1933 under the title La Ville Radieuse; published by Orion Press, New York, 1961.

Table 1. An overview of urban growth, technology and public policy

Year	Type of city	Technology	Prevailing urban transport	Public policy factors	Economic and political factors
1875	Pedestrian	Steel frame construction Electricity (DC & AC motors) Vertical elevator	Cable-car		
1900	Electric railway	Subway Gasoline engine (Automobile)	Electric street car	Federal aid	World War I
1925		Radio Air conditioning Diesel engine Freeway		FHA-housing	Immigration limited Great Depression World War II
1950	Automobile (Urban region)	Nuclear development Television Computers Jet aircraft Space travel	Motor bus & automobile	Interstate Highway system Urban Mass Transit Act	
1975					Energy crisis

Table 2. Transport mode and urban form

Item	Type of city		
	Pedestrian	Electric railway (rapid transit)	Automobile
Population	3,000,000	3,000,000	3,000,000
Area (m^2)	30	200	400
Density (persons m^2)	100,000	15,000	7,500
Jobs in city centre	200,000	300,000	150,000
Development pattern	Compact	Major corridors	Dispersed
Example	Paris, 1900	Chicago, 1920	Los Angeles 1970

An innovative regional transit system in Israel

12

Eliahu Stern   Israel

INTRODUCTION

Small urban centres and their adjacent rural hiterlands are usually faced with a low level of inter-urban bus services. This is considered a rural transport problem where insufficient traffic cannot justify even subsidised transit services. The relatively little work in this area[1] and the solutions proposed[2,3] do not take into account public attitudes to service improvements and therefore no "unorthodox" experimentation has been undertaken. In order to maintain a reasonable level of public transport services, if only because of social norms and government commitment, public preferences in the nature and quality of the service should be examined. However, such an approach was followed for intra-urban transit improvements in New York City.[4] It is expected that an improvement in the service level encompassing consumer preferences will be more significant from the consumer point of view.

The first object of this study is to examine public preferences with regard to inter-urban bus services in a rural area in Israel. The second object is to study public response to a new regional transit system introduced on the basis of the public service preferences. Such information, which can be used to determine service operational standards, is thought necessary in the decision-making process of transit improvements.

The paper is based on broader research conducted by the author in the Northern Negev District.[5] A survey conducted in 1977 supplied information on travel habits, socio-economic characteristics, personal preferences and degree of satisfaction with five quantifiable service attributes: frequency, reliability, travel cost, service network connectivity, and distance to nearest station. With this information, perception and satisfaction profiles were built up by the paired comparison technique, based on Thurstone's Law of Comparative Judgment.[6] Subjective satisfaction scaled values were fitted by the least-squares procedure to operational values of the service attributes in order to determine service standards. The examination of public attitude was based on a questionnaire distributed to 753 citizens in both urban and rural settlements.

PREFERENCE AND SATISFACTION

Preference and satisfaction profiles of service attributes were built, compared and analysed in terms of three classifications. First, profiles based on eighteen socio-economic homogeneous groups resulted in a three-dimensional stratification (sex by age by income) of the sampled population. Secondly, profiles were built of rural and urban population separately and, lastly, profiles were based on personal dominant mode of travel. Comparison of the eighteen preference profiles indicated no significant differences among the profiles.

Figure 1 presents the preference profile of the entire population from which it is clear that frequency was ranked first and walking distance last. One would expect differences in the preference sets between rural and urban populations because of differences in size and location. Figure 2 presents the preference profiles of the urban and the rural populations. The main difference between the two profiles relates to walking distance and network connectivity. On average, the rural settlements are located 1.5 miles from the nearest bus station and the population therefore ranked highly its preference with regard to walking distance, while the need for good connections throughout the trip was ranked last. In addition, the less frequent service supplied to the rural settlements is presented by the relatively higher preference scale value when compared with the urban population profile.

A third type of classification is presented in Figures 3 and 4, where the sampled population is stratified according to personal dominant mode of travel. An examination of the captive riders profile (Figure 3) shows a similarity to the urban population profile. Differences between the profile of the captive and that of the free choice riders primarily concern travel cost and walking distance. Free choice riders consider travel cost of less importance than the captive riders but they are more sensitive to walking distance. The profile of the least mobile people (Figure 4) indicates a low priority for walking distance which can be explained by their minimal acquaintance with the existing transport system. It is also evident that their demand is more responsive to travel cost.

A comparison of all the profiles led to the conclusion that the two profiles of the rural and urban population sufficiently represent the overall variations of preferences.

Following the mutual trends of the satisfaction and preference profiles in Figures 1-4, one would observe that the trends are in inverse proportion to one another. Thus, a relatively low degree of satisfaction to a given service attribute is followed by a relatively high level of preference. For the urban population profiles (Figure 2), for example, a high level of satisfaction for walking distance is followed by a low degree of preference and a relatively low degree of satisfaction for reliability is followed by a relatively high preference scaled value. The same pattern is also evident in Figures 3 and 4. These findings simply mean that the set of preferences is influenced by the service supplied. Moreover, the individual's set of preferences depends on his personal experience and familiarity with a given service situation. A change in the present situation may result in a different set of preferences. It is evident that the urban population ranked frequency and cost first as needing most improvement and the rural population ranked frequency and walking distance.

At this point ordinarily scaled values were introduced into a correlational analysis in which the quantified values of the service attributes served as dependent variables. It was found that in order to be satisfactory, the service in the rural area should provide twenty daily bus departures to and from the area and walking distances should not exceed 0.2 mile.[5] The calculated frequency to and from the urban centres came to "a bus every twenty minutes". Such level of service must be demand-adjustable and therefore the existing bus fleet (fifty seats per bus) would not be suitable for low demand areas. Introduction of the perceived improvements in the existing system would result in oversupply and a high operation cost. This information and conclusions served as guidelines in the derivation of the following alternative transit system.

A REGIONAL TRANSIT SYSTEM

Public bus services are provided in Israel by seven companies, excluding small private Arab companies operating in the post-1967 territories. Of these, only three provide inter-urban services. The inter-city market is served by the largest cooperative company, Egged, which owns 3600 of the 5770 buses in the national system. The company operates 400 different inter-city service lines in a radial pattern from the three largest metropolitan areas. Because of the radial pattern, the inter-regional service involves transfer (i.e. a low degree of network connectivity) and the intra-regional service quality is extremely low. As a result, there is hardly any intra-regional interaction and third-order regional centres in the national urban heirarchy are therefore not functioning. Rural settlements interact directly second-order cities and, even more, with first-order cities while third-order cities remain stagnant in terms of urban and economic development.

The bus companies operate fifty-seat motor buses regardless of the demand. Demand-adjustable, small vehicles operated by the monopolistic company in low-demand areas would probably not reduce operating costs significantly since wages account for over 70 per cent of these costs. Companies using small vehicles would not necessarily hire drivers on a cooperative basis and operating costs might be reduced. This estimation is strengthened by the fact that in 1975 the taxi cab cost per 1000 kilometres was 1226 Israeli pounds compared with 3119 Israeli pounds per 1000 kilometres for buses operated by Egged. Better service quality can be provided by a demand-adjustable system based on small vehicles. The impact of a demand-responsive minibus system, for people immobilised in small urban comunities, has already been investigated and suggests that more research is needed in this area.[7]

A demand-responsive system in Israeli rural areas can be based on existing fleets of minibuses and zotobuses owned by the regional municipalities in those areas. A minibus is defined as an eleven-person vehicle and zotobus as a twenty-person vehicle. There are forty-eight regional municipalities which provide transportation services to regional schools and medical centres. The total fleet, which includes 225 vehicles, is not used for most of the time and the drivers' wage system allows for lower operating costs compared to small vehicles operated by the existing main bus company. Reorganisation of this fleet, which may be enlarged by the local private or public sectors, according to regional demand zones, could be the basis for a demand-adjustable system in the rural areas. This intra-regional service would provide feeders to the existing (but re-adjusted) radial system and improve the service in terms of frequency, reliability and walking distance.

An element of competition will be introduced by opening the market to several operators. Better control of the service quality can be achieved by renewing periodically the concession for a given route or a specific demand zone. In addition, the subsidy can be allocated according to the demand pattern.

Two regional municipalities (owning thirty-two vehicles of varying size) are included in the Northern Negev study area. Each municipality is based on a regional urban centre and adjacent rural hinterland. Over half the total population in both municipalities (27 000 people) is urban. Since the existing public transport service pattern is radial, there is no direct service between the two cities.

The proposed regional system would be based on the fleet of vehicles of the regional municipalities which will provide intra-regional and inter-urban feeder services in the area (Figure 5). Inter-urban feeders would be operated only during peak hours in order to improve the service in those high-demand periods.

Intra-regional feeders focused on the regional cities are expected to strengthen the cities' function as service centres by converting them into regional transfer points. A transfer terminal built in Israel in the CBD of the city would create a multiplier effect, although small, which would increase the economic activity in the city. Another potential advantage is regional integration which has never been achieved in rural areas in Israel. A basic condition for regional integration is thought to be inter-nodal accessibility. Feeder lines between the villages and regional cities fulfil this condition.

With regard to service quality, three potential improvements are expected:

□ Feeders would use the inter-city bus stations in the existing radial service routes so that the inter-city service will be direct. Adjustment of the feeder schedule to the inter-city schedule would reduce the total travel time for those travelling to Beersheva (Figure 5).

□ Reduction of inter-city bus operation time will reduce operating costs without changing the potential number of riders. The saving in inter-city drivers' time might permit an increase in inter-city departure frequencies. The cost of a higher frequency will be mostly dependent on distance related attributes (fuel, amortisation, etc) which account for only 30 per cent of operation costs.

□ Inter-city direct lines will increase reliability since traffic congestion does not yet influence the departure or arrival time in this rural area.

The proposed regional system may also negate some of the service attributes. The rural population may face an increase in travel costs and a decrease in network connectivity. The potential changes caused by the regional feeder system can be summarised as follows:

A comparison of these potential changes with the preference and satisfaction profiles shows that the attributes expected to be improved are those most preferred by both urban and rural populations. Therefore, a second investigation was undertaken in order to study public attitudes on changes in the service resulting from the new system.

PUBLIC ATTITUDES

Public attitudes were studied on the following characteristics of the regional feeder system:

□ the need to transfer throughout a trip compared to shorter travel time and higher frequency

□ willingness to pay more for a more frequent service

□ the technology of the feeder system, and

□ the optimum time for a higher interurban service frequency

Table 1 presents the distribution of public preferences on the first characteristic. The distribution of preferences indicates a high similarity between urban and rural populations, although the rural population may face a decrease in connectivity level with the introduction of the regional system. However, it was shown that the individual's preference is influenced by the existing service situation, and the examination of trip distribution by network connectivity indicated that only 10 per cent of the rural trips require transfers. Most trips (90 per cent) have the regional urban centre as their destination. A similar situation was observed with regard to trips emanating from the urban centres. These had mainly the regional city of Beersheva as their destination. This explains the similarity of attitudes which stress the importance of travel time rather than connectivity.

Some difference in attitude is observed in Table 2. A high-frequency indirect service is preferred by the rural population. Only 24 per cent prefer a low-frequency direct service compared with 32 per cent of the urban population. With regard to higher travel costs (Table 3), we may conclude that the rural population is more willing to pay more for a higher-frequency service, compared to the urban population.

These results concerning cost, frequency and connectivity strengthen the positive attitudes on the potential changes generated by the new regional system. Attitudes on the new technology appeared to be evenly divided between the standard fifty-seat bus and the various types of smaller vehicles. It is noteworthy that the minibus is preferred to the zotobus, probably because it has a better image with regard to convenience. Peak hours for inter-urban service improvements appeared to be early mornings (up to 8 am) and late evenings (after 8 pm).

CONCLUSIONS

The results of this study show a high correlation between the characteristics of a new regional transit system based on intra-regional feeder lines and public attitudes. It is also clear that the urban and rural population allocate different preferences to bus service attributes. This is explained by the fact that the behavioural disposition of personalities in each group is a product of a given service situation. On this basis, recommendations can be nade with a view to experimenting with the new regional transport system. In addition, a second study should be undertaken after the experimental period in order to examine the discrepancies between attitudes and behaviour.

It seems that the reorganisation of public transportation on the basis of complementary regional feeder lines will be to the advantage of the citizens, the feeder operators, and the main bus company. The Ministry of Transportation in Israel has the fiscal right to plan and control public transportation in the country, but the present monopolistic system would make the implementation of a plan such as that described here a daring political act.

REFERENCES
[1] Wragg, R.F., and others, A study of the passenger transport needs of rural Wales (1975), Welsh Council.
[2] Rhys, D.G., and Baxton, M.J. "The rural transport problem: a possible solution", Town and Country Planning (1974), Vol 12, pages 555-8.
[3] White, R.P., Planning for public transport (1976), Hutchinson.
[4] Weiss, L.D., "Citizen opinions on public transportation roles, service and financing", Transportation Research Record (1976), No 590, pages 5-8.
[5] Stern, E., Public transport level-of-service in Israel's developing regions (1977), Ministry of Transportation, Chief Scientist's Office, Jerusalem.
[6] Thurstone, L.L., The measurement of values (1959), University of Chicago Press.
[7] Wiseman, F.R., "Impact of a demand-responsive minibus system for the elderly in a small urban community", Southeastern Geographer (1976), Vol 16.

Table 1. Distribution of preferences (as percentages) to an indirect
but faster service compared with a direct service longer in travel time

Preference	Total	Urban population	Rural population
Absolutely yes	49	49	50
Yes if travel cost is unchanged	24	24	23
Absolutely no	27	27	27

Table 2. Distribution of preferences (as percentages) with regard
to a higher-frequency indirect service, compared with a
lower-frequency direct service

Preference	Total	Urban population	Rural population
Absolutely yes	48	47	51
Yes if travel cost is unchanged	21	21	25
Absolutely no	31	32	24

Table 3. Willingness to pay a higher travel
cost for a higher-frequency service
(percentages)

Willingness	Total	Urban	Rural
Yes	55	51	71
No	45	49	29

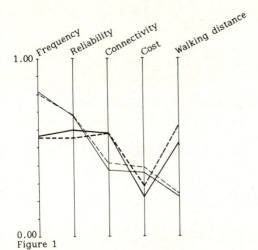

Figure 1
Preference and satisfaction profiles
of total population

—— Preference (demand weighted)
--- Preference (unweighted)
—— Satisfaction (demand weighted)
·--- Satisfaction (unweighted)

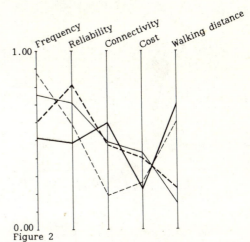

Figure 2
Preference and satisfaction profiles for
urban and rural population

—— Preferences - urban population
--- Preferences - rural population
—— Satisfaction - urban population
--- Satisfaction - rural population

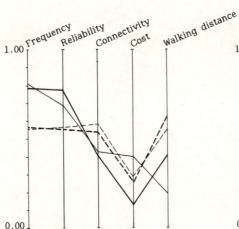

Figure 3
Preference and satisfaction profiles
by travel mode stratification

—— Preference - captive riders
--- Preference - car users
—— Satisfaction - captive riders
--- Satisfaction - car users

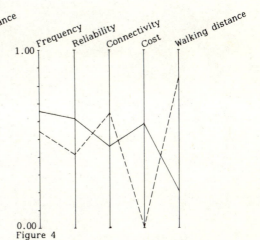

Figure 4
Preference and satisfaction profiles for the
least mobile segment of population

—— Preference
--- Satisfaction

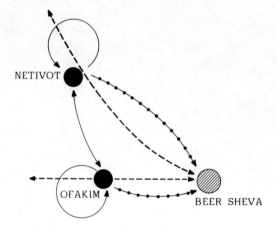

Figure 5

Schematic plan of proposed regional transit
system in the Israeli Northern Negev

--- Existing bus route

⎯ Intra-regional feeder line

•••→ Inter-urban feeder line

⬤ Urban centre-regional
transfer point

V: URBAN DEVELOPMENT IN ISRAEL

The urban system in Israel   13

Michael Kuhn   Israel

INTRODUCTION

Any attempt to formulate an essentially new conception of a familiar phenomenon must, perforce, be based on the restructuring of its elements in a new way. M. Polanyi asserts in his book Personal knowledge that these new structures are always the result of intuition and imagination. They can eventually be elaborated first into tentative and then working hypotheses that can be validated or invalidated by scientific methods.

The current uncritical method of the analytical, as opposed to the conceptual, approach to planning invariably leads to conservative and unimaginative results. A new formulation of desirable future states must be conceptual, based on a creative integration of many existential and "non-scientific" factors. It involves an element of personal knowledge and belief that requires further confirmation by scientific and logical methods. But it is the only way to build qualitative and value-based models for the future, without which planning is reduced to incoherent technological improvements, which are, as we know from experience, insufficient to improve the general quality of life.

The purpose of this introduction is to explain and justify the presentation of this conceptual and hypothetical thesis, in an attempt to revise current conceptions and formulate new and different ones.

The main features of this thesis are: an attempt to use the systematic approach to define complex and dynamic phenomena; formulation of a hypothesis on the transformation of the coastal plain of Israel into a coherently structured system; formulation of a hypothesis on urbanisation in rural settlements and their integration, together with cities and various services, into highly urbanised regional systems; a tentative consideration of the topographical and geographical factors in the form and character of urban settlements and their integration into regional systems; tentative conclusions from these hypotheses, dispensing with the current dichotomy of urban-rural, city-countryside, town-village, and so on; a tentative hypothesis that the degree of urbanisation of rural settlements derives from their level of organisation, which can be achieved without physical transformation into urban settlements as we know them (towns, cities); and a tentative introduction of aesthetics into regional planning through structured and coherent order, correlated with the physical structure of the land and the historically created forms and patterns, shaped by this structure.

As can be noted, the thesis is tentative and hypothetical throughout. Being so, it is highly controversial, but it seems sufficiently important to justify a discussion and be the subject of study and research.

THE COASTAL PLAIN'S PRIMARY ROLE

The city is the product of a complex process that we call urbanisation. It is therefore customary to identify urbanised society with the population residing in cities. The city was, and still is, conceived as a socio-economic, territorial and more or less closed system, limited in space and essentially different from the surrounding rural territory and population. Once it was believed that cities could be contained by green belts and agriculture (British new towns, Abercombie, etc). This proved to be more or less feasible in cities with moderate rates of growth, but failed completely in areas of rapid growth. Recognition of this failure led to the emergence of the concept of metropolitan areas, conurbations, then megalopolis (Jean Gottman) and ecumenopolis (Doxiadis). Metropolitan areas emerged where rural areas around cities and their populations turned from predominantly agricultural occupations to industry, services and administration. But conurbation and megalopolis were phenomena of a higher level: they envisaged the integration of several cities with their metropolitan areas and various national installations and agricultural settlements located between them. Such vast and complex conglomerations have gradually been structured as huge systems whose components are interrelated and interconnected (the Rand in Holland, the Ruhr in Germany, the north-eastern coast of the United States, among many others).

In newly settled countries such as the United States, Brazil and Australia, the new settlers were first concentrated along the coast where contact was maintained with the rest of the world. These coastal areas developed into powerful bases that fed the trickle and then the flow of settlers into the inland areas. In many cases there was a physical and topographical barrier, such as the Appalachian range in the United States that confined the coastal areas. These barriers established a lasting differentiation between the developed coastal cities and the inland towns and settlements which can still be observed both in the eastern and western coastal areas of North and South America.

This universal phenomenon can also be observed in the coastal plain of Israel. Although agricultural settlements were established in the interior from the beginning of Jewish immigration, most immigrants free to choose settled in and around Tel Aviv and Haifa, creating the two metropolitan areas where most of the economic and social activity of the country was concentrated and developed, despite the vigorous efforts by the Israeli government to promote the development of the Negev, Galilee and Jerusalem.

We may still consider the coastal plain cities as separate territorial and functional entities and define them as a chain of cities and towns separated by rural and agricultural areas and sand dunes. But a new trend is already apparent. Large settlements around and between these cities have grown into satellite towns and suburbs. Regional and national institutions and installations, such as air and see ports, power plants, public beaches and recreation areas, as well as universities and regional health services, were located between them.

The developing public transportation networks and the proliferation of private cars have interconnected all parts of the vast region and substantially increased all kinds of exchange between these parts and the various institutions. This process has transformed the coastal plan between Ashdod and Acco into an integrated and coherent system with a holistic character. This system differs from that of other parts of the country not only quantitatively but also qualitatively. The various cities and smaller settlements in this system are no longer separate and discrete units, but components of a vast overall system, despite their partial local autonomy and varied urban forms and social organisations. The system has its heavy poles and concentrations, but it is functioning more and more as a structured and integrated unit.

URBANISATION

This new emerging quality is less apparent visually than it is functionally. The main changes have been in the occupations of the coastal plan population, their mobility and their way of life. They are already highly urbanised, even in the moshavim and kibbutzim where the proportion of agricultural occupations is falling rapidly and is well below 20 per cent. We may consider most of the old and established kibbutzim as highly industrialised and urbanised settlements, despite the preservation of their rural-agricultural form and some patterns of behaviour. Actually, many kibbutzim with a population of only a few hundred are much more urbanised, than many of the small new towns with populations of 5000 to 30,000.

The urbanisation of the moshav and the kibbutz has been described by Berler and others as concealed urbanisation. It is an interesting phenomenon which indicates that it is possible to develop a model of an urban society without the physical and socio-organisational forms of cities with their well-known inner conflicts and shortcomings.

The main criterion of urbanisation is the occupational structure of the kibbutz and to some extent, the moshav. Most if not all the kibbutzim have developed small but highly sophisticated industries. Some have been organised in regional groups and have developed large-scale industries. Even farming has become a highly mechanised process based on research and elaborate organisation. In many of these kibbutzim less than 12 per cent of the people are now employed in agriculture and farming, but there has been no reduction in the extent of the sectors. Very many are occupied in local, regional and even national services and, in some cases, in international scientific and artistic activites.

The kibbutz and moshav movements are represented in the national centres of activity by economic agencies or organisations which buy supplies and sell produce, as well as in institutes for planning, design and research which are well computerised and served by competent technical and scientific personnel. In a way it can be considered a zoning factor, in that the kibbutz and the moshav remain rural and predominantly residential, and do not acquire the street plot structure of the city. Even the moshavim, in which most occupations are urban, have retained the character of garden cities. The residential areas of the kibbutzim are well-kept parks, with no individual plots, no streets and no motor traffic. They have the characteristics of Oscar Newman's defensible space. It is an interesting phenomenon that points to the possibility of developing an urban society without the typical physical and socio-organisation forms of cities with their disadvantages. This possibility deserves to be studied.

ORGANISATION AND AUTONOMY

The highly organised nature of the kibbutz and the moshav, both as socio-economic units and as large organisations of such units, is rooted in their history. The rural and agricultural settlements of the Zionist movement were characterised by strong labourist and socialist ideologies, while non-ideological lower middle class people built and populated the cities. A well-knit ideology can promote organisation and structure. Socialist ideology does it to a very high degree. Eric Cohen suggests that this historical difference may explain the social and economic success of the kibbutz and the economic success of the moshav, compared to the mediocrity and formlessness of Israeli urban patterns.

If we consider the various Israeli settlements from the point of view of personal and collective autonomy (in John F.C. Turner's phrase), they represent a graded continuum. At one end there is the city, with a maximum of personal and a minimum of collective autonomy and organisation. At the other end is the kibbutz, with its very high collective organisation and autonomy, achieved at the cost of personal autonomy voluntarily relinquished. In between there are the various types of moshavim, characterised by their cooperative structure. In principle at least, the Israeli citizen has a choice of different ways of personal and communal life. But, as shown above, all these form of life tend to become highly urbanised without physical change, wherever there is regional integration on a large scale.

TOPOGRAPHY AND THE PATTERN OF SETTLEMENTS

The emergenge of the Israeli coastal plain system as described here is not as an exception but indeed a phenomenon common to countries where a rapid process of settlement has been sustained by intensive immigration. In all cases, the coastal strip of the country was the refuge of arrival, then the base for penetration into the country and the link for communications with the interior and the world at large. In this way, the coastal region became a powerful concentration of activities, population and wealth, as well as a factor of economic and social change. In this respect, the very dense and active Israeli coastal plain concentration was similar to developments in other new countries.

But, as happened in all other cases, local and historical factors shaped the general process and gave it its peculiar form. The physical structure of Palestine, as well as its peculiar history, conditioned the pattern of urban settlements throughout history. The new settlements created by the Zionist movement coalesced into an entirely different pattern, and the old and the new coexisted, mostly side by side but sometimes interpenetrating each other.

This parallel coexistence was, of course, sustained by ethnic and national differences between the two populations, Jewish and Arab, that eventually led to clashes and wars. Eventually, and in spite of antagonisms, a certain new balance emerged from time to time, in which the various parts of the country and their populations performed different complementary functions. As we know now, this transcended political borders and even war fronts.

The basic structure of the country is one of long and narrow zones, extending from north to south. On the west, there is a narrow coastal plain, two to five kilometres wide in the north, and twenty to thirty kilometres wide in the middle and south. The mountain range (Galilee, Samaria, Judea and the Negev) is forty to fifty kilometres wide. Then follow the Jordan, the Dead Sea and the Arava rift (all part of the longest and deepest rift on earth); and the Transjordan plateau extending east into the Syrian desert.

For thousands of years there existed along the watershed of the mountain range a string of towns separated by no more than a day's walking distance. From north to south they are Safed, Nazareth, Nablus, Jerusalem, Bethlehem and Hebron.

In recent times the size and population of most of these towns remained limited. Their agricultural hinterland was poor and relatively sparsely populated. Their contact with the coast and neighbouring countries was not easy, and the rough topography made their extension difficult. The exceptions were Jerusalem and Nablus, which developed considerably faster for political reasons and because the topography made their extension easier.

This discreteness of the towns and cities of the mountain watershed was a strong factor in creating a pattern of activities connecting them to the main centres of activity along the coastal plan and in Transjordan more than among themselves. With the exception of Jerusalem, which fused along the watershed with the nearby towns of Ramallah to the north and Bethlehem to the south, they never came to constitute clusters of towns and cities. Each developed in its own particular way and form, and adapted to its particular topography, with its peculiar crafts and occupations, history and traditions. Endowed with a cooler and drier climate than the coastal plain and with rich religious and historical traditions, some evolved special activities based on these assets: centres of government, study and research (both religious and secular), tourism, summer resorts, health centres, and with crafts and commerce serving the surrounding villages connected with the Transjordanian cities.

These characteristics are in strong contrast to those of the cities of the coastal plain which were built during recent generations and merged into the powerful coastal plain system.

We can, therefore, define two different patterns of settlements: the continuous coastal plain system, with its integrated activities, aligned from north to south; and the string of discrete and individual cities on the watershed parallel to the coastal plain. These discrete cities are connected to the coastal plain by lateral lines of communication, but it is important to note that they are connected to the coastal system as a whole, not specifically with the opposite numbers on the coast. This particular structure was conditioned mostly by the topographic characteristics of the country, although many political and other factors also intervened to distort it to some extent.

In Transjordan there is a parallel string of cities with a major concentration around Amman, the capital of Jordan. Jordan is developing rapidly, especially after the decline of Beirut and Lebanon. Demographically and economically, it is strongly connected with Arab cities of the watershed and, through them, with the Israeli economy and services, located mostly in the coastal system. This has become an additional occupation specific to the watershed cities.

It must be stressed that this description of the overall structure of urban settlements in this region does not amount to a plea for forcible unification. It only points to the fact that, despite the hostility and the state of war between Israel and Jordan, the two countries are interrelated by the initiative and vitality of their respective populations, and that this interrelationship is tolerated and even encouraged by their respective governments.

This description of the existing pattern of settlements is, of course, schematic and simplified. It is more or less true for the country north of Beersheva, but does not apply to the desert part of the country south of it, owing to both a different topography and a change in the direction of the coast. Nevertheless, it can be useful in planning future development that will correspond to both the topographic and climatic structure of the country and to its history and traditions. It can also help in combining desirability with necessity, and order imagined and and created by man with natural order. This way will be essentially different from and more fruitful than the fragmentary way in which all major development has been conceived and implemented in Israel up to now.

COASTAL PLAIN SYSTEM

If the hypothesis of the emergence of a unified coastal system is admitted and confirmed, it can lead to some far-reaching conclusions and guidelines.

First, there is the logical conclusion that cities and other settlements in the coastal plain can no longer be regarded as separate entities, but should be viewed as components of an overall system. The location and special functions of the various settlements must derive from the requirements of the overall system. Local conditions and the topography will influence these overall considerations as well.

The overall system will comprise not only discrete units but sub-systems of various kinds, some of them physically and topographically defined, some functional, some territorially based and some extending over the whole system. The discrete components will not be neatly defined separate settlements, but rather regional and national installations such as harbours, airports, power stations, universities, health centres, monuments and networks.

Conceived in this way, the urbanisation of the coastal plain population can be achieved without mass migration from village to city, and with a reduced rate of concentration in the metropolitan areas of Tel Aviv and Haifa. Most of the services and functions now concentrated in and around the large cities can be decentralised and brought nearer to the population of small rural settlements. This will stimulate growth in some of these settlements without necessarily transforming them into urban settlements.

Obviously, such planned decentralisation requires a considerable increase in the mobility of rural populations, as well as improved communications such as telephone and mail services. The increase in mobility must be achieved mostly by mass transportation, if we are to avoid the congestion of the large cities and the inter-urban highways.

The main lines of transportion must, perforce, be trunk lines running from north to south along the coastal system so that people may commute between its various parts quickly and cheaply. Further delay in providing such mass transportation of a high organisational and technological level will continue to hamper the integration of the coastal system, will further increase the massive concentrations around Tel Aviv and Haifa, and will transform more rural settlements into dormitory towns and suburbs.

The existing trend of consolidation in the coastal system will be accelerated by such a mass transportation system. At the same time, there must be a considerable improvement in the lateral lines of transportation so that the watershed cities may be integrated with the coastal system. These cities are located at distances of thirty to fifty kilometres from the coast. With rapid and inexpensive transportation, they can develop into suitable residential and occupational areas for many people employed in the coastal plain. Access to the foothills will be improved by these lines, and most of the new residential areas could be developed on their slopes at reasonable distances from the beaches and nature reserves, thus avoiding the waste of the best agricultural land in the plains.

So far we have considered Israel's coastal plain system as a self-contained and isolated system. But the coastal system will eventually be connected with the Lebanese coastal system, which is emerging slowly, and later with Egyptian developments along the extensive beaches of North Sinai. This is of importance to the population of Israel whose beaches, already overcrowded, will be further reduced by nuclear power and desalination plants, harbours and urban sprawl.

A NEW PARADIGM

The concept of the linear coastal plain system, with its extensions into the mountainous parts of the country, is not merely a passive acceptance of what is happening spontaneously. It involves acceptance of whatever has happened and cannot be undone, but it proposes a new paradigm for the familiar facts and processes, dispensing with the dichotomy of city-village, urban-rural and town-countryside. It replaces the haphazard conglomerations of constantly changing urban entities with the new concept of a regional system with a complex holistic character. The proposed regional systems will vary according to their topography, climate and ekistics, but they will all be highly urbanised without being urban sprawls, and they will be integrated into an overall structure, extending over most of the territory.

This new concept of human settlements and territory integrated into a vast and heterogeneous system requires a new regional ideology which will replace the fragmentary and obsolete ideologies still operational in various government agencies and in the Jewish Agency's settlement department. These old ideologies consider urbanism incompatible with rural settlements, despite the fact that the latter have become essentially urban in their occupations and ways of life. Cities are still considered as discrete entities that can be contained by green belts, inside which "urban life" is conceived as an unavoidable nightmare. The regional ideology is a way to conceive a region with all its variety as a structured and interrelated entity that allows or even promotes an increase in the autonomy of its components, and one that also increases individual and group autonomy, initiative and responsibility under an overall coordination umbrella of regional and national plans and policies. It provides individuals with a choice of different settlements with different physical and organisational forms and varying proportions of personal-collective autonomy, but with a similar access to complex urban activity.

This means the end of many of the constraints of the city and the possiblity of new forms of urban settlement, ecologically conceived, low entropy, and satisfying the general desire to combine better environment with efficiency and richness of exchange. In this way, a coherent form can also be given to the pattern of settlements in the country.

This proposal should not be considered a plan. It is no more than a proposal for consideration and investigation.

The spatial development of Israel towards the twenty-first century

14

Elisha Efrat   Israel

No country in the world, not even a very wealthy one, can achieve ultimate growth without studying physical development. In any country, physical planning is a very expensive undertaking which needs substantial investments from government bodies. It is impossible to find solutions to, or even to deal with, all the issues that arise in physical planning; yet it is not feasible to ignore them either. Every country goes through many stages of development, each dependent on the emphasis placed at a given time on certain aspects of planning. For example, in the United States much emphasis is placed on the national road system, whereas regional planning is not nearly as well developed. The Netherlands stresses population distribution, water-system planning and soil reclamation from polders as its national development goals. In Great Britain, the emphasis is on town planning and the construction of new towns. In Germany the emphasis is on industrial planning. And in Venezuela and Burma the focus is on agricultural development. Because no country has a budgetary capacity to plan for everything it needs, each one chooses its priorities in development planning according to its ideologies, goals and needs. Israel decides on its development planning in the same way.

DEVELOPMENT PRIORITIES

Because of Israel's special security, immigration and settlement problems, the highest priorities in physical planning have been distribution of the population, building of new towns in the peripherial areas of the country, development of arid zones in the Negev, building of new settlements in Galilee, and populating Jerusalem, the capital. Other important issues, such as metropolitan development, mass transportation, industrialisation and urban renewal, have not as yet been given high priority. Thus, not all issues of physical planning have been solved, and many are in the initial stages, compared with the situation in the Western world.

The question arises whether Israel's list of planning priorities will change in the future. Priorities and their relative importance are decided by the government, together with the relevant municipal bodies. From time to time, they must decide on trends in investment and goals for the implementation of projects. The following is a list of some of the principal issues on which the government and ministries will have to decide in future:

□ Should more money be invested on population distribution? if so, where should it be placed?

□ Should we focus on the development of the railway system rather than highway development?

□ Should efforts be made to encourage growth in all the development towns, or only in those that have been more successful so far?

□ Should we invest in industrial development in Jerusalem, despite its topographical difficulties and distance from the coastal plain?

□ For how long should how much of the agricultural land along the coastal plain be conserved against the need to populate the country and house the people?

□ Which direction should the physical expansion of the metropolitan area of Tel Aviv take in the future?

□ Where should the power stations be located along the coastal strip without disturbing the population and existing settlements?

□ How much money should be invested for recreational purposes? And should it be spent along the crowded coastal plain or in the mountainous areas of the interior?

□ Where should new immigrants be located if they are unable to live in remote development towns?

□ Where should international and domestic airports be located?

□ Should development be encouraged in new regions, or is it better to invest in existing settlements? Should new towns be established in the future? If so, where? Should we create new agricultural settlements in central Galilee?

□ Where and how should we begin using desalinated water?

□ To what extent should minority (primarily Arab) settlements be developed? Is there a need to establish a new Arab town in Galilee? Where should the Bedouins be settled?

Undoubtedly, problems and question such as these are real challenges in the planning and development of Israel and are the issues on which policy will centre towards the year 2000 and even after the beginning of the next century. These challenges put Israel in a difficult situation. Because of lack of experience the country still does not exactly know how to tackle all of them.

As a newly created country, Israel had not reached economic independence, was not able to make use of all its potential and had not yet developed the optimal settlement layout for the future. Israel began its development under very difficult and unusual circumstances, without a basic physical planning background. Thirty years of British rule did not encourage national and regional planning. In fact, the British mandate was against spatial development. At best, when Jewish spatial development occurred, the authorities made sure that it was offset by Arab development. Most British planning and projects took place in the urban sector where the main concern was security. Thus the intention always was to equalise Jewish and Arab incentives.

The establishment of the State of Israel in 1948 occurred after a war of independence. During the first year of statehood there was no comprehensive national planning, as many more crucial and actual problems arose. Finding housing and employment for the waves of new immigrants and establishing supplies and security on the new borders were far more pressing and urgent problems than comprehensive planning.

During the first decade of statehood much intensive work was done in many sectors. It should be mentioned that in those years, much of the initiative and action came from people who had specialities in many fields and which had been unable to express their talents before. New areas in the Negev, in Galilee, and in the corridor of Jerusalem became a challenge for this intensive "doing". Many projects were rapidly implemented, even under conditions of uncertainty. The first signs of comprehensive planning emerged during this period, as did the first planning concepts for the entire country.

One should remember that, at that time, comprehensive planning and physical development was not an advanced discipline in many parts of the world. Its development began after the second world war, when reconstruction in countries such as Britain, the Netherlands and Germany brought a new approach to comprehensive and interdisciplinary planning. Israel, which had attained statehood a few years after, found itself in a period where planning knowledge was neither systematic nor crystallised. Professions such as town planning and town building were much more traditional and employed architects and engineers, whereas experts in the fields of economics and geography were much less in demand. Physical planning in Israel grew after the war of independence, despite an unfavourable economic and demographic climate, but the professionals in town construction had little knowledge of comprehensive planning.

Unfortunately, most of the physical infrastructure of the country was built during this decade, a period distinguished by its maximum uncertainty. The more sophisticated knowledge of physical planning of the next decade (1960 to 1970), could improve somewhat on what had been done previously, but could not bring about any fundamental change.

Many questions arise from the situations created during that period:

☐ Did we have to establish thirty new development towns in order to change the urban layout in Israel?

☐ Did we have to develop agriculture in mountainous areas in order to populate the corridor of Jerusalem and Galilee?

☐ Was it possible to restrain the growth of the Tel Aviv conurbation and prevent its sprawl on agricultural land of the coastal plain?

☐ Could we have prevented the pollution of Tel Aviv's coastline, and blocking off the view of the open sea by high buildings?

☐ Could the pollution of Lake Kinneret by chemicals used in fertilisers near the water have been prevented?

☐ Was it possible to have constructed more railway lines for mass transit and to have made public transportation cheaper?

☐ And what about the urban sprawl on Mount Carmel, the destruction of antiquities and settlement sites in Israel, the misuse of run-off water for agricultural purposes, the urban sprawl in Arab villages?

All these questions indicate that there is a need for reassessment in many of the planning and development areas in order to improve in those sectors where something still can be done.

GOALS FOR THE NEXT CENTURY

What conclusion can be drawn from what was said above on Israel's immediate and distant future? It must be accepted that Israel's future geographic area will not be much larger than it is today. Even after changes in the borders in certain regions, it will have an area of 10,000 to 12,000 square miles (25,000 to 30,000 square kilometres). This is not a very large area and the country will have to find solutions for problems such as a rapidly growing population, the absorption of immigrants, and a rising standard of living which will eventually parallel that of highly developed countries. The enlargement of settlement layouts will be possible in the southern part of the country and in the mountainous regions of Galilee and Jerusalem. In future, urban sprawl and low-density buildings will be permitted in towns. Many development towns will change their urban profiles by having more congested CBDs with higher buildings and better developed infrastructures. Development towns will have more institutions, basic facilities and main transportation arteries. There is no certainty that new towns will be developed in the future, with the possible exception of one in the Negev. Most of the urbanisation will take place inside the towns, inside the conurbations and at their peripheries. In the large cities the population will grow, traffic will be greater and more congested, and more suburbs will arise. Even the Moshavot and veteran villages will experience the pressures of the urban processes. The urban way of life, expressed in high-rise buildings, will spread everywhere.

Access to the larger cities will be much more difficult as the downtown areas will be closed to motorised traffic and the public will have to use mass transportation to a much greater extent. Houses will be built as skyscrapers inside the cities and many engineering projects will be constructed underground. Reconstruction of ancient and historical quarters will occur even in neighbourhoods rapidly built just after the establishment of the state. Undoubtedly, the new construction will be more modern and aesthetic, perhaps eventually culminating in a new type of Israeli architecture.

It will be very difficult to continue with the current trends of population distribution because of the dominant influence of the large cities. The distribution trends will be more difficult to distinguish because the conurbations and large towns have a magnetic effect on people. Towards the end of this century and by the beginning of the next we shall see new forms of settlements, such as industrial villages, homogeneous suburbs, villages incorporating sophisticated industries (i.e. electronics), pensioner villages, military towns and possibly mobile villages.

It can be assumed that the entire development and planning approach will be quite different from what it has been in the past. More and more the professionals will be called on to invent, and sophisticated development of the most basic sectors in the country will be encouraged. Because of soil and water shortages, agricultural exports will be improved by new methods of irrigation and cultivation. Crops will be grown in sand-dunes and will be acclimatised to mountainous regions and deserts. More irrigation will be done with waste or salt water. There will be a constant search to find and grow special vegetables and fruit which are in demand all over the world. In addition, those in the agricultural sector will develop more of an urban style and will also work in light industries and services.

Industry will expand as the means and standards of production increase. The lack of minerals will encourage the development of sophisticated industries which demand little in basic minerals. The electronics, aviation and medical instruments which are being produced today represent the beginning of this trend. Because such industries need specialist manpower, great efforts will be made to encourage education in technology and applied sciences which are the basis for industrial development in any country. In future, scientific exports will be of a high quality, which is typical of a country existing under very difficult physical conditions.

By the beginning of the twenty-first century the population of Israel will have reached the target of six million. This implies that there will be at least one city of approximately one million. Along the coastal plain the population will continue to grow quite rapidly. This trend is already apparent and there is no way in which a very congested coastal plain can be avoided. This will stretch from Hadera in the north to Ashkelon in the south. It can be assumed that one-third of Israel's population will be concentrated in and around the metropolitan area of Tel Aviv which will account for approximately two million people. Agricultural land in the centre of the coastal plain will be gravely threatened and many engineering projects will be forced to move outside the conurbation. The metropolitan population of Tel Aviv will have a quality of life not much better than that of today, and similar to that of other large cities throughout the world.

Air and noise pollution will continue to be one of the major problems plaguing the population, while commuting difficulties will become more intensified. The high standard of motorisation, along with the very sophisticated transportation system, will have social effects on everyday living not experienced in the past. Employment in the service sector will be much higher and this may also apply to domestic aviation.

The main transportation arteries in Israel will be expanded into motorways. New arteries will be constructed in the eastern part of the coastal plain to diminish the pressure on the western section. Metropolitan roads will be developed to the full but will not be able to carry all the traffic. Transportation above and below gound will be developed with cloverleaf highways and assorted junctions. Current ideas on suburban railways combined with mass-transportation will be developed to serve the conurbations of Tel Aviv and Haifa. Major improvements to public transportation vehicles will bring their condition closer to European standards. The frequency of trains and their velocities will be improved. Problems that will have to be solved will include connections between downtown Tel Aviv and southern Tel Aviv; shortening the distance between Beersheva and Ashdod; the construction of a railway between Tel Aviv and Haifa; and straightening the railway line to Jerusalem.

Undoubtedly, the population of Israel will have much more leisure time. The transfer of employment to the service sector, the gradual rise in the standard of living, and increased mobility will bring about a five-day working week, with a longer weekend for most people. Owing to social, religious, health and economic pressures, more public and private institutions will adopt this shortened working week, so that more people will have more leisure and recreation time. This implies that more open space will have to be prepared for the population in the form of national parks, nature reserves, beaches and picnic grounds, and that antiquities will have to be reconstructed to serve as tourist attractions. This increase in the population's leisure time will lead to the development of new ports, playing fields, airfields for private aviation, and more tracks for horse and car racing. The bathing beaches along the Mediterranean, the Sea of Galilee, the Dead Sea and the coast of Eilat will have to be enlarged, as will the capacity of recreation sites inside the country.

The regional picture of Israel will also change, but this is no extraordinary phenomenon. It can be assumed that no new urban centres will arise near Tel Aviv. The country will be able to add to existing developed bases by enlarging them and making them denser by adding new functions. Undoubtedly, in the established metropolitan area of Tel Aviv, the rings of urbanisation will be filled up by more inner migration and economic functions. The town of Ashdod in the south, Lod, Ramla and Petah-Tiqwa in the east and Netanya in the north will be the border lines of this inevitable sprawl.

Jerusalem, which experienced much building activity over the past few years, wants even more construction but this will be difficult to achieve owing to the terrain, the desert border in the east, the sensitivity of the surrounding areas and the restrictions of Arab land ownership around the city. A new suburban area will develop around the city, but it will not be as extensive as that surrounding Tel Aviv.

Haifa will retain its position as the third-largest city in the country. Economically and socially it will continue to rival the other cities in the central part of Israel. Haifa's growth will be mainly inspired by its relationship with Galilee, its economic and demographic hinterland. The population of the city will sprawl towards the small towns along Haifa Bay and satellite towns will develop between Qiryat Tiv'on, Qiryat Ata and the hills of Alonim. The city itself will be very compact while the peripheries will be more sparsely built up.

Galilee and the Negev are the two regions with the highest potential for development during the next century and they will compete for development investment. The positive attributes of Galilee are its population, manpower, climate, beautiful landscapes, water resources and proximity to Haifa. The disadvantages include a high minority population and uneven topography which is difficult to develop. The attractiveness of the Negev lies in its big open spaces which have not yet been exploited, but its major disadvantages are its distance from the centre of the country, its arid climate and its lack of water resources. In these circumstances, it can be assumed that Galilee will receive investments for industrial development that will be based on the existing urban population, while future investments in the Negev will be directed towards projects which need large areas, such as security installations, aviation, power stations and noxious industries which should be located outside populated areas.

From a technical point of view, all the physical development projects described above can be planned and executed, but actual development, the budget for investment funds and the range of priorities for the implementation of these projects are in the hands of the political bodies in Israel who make decisions from time to time. A government concerned about domestic problems, economic independence, social advancement and a higher quality of life for all the people will find a challenge in what has been presented above. An administration that must focus on foreign affairs and security problems as a result of the regional political situation will simply not be able to accomplish this scale of priorities. What this means is that Israel's security problems drain financial resources, thus restricting optimal priorities for development. If the State of Israel can rid itself of these restrictions in future, it will be able to direct more financial resources to issues of physical planning, thus bettering the lives of all its citizens.

Development planning for 15
Mountainous Galilee

Jacob O. Maos   Israel

INTRODUCTION

There is a great deal of similarity in the problems of mountainous regions all over the world. Many civilisations choose to live in the mountains, either for health or for security reasons. Only with the drainage of swamps, eradication of mosquito-borne diseases, and the improvement of security, does human settlement shift to the lowlands, where there are more agricultural resources and the development of physical infrastructure is not hampered by topography. The rapid expansion of human settlement in the plains, due to the accelerated agro-technical progress and modern communications, reduces the mountain to a position of relative retardation and creates a vicious circle of degradation, as the more dynamic part of the population moves to economically more promising regions.

While development problems in the mountains remain vexed in most cases, a social and political dimension is added in Galilee by the coexistence of two heterogeneous population groups in the area. Jewish colonisation in the pre-state period often had to be content with marginal areas, characterised by shallow soil, lack or excess of water (like the Hula valley), where land could be acquired more easily, if at all, and where the new settlers did not complete with the local population. The earlier settlement movement barely penetrated central Galilee, leaving large gaps in the territorial contiguity of Jewish settlements. This spatial and demographic imbalance interfered later with the building of the human and physical infrastructure, and delayed the advancement of Mountainous Galilee, compared with other regions of the country.

Mountainous Galilee is not a conventional geographical entity but is described henceforth as a "planning region" by virtue of its physiographic structure and demographic composition. Its boundaries were determined in order to create a reference area with common characteristics for orderly development planning. The boundaries in the north coincide with the political frontier with Lebanon; in the east, with the slopes of the Galilee hills facing the Hula valley and Lake Kinneret; and in the west, with the mountain slopes parallel to the coast line. In the southern part the region comprises the valleys of Sakhnin and Beit Netofa, and the towns of Nazareth and Migdal Haemek. Similar definitions of Mountainous Galilee appear in the publications of the Settlement Department of the Jewish Agency,[1] [2] [3] the Lands Authority,[4] and the Settlement Study Centre of Rehovot.[5] Within the area thus defined, it is possible to trace four sub-regions which correspond to the towns of Zfat, Maalot, Carmiel and Nazareth, each serving as urban centre to its rural periphery. (See Figure 1.)

DEMOGRAPHICAL BALANCE AND DISTRIBUTION

The described planning region is an integral part of the northern district and covers an area of about 1120 square kilometres with a population of approximately 222,000 of which 32 per cent is Jewish and 68 per cent non-Jewish. The demographic composition of the four sub-regions (Zfat, Maalot, Carmiel and Nazareth) is given in Table 1.

The proportion of Jewish and non-Jewish inhabitants is an outstanding feature unlike any other region in the country. Only in the sub-region of Zfat, the smallest in terms of population, does the Jewish population constitute a majority (88.4 per cent). In the other three sub-regions the Jewish population is a minority: Maalot (30.7 per cent), Carmiel (17.3 per cent), and Nazareth (27.8 per cent). This imbalance and the relative sparseness of Jewish settlements have become a matter of growing concern to planners from the viewpoint of both socio-economic development and national security.

There is a parallel situation in the spatial distribution of the population. Of the total area of 1120 square kilometres, 133 square kilometres lies within the jurisdiction of Jewish settlements and 356 square kilometres within that of non-Jewish settlements. The rest, about 631 square kilometres, is state-owned land, including nature reserves and national parks. However, about 300 square kilometres of state land (nearly one-half) lies within the sphere of influence of the non-Jewish population, and there is a chronic problem of encroachment on these areas through building, grazing and other unlawful land uses.

To what extent do the projections of population growth fit the development plans of Galilee as a whole? The Plan for the geographical distribution of Israel's population of five million (1972) assumes that in the northern district the proportional share of Jewish population will be maintained and will even increase from 54 per cent to 55 per cent (mainly as a result of an increase in the Acre sub-district).[6] This projection is based on the following assumptions: there will be a natural increase of the Jewish population in the northern district at the present level of 1.7 per cent; there will be a decrease in the natural growth rate of the non-Jewish population from 3.9 per cent in 1970 to 2.6 per cent by 1992; about 154,000 new immigrants will be absorbed in the district during the period 1965-92; there will be a considerable inmigration of veteran residents from other parts of the country; and there will be a negative immigration of 80,000 inhabitants during the period 1965-92.

An assessment of the situation since the publication of the plan reveals that the rate of natural growth of the Jewish population in the district conforms to the plan's forecast; the natural growth rate of the non-Jewish population has not decreased, but stayed at the same level (3.9 per cent, or 3.6 per cent after discounting the internal migration, with no change of this trend in sight); and the number of new immigrants is about half of that predicted (3100 instead of 5700 a year). Consequently, by 1976, the proportion of the Jewish population in the northern district had declined from 54 per cent to 52.3 per cent,[7] and there are indications that this downward trend will continue during the next decade. (See Table 2.)

If the number of 2300 new immigrants is assumed correct, some 6500 residents from other parts of the country will be needed annually if the plans for a Jewish majority of 54 per cent in the northern district are to be realised. Under the present circumstances this appears to be a daunting task. But, in any case, how would this policy affect Mountainous Galilee? Table 3 shows the projected population growth in Mountainous Galilee for the years 1977-87, based on the assumption that about two-thirds (1500) of the new immigrants to be absorbed in the northern district and about one-half (3200) of the internal migration entering the district will settle in Mountainous Galilee every year. As can be seen, even such an addition would still leave a proportion of 38.8 per cent Jewish, compared with 61.2 per cent non-Jewish inhabitants in the planning region. A major obstacle in the way of this plan is the backwardness of the northern district, and, particularly Mountainous Galilee. This situation is evident in the emigration from the region, employment in various sectors, output in industry and income, as shown in Table 4.

In order to reverse these negative trends, pragmatic action will be needed in the field of housing, services and basic infrastructure, along with employment and economic incentives, all of which may eventually attract new residents to the planning region.

SPATIAL ORGANISATION OF SETTLEMENT

The distribution of population in Mountainous Galilee highlights another aspect of the demographical problem, namely the relative sparseness of Jewish settlements in the area. The underlying reasons for this are: a broken topography which restricts the deployment and siting of settlements; scarcity of agricultural and other natural resources; lack of attractiveness owing to inferior economic opportunities and low standard of services; and high cost of physical infrastructure owing to the hilly terrain.

Added to these problems are such factors as the expansion of non-Jewish settlements in the region and the difficulty of concentrating state-owned lands into continuous blocks. The non-Jewish settlements are usually located on the slopes of the Bet Netofa, Sakhnin and Bet Hakerem valleys which account for most of the arable land. Other agglomerations of villages and townships are found near Nazareth, the biggest town in the region, and on the fringes of the Zevulun valley.

The economic transformation and demographic pressure in the non-Jewish sector have occasioned the growth and expansion of the traditional village, which in the past was relatively small and compactly built. The increasing demand for single-family houses and the centrifugal expansion of the built-up village area (identical to the forces acting in urban development) have led to unlicensed buildings contrary to authorised plans, frequently on agricultural plots and on state-owned lands. This urbanisation process is intensified by the special idiosyncrasies of the traditional communities which restrain emigration.

The clusters of buildings extending around the villages in the Sakhnin and Bet Netofa valleys already give the impression of a large conurbation. The unlawful squatting and building on farmland invariably leads to problems in the development of municipal services. Nevertheless, this urban-like development proceeds at an accelerating pace and already covers extensive areas.[8] [9]

The Jewish settlements are usually located on the ridges transversing the region from west to east. The location of the principal towns in the planning region (Upper Nazareth, Carmiel, Maalot and Zfat) favours their eventual development as major service centres and poles for industrial, administrative and other economic services. Upper Nazareth, though, is located in an eccentric position in relation to the region under discussion, and may require special treatment for its access problems.

A unique trait of most Jewish settlements is the clear distinction between urban and rural. Unlike the minority villages, the Jewish urban settlement does not sprawl into its periphery and grows mainly by means of compact neighbourhoods of multi-storey buildings. Besides residential areas, the urban settlement needs spaces for industry, workshops or municipal services, all of which are relatively well defined. Rural settlements, on the other hand, are made up of small communities (between fifty and one hundred families), planned in a loose pattern on home plots of 750-4000 square metres per family. Yet, in spite of their limited built-up area and enclosed farmyards, these settlements exercise effective control over extensive tracts of agricultural land scattered in their vicinity.

PLANNING FOR DEVELOPMENT

The situation described above has led to the crystallisation of two planning lines: readjustment of the demographic imbalance, and concurrently, deployment of new settlements in the rural areas of Mountainous Galilee. Implicit in this course of action are the conditions that will attract newcomers, specifically employment, economic opportunities and a fair quality of life, which will be able to compete with those of the central part of the country. Another requisite is an institutional framework able to overcome current coordination difficulties and clear the bureaucratic maze which has thwarted orderly development until now. Equally important is the updating of the official plans for the geographical distribution of Israel's population of five million. These plans serve as guidelines for urban development and spatial organisation and should be evaluated and revised in order to correct the distortions of current development projects.

National and regional planning objectives should include the entire range of socio-economic factors, including organisation, physical and other aspects. In this analysis, special emphasis is given to physical planning aspects, on the basis of the conceptual framework for the physical development of the planning region.

Planning for development in Mountainous Galilee is formally governed by the Master Plan for the Northern District (G-852). This plan, while generally in accord with the National Master Plan and development policy, cannot effectively keep up with regional development plans. Moreover, the plan is not fully operative since it does not set priorities or the pace of implementation. Yet, in spite of its passive role, it gives legal sanction to the diverse development plans. It should be remembered that the master plan contains ordinances derived from national blueprints for roads, public utilities and institutions, as well as data contained in local and subregional plans. Such plans may be either in force, under deposit pending approval, or in the planning stage (Ministry of Interior, 1972). A Master Plan for Central Galilee - roughly congruent with Mountainous Galilee - was commissioned by the Local Town Planning Commission of Central Galilee in terms of the Planning and Building Ordinance (1965), and is at present under perusal before its deposit. It seems from various objections submitted that this plan should be updated in the location of existing and planned rural settlements. Likewise, the plan should be completed in land use for agriculture and forestry, access roads, industrial parks and planned service centres.

In recent years, detailed development plans have been prepared by various government and public entities, such as the Ministry of Housing, the Lands Authority, the Ministry of Industry, Commerce and Tourism, the Settlement Department of the Jewish Agency, and others. As already pointed out, these plans are formally subordinated to the District Master Plan. A summary of some of these plans is given hereunder, with special emphasis on aspects relating directly to the physical planning of the region under discussion.

Accelerated urban development in Galilee - Ministry of Housing and Construction 1977.

This plan draws heavily on the Plan for the geographical distribution of Israel's population of five million (1972).[6] While focusing on Galilee, it also covers a wide range of development aspects in the whole northern district. Although the Ministry of Housing deals with both urban and rural sectors, the plan concentrates on urban development, with a view to speeding up settlement in the region and building an efficient structure of services. The international accent on urbanisation seeks maximum growth of the Jewish population. A corollary objective is the slowing down of urbanisation in the coastal zone of western Galilee.

In order to attain these goals, the plan advocates the concentration of efforts and resources on given urban settlements, in contrast with the thesis of spatially balanced development. The planners' assumption is that a concentrated effort on selected towns will be more effective, since only towns of a certain size will be able to provide adequate services within their areas. The plan identifies the towns of Upper Nazareth, Zfat and Carmiel as suitable in terms of size. A further criterion for determining the scope of urban development in each town is the land available for building.

The planners of the Ministry of Housing selected the lateral axis of Acre-Carmiel-Zfat as the urban centre line of the region. This choice was based on an analysis of the spheres of influence of the major urban centres in the northern district, including the metropolitan area of Haifa. Accordingly, the town of Zfat was to become the principal service centre in the region, with a projected population of 85,000 by the year 2000.

In selecting the town of Zfat, the point of achieving a Jewish majority (or near-balance) may have been missed. It seems that by shifting the gravity centre of urban development to the western part of Mountainous Galilee where the demographic imbalance is most pronounced, the desired change in proportion between the Jewish and non-Jewish population is more likely to be achieved.

There is an ecological factor that should also be taken into account. This concerns the problem of sewage treatment and disposal which has turned out to be a bottleneck that cannot be overlooked. Zfat is located in a sensitive area in terms of eventual pollution of Lake Kinneret, and its untreated sewage today drains directly into the Kinneret basin, before it can undergo such natural cleaning processes as precipitation, filtration, assimilation and evaporation. The water quality of the lake, which is the country's main freshwater reservoir, may become critical when this water is supplied to consumers close to contamination. The problem of sewage treatment and disposal, although technically soluble, requires substantial outlays in plant and installations, the reliability of which is uncertain at times.[10]

Of particular interest in the plans of the Ministry of Housing is the contemplated housing density in the Galilee towns. The distribution of housing types specified for each development phase, high-rise and low-rise apartment buildings and single-family houses, determines space requirements as well as the actual preparations for physical infrastructure works, i.e. roads, water supply, sewerage and power. The planners admit the importance of single-family houses as a means to attract quality residents who may start a development momentum, but such building plans are relegated to later stages. The reason lies probably in the high cost of infrastructure which is not fully utilised in the first years, since single-family houses are usually located on the fringes of the built-up town area.

It is worthwhile re-examining these priorities in the light of past experience which suggests that thriftily constructed apartment buildings attract few immigrants. To date, many flats in such buildings have remain unoccupied, a fact which has given several Galilee towns a negative image and resulted in a waste of resources. It is most probable that this vicious circle can be broken by programmes such as "build your own home", which have aroused keen interest among the public.

A proposed framework for planning - the Israel Lands Authority, 1976.   The   plans elaborated by the planning and development division of the Lands Authority also underline the need for rapid population of Galilee, mainly through pragmatic urban development. The approach adopted by the planners is to augment the attraction of Galilee by developing it as a densely settled residential and recreational area. Since employment is mostly in industrial plants located in the coastal plain and Haifa Bay, the plan calls for an improvement of the network of transportation and communications in order to facilitate commuter travel between home and work. Improvement of the transportation network is also expected to promote the development of the entire region, including Western Galilee, the Kinneret basin, Upper Galilee and Ramat Hagolan.

The reservations about this approach are that it may be difficult to increase the population of Galilee without providing employment closer to the residential area, at least in the medium term. In any case, a modern transportation system is necessary, irrespective of whether the working places are within or outside the planning region. It should be remembered that communting to work in the Jewish sector is not as widespread as it is in the non-Jewish sector. Also, there is a growing tendency in the world to remove industrial plans from overcrowded urban areas to the countryside. In the case of Galilee, light industries can be integrated more easily with the landscape in terms of space requirements and environmental impact. The principle of commuting holds true, however, in the case of heavier industries and long-established plants located outside the planning region.

In addition to its principal role as custodian of state-owned land (approximately 85 per cent of the country's total land area), the Land Authority guards land reserves and ensures proper land use in conformity with approved development plans. The collaboration of the Land Authority is especially important in the creation of territorial continuity, which will enable an effective deployment of settlements, and in preventing urban sprawl and encroachment on agricultural land.

National Master Plan for Tourism - Ministry of Industry, Commerce and Tourism, 1975. The scarcity of natural resources in Galilee underscores the importance of the tourist sector, because of its employment potential and the continuous presence of a visiting population in the area. The Master Plan for Tourism does not set specific targets for Mountainous Galilee, except for the towns of Nazareth and Zfat situated in the planning region. Physical planning concentrates mainly on the periphery of Mountainous Galilee - specifically the coastal strip of Western Galilee, the surroundings of Lake Kinneret,

Upper Galilee and Nazareth. These areas, properly prepared, have a potential for large-scale investments since they can attract foreign tourism, also defined as "intensive tourism". Mountainous Galilee is usually regarded as a transitory visiting spot within the broader system of touring routes in northern Israel. Most of this is local and recreational week-end tourism, also known as "extensive tourism". This activity is based on the region's folklore, cultural and religious values, as well as camping sites and landscape observation points.

The master plan treats in detail two tourist centres - the towns of Nazareth and Zfat. Nazareth contains various historical sites and has become an important pilgrimage centre. Some 540 hotel and hostel rooms are available in the town and 200 more rooms are expected in various current projects. Nazareth has shown remarkable entrepreneurship in the field of tourism, especially notable in the central town area and in the southern approaches to the town.

To date, Zfat, also a unique tourist centre of considerable possibliites, has developed at a very slow pace. The master plan assigns to Zfat an increase from 1070 to 1700 hotel rooms within the next few years. However, lack of local initiative, inadequate tourist services and a deficient urban infrastructure may delay the realistion of these plans. The development of Zfat as an attractive tourist centre entails the rehabilitation of the old town and its historical sites, the building of facilities, as well as the integration of the town with the surrounding region by means of a modern transportation network.

Building up modern facilities for tourism is a vital factor in the development of Mountainous Galilee. Depressed mountainous regions in several advanced countries have been converted into tourist and recreational resorts in which the standard of living of the population is equal to the rest of the country. A similar development may also be possible in Galilee. The master plan predicts a demand for recreational facilities for 1.7 million tourists from abroad and 4.7 million visiting residents in 1985, compared with 625,000 tourists and 3.4 million residents who visited the area in 1974. It is worth pointing out that many of the problems delaying the development of "intensive tourism" areas such as environmental constraints, lack of valid master plans, and conflicting interests, are relatively easier to solve in Mountainous Galilee. The pragmatic exploitation of these possiblities requires the preparation of physical plans to secure the necessary land use provisions in the District Master Plan.

Integrated Rural Development - Settlement Department of the Jewish Agency. The plans of the Settlement Department are directed toward the development of the Jewish rural sector, taking into account at the same time the production factors reserved for the non-Jewish agricultural sector. The activities of the Settlement Department include the establishment and consolidation of agricultural settlements, communal settlements (with a diversified economic basis), and the development of a social and economic supporting system. In recent years the department has dealt with various parts of Mountainous Galilee, i.e. the areas of Segev and Teffen, with a view to increasing the Jewish rural population from 13,000 in 1977 to 21,000 in 1987.[11]

The constraints on agriculture in hilly terrain are well known, and are made more conspicuous by the rapid advance of modern capital-intensive agriculture in better endowed regions. The major problems are scarcity of arable land, few water sources and climatic conditions which limit the range of crops. But there are also constraints bearing directly on the family farm. The collective settlements (kibbutzim and collective moshavim) have made the most of their organisational advantages in applying agro-technical innovations and using distant land and water resources. By contrast, the family farm settlements (moshavim), most of which were established as working villages in the 1950s, found it difficult to manage geographically remote production factors. Only with the introduction of mechanisation in orchards and the modernisation of the poultry branch could the moshav attain comparable economic stability. New developments in agriculture may bring additional solutions, e.g. greenhouse farming, which will rationalise and increase the flexibility of the mountainous family farm. The moshav has to contend with another limitation which prevents the younger generation, except for the "following son", from settling in the village.[12] This situation warrants a continuous search for alternative settlement patterns and additional sources of income.

The expansion of rural settlement activities involves the planning of new villages, elaboration of detailed plans (including the procuring of statutory approval), and the organisation of new communities made up of the younger generation of existing moshavim as well as candidates from other backgrounds, i.e. new immigrants, army veterans, etc.

A new form of planned settlement is the mitzpeh (Hebrew for observation post), usually made up of a small group of families desiring to set up their homes in a small rural community away from the tumult of the city. Various organisations, such as the Settlement Department, the Jewish National Fund and the Ministry of Housing, supply the mitzpeh with basic infrastructure, including access roads, water supply, electricity and housing. In some cases, certain production factors are provided to complement the family income. The mitzpeh permits better supervision of surrounding farmlands and nature reserves, and may help to prevent encroachment on state-owned lands or uncontrolled grazing. A number of such communities have already been established in Galilee and more are being planned.

The planning approach of the Settlement Department is comprehensive and takes in a wide range of aspects, such as the economic basis, supporting services, as well as physical and social planning.

IMPLEMENTATION

Most of the plans reviewed above seek an improved balance between the Jewish and non-Jewish population in Mountainous Galilee and, to some extent, the optimum spatial distribution of Jewish settlements. Either one of these objectives implies the attraction of veteran residents from other parts of the country, absorption of new immigrants and slowing down out-migration from the region. Preparations for such an undertaking require the updating of the Plan for the geographical distribution of Israel's population of five million by means of realistic data which will take into account the changing growth rates and declining immigration in recent years, the stagnant economic situation in the region, and the inferior standard of services compared with the rest of the country.

It would be possible to achieve a numerical majority through accelerated urbanisation. It is important, however, to guide such development, not necessarily by continuing past trends but by improving the demographic balance in each one of the subregions. A typical example is the development of Carmiel or Maalot as principal service centre for Mountainous Galilee instead of Zfat, the only sub-region which already has a Jewish majority. The creation of territorial continuity, on the other hand, depends largely on the expansion and upgrading of Jewish rural settlements. The establishment of new rural settlements may counteract, to some extent, the quantitative weakness and help preserve the necessary space for further development. Exploitation of the attractiveness of Galilee for tourism may also increase the physical presence in the area.

A prerequisite for the advancement of the region, higher income levels and improved facilities, is the building of a physical infrastructure, including ease and rapid access, industrial parks for new plants, land preparation for urban and rural housing, and the development of tourist facilities and recreational resorts. All this must be done with the utmost care for landscape and environmental impact. The housing component offers another important incentive for the younger generation from all parts of the country who look for a solution to their housing problems in combination with an improved quality of life and new economic and social challenges. The integration of new immigrants, too, may succeed better in the context of a veteran population. It is important to point out that the non-Jewish sector should fully share the benefits and duties of all development programmes, according to the proclaimed policy that the entire local population should be incorporated in the country's social and economic life.

How effective is the coordination and cooperation among the various entities engaged in this development process? Unfortunately, there is much to be desired in this respect, despite the high professional standards and levels of sophistication of the diverse plans. Coordination tends to disintegrate after the planning stage and has little effect on implementation. The same applies to the follow-up and evaluation, even the long-term policy-making process. In large-scale projects, in which more than one entity is involved, it is hard to find an institutionalised mechanism for joint decision-making or coordination. The administrative boundaries of the various offices are not congruent and there are cases of duplication in jurisdictional areas.

In many instances, the problems of coordination stem from the lack of a clear policy for Galilee and a priorities system at the national level. Thus, for example, no programme or formulation of intentions has yet been agreed which accords priority to development efforts in the Galilee, or appropriates the necessary means for implementation. In so far as any priorities have been set, they apply equally to other development areas which compete for the same national resources.

A conclusion implicit in these plans and approaches is that the development of the region known as Mountainous Galilee is now in a crucial phase. The complexity of the development process dictates the establishment of a rational and consistent system for planning and implementation, which will be able to translate the objectives outlined in the Plan for the geographical distribution of Israel's population of five million into expedient projects for execution.

REFERENCES

1   The Jewish Agency, Land Settlement Department, The Galilee: A proposed plan for
    settlement and development (Stage One) (1963), (Hebrew).
2   The Jewish Agency, Land Settlement Department, Settlement and development of the
    Mountainous Galilee (1973), (Hebrew).
3   The Jewish Agency, Land Settlement Department, The Mountainous Galilee: A proposal
    for development task and objectives (1974), (Hebrew).
4   The Lands Authority, The Galilee - a proposed planning framework (1976), Division of
    Planning and Development, Jerusalem (Hebrew).
5   Settlement Study Centre, The development of the Mountainous Galilee (1978), Rehovot,
    (Hebrew).
6   Ministry of Interior and Ministry of Finance, Plan for the geographical distribution
    of Israel's population of five million (1972), Jerusalem.
7   Central Bureau of Statistics, Statistical Abstracts of Israel (1977), Annual,
    Jerusalem.
8   Kipnis, B., "Trends in the minorities population and their significance" (1976), City
    and Region (Hebrew; English summary).
9   Sofer, A., "Arab settlement in the north-scope and implications" (1978), Abstracts,
    Decennial meeting of the Israeli Geographical Society, Ramat Gan, (Hebrew).
10 Tahal and Ministry of Interior, Master Plan for the protection of water quality in
    the Kinneret Watershed (1975) (Hebrew).
11 The Jewish Agency, Land Settlement Department, Regional Development Plan: The "Segev"
    Group (1976) (Hebrew).
12 The Jewish Agency, Land Settlement Department, A Proposal for Comprehensive Regional
    Development in the Central Galilee (1978), (Hebrew).

OTHER READING

1   Ardon, Y., "Gloom over the Galilee", The Jerusalem Post Magazine (1979).
2   Bar-Gal, Y., and Sofer, A., "Changes in Minority Villages in Israel" (1976), Horizons
    (Hebrew).
3   Brutzkus, E., "Planning of Spatial Distributon of Population in Israel" (1966),
    Ekistics Volume 21, No 126.
4   Brutzkus, E., "Plan for the Geographical Distribution of Israel's Population of 5
    Million" (1973), City and Region No 3, (Hebrew; English summary).
5   Dash, J., and Efrat, E., The Israel Physical Master Plan (1968), Ministry of
    Interior, Planning Department, Jerusalem.
6   Efrat, E., Changes of Physical Planning Trends in Israel (1971), Ministry of
    Itnerior, Planning Department, Jerusalem.
7   Rokach, A., Rural Settlement in Israel (1978), Jewish Agency, Department of Rural
    Settlement.
8   Weitz, R., and Rokach, A., Agricultural Development Planning and Implementation
    (Israel case study) (1968), D. Reidel Publishing Company.

Table 1. Population of Mountainous Galilee, October 1977

Settlements/sub-region	Total	Zfat	Maalot	Carmiel	Nazareth
Jewish settlements					
Towns with more than 5000 inhabitants	53,800	14,200	-	8,200	31,400
Towns with fewer than 5000 inhabitants	3,500	-	3,500	-	-
Moshavim	8,850	3,900	3,950	800	200
Collective settlements	4,300	1,650	1,800	200	650
Non-Jewish settlements					
Over 5000 inhabitants	73,100	-	-	21,100	62,000
Fewer than 5000 inhabitants	67,900	2,600	20,900	22,800	21,600
Totals	221,450	22,350	30,150	53,100	115,850
Jewish (31.8%)	70,450	19,750	9,250	9,200	32,250
Non-Jewish (68.2%)	151,000	2,600	20,900	43,900	83,600

Source: Development of the Mountainous Galilee, Settlement Study Centre, 1978.[5]

Table 2. Population growth forecast in the northern district for the period 1976-86, according to present trends

	Jewish population ('000)	Non-Jewish population ('000)
Population at the end of 1976	285.8	260.2
Natural growth of existing population*	47.9	121.5
Cumulative balance of internal migration**	-26.0	-15.0
Absorption of new immigrants***	23.0	-
Natural growth of new immigrants	2.1	-
Estimated popultation by 1986 (total 699.6)	332.8	366.7
Percentage of total population in northern district	47.6	52.4

*   Growth rates: Jewish population 1.7%; non-Jewish population 3.9%.

**   Based on previous averages: Jewish population: -2600; non-Jewish population: -1500.

*** Based on average for the period 1974-77 of 2300 immigrants a year.

Source: Development of the Mountainous Galilee, Settlement Study Centre, 1978.[5]

Table 3. Population growth forecast in Mountainous Galilee for the period 1977-87

	Jewish population ('000)	Non-Jewish population ('000)
Population, October 1977	70.5	151.0
Natural growth of existing population*	13.0	70.5
Cumulative balance of internal migration**	32.0	-8.7
Natural growth of internal migration	3.0	–
Absorption of new immigrants	15.0	–
Natural growth of new immigrants	1.4	–
Estimated population by 1987 (Total 347.7)	134.9	212.8
Percentage of total population in Mountainous Galilee	38.8	61.2

*   Growth rates: Jewish population 1.7%; non-Jewish population 3.9%.

**   Based on the assumption that a net yearly average of 6500 residents from other
     parts of the country will be directed to the northern district, and that about half
     of this number will settle in Mountainous Galilee.

Source: Development of the Mountainous Galilee, Settlement Study Centre, 1977.[5]

Table 4. Selected characteristics of the northern district and Mountainous Galilee,
compared with the southern district and the national average

	Northern District		Southern district	Entire country
	Entire district	Mountainous Galilee		
Balance of internal migration per 1000 inhabitants in 1975*	-12.2		1.5	
Number of employed (per 1,000)**				
in public and communal services	22.5	18.8	25.8	27.1
transportation and communications	4.6	5.5	7.7	7.4
financial and commercial services	1.3	1.5	3.2	6.9
Output in industry per employee in 1975 ('000 Israeli pounds)***	186.2	156.6	213.7	197.3
Average free income per farm family (Moshav) in 1977 (Israeli pounds)****		77,925	92,852	88,402

Sources

*   Statistical Yearbook, 1976, Central Bureau of Statistics. (Recent data
     indicate an improvement in the migrational balance.)

**   Manpower survey 1974, Central Bureau of Statistics.

*** Industrial Development Targets, Ministry of Commerce, Industry and Tourism, 1977.

**** Statistical survey of the Settlement Department, June 1978.

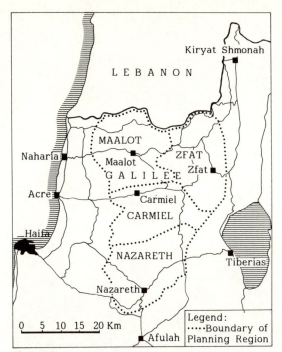

Figure 1

The Mountainous Galilee planning region and
division into sub-regions

The take-off stage in the development of towns in Israel

16

Alexander Berler   Israel

INTRODUCTION

Research into the laws governing the development of towns is an essential stage in creating the tools for the formation of a development policy by government institutions. As the process of urbanisation intensifies, there is a growing realisation that the determination of the objectives of development of towns has far-reaching national implications. It is in the interests of the highest level of social organisation, the government level, to obtain information and control over the strata beneath it, i.e. the local authority and the city. Accordingly, the laws governing the development of towns reach beyond the narrow local framework. The absolute and relative size of the places of settlement, their pace of development, the direction of development and their mutual specific functions - all these create a comprehensive and extensive fabric. The state should exert conscious and deliberate influence on the development of this fabric, in order to direct and channel urban development in such a way that it accords with the demands of the social objectives of the state.

The current research is an attempt to study certain aspects of urban growth, particularly those changes which have a critical significance for the social, economic, spatial, cultural and political structure of the town. This research is aimed primarily at finding out whether in the course of its development a town reaches a definable point of transition from a situation in which the total output of all its activities is less than the volume of demand for those outputs to a situation in which surplus outputs are produced. There are two possibilities in the former situation. Either the surplus demand is satisfied by the artificial inflow of outputs from outside, or the surplus demand turns elsewhere to meet its needs. In other words, if there is no artificial inflow of outputs into the urban set-up, the level of demand will adjust itself to the existing level of outputs, mainly through selective processes of internal immigration, and the town will settle down to a steady low level of activity at which it will reach equilibrium. The point of transition from this situation to a situation of surplus supply which sets in motion a cyclic process of growth has been called the "take-off point". Stimulating the town to beyond the take-off point depends on an "artificial" flow of resources (money, manpower, know-how, policy and leadership, culture and values) into the urban set-up. Such an inflow is the product of an urban development policy at the national level, and for this reason we propose the take-off point as a criterion for the quality and quantity of resources that every town needs in order to stand on its own feet.

The purposes of the research, therefore, were:

□ to examine hypotheses based on the theory of urban growth in terms of which the circumstances of the town are examined at various intervals, beginning with its earliest years, and its status in the entire urban disposition in Israel

□ to identify the functions and estimate their specific contributions to the economic and social basis of the town

□ to describe the systems and sub-systems and the interrelations between these

□ to examine the structural changes in the functions of the town in terms of the changes that have taken place in it, and the relationship between it and other urban settlements in the area and

□ to examine the possibility of using the model (described in the report of the research) as a tool of research in identifying the factors of urban growth, and as an instrument for measuring their contribution to the "take-off" of the town

DEFINITION OF TERMS

A study of a large number of towns shows that they may be divided into two categories: those whose growth is continuous and uninterrupted and not dependent on special circumstances or incentives; and towns whose growth is determined by external or governmental incentives. Furthermore, for at least some towns in the first category a phase can be identified in their past in which they, too, needed outside incentives and supports. It may therefore be assumed that a critical period was reached in which the transition occurred from growth dependent on external incentives to continuous and unconditional growth. We term this period of transition in the development of the town the "take-off" stage.

The purpose of the research outlined here was to define the characteristics, the previous conditions and the results of the specific point of transition from a state of conditional growth to a state of independent growth, in order to develop a theory on the critical changes in urban development.

Another aspect of the same question is the nature of economic and non-economic activities in the town under study. It is possible to distinguish two types of activities: spontaneous activities by which the residents further their own interest, and "guided" activities, i.e. those mainly stimulated by external incentives (governmental and others).

Every town requires a minimal level of activity to fulfil the functions necessary to meet the needs of the population. If this level is not attained a regression sets in, either in the entire urban system or in the specific area of urban activity. In extreme cases, a process of degeneration may set in. In conditions of directed development, this rule generally takes on a somewhat different form, i.e. if the required level is not attained through "spontaneous" activities, it can be attained only through "guided functions" originating from the central government or other external factors. However, if the sum total of "spontaneous" and "directed" activities exceeds the minimum level, it will lead to new spontaneous activities. This may be accompanied by a reduction in the direction of external incentives to the town or by speeding up the extension of activities, providing further stimulus to spontaneous activity and vice versa, until the critical threshold is reached, i.e. the take-off point beyond which any intensification of activities is primarily spontaneous.

METHODOLOGY

There were three stages in the research: crystallisation of the conceptual framework in the light of the main idea, the explorative study, and the main research. However, the theoretical development was not completed at the end of the first stage of crystallising the general conception but continued through the empirical stages.

The explorative study dealt with two towns in terms of the patterns of their development in different situations: Beersheva as an example of rapid and steady development, and Afula as an example of limited and fluctuating development. The findings arrived at in this stage of the research confirmed the hypothesis on the existence and influence of differential factors, resulting in different achievement levels for the two towns. Furthermore, in the case of Beersheva, the behaviour of many variables highlighted the role of the qualitative changes that to a large extent determine the quantitative changes in the variables. But the explorative study did not supply unambiguous proof of the existence of a take-off stage in the process of growth, or of the nature of this stage. Before proceeding to the principal research we therefore had to take certain critical decisions focusing on two major questions: the type and scale of "population" to be studied on the one hand, and the methodological approach in the empirical stage of the main research on the other.

The research team had to choose between two possibilities: either a cross-section of a number of towns at a single point in time, or an in-depth study of one town over a period of at least twenty years. Since one of the aims of the research was to discover the nature and manner of action of the urban system as a general phenomenon, the team preferred the second alternative. Beersheva was chosen as the object of the empirical study. Focusing the analysis on a single town may raise problems as to the scope of the research and the applicability of the findings and conclusions to other towns. However, in principle the conceptual and operative framework of the current research applies to every Israeli town to which the questions being investigated are relevant. In reality, of course, no one town is exactly like any other in its functions, location and social background. However, in the view of the team, a multiplicity of variables with a common basis can be discerned in any urban system. The number of towns in Israel where there is a reasonable chance of a "take-off" is very limited and the number of those for which data is available for a period of at least twenty years is even smaller. The study of a single town therefore not only built the conceptual and operative framework for the research but also supplied the empirical information needed to analyse the subject.

Following the explorative study, it was possible to consolidate the operative framework of the research on the basis of a causal multi-variable system and an interdisciplinary approach, which enabled the team to reconstruct the process of urban growth and to locate the take-off stage. A dummy study was carried out with a stimulation model on the nature and possibilities of the comprehensive model designed to test the sensitivity of urban growth in all its various components to the system of external incentives set in motion at various stages of its development.

In order to develop a comprehensive urban model the team had to obtain data on many different aspects of the life of the town over a period of at least twenty years. The following basic surveys were conducted for this purpose: manpower and population; real estate - prices, areas and uses; development of land uses (on the basis of an analysis of aerial photographs); industry and commerce; and the development of inter-urban public transport in the Beersheva district.

After these surveys and the data had been processed, the team had at its disposal about fifty series of variables (economic and non-economic) on all areas of urban activity for a period of twenty years. They are presented in detail in the report on the actual research. Processing was carried out in several stages, some of which are described below.

A logical analysis to ensure the reliability of the unprocessed data was followed by processing of series of data with a computer in order to prepare them for the next stage of analysis in the research. Then followed formulation of the regressions and choice of the equations needed to describe each phenomenon. The next stage was the preparation of a model of the equations arrived at and solved recursively. All the endogenous variables were solved as a function of the exogenous variables - policy and other endogenous variables, at an interval up to three years. The feedback from the computer offered solutions to forty-one endogenous variables including incomes, production, population, land prices, manpower, internal migration, migration within the town, and many others. The reliability of the model was checked by comparing the solutions with the actual situation. On the whole, the deviations were found to be small. In the last stage, simulation experiments were carried out on the various political variables to check their influence on the growth of the town and on the sensitivity of the urban framework to the policy of incentives and assistance, for this is actually the main aim of the research project.

As stated, the team set out to examine the questions raised by the research by using a growth model which combined various fields - economic, social, spatial, physical and political. This model is recoursive-descriptive, i.e. it acts over a period of time and describes the pattern of causal-behavioural and identity relations and equivalent equations. This structure is represented by a system of equations whose unknown quantities are the endogenous variables that are solved anew every year on the basis of the situation created as a result of the solutions of the previous year, with the endogenous variables of the previous year turned into exogenous elements of the current year, together with other exogenous variables that include, inter alia, factors of policies, prices of capital, and others whose development is extraneous to the town. Comparing the empiric model with the hypothesised model brings out a number of differences which may be attributed to three factors: lack of data or data of low reliability on certain subjects; lack of a reliable empirical link that would negate the assumed links; or the addition of new variables after the formation of the original model.

The model includes forty-one equations, some of which were calculated on the basis of statistical data and others as definitions on the basis of data from various other sources.

LOCATING THE TAKE-OFF STAGE
As stated, the take-off stage is defined as the stage at which it is possible to limit the external incentives given to a town by central factors without bringing the growth process to a halt. The analysis of the take-off was based on a number of simulation experiments carried out with the following four components: directing new immigrants, industrial development (encouragement of investment in large enterprises), development of the physical infrastructure, and housing construction.

For the purpose of the test, the following changes were introduced into each component.

□ The scale of the direction of migrants was diminished to the point of complete cessation (for mathematical reasons a minimum of ten persons annually was set for the number of persons directed). For each of the tests, the addition of large industrial enterprises was stopped. The development of physical infrastructure was reduced to 70 per cent of its actual value because even towns enjoying special support from the central regime get only minimal aid for the development of the infrastructure. Residential building was restricted to 30 per cent of its real value for the same reasons.

□ The chronological range of the test of the take-off was set for the period 1958-69 i.e. twelve years. This was no random decision. The lower limit was determined on the assumption that any town would need a minimum number of years to create a sufficient infrastructure to stimulate unaided growth, while the maximum limit was set in order to allow for a suitable number of predictions for a follow-up on the growth of the town.

□ The simulative examination which tested for the existence (or non-existence) of the take-off stage was confined to five basic tests in each of the twelve years from 1958 to 1969. Altogether sixty simulations were, therefore, conducted to help us locate the take-off stage. The basic tests of the simulation modification or cessation for the four components of the development policy of the central regime mentioned above were conducted, together with a cumulative test of all the components together.

Identification of the take-off stage can be made from two aspects. The first relates to the continuation of the growth of the town even after the cessation or reduction of external supports. The second is concerned with another level, related to the question of the relative status of the town in the countrywide urban framework. Here the following question was examined: does the town continue to maintain the same position in the nation-wide urban hierarchy even after external support is stopped, and to what extent is there a change in the relative weight of the town's population in the total urban population of the country?

BEERSHEVA - A CASE STUDY

After a thorough examination by the method of simulation, we are able to show that in its development the town has gone beyond the take-off stage. This phenomenon was demonstrated in various alternative tests. (The extreme alternative based on the hypothesis of cessation or, at least, modification of all the external incentives given to the town will be described in detail below.)

In time the take-off phenomenon recurs in various alternatives, and we find that 1964 marked a significant watershed in the development of the town. All the simulations carried out indicate that the modification or cessation of external incentives which began in that year would have caused no tangible slow-down in the growth process of the town, while for each of the variables in the period 1958-63, any such slow-down of incentives would have resulted in a far slower rate of growth than that which actually occurred.

Immigrants. It is worth noting a number of points that came to light in the early stages of the project, when the differential influence of each external incentive on the development of the town was being tested separately. It was found that the dominant incentive was direction of immigrant population. Cessation of migration to the town while leaving the other variables unchanged would have led to a substantial reduction in the rate of growth. The influence and impact of the direction-of-population factor is greater than that of all the other incentives. It was measured by the difference between the population figure that Beersheva would have reached by 1972 if the direction of new immigrants to the town had ceased in one of the years 1958-69, and the "original result" i.e. that obtained by using the model on the basis of the actual development of the town. Using the "town size" variable, it is possible to demonstrate the differential influences of each of the factors. If we take the most critical case, i.e. cessation of modification of external incentives in 1958, it will be found that cessation of direction of new immigrants to the town would have caused a scale loss of over 34,000 inhabitants.

Industrial enterprises. The simulative analysis of the influence on the growth of the town of a cessation of the introduction of large industrial enterprises while all the other incentives remained unchanged, showed that if this had taken place in 1958 it would not have significantly affected the continued development of the town and would not have caused a drop in population. This situation implies that the large industrial enterprises set up in the town before 1958 constituted an infrastructure large enough to absorb the population directed to it by the settlement authorities in particular, and the population of the town and the internal migration in general. In other words, this infrastructure was sufficient to ensure take-off, while the directing of immigrants to the town, at least until 1953, was a vital element without which the town could not have reached the "take-off" stage.

According to the simulation study, if the number of large industrial enterprises in the town had been "frozen", a somewhat different employment structure would have emerged from that which actually evolved, and the percentage of people employed in the services would have been higher than those in industry and crafts. This alternative might also have resulted in a certain lowering of the wage level in industry.

To sum up the study of the influence of industrial enterprises, we may conclude that the industrial infrastructure which existed in Beersheva up to 1959 (twenty large enterprises and approximately 2000 employees in industry) was a sufficient basis for continued urban growth, and the influence which would have been exerted by a cessation of support for the further growth of industry would have been in employment structure and wages and not in town size.

On this point it should be borne in mind that Beersheva is the administrative centre for a large region. Consequently, a large number of administrative units and public services are concentrated in the town. Since the bulk of the population is employed in the service sector, the specific weight of industry is necessarily small. In a town with a different structure of employment sectors, a change in the scale of industrial development could have led to far more acute changes, but to arrive at an accurate answer on this question, a special analysis of each case would be required, in accordance with the economic structure of each town.

Critical threshold. It was found that a cessation or reduction of external incentives for Beersheva, if it had started in 1964, would not have curbed the development of the town to a meaningful extent and, in any event, at the end of the period the town would have reached a size level very close to the level actually reached. The transition of 1963-4 is, as it were, a critical threshold in terms of the results that might have arisen from the cessation or reduction of external incentives. Giving external incentives and aid for an extra year in the period 1958-63 would have greatly raised the standard of the town. After 1964 these incentives admittedly contributed to raising the standard of the town, but the marginal additions were on a very small scale. Detailed quantitative data are given in the research itself but here we shall confine ourselves to a very general conclusion relating to the disparity in each one of the possiblities of cessation of external incentives in the period 1958-63, compared with the development that actually occurred. It should be noted that in 1964 when, in our opinion, the take-off process took place, the population of Beersheva was 60,000, constituting the basis for the impetus towards the future.

Relative status. The status of a town in the country-wide urban system was examined by comparing the size of its population in two frames of reference: the country-wide urban system on the one hand, and the country-wide urban framework, excluding the three major cities, on the other. (The second frame of reference was chosen because it is more relevant when one considers the destinations to which the central institutions direct new immigrants.)

It is interesting to note that when the external incentives were reduced before 1964, an actual reduction was discerned in the weight of the town in the total urban population, particularly when the population of the three large cities was excluded. This phenomenon is particularly marked in the years of the recession, when Beersheva suffered from the general effects of the depression in the economy. It seems that the earlier the external incentives are stopped, the more the weight of the town in the total urban population is likely to fall. This finding confirms the hypothesis that a town is more sensitive to unfavourable external situations before it reaches the take-off stage.

Cessation or slow-down of directed incentives. The first test of the take-off stage and the process of growth in its entirety was made on the basis of the population growth of Beersheva in various situations of policy implementation. This test was the basic aspect of all the phenomena of the take-off. At the same time, the process of growth may be presented by a number of other features that reflect the economic and social levels of the town and, above all, its internal structure and the processes of its adjustment. Let us consider the following four variables: wage levels, the level of prices of apartments, surplus demand, and the structure of branches of employment.

Wage levels. The level of wages was calculated in real terms. Since we are considering average wages (average-weighted according to branches of employment), this increase may be attributed at least partly to the changing employment structure, resulting from a transfer from branches with relatively low incomes to branches with relatively high incomes, and from the differential increase in wages in each of the branches. Both these processes took place in Beersheva.

Apartment prices. If external incentives had been stopped in 1967, the rate of increase in apartment prices would probably have been higher than if those incentives had been stopped altogether. This may be attributed to the fact that apartment prices are influenced both by demand and supply, while supply is influenced by the quantity of land developed or earmarked for housing. Therefore, in conditions of growing demand, a decline in the development of land for housing leads to a drop in supply and pressure on prices. In the early years, the pressure of demand is not strong enough to cause a fundamental change in the rate of price increases, even if supply is reduced by a substantial degree. On the other hand, reduction in supply after 1967 - even if at the same time demand is reduced by a not insignificant extent - substantially increases prices for apartments. It may therefore be assumed that around the year 1967 the housing market made the transition from curbs on demand to curbs on supply; in other words, urban land became a relatively scarce asset, a phenomenon that may well characterise the take-off stage. From this stage on, this lends added importance to land development as an element of public policy.

Surplus demand. One of the main hypotheses of the study was that situations of demand pressures in the commodity market are created in the course of growth in a developing town; in other words, the rate of development of incomes and demand growth exceeds the rate of development of supply as expressed in the capacity of the various branches of commerce to meet the demand.

In this study we decided to express this factor as the percentage of potential surplus demand in the town. Changes in the scale of surplus demand are liable to come from two basic sources: a change in the level of demand and a change in the level of supply. According to the original result, surplus demand increased fourfold in the period 1957-66. In the years 1966-8 the model reproduces a 14 per cent drop in surplus demand, while in 1972 the surplus reverts to a level close to the 1966 level. If we test the general tendency in the years 1966-72, we find that the level of surplus demand remains more or less stable, though dropping by up to 4 per cent. When we try to explain the course of development of this variable, we discover that in the early years (up to 1964-66) the level of demand rose far more rapidly than the level of supply, despite the rapid development of sectors such as public services and construction, which create incomes and demand but not a supply of market commodities. From this time onward conditions remained stable: the rate of surplus demand did not change much and even dropped at times. Only in 1964 were conditions in Beersheva right for the establishment of a number of new commercial branches.

The influence of the standard simulations of surplus demand did not significantly alter either the course of growth of this variable or its level at the end of the period (1972). The earlier the external incentives were stopped, the longer the level of surplus demand continued to rise. In other words, the rate of development of supply did not keep up with the rate of development of demand, compared with the original result up to the later period. In general, these simulations led to a drop in the level of this variable. This influence was anticipated, since the basic simulations influence primarily the level of demand while their influence on supply is relatively small, though indirectly they also exert an influence on the supply of market commodities.

We therefore carried out one more simulation. We attempted to examine what would be the likely position of the commodity market if twenty new business enterprises had been added each year throughout the period of the town's rapid growth (1956-60); i.e. altogether 100 units. It emerged that, if this had been the case, there would have been no fundamental change in the pattern of growth of the town in general or of the variable of surplus demand in particular, although there would have been certain changes of degree. In other words, in the framework of this experiment the level of demand surpluses would have been lower than in the original result, while the population of the town would have grown more rapidly than with the original result, reaching a total of over 93,000 inhabitants - a difference of over seven per cent.

In summing up this subject, it should be stated that the analysis of the variable of surplus demand also indicates that the turning-point in the development of the town occurred in the years 1964-66 during which a sufficient threshold was created to enable the town to continue growing without a further increase in surplus demand. At this point we should recall that, as stated above, in the years of the recession there was a temporary sharp decrease in surplus demand, and demand dropped considerably because the purchasing power of the Beersheva population was reduced. A further conclusion reached after studying this variable is that a deliberate (even if temporary) policy of speeding up the development of branches of commerce in Beersheva could have considerably stimulated the growth of the town and enhanced its attractiveness. This assumption, put forward on the basis of the classic theories of location which link the price of urban land with accessibility to urban centres, was confirmed by the present research in the context of the surplus demand variable.

Employment. The employment structure could reflect the stages of the town's development, even though this index does not give an accurate guideline to the structure of the various branches, since it represents only the structure of the labour force, which is only one of the factors of production in any branch, and some advanced industries do not require manpower in large numbers. An analysis of the employment structure of Beersheva in 1956 point to the high weight of those employed in industry (24.7 per cent), commerce (31.7 per cent) and building (25.8 per cent), as against the lower weight of those employed in public services (14.8 per cent) and the very small proportion of those employed in education and health services (4.8 per cent). In 1972 we find that the weight of industrial workers (at 26.4 per cent) remained fairly stable while that of the commercial branch (at 13.3 per cent) declined. There was also a sharp decline in the weight of those employed in building (14.4 per cent), while there was a substantial increase in the proportion employed in health and education services (14.4 per cent) and public services (19.9 per cent).

In the various simulations no great difference was found in terms of the composition of employment, when compared with the original result. However, certain changes may be discerned that are related to the transition of the town from a situation of construction and rapid growth to one of stability with a developed service sector and a broad economic basis, as reflected in the decline in the weight of the building industry offset by a rise in the weight of public services and health and education services, with industry accounting for about one-quarter of the total number of employed.

This structure, found to pertain to Beersheva in 1972, is a mark of a developed town that has passed the stage of rapid growth. A study of the employment structure shows that the process of change in the relative weights of the various branches was a gradual one, continuing throughout the entire period without any outstanding fluctuations in rate.

External crises. One of the tests showing whether a town has passed the take-off stage is its capacity or not to withstand the effects of a nation-wide depression. The period reproduced through the model (1956-72) included just such a period, i.e. the recession of 1966-7 One of the tests of the reliability of the model is its capacity to reproduce this period, which caused a deviation in the pace and direction of change in many of the variables. Indeed, it was found that the model successfully reproduced this period for most of the variables. It is interesting to note that the period of recession is reflected in the solutions of the model for the years 1966-8, and not only for 1966-7.

After the original data gathered in field surveys had been checked, it became apparent that the process of emerging from the recession, as expressed through many of the variables (land prices, demand surpluses, wages and, of course, population) continued in Beersheva until 1968. In essence, the years of recession, both in the solutions of the model and in reality, were reflected in a slow-down in population growth, a drop in demand surplus, a pause in the rise of apartment prices in real terms, and a sharp decline in the average real wage level. On the other hand, there was found to be no decrease in the employment level; in other words, there was no rise in unemployment. But during the years of the recession there was a most significant decline in the porportion of the total labour force employed in the building industry, one of the branches of the economy hardest hit by the recession.

Halting external incentives to Beersheva before 1964 would have led to a decline in apartment prices during the recession years, which would not have occurred had the incentives been stopped after 1964.

As mentioned earlier, demand surpluses also decline in periods of recession, but not at a rate faster than with the original result. In general, it may be said that the period of recession is reflected by a change from a rise to a temporary decline in all the variables. In any case, even in the event of early cessation of external incentives, the town would have reverted to a course of recovery after the recession period, a process that continued until 1968. It can therefore be stated that, although in a situation of early cessation of incentives and supports, a greater sensitivity to economic depression is shown than in a situation where the incentives were not stopped, the town had the capacity to recover in either situation and revert to its original course of growth. Even if external incentives had been stopped before 1964, the town would have successfully reverted to the original course of growth, but the rate of growth would have been insufficient in terms of population size to raise Beersheva to the rung it holds in the national urban grading scale. Furthermore, the rate of growth in supply would not have overtaken the rate of demand growth. A situation was thus created in which demand surpluses continued to rise even after recovery from the recession, as distinct from those simulations in which external incentives and supports were stopped after 1964. If the incentives had been stopped at a later period, the demand surpluses would have stayed at their level prior to the recession.

The behaviour of these variables indicates the level of sensitivity of the town to the harmful effects of economic depressions. It was apparent that a firm economic infrastructure had emerged in Beersheva which permitted the town to overcome temporary depressions relatively unscathed.

CONCLUSIONS

In summarising the test for the take-off stage as a general phenomenon, one may state that Beersheva has gone through the take-off process; and that the take-off process does not comprise a single stage.

The rate of growth of the population and other variables was relatively rapid in the early years of the test, but slowed down from the middle of the sixth year (1963). Furthermore, tests on the cessation of external incentives and supports made in the middle of the model indicated that in most variables there was no fundamental change, compared with the original result in which the cessation of the incentives began after 1964. On the other hand, a significant slow-down in the rate of growth occurred when incentives were halted before 1964. Therefore, from the mid-1960s, there was a transition in Beersheva from a situation of rapid growth to one of more moderate growth. A stable urban structure emerged, as reflected in the employment composition of the town. It should be noted that while the pace of growth has declined, it is relatively high to this day, and in this sense Beersheva differs from the many development towns that suffer from demographic and economic stagnation.

A differential test of the variables shows a number of structural stages in the take-off period, which can be identified in terms of the parts of the system in which they occur - population, the commodity market, industrialisation and the housing market.

Population. As stated, a detailed analysis of the population growth showed that the town had passed through the "take-off" stage in the mid-1960s, as shown in the various simulation experiments. We discovered that cessation of external incentives before the mid-1960s would have seriously affected the rate of population growth, but this would not have happened if the incentives had been halted later. It is therefore evident that Beersheva began to assert itself as a place of residence in its own right from the mid-1960s.

Commodity market. An analysis of the commodity market indicates that the rate of growth in demand was higher than the rate of grown in supply until the mid-1960s. Afterwards the rate of growth in supply kept up with that in demand. This is reflected in the stability of the weight of the demand surplus as a percentage of the total demand for commodities in the town. It is thus evident that in the mid-1960s there emerged a basis for the introduction of new business enterprises at a higher level.

Industrialisation. Apparently the process of consolidation of industry in Beersheva began even before the 1950s. In 1956, the year in which the restoration model begins, there were fourteen large industrial enterprises in Beersheva, compared with twenty large and sixty smaller ones in 1958. In 1956, 1300 people or about one-quarter of the town's employees were employed in industry. The proportion for industry did not fall at the end of this period, even in those branches in the simulation for which the direction of large enterprises to Beersheva was stopped in 1958. It is thus evident that as early as the 1950s favourable conditions emerged in Beersheva for the development of industry, and this may be attributed to the promotion of an industrial infrastructure from the early years of the new town's development.

Housing market. It would appear that a situation of surplus demand characteristic of developed towns arose in the housing market in Beersheva, only by the end of the 1960s. This process may be attributed to the rapid rise in housing prices which would have occurred if the development of land for housing had been stopped from 1967 - something that would not have happened if land development had been stopped in earlier years.

In conclusion it may be said that the take-off process in Beersheva passed through the following sub-stages: emergence of an industrial basis at the end of the 1950s; growth in the attractiveness of the town by the mid-1960s; creation of a basis for the introduction of commercial enterprises by the mid-1960s; and the emergence of surplus demand in housing by the end of the 1960s.

Causes and consequences of neighbourhood deterioration

17

Daniel Shefer   Israel

INTRODUCTION

Neighbourhood deterioration is a dynamic process. It begins when a mature, stable neighbourhood is no longer capable of generating the necessary capital investment and services needed to operate, maintain and replace existing assets. As public and private investment in the neighbourhood falls short of the amount needed to sustain its stability, deterioration begins. The symptoms of this deterioration are quite visible. There is the gradual downgrading of schools, public parks, street cleaning, refuse collection and other public services. The physical appearance of structures begins to show signs of obsolescence and wear. Property values begin to drop, as do rents, and the socio-economic characteristics of the neighbourhood also gradually change.

To a large extent, the changes in the neighbourhood are affected by changes in the structure of the urban area at large. When the urban area is growing rapidly and housing supply generally falls short of demand, a slow deterioration rate may be expected. Thus a "spread effect" may be hypothesised to identify urban areas where economic opportunities and resulting rapid growth occur. Conversely, in urban areas which lose their populations one may expect rapid neighbourhood deterioration. As new residential neighbourhoods are developed in the suburbs and economic activities shift from the central city outward, the locational preferences of long-time residents undergo change. This is the result of the diminishing competitive advantages of the old neighbourhood, in terms of accessibility to work-places and other economic activities, as well as decreased neighbourhood amenities and environmental quality. These factors also tend to hasten neighbourhood deterioration.

In short, the causes and rate of neighbourhood deterioration are complex and certainly not uniform. Remedies aimed at stopping deterioration and the degree of their success are very likely to be different, depending as they do on the unique circumstances and conditions of a particular neighbourhood, as well as its relation to the urban structure in general.

Externalities in urban areas have been recognised for some time as a source of growth as well as decline. Positive externalities play an important role in inspiring positive action by home-owners. Negative externalities, such as congestion and environmental pollution, affect neighbourhood amenities and growth adversely. Moreover, externalities generated by surrounding neighbourhoods may also affect a target neighbourhood. Thus, if the target neighbourhood is declining and bordered by one or more neighbourhoods which are at an advanced stage of deterioration (slums), it probably will be futile to attempt to save this neighbourhood. The reason is that the economic environment surrounding the target neighbourhood generates negative externalities which counteract efforts to assist this neighbourhood.

It is extremely important, therefore, that a neighbourhood selected for rehabilitation should be in an area which is relatively stable. The positive externalities generated by well-maintained neighbourhoods surrounding the target neighbourhood could help much to make the programme successful.

ECONOMIC ASPECTS

From an economic point of view the existence of slum areas points to a lack of efficiency in allocating the limited resources of the economy; and an inequitable distribution of resources between the various segments of the population.

Distressed neighbourhoods are caused by, among other things, inefficient allocation of resources. This includes human resources, which could become more productive and more efficient through vocational training and guidance and the allocation of land and buildings for public services, e.g. education, culture, sport, vocational training and health services, for which the need in distressed areas is so obvious. The availability of these services could greatly improve living conditions in these neighbourhoods. The use of the manpower potential could contribute considerably to the economy of the nation, if proper education and training were made available.

From a social and economic viewpoint, the existence of slums indicates inequality in the distribution of income among the various social strata.

The marginal social cost in a deteriorating neighbourhood is much larger than the private marginal cost. The private cost is limited to the decline in property values, while the social cost is the loss of generations of people who drop out of the productive labour force and even become welfare cases or descend into the underworld of crime.[1] Thus, for society the advantage of improving the situation in the slums will be far greater than for the individual. To bring about an equilibrium between these values, public intervention is needed in the form of subsidies or taxation to stimulate the private sector to act in a direction which is also desirable from a social viewpoint.

Neighbourhood deterioration is a dynamic process. The symptoms of advanced deterioration are clearly discernible: a decline in the level of public services - schools, kindergartens, street cleaning, garbage collection, road and pavement maintenance, public gardens - and in the maintenance of private and public property. The external appearance gradually declines and the lack of care for the environment becomes clearly evident. Social and economic indices react quickly. Families more capable of moving out of the neighbourhood do so and more and more of the remaining families become welfare cases. Groups of "marginal" youths gradually emerge and absenteeism from school becomes prevalent. Loitering, unemployment and laziness lead to moral decay, which deepens with the further deterioration of the neighbourhood into an area of poverty and social and economic malaise.

A number of research papers have tried to describe the processes of change in a neighbourhood.[2][3][4][5][6] This can also be done with the aid of the accompanying illustrations. Figures 1 and 2 are graphic presentations of the processes of change in several neighbourhoods over a period of time. Figure 1 shows four neighbourhoods: a,b,c,d. The quality of "a" gradually improves as time goes on. The reasons could be numerous and varied: public investment in the area and its environment, quality of apartments, the socio-economic composition of the population, etc. Area "b" also improves with the passage of time.

In areas "c" and "d" the situation is different. With the passage of time the quality of these neighbourhoods gradually deteriorates. Area "c" does so at a pace somewhat slower than area "d". In fact, immediately after construction area "d" showed signs of improvement but soon afterwards began to deteriorate.

Figure 2 shows the point above which the situation is still good, and before which the neighbourhoods are distressed. In time the situation changes - some neighbourhoods improve ("c"), some remain stable ("d"), and some deteriorate gradually until at a certain point in time (t_a and t_b) they become distressed neighbourhoods.

DYNAMIC NATURE OF NEIGHBOURHOOD CHANGE

The dynamic processes of residential quarters are ongoing processes and can be classified into four stages: growth and development, stabilisation, deterioration, and decay. (Decay can be either an initial or a final stage. It occurs when an urban quarter is poorly built or in a poor location or is badly populated from a demographic or socio-economic viewpoint. From the very outset, the area was undesirable for living. As a rule, a residential area cannot pass from this stage to another, except in exceptional cases, e.g. unexpected development in the vicinity combined with large-scale investments, leading to unexpected improvement, reconstruction and growth.)

When an urban area finds itself in one of these stages, it is usually the cumulative result of several factors, direct and indirect. Theoretically, it is possible to pass from one stage to another but this rarely happens in practice. Possible transitions from one stage to another may be illustrated by the accompanying matrix.

Transition matrix

(Conditional probabilities of transition - similar to the Markov chains)

Stages ↓From To→	Growth	Stability	Deterioration	Decay
1. Growth	x	x		
2. Stability	x	x	x	
3. Deterioration		x	x	x
4. Decay	x			x

The conditional probability of transition depends on the level of investment at any given period. Large investments, private or public, in or near a residential neighbourhood may lead to improvement and transition from a stage of deterioration to a stage of stability.

The matrix shows how a residential area in a stage of growth may either remain so for some time or move to a stage of stability. Since the transition is an ongoing and not a step-by-step process, it is hard to imagine a sudden change from growth to deterioration during a relatively short period. The sum of probabilities in each row should be equal to 1.0 and the events thus expressed are mutually exclusive.

The probability of transition depends not only on the level of investments, but also on the situation in neighbouring areas. Area A, adjacent to areas 1,2,3 and 4, can be illustrated as shown in Figure 3. When the areas 1,2,3 and 4 are in a state of deterioration, the investments required to save A from a similar fate are far greater than they would be if the surrounding areas were in a state of growth, development or stability. External influences from neighbouring areas are, therefore, a factor in the investment needed to improve the situation in any deteriorating neighbourhood.

Between the two extremes described above, there are, of course, various possible permutations, e.g. areas 1,2,3 are stable but 4 is not, etc.

If the area as a whole is in a state of stability, the treatment of a deteriorating area is relatively cheap and localised. On the other hand, if the area as a whole is in a state of deterioration, localised treatment will be useless and investments will be lost within a short time. In such cases, the approach must be more comprehensive and embrace all affected neighbourhoods.

It follows that the strategy of intervention and the chances of success depend on two basic factors: the state of deterioration of a single neighbourhood, and the condition of the surrounding neighbourhoods.

Changes in urban structure strongly affect neighbourhoods: since urban grown is not symmetrical, urban development is differential. While some districts enjoy public investments in infrastructure and rapid development, others grow slowly or even suffer retardation. In the general fabric of an urban organisation, the relative importance of specific areas changes with time. Preferential treatment of a certain area may lead to prosperity and growth, whereas indifference may lead to decay. When considerable investments are made in the construction of a new shopping centre or in public buildings, the entire district benefits from the favourable effect. Conversely, if polluting plants are erected in a certain area or if a neighbourhood is invaded by noisy trades, the effect may be disastrous.

INVESTMENT THEORY AND NEIGHBOURHOOD DECLINE

Inefficient investment in a run-down neighbourhood causes "disinvestment" or insufficient capital investment in maintenance and renewal. Neighbourhoods can be in one of three stages: growth and development, stabilisation, or deterioration. In each of these stages the marginal efficiency of investment is different. It is at its highest during the stage of growth and development, lower during stabilisation and lowest during deterioration. (See Figure 4.)

It follows that in a deteriorating neighbourhood the volume of private and public investment is insufficient to maintain or replace infrastructures. What may have been sufficient in the first or second stage is insufficient during the third stage. Considerable financial resources are required to reverse the trend and bring the area back from a state of deterioration to a state of stability. It is advisable, and certainly cheaper, to employ a policy of public intervention to prevent deterioration rather than a policy of improvements in a neighbourhood already decayed.

The investment theory described above can be illustrated in the accompanying graph (Figure 4). During the growth stage the volume of net investment ΔI (after accrued depreciation) is positive. During the second stage (stabilisation) the net investment is sufficient to offset depreciation and take care of maintenance and replacements. During the third stage (deterioration) the rate of net investment is negative, i.e. lower than the amount needed to maintain and replace worn-out infrastructure.

To bring a neighbourhood from stage two back to stage one or from stage three to stage two, a higher volume of investment is required because the marginal efficiency of investment is reduced as we move from stage one to stage two and to stage three.

NEGATIVE EXTERNALITIES

Two kinds of negative "externalities" can be found in a deteriorating neighbourhood. The first kind flows from the socio-economic composition of the population which reduced the status of the area and its property values and subsequently its rate of investment. The second is a result of the poor state of repair of the buildings and the neighbourhood infrastructure, which in turn results in a lower return on individual investment. The net result is that residents do not consider it worthwhile to invest in their dwellings and, therefore, cases of individual renewal without public intervention are extremely rare.[7]

Because of the mutual external influences, joint action by a large group is likely to give a higher return on investment than action by individuals. As a rule it is very difficult to arrive at the desired degree of cooperation among owners, some of whom may live elsewhere. Public intervention is usually required to ensure a meaningful return on investment. This can take the form of incentives (subsidies, credits and tax rebates) designed to increase the expected return on investment while at the same time reducing the risk involved. Another incentive is to increase the value of land by measures such as improved communications, changes in the general town-planning design or improved services rendered by the local authorites. This, in turn will encourage further public and private investments.[8] [9] [10]

OWNERSHIP AND TAX STRUCTURE

Many residential areas in Israel deteriorate too rapidly, partly because of faulty planning, partly because of poor quality and partly because of improper composition of the population. Since most distressed neighbourhoods in Israel were designed and constructed by public bodies, it is reasonable to assume that there is a connection between public ownership and deterioration.

In a free housing market the laws of supply and demand may bring about certain changes in the socio-economic composition of a neighbourhood and the quality of services. However, most publicly owned housing projects have been detached from the laws of supply and demand. In consequence, tenants are reluctant to invest of their own resources in properties which do not belong to them, while the authorities find it very difficult to organise public aid for maintenance and improvements. Furthermore, when taxes on buildings are high, there is a tendency to reduce the value, which leads to physical deterioration of the buildings. On the other hand, when taxes on land are high, they are an incentive for the intensive use of the land, hence for the improvement of the structures built on it.[11]

IMPLICATIONS FOR POLICY-MAKING

Neighbourhood deterioration is a dynamic process. It is affected by two principal sets of forces: internal and external to the neighbourhood. These forces can work independently or reinforce each other. When internal and external forces are jointly and adversely affecting the neighbourhood, the process of deterioration is rapid.

The measures required to stop the deterioration of a neighbourhood or, better still, to prevent neighbourhoods from reaching the state of deterioration, are directly related to the internal and external forces operating in and around the neighbourhood.

An old and stagnating neighbourhood could easily move to a stage of decline as investment in infrastructure and other essential social services falls short of the amount necessary to maintain the level of services rendered to the neighbourhood's residents. The type of remedy needed to avert continuing deterioration in a declining neighbourhood may differ from those needed to prevent deterioration or reverse the trend in a decaying neighbourhood, i.e. in a decaying neighbourhood a sizeable public investment may not be the most appropriate intervention.

It seems apparent that there is a need to identify and analyse the processes underlying the socio-economic forces which bring about deterioration, for only then can we identify the key socio-economic variables which may be amenable to change as a result of public intervention. Clearly, prior to any major public intervention in the form of sizeable investment programmes, it is important to understand the underlying causes and policy options. Obviously, this learning process will greatly increase the efficiency of any public or private investment programme.

The investment theory expounded earlier provides a basic understanding of the dynamic nature of neighbourhood change. Furthermore, it helps identify the best set of public intervention policies to bring about an improvement in the neighbourhood's conditions. The amount and rate of private and public investment, we hypothesise, is the most significant variable in causing a neighbourhood to remain stable or to move from one socio-economic and demographic stage to another. Moreover, the marginal productivity of capital, in terms of output and income generated, will vary in accordance with the stage of each neighbourhood.

In a growing neighbourhood the rate of investment or capital formation may constitute a factor limiting growth. In some cases the eagerness of entrepreneurs to pursue investment opportunities in these areas may exceed the capacity of the existing infrastructure. Thus, private investment will lead public investment. In a stable neighbourhood the rate of investment, public and private, is sufficient only to replace the capital consumed in the course of production activities in the previous period. Thus net investment is zero. In a deteriorating neighbourhood the rate of investment, public and private, is less than that needed to replace the capital consumed in the previous period. Needless to say, effective production capacity diminishes over time through this type of disinvestment.

As private investment declines because of low returns, public investment also tends to diminish. This is due partly to the fact that the existing level of economic activity in the area can no longer support and sustain the required public investment in infrastructure or additional public services.

Finally, investment or capital formation is not the main constraint to growth in a decayed neighbourhood. In such an area the major obstacles are more chronic and may be due to factors such as meagre resources in terms of human capital and physical assets or a lack of competitive advantages over other areas. Very often public investment surpasses private investment in distressed neighbourhoods. More often than not, these public investments are made on the basis of redistribution rather than socio-economic development objectives.

Since investment in distressed neighbourhoods does not appear to constitute the limiting constraint to growth, we propose to differentiate between distressed neighbourhoods and the other types of neighbourhoods described above. We hypothesise that the socio-economic condition of an area can be explained by the amount of investment that has taken place. We differentiate between two types of investment, private and public. It is conceivable that to a very small degree one type may be substituted for another. Consequently, a constant production function, such as input-output production function, may be a close approximation to their relationship. Thus, a lag in one of these investment components may diminish the marginal productivity of the other or retard growth altogether, since it will eventually constitute the effective constraint to growth (the limiting factor). Essentially, and in an abstract form, we suggest the following relationship:

Socio-economic and demographic indicators
of neighbourhood's stage,

i.e. growing, stable, deteriorating, and distressed

$$= f[I^P, I^G]$$

where: I^P = private investment

I^G = public (government) investment

Our investment theory is thus in line with the neo-classical economic growth theory and it follows the logic underlying the economic growth models (investment or capital formation). We believe that in any neighbourhood change in terms of socio-economic indicators will be due to the amount as well as the mix of private and public investment. Thus, the objective is to identify the indicators which reflect neighbourhood deterioration. Needless to say, the indicators may not be the same for areas at different stages of deterioration. Consequently, the type of public assistance will vary accordingly.

REFERENCES

[1] Turvey, R., "On the divergences between social cost and private cost" (1963), Economica, pages 309-13.
[2] Smith, W.F., "Forecasting neighbourhood change" (1963), Land Economics, pages 292-7.
[3] Downs, A., "Stimulating capital investment in central city downtown areas and inner city neighbourhoods" (1973), Real Estate Research Corporation.
[4] Sternlieb, G., and Hughes, J.W., "Neighbourhood dynamics and government policy" (1974), American Real Estate and Urban Economics Association Journal, pages 7-23.
[5] US Department of Housing and Urban Development, Office of Policy Development and Research, The dynamics of neighbourhood change (1975).
[6] Cannon, D.S., Lachman, M.L., and Bernhard, A.S., "Identifying neighbourhoods for preservation and renewal" (1977), Growth and Change, pages 35-8.
[7] Davis, O.A., and Whinston, A.B., "The economics of urban renewal" (1961), Land and Contemporary Problems, pages 105-17.
[8] Netzer, D., The economics of the property tax (1966), Chapter IV, Brooks Institute.
[9] Nourse, H.O., "The economics of urban renewal" (1966), Land Economics, pages 65-74.
[10] Shefer, D., Landlords' decision behaviour - a structural analysis (1977).
[11] Schaaf, A.H., "Economic feasibility analysis for urban renewal housing rehabilitation" (1969), Journal of the American Institute of Planners, pages 136-41.

OTHER READING

[1] Bailey, M.J., "Note on the economics of residential zoning and urban renewal" (1959), Land Economics, (August), pages 288-92.

2 Baumol, W.J., "On the social rate of discount" (1968), <u>American Economic Review</u> pages
   788-802.
3 Birch, D., "Toward a stage theory of urban growth" (1971), <u>Journal of the American
   Institute of Planners</u>, pages 78-87.
4 Bloom, M.R., "Fiscal productivity and the pure theory of urban renewal" (1962),
   <u>Land Economics</u>, pages 134-44.
5 Fama, E.F., "Risk, return and equilibrium" (1968), <u>The Journal of Finance</u>, Vol 23,
   No 1, pages 29-40.
6 Farras, D.E., <u>The investment decision under certainty</u> (1962), Prentice-Hall.
7 Grigsby, W.G., <u>Housing markets and public policy</u> (1963), University of Pennsylvania
   Press, pages 84-110.
8 Helliwell, J.F., <u>Public policies and private investment</u> (1968), Clarendon Press.
9 Hirshleifer, J., <u>Investment, interest and capital</u> (1970), Prentice-Hall.
10 Kain, F.J., and Apgar, W.C. Jnr., <u>The modelling of neighbourhood changes</u> (1977),
   Discussion paper D77-22, Harvard Universty, Department of City and Regional Planning.
11 Krumm, R., and Vaughan, R.J., <u>The economics of urban blight</u> (1976), Rand Corporation,
   P5712.
12 Schaaf, A.H., <u>Economic aspects of urban renewal: theory, policy and area analysis</u>
   (1960), Research Report No 14, Centre for Real Estate and Urban Economics, University
   of California.
13 Schaaf, A.H., "Public policies in urban renewal: an economic analysis of
   justifications and effects" (1964), <u>Land Economics</u>, pages 67-78.
14 Schaaf, A.H., "Effects of property taxation on slums and renewal: A study of land
   improvement assessment ratios" (1969), <u>Land Economics</u>, pages 111-7.
15 Smith, W.F., <u>Filtering and neighbourhood change</u> (1964), Research Report 24, Centre
   for Real Estate and Urban Economics, University of California.

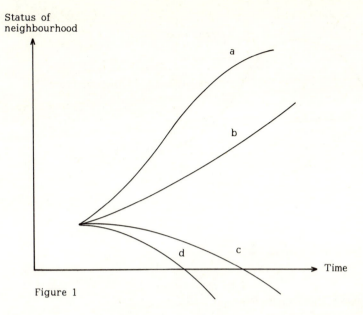

Figure 1

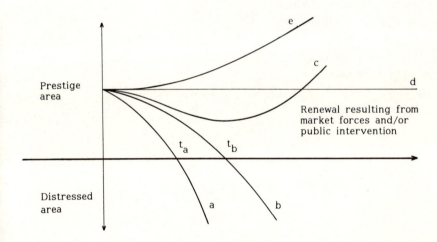

Figure 2

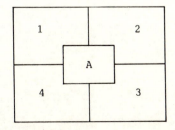

Figure 3

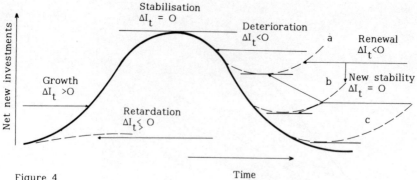

Figure 4

$$I_t = I_0 e^{(\delta-\rho)t}$$

$$\Delta I_t = I_t - I_0 e^{(\delta-\rho)t}$$

ΔI_t - new net investments (new capital vintage)

I_t - final stage, value of I during period t
   (or residual investment during t)

I_0 - starting position. Value of I during O

ρ - annual capital depreciation

δ - exponent of annual investment

e - natural Logarithm base

The Israeli experience 18

Naomi Carmon and Moshe Hill   Israel

INTRODUCTION

Deteriorated residential areas are a world-wide urban problem. A deteriorated area is a territorial concentration of households with individual and collective social or physical problems. In such an area there are many households with standards of social or economic or physical living conditions considerably lower than those accepted in that society. Since these inferior living conditions frequently disturb the functioning of individuals, families and communities, they are usually defined as "problematic" and governments frequently initiate remedial programmes to upgrade the deteriorated areas.

On the assumption that it is necessary to identify the causes of neighbourhood deterioration in order to prevent it or help slow it down where it has already developed, this paper opens with an analysis of the causes of deterioration. The presentation is based on the Israeli situation, but the framework of analysis can be adapted to analyse and understand the process of neighbourhood deterioration in other countries.

The second part of the paper gives a brief description of the characteristics of deteriorated and distressed neighbourhoods in Israel and explains the strong commitment of the government to the improvement of the living condtions of the disadvantaged groups through a national project of neighbourhood rehabilitation.

Acquaintance with the underlying causes of neighbourhood deterioration, together with the aggregate experience of the planning profession in general and renewal and development in particular led to the formulation of an approach to these multi-problem residential areas, which is presented in the last part of the paper.

CAUSES OF DETERIORATION

For purposes of analysis we shall divide the causes into three groups: first, basic conditions in the country (demographic, social, economic and physical characteristics of the people and their environment); second, ideologies and bureaucratic practice in the field of physical and social planning; and third, the spontaneous social and economic processes found in most urban situations which cause urban slums and deepen their distress.

Basic conditions. When the state of Israel was founded in 1948, hundreds of thousand of refugees arrived and the population was doubled within three years. About half of the immigrants had fled from the holocaust of Europe of the second world war and the other half were refugees from Arab countries. With the arrival of these masses of newcomers, especially those from the undeveloped countries of North Africa and the Middle East, illiteracy, unemployment, poverty and accompanying social problems increased significantly.

Initial housing conditions in Israel were very poor. A survey of the urban population a year before the foundation of the state found an average density of over three persons per room.[1] In order to overcome the severe shortage of housing caused by the initial conditions and the mass immigration, the government began to play a central role in supplying new apartments and constructed about half the housing units built during the years 1949-72.[2] Since the needs were enormous and the resources of the new state limited, the standards of construction, including building materials, dwelling size and infrastructure, were very low in the first years. This was especially so in the transit camps (ma'abarot) which were built for the hundreds of thousands of immigrants who usually arrived with no material possessions at all. The temporary shelters were to be replaced by solid structures within a few months, but the government could not afford to provide such structures for many years. Thus, many transit camps, as well as areas with structures of the pre-state period and neighbourhoods quickly and cheaply built by public authorities in the 1950s, deteriorated physically within a very few years.

Urban environments which were considered adequate some twenty or even ten years ago, are today regarded as sub-standard, not because the level of housing and services has dropped but because the level in other urban areas has greatly increased and the inter-neighbourhood differentials have grown. This fits the thesis of Titmuss, who sees the problem of poverty as the social pathology of groups of people which stems from the advancement of other people.[3] According to this thesis, economic activity and technological development have their social costs which are borne by those groups which benefit little, or not at all, from this progress. One of the social costs is the deterioration of the relative position of the poor and their residential areas, caused by the rapid social upsurge of the other groups and areas.

Ideologies. The image of Jewish society in the land of Israel, as conceived by the pioneering Zionist leadership, is a unique example of a social philosophy which envisaged a modern society based mainly on agriculture, leaving hardly any place for the city. In actual fact during all the periods of Zionist settlement, some 75 per cent of the Jewish population of Israel lived in urban areas. The negative ideological attitude to city life remained, however, and left its mark on urban development. Per capita allocations of national resources favoured the rural sector, and the older cities and towns were allowed to grow without planning. Thus, their functional problems increased and distressed neighbourhoods developed in their hearts and on their outskirts. For a few decades these problems did not receive any public attention because government leaders were concerned almost exclusively with rural development.

Another contributing factor is the preference for new development which is rooted in a long historical process which started at the beginning of the modern Jewish settlement in the land of Israel, when the ideal of "pioneering" began to dominate the national consciousness. An institutional structure was established which served the values of pioneering, while preservation and renewal of the old were neglected. Some thirty new towns were established, most of them in remote development areas. Most resources allocated to construction in the urban sector were invested in these new development towns. Very little was set aside for maintenance and rehabilitiation of the old cities and towns.

Some of the publicly built neighbourhoods suffered heavily from planning deficiencies which contributed to their deterioration. These included a lack of flexibility and space for changes in the future, inadequate infrastructural facilities, a delay of years in the provision of accessible social services, and the low standards of such services. In several cases whole areas were populated with homogenenous low-income families, thus creating a distressed area from the start.

Social and economic processes. When a neighbourhood starts to deteriorate because of one or more of the conditions described above, the return on investments decreases and, as a consequence, the amount of investment decreases until it is not adequate to maintain and renew the various systems. Hence, the process of decline is sharpened, investments become even less profitable and the cycle is repeated.

Social problems which are territorially concentrated are aggravated. Many social problems, such as those related to the functioning of families, child education, social apathy, and crime and deliquency, reflect deviate social norms, compared to those accepted by the surrounding society. When such problems are goegraphically concentrated, those who uphold the deviate norms are supported by the people in their environment. Such social support, especially in an environment of social anomie which is typical of groups of immigrants, aggravates the deviance and promotes its spread through the community and from generation to generation.

Another major cause of deterioration is the process of spatial separation of socio-economic groups whereby a residue of weak and problematic families is left within certain neighbourhoods. Voluntary ecological segregation occurs when an individual or a family decides to move away to an area populated by people whose status is more similar to their own or to whose status they aspire. This usually happens when a household is in a state of upward mobility and strives to express its improved condition by residence in an area of a higher status. There is evidence of segregation in all urban residential areas, but its processes are sharpest in urban neighbourhoods whose relative image has started to deteriorate as a consequence of one or more of the above factors. Strong households, i.e. those with relatively more economic, social and psychological resources, tend to leave these less desirable environments. Hence, a voluntary process of segregation begins. On the other hand, involuntary segregation operates when weak households, those which cannot afford other choices, are obliged to continue living in the neighbourhood or to enter it because its prices are decreasing. As a result, the surrounding social and physical conditions deteriorate, the area becomes even less desirable and the process of negative selection of residents accelerates.

Although this is only a secondary cause which follows one or more of the primary causes mentioned above, it is a most powerful factor and may cause a neighbourhood to die. In South Bronx, New York, these processes have reached their peak resulting in ghost neighbourhoods, in the midst of the big city. In certain areas most buildings are deserted, even though it would be physically possible and even economic to repair them. Only a few apartments are occupied, usually by elderly people, often without connection to energy sources. Other residents are delinquents and gangs who constantly harass the remaining population and passers-by.

REHABILITATING SLUMS IN ISRAEL

These conditions, practices and processes caused the deterioration of many urban neighbourhoods in Israel as well. In 1965 the Israeli parliament passed the Slum Clearance and Redevelopment Act, but the agency founded in terms of this law accomplished very little throughout the twelve years of its existence. Meanwhile several governmental-municipal companies were relocating poor families. But this assistance to individual families was usually restricted to their housing and had very little to do with their social problems and the problems of the whole community. Thus, the processes of deterioration of residential areas continued and accelerated and in 1975 the Ministry of Housing published a list of 160 neighbourhoods which qualified for rehabilitation. These accounted for half a million people, about 15 per cent of Israel's total population.[4]

According to our definition, deterioration and distress are relative conditions, measured against what is acceptable in a certain society. Since the Israeli standard of living is not low by international standards, the general circumstances of the "distressed" neighbourhoods are not desperate. Most residents of these neighbourhoods are members of stable families. In most of these areas there are still a considerable number of "strong" families of blue-collar or even white-collar workers. In many neighbourhoods there is also a high percentage of welfare-dependents. Many have a more or less organised local leadership. Crime, especially juvenile delinquency, is a common problem, but the rate of law violations is relatively low.

There are several distressed neighbourhoods in which most housing units are owned by their occupants, but the most frequent form of tenure in these areas is that of renting public housing. Usually, the neighbourhoods are not located on very expensive urban land. Only a few are close to the CBDs and a few more are in desirable residential quarters, but most are found on land for which there is medium or less than medium demand. Most dwelling units are neglected but still structurally sound and have the basic facilities of toilet, bathroom and kitchen. Neglect is mainly visible in the public parts of the building, the yards and in the public areas.

After the election of May 1977, a new coalition of parties took over the government of Israel. Within a few months this new government announced a plan for rehabilitating the 160 slum neighbourhoods. There are three kinds of motivations behind this plan. The first is a political motivation. The new government was widely supported by residents of the slums in the big cities and the development towns. It therefore has a political debt to pay. Secondly, there is a social motivation. There is a sincere wish by all parties to narrow the gap between the haves and have-nots. Some are inspired by concern for equality in the society, while others are concerned by the fact that most of the haves are of Western origin (Europe and America) while most of the have-nots are of Eastern origin (Asia and Africa) and this threatens national unity. The result is that all parties are genuinely interested in improving the living conditions of low-income families. Finally, there is a special motivation. In order to mobilise the Jewish people through the world to help Israel deal with its pressing problems, it was suggested that specific Jewish communities abroad adopt a slum neighbourhood in Israel and participate in its rehabilitation. Hence, the project also served to strengthen the bonds between the Jews of Israel and those of other countries.

These motivations are very different from those behind urban renewal in other countries. In the United States, objectives such as the expansion of the economic base of the city, an increase in the real estate tax base, and the rejuvenation of the central business district play a central role.[5] In England, concern for the deteriorating housing stock is the main motive.[6] None of these motives had much weight in the Israeli government's decision to invervene in distressed neighbourhoods. Here the issues remain social and political, and neighbourhood rehabilitation, currently the main domestic project of the government, is actually a social experiment in solving the problems of families in distress. There is a strong political commitment by the government to achieve some success in this experiment.

PRINCIPLES OF REHABILITATION
Based on the analysis of the causes of deterioration and the accumulated experience of planners, a list of principles for neighbourhood rehabilitation was developed.

Comprehensiveness. Since the processes of neighbourhood deterioration are multi-faceted, the approach to their rehabilitation must be likewise. According to Ashby, as quoted by McLoughlin, "the variety of a set of outcomes arising from disturbances to a system can only be reduced in proportion to the variety of a regulator associated with that system".[7] The interaction between the various causes of deterioration calls for a comprehensive approach, involving a combination of physical and social rehabilitation.

Physical rehabilitation is concerned with all the various levels of the physical hierarchy - the dwelling, the building, the block and the neighbourhood. At each level, the rehabilitation improves the substandard or malfunctioning structures and infrastructure and provides the additional facilities necessary to bring the physical environment up to acceptable standards.

In the past, social rehabilitation focused on the community organisation necessary to promote and maintain the physical rehabilitation. At present it relates to the treatment of all the social and economic problems in the neighbourhood. There is a social problem in a neighbourhood when the proportion of people suffering from a particular problem is significantly greater than the proportion of people suffering from it in the society as a whole. Typical social problems may be illiteracy, unemployment, poverty, dependence on social welfare payments, health and educational problems, problems relating to the structure and functioning of the family, violence, delinquency and crime, feelings of relative deprivation and expressions of alienation from society in general. Programmes aimed at improvement in each of these areas may be part of the rehabilitation project.

While it is not feasible to solve all social problems in these diverse areas in the context of neighbourhood rehabilitation, it is possible to identify those areas in which the gap between the neighbourhood and Israeli society in general is especially wide. Such neighbourhood improvements will be oriented to the needs of its residents. Indeed, it is possible, sometimes desirable, that several neighbourhood facilities should serve the needs of people in adjoining neighbourhoods as well. As a rule, the facilities will be funded by the rehabilitation project only if the main beneficiaries are the residents of the rehabilitated neighbourhood.

The comprehensiveness of the approach also has a bearing on the composition of the planning team. Since the rehabilitation of the neighbourhood covers diverse aspects, it is imperative that the planning be carried out on a multi-disciplinary basis. Hence, planning teams should be composed of experts in urban planning, economics, sociology, psychology, education, social and community work, urban law and urban administration, who are able to communicate well with one another to ensure that proposals are well integrated. The comprehensive approach is achieved by the participation of governmental planning authorities responsible for housing and infrastructure, education, health, welfare, labour, community and other services at the national and local levels. At the same time, it is recognised that implementation in the field may be the responsibility of individual sectoral authorities.

Neighbourhood focus. In a departure from other traditional social welfare programmes whereby funds are allocated on a national and sectoral basis for education, vocational training, housing, health and other services, the new government plan provided for the allocation of resources in the rehabilitation programme on a geographical, i.e. neighbourhood, basis.

This decision was based mainly on the accumulation of experience in providing various social services, where those responsible had come to the conclusion independently that they might achieve better results if they treated the neighbourhoods as the administrative and planning unit for the provision of services, particularly in distressed neighbourhoods. For example, the Israeli educational authorities, which had for many years conducted special programmes at the national level for the socially and culturally deprived, recently adopted a neighbourhood focus in a welfare programme which converges on specific neighbourhoods and bestows considerable authority on the local educational community. The Ministry of Welfare is gradually devoting more resources to community work in residential areas, in preference to individual case work. The social workers' association has even proposed a reorganisation of the national welfare services based on neighbourhood roof managements.[8]

Another basic argument is that by focusing on neighbourhoods one is likely to open social mobility channels to their residents. Also narrowing the social gap by raising the status of the distressed population is a central purpose of the rehabilitation project. Thus, residents are provided with employment opportunities related to the rehabilitation process in the neighbourhood (workers, contractors, para-professions, etc) and they are involved in the political process by establishing community committees as part of the rehabilitation effort. Furthermore, as sociologists (for example, Dobriner[9]) have pointed out, the social status of an individual is, among other things, a function of his residential neighbourhood. Hence, by improving the image of the neighbourhood the social status of the residents is likewise enhanced.

Rehabilitation rather than redevelopment. In the middle of the 1960s the government of Isreal set up the Slum Clearance and Redevelopment Authority which initiated projects in neighbourhoods in various parts of the country. At the same time, several municipal-governmental companies were engaged in some major relocation projects in the larger cities of Israel. The lessons of these activities slowly accumulated and it was realised that while in almost all cases the standards of housing of the relocated people were clearly raised, their social problems were not eased. Furthermore, the positive social features of the slum neighbourhoods, such as the supportive extended family structure, and community facilities, such as the small synagogues whose congregations were composed of people coming from the same area in the old country, disappeared when the slum residents were relocated. The destruction of these institutions aggravated the social problems of the young as well as the elderly people. Moreover, the relocation of the slum population usually removed them from city centres and imposed additional transport costs and greater travel time to job opportunities and to traditional shopping areas such as open-air markets that were previously easily accessible. In this way, their economic situation was made more difficult. Thus, new neighbourhoods built for the relocated population rapidly deteriorated, and where these people were introduced into established residential areas, their neighbours dissociated themselves from them and the social image of these neighbourhoods gradually deteriorated.

In the light of the above it was decided to minimise slum clearance and relocation in the new programme and to emphasise the rehabilition of existing neighbourhoods, thus enabling the residents to stay on in their familiar physical and social environment.

Resident participation. Participation by residents in the rehabilitation process is seen as an important element of rehabilitation. Thus, while it is recognised that resident participation will both complicate and extend the process, it is considered an essential principle. In this way the residents are made to realise that they have the right and ability to decide and do things for themselves and for their neighbourhoods. This is designed to break the psychological state of dependence, in which they tend to rely on various government agencies to do things for them while their only initiative is in making demands for more assistance.

Involvement of the residents is expressed in different ways and at various stages of the rehabilitation process. Resident participation in the overall planning of the rehabilitation of each neighbourhood is achieved by setting up local steering committees in which local representatives vote side by side with representatives of local and central governments. The steering committee is sometimes assisted by subcommittees of residents and specialists preparing specific programmes on selected aspects. In this way, residents participate directly in the decision-making process, from the initial stages of problem definition to the adoption of the integrated rehabilitation programme.

Participation in the planning and implementation of housing rehabilitation varies according to the housing tenure. Where the dwelling units are owned by the residents, owner-initiated physical rehabilitation is encouraged. In many distressed neighbourhoods, such self-initiated extensions and renovations are frequent and methods for stimulating these activities are being studied. Where the housing units are publicly owned, residents are to participate in planning and partly in financing the rehabilitation of their individual apartments as well as their residential block and courtyard. Voluntary work by residents (adults, youths and children) is encouraged, especially in jobs such as cleaning, painting and gardening or assistance to the aged and disabled, thus developing and giving expression to a sense of mutual responsibility. It is recommended that residents be employed in the rehabilitation work as workers (skilled or unskilled), as contractors for construction and infrastructure, and as para-professionals in health, education and welfare services. Thus, residents will be direct beneficiaries of public investments in the rehabilitation and will have a greater sense of identification with the entire rehabilitation effort.

Meeting the aspirations of all. In the rehabilitation of distressed neighbourhoods it is customary to focus only on the needs of the disadvantaged families in order to improve their situation. We consider this a mistake. Our analysis of the causes of deterioration showed that the negative selection of residents in a neighbourhood, i.e. the exodus of its stronger elements, is the crucial factor that may lead to further deterioration and total abandonment. Hence, if one wants to stop the process of deterioration, this exodus should be stopped by providing opportunities for the people to realise their aspirations for social mobility within the neighbourhood. If this is not done, and the stronger elements leave the area, the neighbourhood will deteriorate further even if heavy inputs are provided, because services solely provided for a poor population are usually poor services.

This implies that success in rehabilitating a neighbourhood depends on its having such strong elements, i.e. people with relatively greater economic, social and psychological resources, among its residents. As has been stated, such people can be found in most distressed neighbourhoods in Israel. They have stable families with one or more breadwinners who are skilled blue-collar or even white-collar workers. In many cases, they own their homes and care for their immediate environment. Usually, their desire for social mobility is strong and therefore they tend to leave the distressed areas in due course. This tendency can be reversed if these people can realise their aspirations in their current areas of residence, if they are given subsidies for better housing in the same area if not in the same building, and if they are provided with openings for local leadership and opportunites for better jobs.

At the same time, help should be provided for the disadvantaged residents of the neighbourhood. It is immoral to help those better off and neglect those worse off, even if the assistance to the stronger people will indirectly help the weaker ones. Secondly, if the gap between the living conditions of the more affluent and those of the poorer segments of the population in the neighbourhood is too great, no incentives will keep the former in physical proximity to the latter.

By raising the standard of living of the weak families and keeping the existing stronger families in the neighbourhood, relatively strong new people may be attracted to live there. If this happens, then the process of rehabilitation is well on its way.

Flexibility. Adaptability in the planning process in the face of an uncertain future is desirable in any event. This is particularly so when dealing with something as complicated as a slum neighbourhood. As has been suggested by some writers (for example, Cartwright[10]), the more complex the planning problem, and the comprehensive rehabilitation of slum neighbourhoods is undoubtedly a complex problem, the more the planner should proceed incrementy. This permits the planner to learn the effects of the implementation of small and short-range changes, pointing to other changes which become necessary as the programme evolves. The concept of the growing programme is in good currency in Israel. This implies that the planning leaves room for future changes, not only in the policies and courses of action to be implemented, but also in the general orientation and objectives. Such changes are apt to flow from the development of ideas, from experience gained and from transformations in the social and political environments. It is therefore important to leave future options as open as possible.

A second aspect of flexibility relates to the avoidance of model solutions. Each neighbourhood is approached independently and its programmes are determined according to its peculiar characteristics and problems by an independent steering committee and planning team.

A third aspect of flexibility relates to the planned physical system. It is recognised that the very rigidity of the physical systems has been responsible for the poor fit between the changing needs of the population and the physical environment, which detracts from the quality of life and contributes to physical deterioration. In order to overcome this, flexibility should be introduced in the housing systems, and multi-purpose and adjustable uses should be planned for the semi-public and public spaces in the neighbourhood. [11]

Administrative structure. In Israel, bureaucratic structures serving urban and regional development tend to be concentrated at the central government level. By contrast, the statutory planning system is hierarchically structured with specific responsibilities divided among the national planning council, district councils and local planning councils. [12] [13] [14]

The neighbourhood rehabilitation programme has been based on an administrative structure that is vertically decentralised and horizontally centralised. The vertical decentralisation implies that the authority to plan and implement the rehabilitation programme is shared between various levels of government - the central government and the neighbourhood steering committee. Horizontal centralisation means that a central body coordinates the decision-making at each level. In this way, decision-making is shared by various levels of government, but coordination and accountability is assured.

At the central government level there is a coordinating committee representative of both the government ministries involved in neighbourhood rehabilitation and the Jewish Agency. The agency, representative of Jewish communities throughout the world, provides half the budget for the rehabilitation programme, the other half being allocated by the Israeli government. The coordinating committee is jointly headed by the deputy Prime Minister and the chairman of the Jewish agency. Other participants are the Ministers of Housing, Welfare, Labour, Education, Health and the Interior. In the larger cities of Jerusalem, Tel Aviv and Haifa, there is a committee to coordinate all rehabilitation projects in the city. Special companies, jointly owned by the municipalities and the Ministry of Housing, oversee the implementation of these projects. At the neighbourhood level, there is a steering committee responsible for preparing detailed social and physical plans with budget proposals. The neighbourhood steering committee is headed by the mayor and includes representatives of relevant municipal departments, such as engineering, education and welfare, and local representatives of relevant ministries such as health, education, welfare, housing, as well as representatives of the residents in the neighbourhoods.

CONCLUSION

The characteristics of slum neighbourhoods in Israel are peculiar to the country, but the causes of their deterioration are similar to those of other countries. Socio-economic segregation and negative selection of residents in less desirable neighbourhoods are evident in every city, as well as disinvestment in deteriorating areas. Social and physical conditions may differ in detail. For example, in Israel the problems were caused by the mass immigration of refugees, especially from the Arab countries, while in other countries they are generated by internal migration, especially from rural regions. In fact, the problems are similiar because they are caused by difficulties in adapting to work, housing and generally to life in the modern city on the part of residents who have grown up in different cultures.

If the problems and their causes are similar, the principles developed for the rehabilitation project in Israel may very well be relevant to other countries. Indeed, several of them were suggested by previous programmes elsewhere, especially the Demonstration Cities Programme (Model Cities) in the United States of the late 1960s. But the Israeli approach is distinctive at least in two respects.

First, while former programmes focused on the disadvantaged in the neighbourhoods, the Israeli project is intended to meet the aspirations of the strong population as well, in an attempt to counter the most powerful cause of deterioration: the negative selection of residents in deteriorating areas. Secondly, all these principles are being transferred from the heads and desks of the planners and the decision-makers to the distressed neighbourhoods. The process is slow and fraught with many obstacles at all levels of planning and implementation. But there are built-in evaluations at various points in the process, and in due course we shall have empirical evidence on the successes and failures of the programme in realising the social and physical goals of the project of neighbourhood rehabilitation in Israel.

REFERENCES

[1] Carmon, N., Attaining social goals through housing policy (1975), Dissertation submitted to the Senate of the Technion-Israel, Institute of Technology, Haifa (Hebrew); and Carmon, N., and Hill, M., Rehabilitation of distressed neighbourhoods in Israel (1979), Research report, Samuel Neaman Institute, Technion-Israel Institute of Technology, PN 02/79/100.

[2] Haber, A., Population and building in Israel: 1948-73 (1975), Ministry of Housing, Programming Department, Jerusalem.

[3] Titmuss, R., Social policy and economic progress (1966), paper presented at the National Conference on Social Welfare, Chicago.

[4] Ministry of Housing, Neighbourhood rehabilitation (1977), Jerusalem (Hebrew).

[5] Rapkin, C., An evaluation of the urban renewal experience in the United States, Research report, Samuel Neaman Institute, Technion.

[6] Rose, E., Urban renewal in the United Kingdom: a criticial review and evaluation (1979), Research report, Samuel Neaman Institute, Technion.

[7] McLoughlin, S.B., Control and urban planning (1973), Faber, page 218.

[8] Hahistadrut Halkalit Shel Haovdim Be-Eretz Israel, Social Workers Association, and Jerusalem Committee for Social Policy, A proposal for comprehensive organisation of local welfare services (1977), Jerusalem

[9] Dobriner, W.M., Class in suburbia (1963), Prentice-Hall.

[10] Cartwright, T., "Problems, solutions and strategies: contribution to the theory and practice of planning", Journal of the American Institute of Planners (1973), pages 179-87.

[11] Hill, M., and Alterman, R., Land use planning standards: open space (1977) Research report, Centre for Urban and Regional Studies, Technion (Hebrew).

[12] Akzin, B., and Dror, Y., Israel high pressure planning (1966), Syracuse University Press.

[13] Hill, M., Planning in turbulence - physical planning in Israel (1978), Working Paper 78, Centre for Urban and Regional Studies, Technion.

[14] Oxman, R., Meyer-Brodnitz, M., and Amit, Y., Planning and development of dynamic housing systems (1978), Research report, Centre for Urban and Regional Studies, Technion.

Community participation in urban renewal

19

Dan Soen   Israel

INTRODUCTION

Urban renewal as a government programme is a widely discussed and most controversial issue in more than one country. James Wilson writes that the United States spends much more on farm subsidies and highways than on urban renewal, yet these programmes - except for an occasional scandal - are rarely debated outside the circle of immediate participants and their scholarly observers.[1] What is more, there are other federal housing programmes in the United States, the collective impact of which has in the past been considerably greater than that of urban renewal, yet only seldom in recent years have they been the objects of general public discussion. Last but not least, the decisions of a variety of more or less obscure regulatory commissions in Washington more likely than not affect the lives of more people than does urban renewal, yet very rarely does one encounter the names of these agencies in print, much less an argument over their politics.

On the other hand, for years now urban renewal has been the object of the closest scrutiny in learned books as well as in the pages of both popular and esoteric magazines, in newspaper editorials as well as in news accounts of citizen meetings and city council hearings.

According to Professor Rapkin, in recent years urban planning throughout the world has become much more comprehensive in scope, adding economic, political and social policies to its basic concern with the built environment.[2] At the same time there has been a shift away from end-state plans to a greater flexibility of efforts designed for a more immediate future. These changes have brought urban planning closer to the interests, concerns and comprehension of the general public, particularly the poor and the minorities. These groups have become more politicised by the civil rights movement, the effort to decentralise education, and the example of student protests. In this process, the role of the planner has been converted from that of the technical expert whose decisions are final to that of a formulator of alternatives, leaving urban policy to emerge from the interplay of conflicting interests in the political area.

Citizen or community participation is now generally taken to be a necessary precondition for the successful implementation of any renewal or rehabilitation project. Whereas the slogan "planning is for the people" has been part of the professional jargon for many decades, in recent years the leaders of the rebelling inhabitants of urban American ghettos have vociferously made it clear that nothing can be done for them, only by them and most certainly with them.[3] During the past year, similar voices have been heard from the leaders of several renewal neighbourhoods in Israel. H.W. Eldredge has stated that "this is merely an extreme underlining of the new mood in urban planning, the somewhat belated recognition that for new cities, new people are necessary".[4]

On the whole, it is now accepted that community participation in the decision-making process on renewal and rehabilitation is desirable. Many regard the involvement of citizens in this process as a manifestation of participatory democracy and, as such, it is seen as a highly commendable activity and an end in itself.[5] Others see in community participation a superior strategy for successfully enlisting popular support for projects concerning the community.[6] D.R. Hunter has stated that "the process of improvement is not likely to strike very deep unless the target people themselves are part ot it. In practice this means that parents must support, or at least not resist, efforts to improve slum schools and the performance of their children in those schools. The adults of a neighbourhood must cooperate with and help the efforts to control delinquent behaviour. They must support the pressure and political tactics designed to persuade decision makers to make the decisions that will tend to improve slum conditions".[7]

CHANGE FROM ECONOMIC GROWTH TO SOCIAL CONCERN

Community participation has been promoted by a number of changes in general public attitudes.[8] First, there has been a shift away from emphasis exclusively on economic growth to a greater degree of concern for an equitable distribution of the aggregate product. In the United States this has been linked to a subtle but discernible trend in attitude away from equal opportunity towards equal shares. It has also been associated with an increasing demand for an improvement in the quality of life, even at the expense of the quantity of income. Finally, it is also manifest in the declining premium on economic efficiency and the rising concern for human welfare and a more humane scale.

There has also been a devaluation of the earlier achievements of urban planners. Public housing estates once considered commendable efforts to change the residential environment of the poor on a massive scale are now viewed as ghettos for the minorities and the indigent. High-rise buildings and super highways have had a similar decline in applause because they achieved their original purpose all too well or because the value system on which they were based has changed.

The actual problems of implementing community participation in practice are numerous and complex. In fact, many of those who at one time were committeed to the idea have become frustrated and have given it up as a bad job. Others have oversimplified the issues by describing and tackling them in terms of a power struggle between the haves and the have-nots.[9]

The United States Workable Programme for Community Development demands that a community demonstrate that it has made provision for the participation of citizens in its renewal effort. This requirement presupposes that all individuals and groups within a community are equally capable of participating in the renewal process. This assumption is, of course, highly questionable. In fact, it is now taken for granted that there are prerequisites for participation not possessed by all groups and strata within a community.[10] One expert has gone even further by claiming that the rehabilitation and renewal process depends on a miniscule segment of the local population, "the indispensable one-hundredth of one per cent".[11] In any event, it used to be assumed that a citizen should have direct and continuing opportunities to influence the administration of a programme, all the more so if he is a prospective beneficiary of the programme.

Yet the alternative structures created have repeatedly encountered similar problems and have ultimately failed to serve programme beneficiaries. These problems include, first, that unavoidable conflict for control exists between lay participants and the often technically trained providers of the service; secondly, that existing local organisations do not appear to provide normally for participation by anyone other than members of local élites who themselves are not usually beneficiaries; thirdly, that the development of participation in new local organisations often leads to excessive community conflict and possible cooptation by the local élites; and fourthly, that where participation has been dominated by beneficiaries, they have usually been concerned with the transmittal of information or some other perfunctory activities, not actions permitting the beneficiaries to exert any real influence or control.[12]

PARTICIPATION AS COUNTER TO CENTRALISED CONTROL

All other things being equal, it is still asserted that the need for effective citizen participation in the rehabilitation process is as great as ever, for two reasons in particular: the continued centralisation of power within the government on the one hand, and the increased technical specialisation required to administer public programmes on the other. It has been claimed that these trends have helped to widen the gap between the decision-making process for public programmes and the programmes' beneficiaries.[13] The result is the phenomenon referred to as alienation.

One way of successfully combating this alienation is through citizen and community participation. Citizens show up in the planning process at three levels: as individual objects, as individual participators or actors, and as group participants.[14] As objects, citizens can be the target of public relations and public education, or participants in the planning process. It is now customary in the United States to involve them at the community level in boot-strap operations.

Community participation is a means of involving people outside government in the planning process. It is particularly aimed at poor people who frequently are the uncompensated and powerless victims of city rebuilding. The powerlessness of the poor is nowhere more vivid than in public or private urban renewal. In the past this process has often asserted that the land under the homes of the poor is more valuable if used for some other purpose. The planning decisions are made by others for the benefit of still others. The exclusion of the poor from the process make them suspicious of government action and the planners' purpose, particularly when the purpose is not clear or the time lag too long. In the past it has meant withdrawal or, if the political climate was right, violence. Powerlessness breeds frustration and frustration leads to explosion.

Urban planning, particularly at the neighbourhood level, provides an opportunity for residents to participate in setting their own goals and building their own future. The local residents know their own social and economic needs best. These have budgetary and land use implications and planning helps translate them into operational terms.[15]

Sherry R. Arnstein maintains that "citizen participation is a categorical term for citizen power...participation without redistribution of power is an empty and frustrating process for the powerless. It allows the power holders to claim that all sides were considered but makes it possible for only some to benefit. It maintains the status quo".[16] To illustrate her point, she arranges the eight levels of participation in a ladder pattern with each rung corresponding to the extent of citizens' power in determining the end product.[17] The bottom rungs of the eight-runged ladder are (1) manipulation and (2) therapy. They describe levels of "non-participation" contrived by some to substitute for genuine participation. Their real objective is not to allow people to participate in planning or conducting programmes, but rather to permit the power-holders to "educate" or "cure" the participants. Rungs 3 (informing) and 4 (consultation) represent levels of "tokenism" that allow the have-nots to hear and have a voice. When this is the total extent of participation, citizens may indeed hear and be heard, but they lack the power to ensure that their views will be heeded by the powerful. When participation is restricted to these levels, there is no follow-through, no "muscle", hence no assurance of changing the status quo. Rung 5 (placation) is simply a higher level "tokenism", because the ground rules allow have-nots to advise but retain for the power-holders the continued rights to decide. Further up the ladder are levels of citizen power with increasing degrees of decision-making clout. Citizens can enter into a partnership (6) that permits them to negotiate in trade-offs with traditional power holders. At the topmost rungs, (7) delegated power and (8) citizen control, have-not citizens obtain the majority of decision-making seats or full managerial power.

FUNCTIONS AND TECHNIQUES OF PARTICIPATION CODIFIED

As community participation has grown, the functions performed and the techniques used have increased in number and variety. Judy B. Rosener has compiled a list of fourteen functions and thirty-nine techniques and has cross-tabulated them in order to determine which functions a specific technique will serve.[18] The most frequent functions are identification of attitudes and opinions, facilitation of participation, classification of plan process and the determination of the plan programme and policy review. The most versatile techniques determined by the number of functions served are the following:

□ Charette: the assembly of interest groups for intensive meetings.
□ Citizen's advisory committee: an ad hoc organisation of citizens to present the ideas and attitudes of local groups.
□ Citizen employment: the direct employment of client representatives.
□ Coordinator: a focal point for citizen participation in a single individual.
□ Design-in: a technique which allows citizens to see the effect of a project or plan on their community.
□ Fish-bowl planning: an open planning process in which all parties express their views before a proposal is adopted.
□ Meetings (community sponsor): organised to focus on a particular plan or project.
□ Open-door policy: encouragement of citizens to visit local project office without prior appointment.
□ Short conference: intensive meetings organised around a detailed agenda.
□ Workshops: working sessions to discuss an issue and to reach an understanding of its role in the planning process.

Once the question of power and control has been settled in favour of community participation in decision-making, one is faced with a second type of problem, namely that of reconciling participatory democracy with rational management procedures and professional expertise.[19] George Bernard Shaw, in the pioneering days of broadcasting, pinpointed the basic issues with his accustomed lucidity and wit. Speaking of democracy as "government of the people...for the people and by the people", he declared: "...we repudiate number three (i.e. government by the people) on the ground that the people cannot govern. The thing is a physical impossibility. Every citizen cannot be a ruler any more than every boy can be an engine driver or a pirate king...If you doubt this, if you ask me, 'Why should not the people make their own laws?' I need only ask you, 'Why should not the people write their own plays?' They cannot. It is much easier to write a good play than to make a good law. And there are not a hundred men in the world who can write a play good enough to stand the daily wear and tear as long as a law must."[20]

There is an obvious parallel with planning here.[21] Quite apart from the fact that not even a majority of citizens can be expected to possess the required knowledge and skills, it would make the process of planning too cumbersome and unwieldy. Clearly, total community participation, in the sense of the early American town meeting, is impossible. Participation must, therefore, take the form of representation.

While it is by no means certain that the elected representatives of a community will be any more qualified professionally to participate in the planning process than their constituents, there is at least the chance that, given sufficient time and direct effort, they may become so qualified. Besides, professional qualification is not the real issue, but rather the legitimacy and relevance of non-professional considerations to the decision that has to be made. These problems have received much attention, and various strategies have been suggested to make such participation more meaningful and effective.[22] Basically, the problem here is communication. It is notoriously difficult for professionals to make themselves clearly understood by anyone outside their discipline, or to make others follow the logic or see the necessity of one way of reasoning as against another. Conversely, the community representatives are at a disadvantage when trying to present their case, since by definition theirs is a layman's view of the issues, with all the prestige of professional expertise pitted against them.

THE HALAMISH EXAMPLE: TEL KABIR AND THE CHARETTE TECHNIQUE

Frustrating as these difficulties may be, they can be overcome, provided there is sufficient goodwill on both sides. A case in point is the substantial participation initiated a few years ago in Tel Aviv by Halamish, a public corporation entrusted with the task of urban renewal and rehabilitation in the biggest metropolitan centre of Israel.[23] The project - so far the only one on this scale in Israel - involved the planning of a central community centre in a new neighbourhood, Tel Kabir, populated by roughly 6000 people, most of them blue-collar workers and their families, transferred to the location from their substandard dwellings. The Tel Kabir quarter is located in the south-eastern part of Tel Aviv. The western boundary lies on the road to Holon, a satellite of Tel Aviv. Construction of the neighbourhood began six years ago and is not yet complete. Most houses are four storeys high and surrounded by decorative plants.

Residents came from southern and central Tel Aviv, and from various parts of Jaffa, the old part of Tel Aviv previously inhabited by Arabs. The majority are families with children, the remainder being young couples and senior citizens, while several blocks are occupied by new immigrants. The services available in the quarter include sick fund facilities, an infant care centre, day nurseries, kindergartens, two elementary schools, a youth club, a women's club and several shops. Because of the considerable distance to the centre of town, the neighbourhood itself has to provide services for residents.

In July 1976 a meeting was held between the director-general of Halamish, head of the company's department for community work, and the chairman of the Institute for the Development of Educational Buildings. The latter informed the meeting of the intention to establish a community centre in one of Tel Aviv's neighbourhoods and asked the director-general and the community work department head for their advice on the choice of neighbourhood. They came to the conclusion that the need for such a centre was most urgent in Tel Kabir where the prospect of success was also fair. The neighbourhood was attractive and well developed, but rather remote from the town and its services and therefore evinced a low self-image. The residents wanted to counteract this image and the establishment of a community centre with their participation from the very first stages of planning would make a contribution. The fact that the neighbourhood was new and the residents were powerfully motivated for improvement, improved the prospects for the success of a community centre. Resident participation in planning might ensure that the building is put up in accordance with the specific needs of the Tel Kabir population and would thus become a focus of active communal life.

After the acceptance of the idea in principle, members of the Institute for the Development of Educational Buildings proposed the charette technique for involving the residents in planning. Charette is a French term meaning "carriage". After students of architecture had worked for many days on a building plan, they travelled in a carriage to the university to submit their drawings, and during their journey introduced final amendments in the plans while helping one another. Since then this term has been used to describe a process of intensive group work on a plan, limited to a given period of time. Intensive activity in a limited span of time is the most important characteristic of the charette process. It brings many community members into involvement in defining the public needs and in the efforts to find adequate solutions.

The idea was to involve the groups in studying and solving problems arising in the development of public buildings in the context of public needs. The principal characteristics of the techniques as applied here were maximum participation by residents and representative of the public, and brief, intensive work periods.

The initiators of the project envisaged three stages in the citizens' participation:
☐ Preliminary planning - outlining a general framework for the proposals while defining accurately the purposes and targets.
☐ Steering committee - setting up a committee of residents to take the project through all its stages, organising the charette, publicising the idea in the neighbourhood, examining the needs, defining the aims, considering the issues associated with communal activities, appointing the participants of the charette and its timetable.
☐ The charette - after a period of preliminary preparation, the charette would be held as a day of intensive workshops, with the participation of residents and representatives of the relevant government and municipal offices, planners and financiers, discussing the issues raised during the period of preparation and arriving at final conclusions.

Several aspects of the project were examined before work began. While the charette offered a basic technique for involving the population in the planning process, the initiators had no idea how the residents could be given the mental tools to think through and consider involved subjects in the field of architecture and planning, or how they could be imbued with the courage to discuss such subjects with architects and heads of the various public agencies. Nor was there any certainty that these professionals and public servants would agree to discuss these professional matters with laymen or to consider non-professional opinions seriously.

The community workers were aware that the idea of a community centre originated from the establishment, although it was in essence designed to meet the neighbourhood's needs. It was not even certain that the neighbourhood's residents would accept the proposal. In spite of these initial doubts, the community workers considered an additional aspect of the project. The residents' activities in establishing a community centre could lead to more community purposes, e.g. the organisation of the residents and attention to their needs, and a definition of priorities. Such consideration and examination of the mode of life at Tel Kabir could create a sense of identification with and belonging to the quarter among its population and enhance their cohesion.

During discussions held by the community workers in November 1976 with members of the Institute for the Development of Educational Buildings it was unanimously agreed that it was of vital importance to work closely with the population and the establishment. The need was recognised of interaction between these two. As a result, two areas of activity were outlined. Coordination with the relevant government and municipal agencies was seen as of decisive importance to the success of the project. The bodies concerned were the Ministry of Housing, the Ministry of Education, the City Council of Tel Aviv, the Halamish Corporation, the Community Centres Corporation, the plan's architect and the Institute for the Development of Educational Buildings. Their cooperation ensured that all grades of participants - top, intermediate and local - would work in parallel towards the common goal.

Before the operating team was chosen and while action was proceeding on coordination with the agencies concerned, publicity on the project was launched in the neighbourhood to arouse the residents' interest and encourage their future participation. An unconventional idea, the project drew varied reactions. A very small number of people welcomed the proposal right from the beginning, but the general feeling was that there were more urgent matters to be dealt with. The majority were not convinced that such a centre would indeed be built in the neighbourhood. There was also opposition to "the establishment imposing responsibility on the residents", in the phrase of one Tel Kabir inhabitant.

To give the people a clearer picture of what was going to happen and to begin activating them, explanations were given to prominent people in the neighbourhood. The community workers also discussed the project with numerous inhabitants, exhibited films on the subject to the youngsters, and then held a general public meeting at the neighbourhood school which was open to all residents. The meeting was attended by one hundred people. The subject was explained in detail and a film was shown illustrating the activities of a community centre. The architect of the project then showed his preliminary sketches and explained them. The sketches were accepted as proof of an actual plan and the readiness to let the inhabitants participate in decisions even on architectural matters, though it was stressed that "no responsibility would fall on them", except to the extent that they would be partners in making the decisions.

After it had become clear to all what the issues involved were, it was decided to elect a small team that could work effectively and intensively on the project. A group of some twenty-five persons was elected from among the residents and named the Tel Kabir Steering Committee. The work of the steering committee took about six months and passed through numerous stages and developments. The following functions were defined and carried out:

□ Study of the population's needs - by special questionnaires, distributed among youngsters and adults, and summarising the findings.

□ Meetings and discussions with house and block committees, neighbours, friends and youth groups.

□ Visits to youth clubs in Jaffa and towns with community centres.

□ Meetings at which conclusions were drawn and ways outlined of continuing the work.

Following these stages, formulation began of the general lines of the plans for the community centre. Questions considered included that of a swimming pool large enough to serve all the residents, but still kept within the limits of the budget; dual-purpose use of different rooms at the centre; and matters not considered by the architect, such as the need for a senior citizens' club.

In the course of its work the committee developed into a homogeneous, self-assured body whose members trusted and reassured one another. The unity of purpose did not turn the group into a self-important body, however. On the contrary, openness of a high degree evolved. With the progress of the group's work and the first signs that the ideas were being accepted by the members of the establishment, personal development and improvement became apparent in several committee members, who learned to speak better, have more patience, and be better able to think in the abstract. Personal tension among members was relieved by persuasion and candour. The members abstained from pursuing personal interests. Attention was given to the needs of population groups not represented on the committee and the need to contact them was stressed.

The steering committee's preparatory work took five months and at the end of June 1977 the charette, the combined workshop day, was held. The meeting took place outside the neighbourhood to ensure an intensive working day unaffected by interference from the surroundings, and to offer the participants a departure from accustomed routine. The discussions lasted from 9 am to 5 pm. Apart from members of the steering committee and several additional residents, the meeting was also attended by representatives of the Ministry of Education and the Ministry of Housing, the architects, members of the municipal staff including the deputy mayor of Tel Aviv, representatives of the Halamish Rehabilitation Corporation, the Community Centres Corporation, the Institute for the Development of Educational Buildings and the executive team's consultant who had given professional guidance on the project.

The meeting split up into four workshops to deal with the following issues: development of community life, social activities, sport, and group activity rooms. Representatives of the neighbourhood and the various public agencies took part in every workshop. The dialogue between the members of the establishment and the inhabitants of the neighbourhood was held in the spirit of a joint effort towards a common goal. Serious consideration was given to the views of every participant.

In the afternoon the workshops were dissolved and the work proceeded in two ways. The architects, members of the various public agencies and representatives of the neighbourhood gathered around the programme, and sketches and the recommendations agreed to by all the workshops to discuss how these recommendations could be realised.

The success of the charette day was assured by the willingness of the residents to devote their time and energy and by the helpfulness of the members of the establishment. The preliminary coordination of all factors involved in the project markedly contributed to its success.

The remaining members of the neighbourhood team formed two groups to discuss the cultural programmes to be carried out between that stage and the establishment of the community centre. A recommendation was adopted to sponsor group activities for all ages using existing facilities in neighbourhood schools, shelters, the women's community centre and the youth club; to appoint the director of the community centre there and then; to publish a local paper; to open courses for youth leaders from Tel Kabir so as to prepare cadres for the future.

At the end of the day all the participants met in plenary session. The neighbourhood's representatives read out their recommendations for the period up to the establishment of the centre and the deputy mayor acknowledged their statements. A report was presented on the conclusions reached at the meeting of the architects and the heads of the public agencies in respect of the recommendations made on the plans for the centre. In view of the wish expressed by members of the steering committee to keep up their work for the benefit of the neighbourhood even after the conclusion of the centre, the community workers continued to guide and organise their activities. The Institute for the Development of Educational Buildings left the stage and the community workers, together with the neighbourhood's administrator (appointed by Tel Aviv Municipality) continued to work with the committee members.

To avoid an impression of stagnation, the first issue of the neighbourhood's newspaper appeared on the day the charette was held. In it the residents were told of the activities of the steering committee and the developments concerning the community centre. The members of the steering committee deemed it their duty to ensure the fulfilment of promises made by the establishment and to realise their plans. They took care to follow up plans for the community centre and pressed for the immediate election of the centre's director and the construction of temporary huts for social and cultural activities. They also initiated their own progammes for social activities in the location. For an interim programme pending the arrival of the community centre director in the neighbourhood, the committee decided to show films, organise various public competitions, present lectures and continue publication of the paper. Not all their plans were realised. Some remained unrealised for lack of time available to the initiators, and others for lack of financial means or suitable sites. What is of major importance, however, is that they became conscious of the environment and the neighbourhood's needs, so that at their own initiative some members took up the matter of transportation and one even volunteered to work with one of the street-corner gangs in the neighbourhood until the municipality found a suitable social worker to do the job. This was a valuable achievement. During the months of work with the neighbourhood's residents within the steering committee gradual progress was made toward the present situation where individuals and groups show concern for what is taking place around them and show initiative for change.

Various lessons were learned. The employment of consultants in various disciplines proved useful and productive. Cooperation with the various public agencies and the efforts made to win their consent and ensure coordination with them proved as vital and decisive for the success of a process of the present kind. There was insufficient reporting by the steering committee to the population at large on developments in respect of the community centre. The community workers urged the steering committee to show responsibility towards a wider group within the population in order to give greater legitimacy to their activities.

During all the months of the steering commmittee's work prior to the charette day and up to its conclusion, the organisers feared that the committee would see its function as limited to the planning of the community centre and would not find the time, strength and will to continue being active in the location. The community workers saw the need to encourage them to adopt a wider definition of their function and to see themselves as the neighbourhood's cultural committee that should initiate, before the centre was opened, activities for youths, adults and senior citizens in the location,

The community centre was duly completed and turned out to be the main focus of local community life. The charette technique was therefore quite a success.

CONCLUSIONS

Israel, of course, is not the only place in the world where citizen participation has started to play an active role in the planning process. In fact, as already mentioned, in the United States more and more public bodies are developing formal procedures for citizen participation in order to ensure a direct hearing for local sentiments.[24] Not only are planning departments making a greater effort to involve citizens in their day-to-day work, but local governments are setting up special advisory groups which counsel decision makers on final policy determination. In New York, for example, a codified system of community boards has been established to overcome the seeming remoteness of government. These boards advise city agencies on programmes and projects affecting their district. They may hold hearings and arrive at policy positions on the basis of majority vote. Members are appointed for overlapping terms by the presidents of their respective city boroughs. There are sixty-two boards in all. The record of these boards is mixed. Their greatest contribution has been to sharpen official understanding of local needs and wishes by pointing out facets of problems overlooked by city hall. Many times, though, local criticism is purely negative in nature, offering few constructive suggestions based in reality. To some observers these boards merely provide an opportunity for local people to vent frustrations of a general nature.

In contrast to this practice of supplying the public with an opportunity to vent frustration, a real attempt was made by the Halamish Rehabilitation Corporation of Tel Aviv to provide the citizens with increasing degrees of decision-making clout. The organisational model, now applying to all Halamish renewal neighbourhoods, involves the local citizens both vertically and horizontally in all the planning processes, as illustrated in Figure 1.[25]

Frustrating as the difficulties of communication between community representatives and the professionals may be, they can be overcome, provided there is sufficient goodwill on either side. In this regard it may not be amiss to quote George H. Sabine:

"Communication and negotiation, however, have moral as well as semantic presuppositions. They assume in a society a factor of free intelligence, not bound either to race or to social position, that can take cognisance of social forces and within limits can direct them. They assume in addition a factor of goodwill, not unrelated to intelligence and also not bound to race or social position, that intends in the direction of social forces to adjust them to one another with a minimum of friction and coercion...A genuine meeting of minds may result if each party in the negotiation will concede to the other the honour of believing, at least as an initial assumption, that its point of view is not merely vicious or silly. Without that attitude, understanding will almost certainly not result, and in a very real sense to assume that attitude is the meaning of treating another person as an equal...These attitudes make it possible that communication should issue in understanding and that negotiation should end in agreement. They are not guarantees that the process will succeed, but their absence is a guarantee that it will fail."[26]

REFERENCES

[1] Wilson, J.Q., (ed) Urban renewal: the record and controversy (1966), MIT Press.
[2] Rapkin, C., "Recent development in community participation in urban planning in the United States" (1979), ITCC Review, page 46.
[3] Eldredge, H.W., (ed). Taming megalopolis (1967), Vol II, page 954.
[4] ibid
[5] Cahn, E.S., and Cahn, J.C., "Maximum feasible participation: an overview", in Cahn, E.S., Passett, B.A. (eds) Citizen participation: effecting community change (1971), page 31.
[6] ibid, pages 16-25
[7] Hunter, D.R., The slums - challenge and response (1964), pages 174-5, The Free Press.
[8] Rapkin, C., "Recent development in community participation in urban planning in the United States", (1979), ITCC Review, page 46.
[9] Arnstein, S.R., "Eight rungs on the ladder of citizen participation" in Cahn, E.S., and Passett, B.A. (eds) Citizen participation effecting community change (1971), pages 69-91.
[10] Bellush, J., and Hausknecht, M., "Planning, participation and urban renewal" in Bellush, J., and Hausknecht, M., (eds) Urban renewal: people, politics and planning, (1967), pages 278-86, Doubleday Anchor.
[11] Bodine, J.W., "The indispensable one-hundredeth of one per cent" (1967), in Eldredge, H.W. (ed) Taming megalopolis, Vol II, pages 956-91, Doubleday Anchor.
[12] Mann, S.Z., "Community development decisional process in an urbanised world - some reflections and observations as related to citizen participation and decentralisation issues" in Soen, D., (ed) Decision process in development (1974), Association of Engineers and Architects in Israel, International Technical Cooperation Centre, Tel Aviv, page 3.
[13] Yin, R.K., Lucas, W., Szanton, P.L., and Spindler, J.A., Citizen organisations: increasing client control over services, (1973), pages 1-3, Rand Corporation.
[14] Eldredge, H.W., (ed) Taming megalopolis (1967), Vol II, page 954.
[15] Rapkin, C., "Recent development in community participation in urban planning in the United States" (1979), ITCC Review, page 47.
[16] Arnstein, S.R., "A ladder of citizen participation" (1969), Journal of the American Institute of Planners, Vol 35, page 216.
[17] ibid, page 217.
[18] Rosener, J.B., "Citizen participation: tying strategy to function" in Marshall, P., (ed) Citizen participation certification community development (1977), National Association of Housing and Redevelopment Officials, Washington, D.C.
[19] Jacobsen, C., "Problems of community participation in the planning process", in Soen, D., (ed) Decision process in development (1974), Association of Engineers and Architects in Israel, International Technical Cooperation Centre, Tel Aviv, page 16.
[20] Shaw, G.B., The apple cart: a political extravaganza (1930), pages XIV-XV.
[21] Jacobsen, C., "Problems of community participation in the planning process", in Soen, D., (ed) Decision process in development (1974), Association of Engineers and Architects in Israel, International Technical Cooperation Centre, Tel Aviv, page 16.
[22] Burke, E., "Citizen participation strategies" (1968), The Journal of The American Institute of Planners, Vol 35, pages 287-94.
[23] Lerner, R., and Wexler, N., "The charette project in Tel Kabir - resident participation in the planning of a community centre" (1979), Meydaoss, Organ of the Social Workers Association in Israel (Hebrew).
[24] Rapkin, C., and Ponte, R.W., "The decision process in urban development: the interaction of planning and politics in the US and the less developed countries", in

     Soen, D., (ed) <u>Decision process in development</u> (1974), Association of Engineers and
     Architects in Israel, International Technical Cooperation Centre, Tel Aviv, page 58.
25   Soen, D., and Hirsch, A., <u>Shen Ari neighbourhood, Jaffa D - renewal and</u>
     <u>rehabilitation programme Part 1: discussion of problems and guiding lines for</u> action
     (1979), Halamish Corporation, page 98 (Hebrew).
26   Sabine, G.H., <u>A history of political theory</u> (revised edition, 1956), pages 908-9,
     Henry Holt.

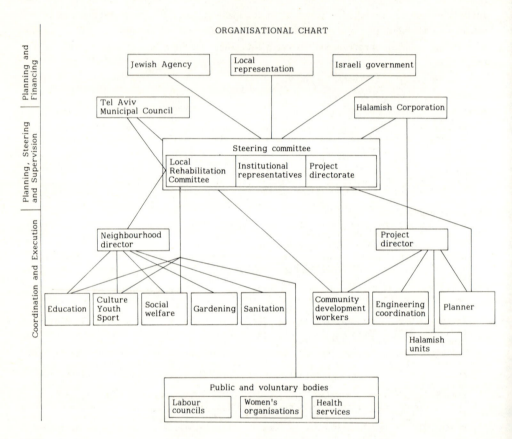

Figure 1

VII: INSTITUTIONAL RENEWAL

Urban renewal and employment initiatives at the local level

20

Edgar A. Rose   United Kingdom

INTRODUCTION

The context for United Kingdom employment studies generally, and local government employment initiatives in particular, is the attempts to regenerate the declining inner areas of our great cities, and the rise in unemployment. There is growing local authority concern about employment within their areas, especially where manufacturing industry is contracting and factory closures have had a pronounced politicial and social impact. The spatial or localised aspects of reduced levels of economic activity are no longer seen simply in terms of regional policy, or "fortunate" and "unfortunate" regions. Concern is focused on relatively small, deprived parts of cities, where concentrations of unemployed people are now to be found in juxtaposition with a physical environment of obsolete housing. Such problems have a local dimension which many believe calls for local policies and action.

Nevertheless, the extent and nature of the role which local authorities can usefully play in the local economy is arguable. There are both political and technical considerations which have to be taken into account. Central government in Britain has generally resisted the extension of powers to local authorities, partly on the grounds that general powers are adequate, and partly because of the potential conflict with regional policy. There are probably also doubts, not confined to the civil service mandarins in Whitehall, as to the capacity of many local authorities to develop this relatively new field. It is interesting to note that, ever since the formation in 1974 of the metropolitan county councils in terms of a new two-tier system of local government, the ambitions of these councils have been directed towards extending their relatively circumscribed roles and powers. They are the majority among the local authorities which have suggested Bills to Parliament for extra employment powers.

We suggest that the real test of interventionist measures does not lie in the elegance or otherwise of formal administrative structures, but in the way such structures function in respect of employment and related economic objectives. The difficulties experienced are those arising in translating policies and proposals into practical programmes of action which can be implemented so that the effects can be measured and evaluated against some explicit criteria.

Our own research has explored some of the conceptual and practical difficulties through desk and case studies of the local economy. Two studies co-directed by the author were carried out in 1978 by a multi-disciplinary team of the Joint Unit for Research on the Urban Environment at the University of Aston (JURUE). The first was a preliminary investigation of planning by local authorities for employment within their areas carried out with a grant from the Social Science Research Council and reported in

January 1979.[1] Much of this paper derives from the work carried out for this study. The second was concerned with public action to alleviate employment problems and was sponsored by the Department of the Environment.[2] This study was directed specifically towards local employment initiatives in the West Midlands. The final report was delivered in May 1979.

Local authorities have made only a few partial attempts to evaluate their initiatives and because many of them are new and exploratory, no universally valid generalisations can be made. Circumstances differ greatly from region to region and within different areas of regions and cities. For example, in the West Midlands Economic Planning Region the local economy's performance, judged by a number of major indicators, has fallen behind. The rate of unemployment more than doubled between 1971 and 1976. It is now above the national average instead of below, and over a similar period the region experienced a net job loss of 61,000, the largest percentage job loss in the country. The heartland of manufacturing industry once enjoyed personal disposable incomes well above the national average. By 1975, the West Midlands had fallen behind assisted areas such as North-West Scotland.

In the first part of the paper, the scope of local authority initiatives is discussed. In the second part, some of the more important actions which may be and are taken to alleviate employment problems are listed and discussed briefly. Considerations affecting policy formulation and implementation are emphasised. In the third and final part of the paper, an interim assessment is made of the extent to which the various measures appear to have been effective. The conclusions focus on the methodological problems, conceptual and operational, of understanding the workings of local economies better, of evaluating effectiveness and devising systematic organisational and procedural routines which bring together the principal actors necessary to ensure more effective implementation of policy measures.

SCOPE FOR LOCAL GOVERNMENT INTERVENTION

Local authorities may adopt one or more of three main approaches in intervening in their local economies. They have only limited scope for taking local employment initiatives within the constraints imposed by institutional and administrative factors, by existing powers and other factors, not least those concerned with expenditure levels. It is necessary to examine the parameters within which they must operate before examining what they do.

It has been said that regional policy in Britain has moved too far ahead of "regional science" for all its components to be sound and consistent with its objectives.[3] Much the same could be said of local authority policy in the field of employment planning - perhaps with greater justification, given its relative newness.

It is axiomatic that effective, sound and consistent policy requires a greater theoretical understanding and knowledge of the practical effects of such policy than there is at the present time. Tested factual knowledge is a prerequisite for adequate policy making, but if we insisted on an adequate empirical base we would never start. But a start has been made and it is important not to make the mistake of assuming that the measures taken stem from a well-worked out theory or knowledge of what the outcome will be.

The position taken here is that greater rationality is needed in policy-making. Political rhetoric and ideology may be necessary, but they are not sufficient conditions for a social democracy faced with real problems of falling production, rising unemployment and social choices. Greater rationality is a normative ideal and in no way implies that the structure or nature of decision processes, within and outside government, actually correspond to such a model. Nevertheless, if a rational approach is to be pursued, however bounded, information is obviously needed on employment measures corresponding to the successive stages of a rational process model.

The focus in this paper is the local authority planning unit, either at metropolitan county or metropolitan district level, and its relationship with both national and regional levels of government. The approach relates social organisations and the individuals comprising them to their spatial environment and recognises conceptually the pattern of constraints which operated differentially in given localities. In essence, the notion of intra-regional differences is no different from the notion of inter-regional differences which for many years now have provided the basis for regional policies and employment initiatives of various kinds.[4] Such an approach values equity principles highly and seeks to overcome areal differences thought to be undesirable, whether related to people, goods, services or physical and natural environment, by redistribution resources and sometimes by institutional reform.

Definitions. We use the term planning or employment planning to mean a relatively loose programme of measures, coordination of public policies in several overlapping economic and social realms, as well as levels and varieties of decision-making agencies. In this sense coordination leads to planning, and is indeed needed because the individual acts of government intervention are increasing in number and tend to be taken without due consideration of their interaction. The subsequent discussion of statutory powers and obligations highlights the growing complexity of government, inter-agency powers and procedures.

A local employment problem is said to exist when some employment objective or standard is not attained within the administrative area of a local authority. An employment measure is any action or series of actions taken by local authorities, independently or in association with other public or private bodies, to alleviate local employment problems.

Three approaches. Three distinct approaches by which local authorities may influence the local economy and economic behaviour may be identified. The first is by effecting changes in supply, price and efficiency of factors of production - land, labour, capital and raw materials and quantity and quality of information available on such factors. The scope for the manipulation of such factors is limited by legal, administrative, political and resource constraints; and information requirements are vast. The second is by inducements which assist decision-makers and encourage entrepreneurial activity. Inducements involve costs and benefits. For example, industrialists might be persuaded of the locational and environmental advantages of an area by promotional and environmental improvement measures. Thirdly, authorities may produce marketable goods and services or become involved in setting up firms that do so, using local resources.

It is not difficult to find examples which illustrate one or more of these approaches, used separately or in varying combinations. The problems which arise in assessing such measures include the identification of inputs, technical problems of measurement, obtainable and useful information, the identification of relevant variables, causal relationships, multiplier leaks, and spill-over effects.

Several additional points deserve emphasis. The component of unemployment that may be attributed to structural changes in the economy is of critical importance to any understanding of appropriate action. Information is required on the inputs of a specific measure and its effects as well as on the contribution made by the local authorithy in meeting the specified objectives, compared with the efforts of other agencies.

It may be concluded that in fact we have a relatively poor understanding of the way local economies work. And to compound the difficulties of acting on something we do not fully understand, we have to acknowledge that in seeking the best mix of policies to alleviate problems and achieve objectives it is also necessary to define the administrative, institutional, statutory and financial constraints to any actions we may deem desirable. Likewise, we have to acknowledge the interdependence of measures, the unpredictability of second-order effects and the need to resolve conflicting objectives, all of which lead to considerations of policy coordination and programming of employment measures.

Range of actions. The statutory context and financial resources available over time are the major constraints for local authority action. They may be listed as follows: the powers available to local authorities, their statutory obligations for employment and related responsibilities and duties; the doctrine of ultra vires; and central government financial control, key sector spending limits and financial guidelines for policy and expenditure.

Local authorities have a statutory duty to provide four employment-related services and measures: a careers advice service for students leaving schools and colleges; facilities for vocational and industrial training; land-use plans allocating land for employment and related purposes; and sheltered employment and workshops for disabled persons. Local authorities have some discretion in discharging these statutory obligations, which is relevant to the quality and scale of associated employment measures.

In discharging their statutory responsibilities to provide education, housing, transport, planning, social and environmental services, local authorities may initiate a range of related employment measures and policies. They may tailor educational initiatives to employment objectives; allocate public housing to key workers moving into their administrative areas; and subsidise public transport in various ways on specific routes in order to extend the labour market by improving accessibility to certain groups. Employment considerations may be given high priority in evaluating policies and programmes for roads, traffic management and public transport.

In discharging their planning functions, local authorities are operating employment measures primarily relating to land. The Community Land Act and the Planning Act empower local authorities to acquire and service land and make sites available for development. Various planning Acts, the Inner Urban Areas Act (1978), and local Acts empower them to designate industrial improvement areas and to permit special grants and loans to be made available for improvements to premises and amenities within the area. And planning Acts and the Local Authorities (Land) Act (1963) empower them to make environmental improvements such as the reclaiming of derelict land and making areas more attractive for the location of businesses. Other local authority planning functions may be relevant to employment policies and objectives. They are development control and settlement policies, relocation, and employment density standards.

Social and environmental services could have indirect effects by providing facilities such as day nurseries which could affect female activity rates. The discretion exercised by local authorities over river pollution control standards has implications for the costs of firms affected.

Two other groups of measures are the temporary employment measures operated across local authority services at the behest of central government's Manpower Services Commission (MSC), and enabling and permissive powers aimed at increasing the supply of, or improving access by local firms to, finance and fixed capital. The Inner Urban Areas Act (1978) and certain local Acts allow local authorities to make grants to firms to cover some costs of job-creating works, or in the form of rent reductions or rent-free periods on land and premises. Powers designed to disseminate information and advice to firms and promote campaigns to attract investment and firms allow authorities to appoint industrial development officers and provide advisory services on land availability, premises, labour and economic intelligence generally.

Financial control and resource availability. This is critical. In the year 1975/76, expenditure on economic development in the six metropolitan counties of England and in Greater London was estimated at around £5 million. Primarily this went to the provision, acquisition and preparation of land, factory construction, loans and grants to industrialists, promotion and publicity. This may be compared with the £300 to £400 million a year paid in regional development grants and regional employment premiums (abolished in January 1977) by central government in the mid-1970s.

With the advent of a Conservative government at Westminster, reductions in public spending, including major cuts in central goverment support for local authority rates (property taxes raised locally) are continuing. The effects are already being felt by those very authorities with inner area projects that had been asked to "bend" their programmes to make the small sums of money awarded by central government go further. In fact, only a small part of inner area programmes is directed towards economic objectives, despite the political rhetoric which often gives the contrary impression.

Despite the verbal emphasis on the weaknesses of the regional economy, the economic content of the Inner City Partnership programme for Birmingham, for example, relates primarily to policies on development and falls within the traditional responsibility and powers of physical planning. Little consideration has been given to the wider range of powers and initiatives available.

The issues may be summarised briefly. Financial uncertainty, even in the short term, is reflected in the absence of information on strategic plans for expenditure levels. No effective priorities are therefore contained in such plans. Open-ended "commitments" become the norm, and the "plans" the vehicle for the advocacy of policies authorities would like to see. Such special pleading is to be found in many structure plans.

In such a climate it is difficult to know how much capital is to be allocated to specific employment measures; what the opportunity costs of interventionist measures are; or how projects to promote employment or the local economy should be chosen in relation to the resources available. It is difficult to assess how well an authority is doing. Answers, however imprecise, are needed to such questions if monitoring and evaluation are to be valid. The answers may depend on the number of jobs created or on rates of return but, in any event, measures of output are required. If we ask how much money is being directed towards employment objectives by local authorities, the answer is very little indeed. This conclusion is a necessary if not sufficient consideration for separating employment and economic issues from other matters - a first step towards linking measures with objectives.

INITIATIVES AND PROBLEMS OF COORDINATION AND PROGRAMMING

The scope and character of employment initiatives and the problems of coordination and programming which arise need to be seen in the context of four basic premises. Employment policies and initiatives have grown incrementally, shaped by and shaping the administrative procedures and institutional context within which they are embedded. These policies and initiatives do not stem rationally and logically from the experience of implementation. Such policies and initiatives undertaken at various levels of government and relating to different geographical areas within metropolitan regions tend to result in a degree of conflict between levels and areas on priorities in time and resources. The main problem of inter-agency linkage is the interface between private sector and local government, which raises important political as well as managerial questions.

Initiatives may be considered in either of two ways. We may refer to a selection of "representative" or "active" authorities and look at the policies and measures they put forward; or we may categorise measures in four broad groupings. These are supply-side initiatives (provision of sites, the supply and quality of labour, and the provision of information and advice services); provision of premises and finance, and local purchasing policy; promotion and advocacy of measures with the main focus outside the administrative area; and initiatives to increase employment directly within local government.

The vehicles for policy statements within local government are structure plans prepared by county or top-tier authorities, or local plans prepared by lower-tier district authorities. A central paradox is that the more recently produced regional strategies, though not statutory documents, provide the clearest statements of the economic problems and opportunities of the planning regions to which they relate. The relationship between structure plans prepared by elected local authorities and the regional strategies prepared by civil servants under the guidance of appointed regional economic planning councils, so far as employment policies are concerned, is often unclear. The relationship between structure plans and local plans is likewise ambiguous. There is little doubt that the variety of approaches adopted in each category of plan reflects the differing perceptions of the scope of plans and the effectiveness of the measures which they might contain. The employment content of plans varies considerably. District or second-tier authorities are playing an increasingly important role in promoting and implementing policy initiatives, although the evidence suggests that little use is made of existing powers to influence local employment provision by housing, educational and transport measures, for example.

In the most detailed employment planning programme in Newcastle, where the council has pioneered attempts to intervene in the employment field and secured powers under the Tyne and Wear Act (1976), measures taken or advocated were concerned solely with physical policies and were directly relevant to local plan making. There is little evidence of coordination between programmes or agencies. The contrast between the London Borough of Islington's primary aim - to solve the problem of industrial decline - and the absence of measures to do anything more than apply negative physical development control is not untypical. That borough in 1977 had no policies for building factories or small workshop units or for assisting with loans; no policies relating to partnership or dialogue between agencies or sectors, and little indication of resource commitment.

Nevertheless, there is a growing number of initiatives designed to assist small firms, and the evidence suggests that there is effective demand in many localities. For example, the conversion of housing and other accommodation in Nottingham, especially where supply may have fallen as a result of earlier planning policies involving widespread demolition and clearance, may well be justified and may meet a need which the private sector has not met. But the extent to which such pilot projects can make any significant quantitative contribution to meeting employment needs depends on the scale of effective demand and the time taken to implement such projects and overcome the procedural and other delays. There is little evidence of widespread demand for flatted factory space. Such often cited examples as Wandsworth, where such an initiative may be found, suggest that it is the very smallest units that are in demand, where there are individuals who seek the opportunity to innovate. In the case of workshops provided with finance in terms of the Urban Aid and Job Creation Scheme, essentially a central rather than a local government initiative, experts from industry and commerce will need to make a major contribution and more land, buildings and resources could be required if the pilot scheme (Glasgow) proves successful. The concept of the industrial park mooted in a number of cities, and sometimes linked to a technological university, is a seed-bed approach with initially few jobs provided. But no major initiative appears to have reached even the initial stage of implementation.

One activity that is steadily growing and involves new organisations within town halls is promotion. The inevitable competition for the limited amount of mobile industry and the relative inexperience of many local government organisations in this entrepreneurial work, the growing budgets and ill-defined Industrial Development Officer jobs being created - all this suggests the need for further study of the effectiveness of such measures.

Industrial regeneration initiatives are characterised by the emergence of new bodies, whether joint officers' teams drawn from local government department heads with industrial or commercial expertise or new business panels composed of high-powered leaders and managers drawn from beyond the town hall. The experience of the London Borough of Southwark illustrates the possibilities of public-private partnership arrangements to provide factory accommodation. But it remains an isolated example.

Industrial improvement areas and inner-city partnership programmes deserve closer scrutiny. They are conceived in spatial and environmental terms. These approaches assume that after initial efforts by the public sector to halt physical obsolescence and economic decline, the private sector will be induced to invest. Other area-based initiatives emphasise job priority areas (South Yorkshire) and employment areas (Cheshire). There is some evidence that industrialists and public officials differ widely on what industrial improvement areas should be. The former think in terms of criteria appropriate for capital-intestive, high-productivity activities, which can compete with areas on the periphery, while the latter are preoccupied with the physical obsolescence of the area and the need to minimise its inherent disadvantages for modern industry.

Local authorities appear to be working on the assumption that they can assist small firms working in older premises. The actual criteria used to designate industrial improvement areas vary and are often vague. They include levels of vacant land, unused buildings, high unemployment, serious obsolescence, lack of room to expand, and the age of buildings.

The most ambitious area-based approach is the inner-city partnership programme, the most comprehensive plan designed to stimulate activity in the inner areas. Government policy is set out in the White Paper Policy for inner cities (1977) and the Inner Urban Areas Act (1978) gives forty-three designated authorities in England increased powers to assist industry and commerce and to improve the environment. In summary, the economic content of the programme is as follows: industrial improvement areas, refurbished industrial premises, advanced factories (new units on refurbished sites), new enterprise workshops, environmental works, industrial promotion, and support for new enterprises.

Area-based improvement raises question of policy emphasis. Any area initiative requires political decisions and progress through collective action which implies shared values and positive consensus. The difficulty, conceptual and practical, is that it is difficult to define political boundaries - within which consensus has been established for the purpose of decision processes - which are co-terminous with "community" area boundaries - within which problems, including employment, may be identified and possibly different sets of interests and values found. "Communities" are open systems. Political and other boundaries may be defined, but activities transgress and cross such boundaries and are influenced by exogenous factors.

The purposes of area coordination activities are not easily defined or agreed upon - certainly not in terms of specific programmes, resource costs, priorities and timing. The implicit purposes of area coordination relate to concepts of justice and equity. The purposes or ends in view often assume that less advantaged communities, the victims, shoud be aided to become more self-sufficient and to have more control over their own development. But the objectives must be linked to means for their realisation, and resource costs are involved. Political and other interests are in conflict, if not within such areas then certainly between a number of areas or groups of people within a city or region. Problems of strategic choice remain to be resolved, usually through bargaining and political routines.

Several questions are pertinent. If new employment opportunities are created in such areas, would they be taken up by inner-city residents or others? How will areas designated for special treatment affect similar areas not so designated? Would the effects, real or imagined, exacerbate problems in areas where political boundaries hardly coincide with "community" boundaries? How far will grants and loans be made to "high rank" enterprises? Will decison rules be different across industrial improvement areas or inner-city partnership programme boundaries?

Decision processes. Joint working has become the norm in a number of economic planning regions concerned with strategy review. It remains to be seen what the effect of abolishing the regional economic planning council will be. Area initiatives bring new problems. The bargaining and advocacy routines identified in the casework will require management of a high order. Implementation agencies will require hard technical skills to secure results. Questions of organisational design to meet new functions and issues of networking require further study. The outcome of policy is seen as the central question. Planning is judged by its results. Improvements in inter-organisational learning and strategic choice routines are only a means to an end. They will be of little value if the real needs of those adversely affected remain unmet. The tendency to emphasise research on decision processes at the expense of substantive policy issues is to risk underestimating the need to ask questions about supposed relationships between processes on the one hand and outcomes on the other.

Implementation is the "missing link" in areas of weak linkage between stimulus and policy, stimulus and programme, policy and programme. Information on implementation or the failures in implementation is inadequate so that feedback is not yet available to assess effects. What can be implemented is confused with what should be implemented. The effect of techniques on organisation behaviour tends to be minimal and the decision process is characteristically novel, complex and open ended. Decision-making takes place in contexts which are ill defined and not well understood, in conditions of ambiguity with little regard for the analytic mode. Bargaining and political routines are the norm. There is no single acceptable theory to describe how decision processes flow through organisation structures.

Studies of policy evaluation, plan development and programme implementation have been carried out largely in isolation. The linkages between the stages need to be studied to understand why and at what stage plans are shelved or aborted before implementation. The rational decision model we now know is unsatisfactory on a number of counts, primarily because it fails to describe what ought to happen and manifestly fails to describe what is happening in decision processes.

The role of agencies and their linkages deserves further study by local authorities and the agencies themselves. Understanding and knowledge of their roles vary. The absence of any explicit consideration of formal linkages required for implementation is seen as a deficiency in the operation of most organisations. Specific questions of coordination of employment programmes receive virtually no attention. There is little experience of interacting relationships between strategic or structure plans on the one hand and local plans on the other, and equally little experience of employment initiatives. The collection and coordination of relevant information raises both technical and political issues. Information must inform the growing dialogue between the various levels of government, and in turn between the public and private sectors. The various authorities have different priorities and therefore perceptions of what information is useful. The cost-effectiveness of information services is differentially valued. The barriers to inter-agency linkages are organisational and increasingly political.

Finally the complexity of joint action raises the gravest doubts as to the effectiveness of policy that depends on such an operation. Where organisations have relative autonomy and both the authority and resources to carry policy through, and where the issues of external demand appear less relevant, the chances of success are greater. An evaluation of United States programmes, especially those in the Model Cities Programme, has shown that economic as well as social programmes are characterised by deeply rooted conflicts of interest. Apparent agreement among agencies on ends is no guarantee that these same agencies will not actively oppose or stand in the way of the proposal being acted upon. There are common interests as well as conflicts between central and local government and other actors. Consensus may be bought at the cost of delay to programmes.

Joint operation and the proliferation of agencies serve to obscure problems and hinder implementation, which becomes even further separated from policy. Learning fails because the organisations which cause the events and those which feel the consequences are not the same. Means and ends can be brought into closer correspondence only by making each partially dependent on the other, by closing the gap between design and implementation, by gearing programmes more directly to the demands of executing them. Simplicity in policies is desirable, and the fewer the number of steps in implementation the less the likelihood of failure.

It is evident that the decison process is inadequately structured and understood. Other problems are hardly addressed: the widespread emphasis on reversing the decline in manufacturing industry, and the conflict between this objective and the creation of new jobs; the widespread emphasis on short-term remedial measures, which obscures the need for new types of economic activity and a work force with skills very different to those of today; a planning participation process that raises issues beyond the powers of the plans and calls into question the very idea of local authorities extending their intervention in the economies of their area until much more is known about current efforts. For this we need an assessment of what has been achieved to date, which in turn requires a framework for monitoring and evaluating local employment measures.

THE EFFECTIVENESS OF MEASURES:. AN INTERIM ASSESSMENT

We have described the groups of initiatives being undertaken and we now have to make an interim assessment - interim, because there is still no adequate information on the extent of implementation of measures or knowledge of their effects. Moreover, few authorities have a systematic monitoring capability which remotely covers the range of factors identified earlier as being capable of manipulation by a local authority seeking to intervene in the local economy. Without such a capability and the information categories to serve it, rigorous methods of evaluating the effectiveness of measures are a pipe dream.

Before discussing how we can move towards an operationally valid system of evaluation, we should list a number of general conclusions on the employment content of plans which vary considerably. Central government advice on what local authorites can do has not been given and the limited land-use role of the structure plan appears to have been emphasised. Few structure plans had been approved by the Secretary of State by 1978. The statutory and resource constraints applicable to planning for employment are not understood very well nor are they perceived and evaluated in the same way. Much the same could be said about conceptions of an employment or economic problem. Policies often cannot lead to action: they are statements of need; the need for more resources, for a climate of confidence and for government to act. Authorities adopt an advocacy role on many policy issues and recognise implicitly, and sometimes explicitly, that they cannot intervene in their local economy as they would wish. Some authorities seek a greater role in the operation of employment policy. Authorities generally focus on the perceived problems of small firms. This perhaps reflects the relative ability of local authorities to intervene effectively in this area. The emphasis in policies is remedial and tends to focus on the loss of manufacturing employment rather than the creation of new forms of employment, especially services. Authorities tend to rely on a traditional land-use area-based approach which reflects perceptions of what can be done and seen to be done - the provision and servicing of land and the refurbishing of buildings. Structure plans are not explicit in specifying which policies can and cannot be implemented by the planning department. The role of other departments or agencies in implementing policies is often ill defined. The procedures adopted within local authorities for preparing policies, including employment, influence the scope and character of the employment measure.

The existence of an economic intelligence capability, whether situated within a corporate framework or not, leads to a greater understanding of the limited instrumental role of physical plans in achieving economic objectives. Likewise, the greater the perception of uncertainty in the policy environment the greater the awareness of limited control. There is little assessment of what policies might achieve and even less of an ateempt to evaluate the likely consequences of any employment measure taken. Policies are "leaps in the dark", accompanied by minimal understanding of their potential effect.

Four groups of questions may be identified. The first concerns the utility and effectiveness of the statutory structure plan as an instrument of policy so far as economic and employment issues are concerned. The second relates to the character of local authority management structures and the extent to which employment policies require to be formulated in a corporate environment in which policy formation is informed by adequate economic intelligence and forecasting. The third relates to the hierarchy of plans and their relative importance for employment strategies and separate initiatives. The final group concerns the role of non-governmental organisations, especially private industrial, commercial and financial interests, the formulation and evaluation of measures. Do they have a role? And if so, at what stages in the process? Should they have a formal consultative role built into any procedures? On the evidence of our research it is possible to draw the following conclusions.

□ In encouraging local firms and establishments to retain and create jobs, the most effective initiatives are associated with the provision of sites, information and advice services and the supply and quality of labour.

□ Initiatives to increase local employment directly by local authority manpower policy run counter to government policy and, like the formation of local cooperatives or other enterprises, are not likely to be cost effective.

□ Local authorities taking employment initiatives appear to have sufficient general powers and the evidence suggests that full use is often not made of such powers. There is little evidence to support the granting of extra powers to local authorities to tackle local employment problems.

□ In order to evaluate the effects of policies and measure their net benefits one needs a monitoring capability. The measurement of output remains a significant problem area and progress may be made within a policy framework and on a partial basis to establish criteria for the selection of measures and a choice between sites for measures such as industrial improvement areas. The need for eligibility rules requires an attempt to design measures that may be monitored. It follows that local authorities require a systematic and explicit procedure for monitoring their local economies and evaluating employment initiatives.

□ Effective implementation requires an appropriate procedure for implementation which recognises the roles of the various departments and agencies, public and private, that are likely to be involved in the process.

REFERENCES

[1] Joint Unit for Research on the Urban Environment (JURUE), Planning by local authorites for employment within their areas (1979), University of Aston, Birmingham, Report, (two volumes) to SSRC.

[2] Local authority employment issues (1979), University of Aston, Birmingham, report to the Department of the Environment. This report contains an extensive list of government publications and other references which have informed the author.

[3] Richardson, H., Elements of Regional Economics (1969), Penguin.

[4] Falk, N., and Martinos, D., Inner City (1975), Fabian Research Series, 320.

Urban renewal in developing countries

21

P.A. Oluwande   Nigeria

INTRODUCTION

Most of the environmental problems of the developing countries are due to lack of development. Such problems are caused by the unavailability of adequate drinking water, insanitary methods for the disposal of human wastes, proliferation of various types of disease vectors, and poor housing in both rural and urban areas. These problems are being aggravated by a rural-urban population drift which is concentrating the people in the urban centres at the expense of the rural areas. An opportunity to visit Uganda, Kenya, India and Lebanon was provided by the World Health Organisation in 1970, and an opportunity to visit China was provided by the IDRC of Ottawa, Canada, in 1975. China is the only developing country visited which applies an effective check on rural-urban drift. Between 1967 and 1975 about a million youths moved from Shanghai to the rural areas in response to Chairman Mao's call.

The adverse effects of the population drift from rural to urban centres of the developing countries cannot be overemphasised, particularly when it is realised that these countries are dependent on agriculture. Apart from the adverse effects on the environmental qualities of the urban centres, the drift is also affecting the economy and food supply of the countries. Although modern techniques are being introduced to increase food production, the rapid growth of urban population at the expense of rural population is still reflected in the high cost of locally produced food in most of these countries.

For many reasons, the various methods employed to tackle the problems are not effective. One such reason is the fact that the people are often not consulted when the authorities are planning these schemes. For this reason, the people consider these schemes as schemes of the government, not their schemes. This makes the effects of poverty on environmental development truly overwhelming. Well-to-do individuals and communities which are in a position to solve their environmental problems with little or no assistance from their governments, often look to their governments to provide the services and facilities which they themselves are better placed to provide. The effect of this situation is serious when it is realised that government establishments often lack adequate funds because of inefficient taxation methods which fail to make rich people pay taxes commensurate with their income.

THE SLUMS

The majority of the people living in urban areas in developing countries are to be found in the slum areas. The location of the slums varies from one country to another. In East

Africa, the slums are found on the peripheries of the cities, while in West Africa and Asia, they are in the older city centres. Slums on the outskirts of cities are commonly inhabited by people who have moved to the cities to look for employment. Thus, such slums are younger than those in the city centres.

The environmental problems and human misery associated with slums are well known.[1] [2] [3] [4] The slums of the cities and towns of developing countries are characterised by high disease and death rates, social disorder and absence of comfort. The majority of the people who live there are rich enough to do so. In an area of Ibadan within a period of seven years (1970-77) more than 10 per cent of the families moved out of the traditional slum areas to new areas on the outskirts. The irony of this is that most of them merely moved to new houses in badly planned areas which are themselves fast developing into new slums. Also, the space vacated by them in the central slums was partly occupied by other people, mainly from rural areas. More recently studies in Ibadan revealed that more people move out of slums in the city core than move in.

Town planners, government authorities, and others who have anything to do with environmental development agree that the elimination of slums is the ideal strategy for urban renewal in the developing countries. This solution, however, is not practicable because nearly all the developing countries are poor. They have slum clearance programmes but the rate of progress is so slow that the effects are almost nil. The conventional approach to slum clearance which nearly all the developing countries adopt cannot eliminate slums from their cities, mainly because the governments do not have enough resources to do it. Moreover, in many countries the growth of slums is not static. The land tenure systems in countries such as Nigeria, India and parts of Uganda make it easy for the people to acquire land to build all sorts of houses. The town planning authorities are often unable to exercise effective control over the physical growth of communities, with the result that slums keep on growing.

NEW APPROACH TO SLUM CLEARANCE

If slums are to be eliminated from the urban centres of developing countries, the clearance cannot be done by the governments alone. Private developers, industrialists, both local and foreign, must be encouraged to acquire land in the slum areas. Also, governments must develop policies which will allocate land available in the slum areas to government projects such as schools, hospitals and other institutions. Only when there is no suitable land for such projects in slum areas should fresh land be acquired in other areas.

This approach will accelerate the pace of urban renewal in many ways. It will remove the constraints which shortage of funds imposes on the conventional approach to slum clearance. The money paid by private property developers and industrialists will subsidise the government efforts to provide adequate compensation for the owners of the land acquired. It will also assist the government in its efforts to resettle the slum dwellers in planned areas which have the required infrastructural amenities. The approach will also help to conserve land. The existing practice encourages the siting of industries, schools and other development schemes in vacant or semi-vacant land on the outskirts of urban centres. Thus, land which can be used for agriculture is rapidly used up, while vast areas of slum land remain poorly and inefficiently used.

Investigations show that poverty is the main factor compelling people to continue living in slum areas. Family ties or social connections have little or no effect. Once a family has funds to build or rent accommodation in the well-planned areas, it moves out from the slum area. The approach being advocated here can be executed in such a way that groups of people who have been living together in slum areas can be moved together to new areas where they can continue living together. In this way, emotional problems often associated with resettlement can be minimised.

ELIMINATION OF OPEN DRAINS

Since there is no central sewage system in many communities of the developing countries, "grey water", i.e. waste water from laundries, kitchens, bathrooms, the overflow from soak-away pits and industrial waste water, is discharged into the open drains. Apart from the grave danger which the drains constitute to public health (all types of pathogenic organisms find access to the drains), they are unsightly and a nuisance owing to bad odours. They also breed mosquitoes and the snail vectors of bilharzia. Wherever they exist, open drains are symbols of poor environmental sanitation, underdevelopment and poverty. It is widely accepted that more than 90 per cent of diseases treated in hospitals and clinics in developing countries are due to poor sanitary conditions. Open drains are the source of many infections that cause misery and debility.

As in the case of slums, the governments of the developing countries are unable to remove open drains as quickly as the hazards from them justify, simply because funds and materials are not available. It is possible to remove the constraints imposed by the unavailability of funds by following an assisted self-help approach.

In many developing countries, land belongs to private families who are often free to sell the land to people to build homes. In such communities, the town planning authorities are often unable to control the rate at which people put up houses. Even where the planning authorities are able to regulate the standard of housing, infrastructural facilities such as electricity, telephones, water, roads, refuse, and sewage disposal programmes of the government are often not able to match the rate at which houses are built, with the result that environmental conditions and public utilities are of very poor standard. The people are eager to build houses but leave the provision of infrastructural amenities to the government. In such communities there are no effective property taxing systems, with the result that the government is unable to provide efficient services. Costly modern houses are often surrounded by open drains, poor access roads and inefficient public utilities. Assisted self-help schemes will enable the landlords to provide the capital outlay for sewers and other facilities such as access roads during the period the houses are built while efficient taxation will provide the local authorities with adequate funds to maintain the facilities. In Ibadan and some other urban centres of Nigeria town planning authorities now insist that access roads on private land destined for residential development must be built before the layout is approved.

Investigations have shown that open drains and scattered refuse are the main causes of poor environmental conditions in such areas. Public works authorities will have to adopt a plan whereby the open drains on both sides of roads are replaced by modern sewers. The size of the sewers and their gradient must be determined by the engineers of the public works authorities. Landlords are to be responsible for the construction of the sewer in front or around their property. The construction must be carried out to comply with specifications laid down by the public works authorities. The same principle must be adopted in new areas to be developed. However, there will be no need for sewer lines on both sides of the road. If separate sewerage systems are intended, one storm-water line and one foul-water sewer line can be suitably located for housing on both sides of the road. All that is required is that the sewers should be designed and constructed before people move into the areas.

If this approach is followed, it will be possible to provide sewers in all those areas where open drains are in existence, and new areas will be provided with modern sewers right from the start. By making landlords pay for the construction of sewers in front or around their properties, the constraints imposed on government authorities by the prohibitive costs of sewer construction will be removed. For most developing countries, cheap sewage treatment methods such as oxidation ponds, aerated lagoons and oxidation ditches are very appropriate and efficient.[5][6][7][8][9][10] In particular, oxidation ponds are simple, cheap and most appropriate for tropical countries. Experience in India, Kenya, Uganda and other areas shows that oxidation ponds can be imployed in most communities in developing countries. Once simple and cheap sewage treatment methods are adopted, the money collected from property taxation should be sufficient for efficient refuse disposal and other infrastructural amenites.

THE USE OF AQUA PRIVIES

The aqua privy may be described as an imtermediate arrangement between the pit latrine and the septic tank system. Much has been written on the technical aspects of the aqua privy.[3][8][11][12][13] Unfortunately, many developing countries which can make use of the potential of the aqua privy to solve sewage disposal problems among low-income people do not yet seem to be aware of its advantages. It is common to find engineers and architects in developing countries specifying flush toilets for people who do not have a regular supply of water. For such people the aqua privy is more suitable. While the aqua privy combines the characteristics of a water closet with the simplicity of a pit latrine, it does not share the disadvantages of both. Above all, communities using the aqua privy may eventually upgrade the system by connecting all the privies with sewers discharging into central treatment centres. This type of sewered aqua privy system discharging into an oxidation pond has been functioning in New Bussa, Nigeria, a resettlement town founded for people from Old Bussa which was submerged by Lake Kainji.[14] Sewers carrying aqua privy effluents are susceptible to frequent blocking but this problem can be eliminated by the correct design of the outflow from the aqua privy tanks to ensure that floating solids remain inside the tanks, and by good maintainence of the sewers. The sewered aqua privy system in New Bussa ensures a healthy environment for the community.

Another way in which the aqua privy system can be employed in urban renewal is in comfort stations, which may be defined as places where people who live in crowded urban centres have toilet, bathing and laundry facilities.[3] These have been introduced in Ibadan, Calcutta and some other cities in developing countries to solve sanitation problems in slum areas. Comfort stations belong to groups of families, and only members of the families owning a particular station may use it. In Ibadan, more than forty comfort stations have been built in the slum core areas of the city. Since the introduction of comfort stations in 1972, the standard of sanitation in the slum core of the city has improved considerably.

CONCLUSION

Finally, it is important that all developing countries should have effective qualitative control of the growth of their communities. This can be effected in many ways. Industries and other employment-generating institutions should not be concentrated in urban areas only. Town and country planning authorities must have control over the physical growth of the communities. The people must be educated to appreciate the importance of a sanitary environment to community development. Taxation systems must be overhauled, as in developed countries, to compel landlords, property owners and others to pay taxes commensurate with their incomes.

REFERENCES

[1] Salvato, J.A., Environmental sanitation (1958), John Wiley.
[2] Newcombe, V.Z., "Emotional stress and strain in urban areas" (1973), ITCC Review, Vol 11, No 4, pages 16-25.
[3] Maclaren International, Feasibility study for waste disposal for Ibadan (1971), WHO/UNDP-assisted project, Ibadan.
[4] Salami, M.Y., "The environment of cholera patients in Lagos" (1975), Nigerian Medical Journal, Vol 5, No 1, pages 57-61.
[5] Gloyna, F.E., Waste stabilisation ponds (1971), WHO, Geneva.
[6] Marais, G.V.R., WHO Bulletin (1966), Volume 34, pages 737-63.
[7] McGarry, R., Developing countries sanitation (1975), Report prepared for IDRC, Ottawa.
[8] Oluwande, P.A., Sewage disposal in developing countries (1978), Ibadan University Press.
[9] Mara, D.D., Sewage treatment in hot climates (1976), John Wiley.
[10] National Environmental Engineering Research Institute, Nagpur, India. Papers for Symposium on low-cost sewage treatment (1969), Nagpur.
[11] Wagner and Lanoix, Excreta disposal for rural areas and small communities (1958), WHO, Geneva.
[12] Vincent, L.J., Algie, W.E., and Marais, G.V.R., "A system of sanitation for low cost" high density housing", Symposium: Hygiene and Sanitation in Relation to Housing (1961), CCTA/WHO, Niamey.
[13] Oluwande, P.A., "Development of aqua privy for urban sanitation" Proceedings: International Conference on Water, Waste and Health in Developing Countries (1975), Loughborough University of Technology, pages 109-22.
[14] Waddy, B.B., Journal of the Society for Health (Nigeria) (1970), Vol 5, No 2, pages 28-32.

VIII: OVERALL CITY REJUVENATION

A planning analysis for the renewal of Tel Aviv

22

A. Mazor and M. Gluskinos   Israel

This paper describes the methodologies developed during the preparation of a new master plan for the city of Tel Aviv, Israel, specifically for the renewal and revitalisation of residential areas.

PRELIMINARY STAGES

The city, although relatively young, has been affected by processes common to many metropolitan centres. Like other large urban communities, Tel Aviv has experienced an invasion of its residential areas by business and commercial activities. This has been accompanied by a decline in environmental quality, out-migration, deterioration of public services, blight of the housing stock and a constant weakening of the socio-demographic composition of its population.

The purpose of the analysis was to identify specific features of the process of deterioration, quantify them and determine their causes. On the basis of this characterisation, it was possible to outline the specific rehabilitation activities required in each residential area in terms of type, urgency of action, availability of land and organisational structure. Within the framework of the study, rehabilitation activity was defined as activity initiated in order to bring a certain zone to a desired level, or at least an improved stage towards that level, in terms of both its population and its positive integration in the complex urban structure, as outlined in the master plan. The process of rehabilitation is comprehensive and wide ranging and should not be defined by type (physical, social, economic, etc). At the same time the rehabilitation activity is limited. It ends whenever active intervention is no longer necessary, because the dynamic action taking place in the area is in the direction of accomplishing the planning goals.

The desired level of improvement is determined in two ways: matching the characteristics of the zone, and the preferences of its inhabitants to various agreed norms; and integrating the zone positively in the urban structure in terms of both the attainment of its designated functions and the types of interaction with other zones, such as in-migration, stability of businesses, and the achievement of any desired specialisation.

The preliminary analysis led to the conclusion that the direction of rehabilitation activities should be based on three sets of characteristics:

□ Severity characteristics. These define for each residential zone the type of the problem and its severity relative to the city average.

☐ Externality characteristics. These define the impact of rehabilitation activities within each zone on outer development and the implementation of the desired urban structure; and they specify outside activities on which the zonal rehabilitation will depend.

☐ Urgency characteristics. These define the urgency of an induced intervention and they set priorities for zones in which rehabilitation activities should immediately begin.

The complexity of the three sets required the incorporation of a multitude of characteristics: socio-demographic, economic, physical, transportational and environmental. At attempt was made to determine the main characteristics within each set, and to examine the mutual relationships among the sets. The analyses were based on data available from the various statistical areas. This information was stored in the data bank of the Ramat Gan Institute of Urban Studies so that it could be used for additional comparisons among the zones. While it is not sufficient to classify residential zones solely according to the relative conditions in comparison with other zones in the city as in every residential zone there are unique problems stemming from singular processes in the area, the framework of the study did not allow the inclusion of these problems. However, zones suggested for priority action should undergo a detailed examination designed to locate special processes and to clarify suitable actions. A detailed examination could lead to changes in the priority classification arrived at in this work.

THE STUDY

The study was undertaken in eight sequential parts, detailed below.

Definition of the study area. Ninety-two residential zones in Tel Aviv were selected, based on statistical areas for which updated information exists. Areas in which residential activity is marginal or absent were neglected. Similarly, zones in which residential development has been recent and swift were omitted, since these phenomena are inconsistent with the need for rehabilitation.

Selection. Twenty-five characteristics, relevant to all aspects of rehabilitation, were selected, quantified and grouped into the following categories: socio-demographic, population trends, socio-economic, housing, residential activity, transportation activity, building intensity, level of public services. The twenty-five characteristics were quantified for each of the ninety-two zones. Each zone was then defined in terms of these categories.

Correlation. Correlations among all characteristics were tested. The statistical analysis was aimed at clarifying the following two aspects: the "centrality" of each characteristic within its category; and correlations among characteristics of different categories. This examination permitted the identification of primary variables, by which a complex group of characteristics could be represented. In addition, it allowed for the testing of "dependency" among variables. Table 1 shows the statistical analysis of the rehabilitation variables. This technique made it possible to identify the major factors whose change could increase the residential attraction and thus improve the migration balance of each zone in the city.

Factor analysis. In order to simplify the analysis, the various characteristics were combined by means of factor analysis into a small and significant number of groups. This technique produced five principal factors, each composed of a vectorial arrangement of various characteristics: low socio-economic level; negative environmental impact; physical deterioration and out-migration; aging; and low level of public services. Table 2 shows the rehabilitation factors and their component characteristics in terms of which each zone is characterised.

Spatial distribution. Five maps were prepared, on the basis of the deviation of the various factors from city-wide means. In these maps, the spatial distribution of the factors was analysed in terms of the characteristics of each factor (its amplitude), and those of the specific city section, such as conditions in the north compared with the south, the centre and the outskirts, for example. Figure 1 shows the spatial distribution of Factors 1 and 3 (low socio-economic level, and physical deterioration and out-migration).

Externalities. The role of each zone in the complex urban structure was defined according to the master plan. Zonal roles specially emphasised functional specialisation, limiting of industrial expansion, bordering on CBD extension, development of urban access routes through the zone, and the location of urban nodes within the zone. In addition, an evaluation was made of the contribution of rehabilitation activities in the zone to the accomplishment of the master plan objectives, not necessarily within its boundaries. Consequently, it was possible to define the relative contribution of each zone to the implementation of the master plan - by activities within that zone along with externalities resulting from them.

Urgency. While the characteristics mentioned above indicate the relative severity of the problems and the external contribution made by their solution, the purpose of the urgency factors is to specify the need for priorities in rehabilitation activities. The priorities arise from the dynamic processes taking place in the particular area and are based on three considerations:
□ The degree to which lack of action will change the situation in the zone for the worse and consequently make future rehabilitation attempts more difficult.
□ The extent to which delays in action might prevent achievement of planning goals in the target year, particularly if the implementation of the development plans is long and complicated.
□ The feasibility of initiating rehabilitation activities in the zone in terms of land available for rehabilitation.

Synthesis and conclusion. In order to compile a comprehensive list of zonal characteristics, severity, externality and urgency characteristics were synthesised. A list of zones for priority action was drawn up on the basis of this synthesis. In Israel, both national and municipal organisations deal with rehabilitation problems, but from different aspects. Further analyses were therefore carried out in order to classify every zone according to the organisation best qualified to lead the rehabilitation activities within it. Obviously, cooperation between state and local organisations is always essential and the purpose of the analysis was merely to indicate who should head the rehabilitation team. Another priority list was produced at the end of this stage. The list distinguished between zones to be rehabilitated under the direction of the national government (essentially the Ministry of Construction and Housing), and those to be rehabilitated under the direction of municipal organisations. The analyses and the lists resulting from the study should serve as a guide to plan, outline and budget for rehabilitation activities in the city of Tel Aviv on a zonal basis in both the short and the long term.

Table 1. Statistical analysis of revitalisation characteristics

CATEGORIES			KURTOSIS	SKEWNESS	LARGEST STANDARD SCORE	SMALLEST STANDARD SCORE	MAXIMAL VALUE	MINIMAL VALUE	COEFFICIENT OF VARIATION	STANDARD DEVIATION	MEAN
1. SOCIO-DEMOGRAPHIC	11.	Mean age	-1.48	0.01	1.51	-1.67	54.00	19.50	0.29	10.86	37.64
	12.	Family size	0.96	1.13	3.65	-1.14	6.00	2.00	0.28	0.83	2.94
	13.	% of 65+	-0.70	0.12	2.21	-1.88	39.75	3.89	0.43	7.98	18.14
	14.	% of 0-14	-0.89	0.54	2.33	-1.49	2.09	0.47	0.38	0.44	1.19
2. MIGRATION AND MOBILITY	21.	Natural increase	0.80	0.95	3.52	-1.58	20.09	-7.05	3.89	5.32	1.36
	22.	Migration	14.16	-0.99	4.60	-5.72	30.58	-58.75	-0.93	8.65	-9.22
	23.	Mobility	3.34	-0.71	2.39	-3.69	15.78	-30.98	-2.93	7.69	-2.62
3. SOCIO-ECONOMIC	31.	Composite CISEL index	-1.20	-0.51	1.02	-1.87	9.00	1.00	0.45	2.76	6.18
	32.	Disadvantaged students	-0.68	0.62	2.38	-1.30	85.00	0.00	0.77	23.09	30.07
	33.	13+ years of education	-1.07	0.49	2.24	-1.10	54.00	0.00	0.91	16.18	17.81
	34.	Asia-Africa origin	-0.07	0.92	2.64	-1.10	91.00	3.00	0.82	23.53	28.82
	35.	Low income	-0.43	0.04	2.43	-2.47	77.00	2.00	0.38	15.30	39.85
4. HOUSING	41.	% of small apartments	-0.46	-0.42	1.73	-2.52	84.60	3.80	0.37	19.03	51.67
	42.	Median persons a room	-0.86	0.77	2.55	-1.48	2.30	0.70	0.31	0.39	1.28
	43.	% of 3+ per room	1.90	1.64	3.44	-0.79	42.90	0.00	1.27	10.14	7.98
5. RESIDENTIAL DEVELOPMENT	51.	% of res. floor area	-0.46	-0.85	1.22	-2.30	95.39	1.33	0.42	26.69	62.85
	52.	% of res. apartments	0.77	-1.36	0.97	-3.22	97.80	8.80	0.27	21.21	77.16
6. URBAN NON-RESIDENTIAL ACTIVITY	61.	Employment in the area	37.89	5.76	7.69	-0.35	36.09	0.04	2.81	4.48	1.59
	62.	Zonal O-D of trips	9.98	3.04	5.09	-0.55	37.24	0.00	1.82	6.60	3.62
7. TRANSPORTATION AND ENVIRONMENTAL	71.	Urban trips	8.08	2.56	4.93	-0.80	265.20	0.57	1.24	46.23	37.40
	72.	Metropolitan trips	11.20	2.86	5.58	-0.77	17.54	0.00	1.29	2.76	2.13
8. DENSITY OF DEVELOPMENT	81.	% of built-up land	-1.10	0.27	2.51	-1.47	135.40	2.60	0.64	33.32	51.65
	82.	% of empty apartments	3.60	1.85	3.95	-0.97	12.50	0.00	1.03	2.53	2.46
9. PUBLIC SERVICES	91.	Level of infrastructure	3.41	1.64	3.83	-1.08	2.50	1.20	0.18	0.26	1.48
	92.	Level of pub. services	-0.74	0.27	2.18	-1.69	2.30	1.40	0.13	0.23	1.79

Table 2. Revitalisation factors

CATEGORIES			LOW LEVEL OF PUBLIC SERVICES	AGING	PHYSICAL DETERIORATION AND OUT-MIGRATION	NEGATIVE ENVIRONMENTAL IMPACTS	LOW SOCIO-ECONOMIC LEVEL
1. SOCIO-ECONOMIC	11.	Mean age	0.05180	0.48522	0.10651	0.21078	-0.81036
	12.	Family size	0.08040	-0.39169	0.10152	-0.11312	0.74880
	13.	% of 65+	-0.01657	0.86551	0.05616	-0.01188	-0.25117
	14.	% of 0-14	0.07148	-0.86507	-0.12225	-0.13600	0.34547
2. MIGRATION AND MOBILITY	21.	Natural increase	-0.08951	-0.40524	-0.45875	-0.01551	0.58549
	22.	Migration	-0.10989	-0.02597	-0.59203	-0.19455	-0.22914
	23.	Mobility	0.02579	-0.03709	-0.77503	-0.20026	-0.07518
3. SOCIO-ECONOMIC	31.	Composite CISEL index	-0.22989	0.18826	-0.35153	-0.03928	-0.87617
	32.	Disadvantaged students	0.26347	-0.06316	0.37896	0.03725	0.85405
	33.	13+ years of education	-0.30283	-0.02708	-0.21868	-0.10925	-0.69956
	34.	Asia-Africa origin	0.12349	-0.09865	0.12989	-0.02950	0.87929
	35.	Low income	0.43933	0.28051	0.49544	0.19555	0.38762
4. HOUSING	41.	% of small apartments	0.20231	0.22176	0.73624	0.13067	0.29058
	42.	Median persons a room	0.06077	-0.14504	0.39374	-0.04932	0.76863
	43.	% of 3+ per room	0.23072	-0.16437	0.49184	-0.07133	0.67247
5. RESIDENTIAL DEVELOPMENT	51.	% of res. floor area	0.03929	0.11178	-0.42337	-0.67296	-0.98040
	52.	% of res. apartments	-0.08875	-0.05739	-0.43341	-0.77394	-0.02381
6. URBAN NON-RESIDENTIAL ACTIVITY	61.	Employment in the area	0.01063	0.02889	-0.01562	0.89739	-0.02899
	62.	Zonal O-D of trips	-0.03424	0.01650	0.16333	0.95087	0.01003
7. TRANSPORTATION AND ENVIRONMENTAL	71.	Urban trips	0.29677	0.27895	0.07471	0.74908	-0.32927
	72.	Metropolitan trips	0.23663	0.24525	0.01381	0.81901	-0.35938
8. DENSITY OF DEVELOPMENT	81.	% of built-up land	0.22245	0.45954	0.12986	0.21421	-0.63997
	82.	% of empty apartments	0.42589	-0.09743	0.02615	0.55508	0.17852
9. PUBLIC SERVICES	91.	Level of infrastructure	0.53224	-0.27917	0.26629	0.21266	0.35295
	92.	Level of public services	0.69036	0.03732	0.07054	0.08819	0.13406

Figure 1. The spatial distriburion of factors 1 and 3 (low socio-economic level, and physical deterioration and out-migration)

City renaissance 23

Alfred A. Wood   United Kingdom

INTRODUCTION

Man has always altered his towns and cities: his needs have been changing throughout history and this has been shown by modification of the urban fabric. In the Middle Ages and during the Renaissance these changes were relatively slow and in tune with the tempo of life. During the nineteenth century, the industrial revolution produced rapid and violent changes in towns, particularly in Britain. Large new cities developed quickly as workers from the countryside crowded into the urban areas for the higher wages that industrial employment offered. This rapid change has continued into the twentieth century; larger populations have had to be housed and employed, and the advent of easy transport, initially public and later private, facilitated the urban sprawl which has become one of the greater problems of today.

All this has had the effect of turning our cities inside out. Those who could afford to do so left the inner city for better surroundings in the suburbs or villages outside the built-up areas - a serious social loss to the increasingly deprived inner areas. Industry has also tended to reorganise, finding locations offering much more space and better road communications, and sites closer to much of its skilled labour force. Commerce, too followed the exodus to be closer to the higher purchasing power of the commuter settlements, and to be free of the unpleasant environmental conditions for shoppers and growing congestion created by increased downtown motor traffic.

In addition, there has also been planned dispersal, partly by the development of large public sector housing projects on peripheral sites intended to rehouse those living in slum areas in the inner city. There is little doubt that these forces of dispersal have had a devastating effect on the inner areas when added to the problems of obsolescence that already affected those districts. There is a growing recognition of the fact that peripheral sprawl and inner city decay have a direct relationship. In the gloomy mid-town areas of Detroit, something like forty square miles (say 200,000 hectares) lies under-used and largely derelict. The sight of vast used-car lots, old empty factories, wired-off car parks, waste land, decaying and dead housing areas, and boarded-up local shops is familiar enough in too many European cities, but the enormous scale of this dereliction has a macabre fascinatiuon and gives us an awful warning that we must heed. This is not entirely a town planning and economic problem for there are obvious social factors at work, but the plain fact is that this tremendous decay is exacerbated by the forces of dispersal: the new freeways and the thriving suburbs are the means and the end of people voting with their wheels. It is being paralleled in some European cities where the soft option of peripheral expansion fuels the fire of inner area decay. In both the Detriot and European cases, the artifically high values of inner area land are basic causes of low land usage. A short-term use of land as a used-car lot employing two or three people provides an economic return probably much greater than that of a factory employing perhaps fifty people. The new America is in the suburbs. Near the Ford headquarters the Fairlane Centre is a fascinating mix of the urban and the suburban. A large three-level enclosed shopping centre is linked to the nearby Hyatt Hotel by an automated minitram running on an overhead guideway which passes over the 10,000-space car park on the way - surely the most muddled bit of transportation thinking even for the twentieth century.

Detroit is, of course, a car-dominated city. There are only about two hundred buses. Ironically, many of the commuters (leaders in the city community) who use the freeways may well be unaware of the extent of the growing dereliction of the city for the simple reason that they are not exposed to it. Mose of these freeways run in cuttings and the decay is a bad dream the traveller never sees.

In many ways, the Detroit experience has arrived, perhaps on a smaller scale, in some parts of late eighteenth and nineteenth century cities of Europe. London's docklands, parts of Liverpool, Glasgow, Manchester, Birmingham, Lille, Naples, Antwerp, Ghent, Amsterdam, all exhibit in differing ways symptoms of the same disease.

THE ENERGY DIMENSION OF DECAY

Western nations based their nineteenth century industrial democracy on the twin planks of relatively cheap labour and relatively cheap materials. Cheap labour gradually disappeared in the 1940s and 1950s and during the past few years labour cost has become the major element in the price of any article or service. Cheap materials stayed with us rather longer and it was only in October 1973 when King Feisal, the Shah of Iran and the other oil sheikhs flexed their economic muscles that we realised the second plank had been taken away. The disappearance of cheap oil affects every aspect of life and will force us to reconsider our lifestyle in a fundamental way. The oil sheikhs will do us some good if they compel us to reappraise our resources and hence our planning attitudes. Since 1945 we have based our whole economy on cheap and plentiful energy and this has affected our planning policies. Almost all our actions have been to make personal mobility easier and the use of a private motor car obligatory to an increasing extent.

We have cleared older terraced houses and rehoused the occupants in new housing on the periphery of our towns and cities. Much social damage has been caused by this over-enthusiastic slum clearance and its resultant decay (based on the idea that comprehensiveness is better than an incremental approach). We have also dispersed employment from the central areas which could be served by public transport, and allowed the development of suburban office blocks all too often in locations where the private car is the only means of access. There has also been a move towards grouped shopping centres to replace the general corner shop in housing areas. The paradoxical situation is that more restricted journeys for the few (the suppliers) mean greater journeys for many (the shoppers). Who really benefits? The same trend towards what the economists call the economy of scale has led to the development of hospitals in larger and no doubt better equipped units. For a number of reasons, schools have been similarly grouped. Indeed, for academic and other reasons, the new universities have appeared on the edges of our towns and cities instead of being insinuated into the fabric of our towns as was the case in the past. All these trends may have been perfectly sensible from the point of view of the developer, the superstore owner or the supplier, but I wonder if it has been so sensible from the point of view of the common good?

According to the British Institute of Fuel, oil supplies will last between thirty-two and thirty-six years if they are used at 1971 rates, but only half that time if the present increase in consumption is projected into the future. Indeed there are limited reserves of all other fuels as well. Coal is in the best position, with reserves sufficient for up to 150 years. Reserves of copper, lead, bauxite, silver, tin and zinc are also very limited (sufficient for thirty-six years, according to the OECD) and vulnerable to the same pressure as that applied to oil. The recent instability in Zaire highlights the difficulties facing the Western consumer.

It seems to me that the message is very clear. It is not easy to be pessimistic about resources, but it is important not to over-compensate by way of mindless optimism, as seems to have happened in connection with North Sea Oil, which is seen as the cure for British economic ills in the 1980s. It is conveniently forgotten that borrowings abroad will have to be largely paid for with that oil and that the inevitable remedial action must be a reduction in consumption. However, President Carter's inability to convince his countrymen that there is an energy crisis just round the corner underlines the problems faced by all political leaders attempting to follow prudent energy policies. We all tend to hope that something will turn up to make the problem go away, even when we know the facts very well.

Man has proved himself to be a better taker than giver of resources, but unaccustomed as he is to conservation he is nevertheless going to be forced into a position where he will have to be economical with the world's resources, and considerations of this kind must therefore condition our approach to urban restoration. Clearly, if only from the energy point of view, we must re-examine our plans and policies and take account of the changed situation in which we find ourselves. This reappraisal must include transport plans, settlement patterns, housing locations and so forth in order to aim for a society consuming much less energy. This will extend the period during which resources will be available to us but it will inevitably lead to a reduction in mobility. I believe that we must also begin to plan to maximise renewable resources. Agriculture and forestry will probably emerge as being more important than central área redevelopment and new buildings must be designed on an energy-conserving basis. Surely, by this token, we must renew the inner areas rather than allow green fields to be used, particularly at a time when population estimates are declining, the birthrate is starting to fall and for the first time in over a hundred years we have the prospect of relative population stability.

URBAN TRAFFIC AND TRANSPORT

The private motor car has become a virtually indispensable convenience for many people and has certainly widened the horizons and range of activity of many owners. Moreover, present patterns of manufacture and distribution rely on the growing use of goods vehicles, increasing year by year in size and capacity as well as impact on our surroundings. Indeed, the economies of many countries of Western Europe rely heavily on the motor vehicle industry. In spite of continuing increases in fuel costs, made inevitable by shrinking supplies, the demand for private motor vehicles has continued to grow, although at a slowing rate.

Whether or not other forms of energy are developed and translated into new methods of propulsion is in many ways irrelevant as it is the very numbers of motor vehicles which create the problem. The effects of the growth in traffic are obvious to even the most dedicated of vehicle users: most of our towns and cities are suffering from the impact of modern traffic. Danger to life and limb, damage to buildings, noise, fumes and visual intrusion are universal and are adding to the problems of retaining character in older towns.

It has become increasingly difficult to find occupants for town houses on busy routes. A fine house on a main street used to be a very desirable place in which to live, but now such a location would be intolerable for many people. The enduring pattern of streets in old towns is at once the key to their charm and the reason for their present-day traffic problems. Motor vehicles can penetrate into the confined streets and spaces of our towns; parked vehicles in market squares or formal spaces obstruct fine buildings, clutter the townscape and obstruct the movements of people on foot. Continuous streams of traffic overwhelm the town and utterly destroy the sense of history. Harassed highway authorities, usually under pressure from motorists and traders to relieve congestion and speed the flow of traffic, have often resorted to new road building in sensitive areas or street widening in historic thoroughfares. The result has been loss of buildings of character, damage to attractive areas, and planning blight in the small shopping streets on the fringes of old town centres. Even where there has been little new road building, traffic measures can in themselves damage the environment. Signs to indicate restrictions, one-way systems which very often allow an increase in volume and speed, and the paraphanalia of conventional traffic management merely add to the overall visual damage. Pedestrians suffer, too: town centres are no longer places to be enjoyed by people on foot and there are still too few areas where shopping can again be the civilised pleasure our grandparents knew. An excursion to the traffic-dominated central area of many towns and cities is an unpleasant, frustrating and tiring business for many people. But cities are by their nature places of congregation and congestion: they have to support life, they must be accessible to people and goods. A free-standing historic town set in a rural hinterland with little public transport has to accept a different proposition of traffic access, compared with a metropolitan area with a good public transport system.

The dilemma is, therefore, to avoid towns either becoming amiable but dead museums or being relentlessly destroyed by the onslaught of modern traffic. The very fact that many people have rebelled against some of the physical changes that have occurred in towns - too many high-rise flats, depressing housing estates, too much traffic, the sterile architecture of too many new buildings - coupled with their desire to retain those buildings and amiable eccentricities which make their town different from all others, indicates that there is a pressing need to develop sensible and sensitive management of our surroundings in older urban areas.

In future it will probably no longer be possible and certainly no longer desirable to redevelop our cities on the multi-level basis which at one time was considered de rigueur in order to accept as much traffic as possible. The move away from the "throw-away" society and the need to retain historic buildings and areas of character imply that future attempts to improve town centre conditions must be made on the basis of a sensible coexistence between conflicting road uses, without contrived changes of level and with minimal alteration to the urban fabric.

The bus, the tram, the goods vehicle, the private car, the cyclist and the person on foot tend to get in one another's way; means must be found to deal with these conflicts by way of low-cost environmental measures which will allow the city to function as a living and intricate organism.

ACCESSIBILITY

There can be no standard solution since all towns are different. It is nevertheless possible to indicate certain principles which might be observed. Car access to central areas should be limited to the periphery of the main central shopping area, which itself may well be improved by restriction or removal of traffic, provided the distance from car park to shop is relatively short, say no more than three minutes' walking. There should be arrangements to allow vehicles for the disabled to be driven into otherwise traffic-free zones, and attention must be given to safety and convenience at junctions with the general road system.

As there must probably be a general presumption against major new road building or street widening, vehicle access to the town centre will be by way of existing streets, and particular attention should be paid to the environmental capacity of those streets to accept the volume of traffic intended. This may well be somewhat below the overall crude capacity of the street system and must be judged against the function of buildings in the street and sidewalk widths, the capacity of car parks served by the streets, routes for public transport or access requirements for goods vehicles. It is probably sensible to try to separate, as far as it is possible car, public transport, goods vehicles, cycle and pedestrian routes by means of selective traffic measures.

Street and surface car parking should be reduced as much as possible, particularly in environmentally sensitive areas. There should also be measures to discriminate in favour of shoppers and those who live in the central area, while commuter parking should be sited further out. The manner in which multi-storey car parks are insinuated into the fabric of the town is critical to their environmental acceptability. Generally, a good rule is that small units, possibly tucked away behind other buildings, are easier to absorb and have less impact on the surrounding streets.

Improvement of the surroundings through traffic reduction can serve to retain existing housing in town centres. It does imply, however, that special measures must be taken to ensure relatively easy vehicular access and parking space for residents close to their homes. This is not incompatible with overall traffic commonsense and is another example of the need to separate conflicting road space requirements.

Access for the cyclist may well become more important in future. It is probably necessary to allow cycle access and provide safe storage in traffic-free areas and to develop a network of quiet but not necessarily completely segregated routes between the centre and outer districts and between districts. Generally speaking, mopeds are not entirely compatible with cycle routes, and should not be given the same advantages.

Access for pedestrians is an important traffic consideration in every town and attention should be given to the need to link nodal points by safe pedestrian routes, the town centre with the surrounding residential districts and district to district, and to provide convenient access to schools, colleges and cultural features as well as local shops and factories. There should be a real attempt to avoid excessive detours or daunting changes of level for the person on foot. Unpleasant pedestrian underpasses merely provide the mindless aerosol vandal with a quiet free gallery and can be a nuisance for the ordinary person on foot. Overall, the aim should be to give the person on foot as much advantage as possible over other road-users where the nature of the zone indicates that pedestrian priority is an overriding need.

Access for delivery vehicles to shops can be provided in a number of ways. Access-only routes can be designated in the environs of the town centre, and limited-time servicing, selective permits, trolley servicing or unlimited access are among the techniques which may be employed in town centres. It is probably environmentally damaging to provide rear access to existing premises by extensive modification of the area, and certainly not always necessary, to judge by many towns with traffic-free central areas. If rear access is a fundamental requirement it is probably best provided by existing routes without widening the spaces which provide a sense of enclosure in the minor street network.

Public transport should have easy and direct access to the town centre and between districts, and should as far as possible have priority over other road users. This priority might be shared with taxis. It is sometimes possible to allow public transport to traverse part of a pedestrian area and to designate special bus-only or tram-only streets. For the sake of pedestrian safety, speed control devices, such as "sleeping policemen" may be necessary in bus-only streets. The location of public transport routes and the siting of stops should be determined by passenger convenience. This is merely stating the obvious, but the obvious is by no means commonly observed.

Public transport schemes for old towns must of necessity consist of an overall package of measures which will include bus or tram priority, traffic restraint, transport interchange stations, park-and-ride schemes, links with traditional pedestrian routes, and so forth.

The overall approach must obviously vary from town to town but the main principles of sensible and as far as possible separate access for different road users will clearly be acknowledged by most people as essential. Discussions with interested parties as well as general public participation are important first steps in dealing with traffic matters. Public participation is perhaps best ensured by the authorities publicising their proposals as widely as possible. At the same time they must make it clear that if the schemes do not look like achieving the desired results after a period of experiment, the project will be modified or discontinued. It is not a failure to admit that a mistake has been made.

SHOPPING IN COMFORT

There is a great deal to be learned from the experience of the many European towns and cities where great environmental and commercial improvements have been achieved by the development of traffic-free areas.

For the most part, these pedestrian streets have been created by closing existing streets to motor vehicles for the major part of the day or even permanently, very often in situations where no rear servicing was possible. Pressure for these pedestrian streets very often came from commercial quarters, often after initial fears had been expressed that local shopkeepers would lose trade if traffic were to be excluded from their streets - fears which in the vast majority of cases proved to be groundless.

The idea of setting aside existing streets for pedestrians is by no means a new one, especially not in Germany. Limbeckerstrasse in Essen was closed to vehicular traffic in 1927 and in nearby Cologne, Hohestrasse and Schildergasse were converted to pedestrian streets for specific periods (there were almost no facilities for rear service access) just before the second world war. After 1945, there was renewed of interest in pedestrian streets and those in Cologne were restored as traffic-free zones in 1949 and in Essen, Limbeckerstrasse and Kettwigerstrasse formed part of a major pedestrian area developed in the city from the early 1960s.

Today, there are more than two hundred towns and cities in West Germany with extensive traffic-free central areas, the great majority of them created without the extensive road building often thought to be necessary to accommodate traffic displaced by street closures. Sixty more traffic-free areas were due to be completed in 1976 and a further 150 were planned for early subsequent years. Now nearly every West German city with a population of over 100,000 has all or a major part of its central area set aside for pedestrians. The tragic 1972 Olympic Games in Munich also had a happier side. They drew the attention of a wide international audience to the undoubted virtues of a city centre without traffic. Visitors to Munich enjoyed the civilised quality of life created when the heart of a great city is given over to the person on foot and public transport is specifically arranged to complement the new role of the centre.

Consideration of the factors affecting traffic-free areas will include function, character, comfort and aesthetics as well as the question of access and public transport. The choice of the area to be closed to motor traffic is to some extent dictated by opporutnity, but the potential commercial and physical attractiveness of the streets must also be taken into account. Those streets which attract most shoppers are clearly good candidates, but efforts must be made to minimise commercial disadvantage in areas just outside the traffic-free zone. There should be sensitivity to the need to retain desirable trades in the area - the small shops, craftsmen, cafes and so forth. A liberal attitude to forecourt and kerb-side trading can be a significant help in creating a lively street.

It will be possible, too, to improve the environment by introducing recreational features into a pedestrian street system. Street cafes, proper seating and the exploitation of water and vegetation are important. The aim should be to exploit the particular character of the area so as to create a zone which is unique to the town. As a craftsman works with a piece of wood, so should the designer work with the grain of the area. Conservation of buildings of character and features which can best be described as amiable eccentricities should be considered part of the process of pedestrianisation. New uses for old buildings will also help to emphasise the character of the area. As much of the town's visible history as possible should be brought into the pedestrian street system. Statuary should be employed as part of the visual experience. Lighting, too, can play its part in emphasising important buildings and the townscape.

One of the main benefits derived from pedestrianisation is the sense of relaxation brought to the town centre, which becomes a sort of open-air living room. The spaces must be furnished with this in mind. There must be plenty of seats, well-designed and preferably with backrests and armrests. There is a great deal to be said for individual chairs (as in Munich). A sensible and sensitive planting scheme can add greatly to the sense of relaxation. Seating areas should generally be protected from the main pedestrian routes, and should cater for those who like sun and those who prefer shade. They must also permit the occupants to indulge in one of man's favourite activities - watching the passing crowd.

Safety from traffic is obviously achieved without difficulty in most traffic-free areas, but there must be special attention to the problem if public transport or other vehicles use the pedestrian street system. Speed control devices should be considered and street furniture used to protect the pedestrian from unexpected traffic. Protection from crime is usually achieved by increased pedestrian activity. A resident population in the area also increases the number of eyes on the streets. Banks have found it advantageous to be included in a traffic-free area, as a "get-away" car outside their premises in a pedestrian street is immediately obvious. Thus, the site becomes safer than a position in a conventional street.

The need for shelter must be related to climate. In some countries it may be sensible to construct free-standing canopies linking the frontages or, as in Gotgatan in Gothenburg, to cover the whole street. In such a case, the fire-brigade must be given access to existing roofs. In both cases it is important to consider whether or not the appearance of existing buildings will be harmed by the shelter provided. Obviously, bus-stops should have weather protection, as should street cafes. Equally, in some climates the sun may have to be considered an enemy.

There should be well-sited and signposted lavatories, pillar boxes, telephones, left-luggage lockers (in large areas), storage for bicycles, and a spectrum of facilities for food and drink. Automatic vending machines should be sited at nodal points or grouped by existing shops. The larger schemes might even provide supervised child care coupled with a small play area.

Although circumstances have changed and there is perhaps no longer quite the same degree of commercial opposition to traffic-free streets, it is nevertheless as well to recognise that discussions beforehand can be complicated and protracted. In Norwich, fifteen separate interest groups were consulted at three stages, twice during the preparation of the scheme to close London Street to traffic and once during the experimental closure period. In subsequent street schemes discussions were generally less difficult or lengthy, but the same groups were involved and inevitably the process took time.

INNER-CITY DECAY

Usually (but not always) located immediately around the city centre, inner-city decay is easy enough to recognise but the reasons for decline can vary from city to city. Usually, the obvious physical characteristic is rundown, ill-maintained housing, often occupied by the unskilled and their families or immigrants. The shopping areas with unoccupied space on the upper floors show environmental decline. Often there is a reduction in the type of shop useful to the population, accompanied by an increase in service industries, filling stations and the like. In general, land tends to be under-used. There are often large areas of dormant land owned by public authorities, and brick-strewn gaps in the urban fabric caused by demolition without replacement. Many such gaps are used as car and truck parks. Open space and small landscape features are often ill-maintained and sometimes have a dreariness which is daunting even to the insensitive. I often think that the two dullest words in the English language are recreation ground. The connotation of boredom, dull landscape, worn grass, wire fences and an atmosphere of despair describes local parks in far too many inner areas. Recreation planners all too often believe that if they provide so many hectares of open space per thousand population, they have catered for the needs of the people. Quality rather than mere arithmetic should be the measure.

The inner areas are probably the zones where employment prospects for the resident population have declined radically in the past few years. The old nineteenth century intermixture of housing and factories has suffered most from age. Some industries have moved to find more space for their processes and better access for their transport arrangements, predominantly by road today. Other industries have quietly died, overtaken by competition or because their unpleasant characteristics (noise, fumes and smoke) attracted the unwelcome attention of town planners or public health authorities. In many areas land has been made derelict by the industrial processes carried out previously.

The impact of traffic is usually devastating. Commuters in their cars find short-cut routes through terrace-house streets, a phenomenon known in Britain as rat-runs. Heavy goods vehicles servicing the factories which remain in the inner areas add to the unpleasant environment. Often, too, they are parked overnight on cleared sites in residential areas. Public transport, necessary for a higher proportion of people than in outer areas, is generally confined to the major radial routes passing through the zones.

The inner areas, too, are the districts where the redevelopment of older housing and its replacement have led to the development of large districts where there is only one class of tenure. It could be said that large areas of social housing lead to increased division of the city as a whole.

There is also the danger of treating the problem of inner cities as self-contained issues, whereas they are closely associated with planning policies for the city as a whole. Equally, it is easy to forget that cities have always changed and there can be a natural but misplaced desire to return the inner city areas to their nineteenth century role, but in architectural modern dress, as it were. In finding remedies it will probably be necessary to reverse some of the forces of dispersal while accepting that the reduction in population can improve the surroundings for those who remain and serve as a magnet to attract other social groups. In short, inner areas must be given self-confidence in order to obtain investment from house owners and companies.

INNER-CITY REVIVAL

The immediate need is for direct action. We have been buried in the vast flood of reports analysing the problems of inner areas, but even as these studies are prepared the plight of the inner areas grows worse. In Britain action is being taken in Lambeth, Liverpool and Birmingham, among other places, by a tripartite partnership comprising the government, the county councils and the district councils. This Inner City Partnership Programme (ICPP) is the vehicle for public projects designed to improve the economy, environment and transport infrastructure. Although it is too soon to expect results, the cores of our cities are continuing to decay while central government, counties and districts all attempt to make an elaborate bureaucratic machine respond to immediate needs. Already there is criticism that local residents are not being properly consulted. On the other hand, we all know that the price of public participation is that the whole planning process is delayed. Speedy and effective action is rarely compatible with democracy and full consultation.

We must also bear in mind that these issues are not merely physical planning problems. Virtually all arms of government have a role to play and their actions should be coordinated. Personal social services are particularly important. Our role is inevitably confined to physical measures, but low incomes are the greatest single problem. The impact of planning on social issues is at best indirect.

It should also be borne in mind that the objective is to revive our inner cities. It is neither realistic nor desirable to try to reproduce in modern building materials the inner cities as they were. The forces which shaped nineteenth century development have changed and the inner cities must reflect those changes. Their regeneration will succeed only if it is related to our needs today, particularly as the private sector will have a major part to play in bringing about that revitalisation.

Perhaps the greatest role that government can play is to promote confidence so that employers will invest and individuals will be happy to spend money on maintaining and improving their homes. The building societies or other agencies, too, can assist by being a little more responsive to the needs of inner area home-buyers. One suspects that as the exodus from inner areas was inspired by a desire for better housing, the reverse trend may well be one of the best ways of stimulating revival, provided that improvement of the surroundings and a relaxed attitude to home-ownership funding can be achieved. Promotion of confidence also requires that town planners return to their main role, that of giving creative stimulus to town improvement, as opposed to the more negative aspects of control and restriction of development, which has become endemic in some circles.

The decline in population and employment in inner areas is not undesirable in itself. The centres of some of our cities have been too crowded, and we now have the opportunity to give people living and working there more room. In our anxiety to prevent the total collapse of inner areas we should not become obsessed with number or with population levels for their own sake. Our concern should be for quality, not quantity.

As pressures fall, land resources should become less of a constraint. The West Midlands is not typical in this respect and in some other areas the problem is one of too much land even now. There are however major problems in utilising land in inner areas. The first problem is land values. In the absence of a proper market owners often value their land too highly: we must establish its true value. Local authorities could perhaps release land in their ownership by Dutch auction methods. Some sites may well have negative value and authorities may have to pay developers to take them. Major landholdings are the second problem. Public bodies, including local authorities, own large areas of land, particulary in inner areas. In the Birmingham Partnership area 77 per cent of all vacant land is publicly owned. In many cases this land is no longer required for the use for which it was purchased, e.g. major road schemes now abandoned. Local authorities are unlikely to be able to develop much of this land in the near future, and if it were released for private development it would not only be developed quickly, but it would also help to bring down the market price of inner area land.

In Britain, local authorities are by no means the only public bodies owning land. British Rail has been able to release some former sidings for development, but there have been major problems in releasing land owned by the Gas Corporation. Some sites of former gas plants which are now redundant are being held in reserve in case they are required after North Sea gas has been used up. This is a very curious attitude. Coal gas is surely more likely to be made at or near the coalfield and piped round the country via the gas grid which was one of the benefits of North Sea gas. Dormant land in public ownership is incompatible with the urgent need to use land creatively - it has a disastrous effect on the surroundings of inner areas.

The third problem is physical constraints. Many sites are difficult to develop because of physical constraints. Derelict land can be a major influence in inner areas. While in some cases such land does provide valuable opportunities for informal recreation, the use of derelict land, often with hidden mine-shafts, deep quarries or dangerous chemicals, as unofficial playgrounds, can be extremely dangerous. The influence of derelict land varies from area to area, but it is perhaps the biggest single environmental factor in parts of the Black Country. The significance of recent government action in declaring most of the West Midlands a derelict land clearance area with 100 per cent grants for reclamation should not be underestimated. We have already achieved a great deal of reclamation in collaboration with the districts. About 1000 acres of derelict and waste land has either been reclaimed since 1974 or is in the pipeline, and as a result of increased grants the pace of reclamation will increase. Apart from the improvement to the environment, land will be released for development in some but not all cases. In any event, improvement of the surroundings is crucial to restoring confidence. The reclamation of large tracts of land in the Rühr region has had an important effect on the surroundings of many millions of people, and has probably been one of the main factors in the successful industrial regeneration of the area.

I have already emphasised the major role that the private sector will have to play, but experience has shown that we can influence and mould trends but not direct them. We must therefore begin by making inner areas more attractive to investors, whether they be financial institutions, companies or individuals. Confidence is perhaps the biggest single factor in investment decisions, and at the moment nobody has confidence in the long-term future of inner areas. Local authorities have themselves often contributed to the lack of confidence by producing unrealistic plans which create an atmosphere of uncertainty because they cannot be carried out. As a result, industrialists are unwilling to expand or improve their premises, and people are unable to obtain loans to carry out housing improvements or to buy houses. Authorities could, therefore, remove one constraint on investment by making a vigorous examination of their own published plans, implementing those which are capable of early action, and deleting those which cannot be started quickly. In the West Midlands, for example, we are reviewing all road improvement lines and major road schemes to remove blight wherever possible. Even in this one area the potential contribution is very great, as is reflected in the fact that capital expenditure on highways in 1977/78 was only a quarter of that envisaged in the structure plans.

Currently, almost endless difficulties are placed in the path of the developer in inner areas. I have already referred to the problems of acquiring land and removing physical constraints. The problem of administrative red tape persists and, if anything, the new partnership machinery will not make matters easier. While it is obviously important that all our efforts should be coordinated, the partnership arrangements are more likely to frustrate and delay development than stimulate it. This is simply another symptom of the difficulties of the two-tier local government process which is totally unsuited to the creative management of complex urban areas.

In reviewing inner areas, government in its widest sense should establish very clearly what direct action it can take and stop interfering elsewhere so that other people can act with the maximum freedom. Obviously, control of development must continue in order to prevent the worst excesses, but if we are to make inner areas more attractive to industry our policies and procedures must be more responsive to its needs.

Most authorities in most countries have the powers necessary to assemble sites for development, and they can use their powers effectively to encourage development in inner areas. Local authorities can make a significant contribution even if they only concentrate on land and buildings already in their ownership. I have already suggested that there should be major programmes of land release. Similarly, houses which are at present vacant or occupied by short-term tenants could be placed on the open market. Some experience in homesteading is already available in the United States, and a different scheme bearing the same name has been suggested by the Greater London Council. Probably the most effective scheme of homesteading was carried out in Baltimore, where the city in the early 1970s bought an area containing 580 houses with the intention of demolishing them in order to create a new downtown commercial zone. In 1975, however, there was a significant change of heart. The houses were offered for $1 each to families, provided that certain specified repairs and improvements were effected within two years. The imaginative approach to homesteading has paid off handsomely and could be copied with advantage in other countries.

This would not only make good use of virtually derelict housing but also bring a different group of people into inner areas and reduce the obvious social differences between them and the suburbs. There is no reason why the same approach could not be adopted for other buildings, such as shops and small factories. In many places, for example, civic buildings, long since abandoned, are still unused or underused. These buildings were put up by the local community and belong to that community in the fullest sense. They are often the dominant feature of the local scene and could be the focal point of local activities if effective measures were taken to restore the structure and find new uses for it that are suited to the fabric and the needs of the area. We need a much more flexible approach to alternative uses for existing buildings. If necessary, they could be given to community groups, or we could at least allow them to be used almost free of charge. Creative conservation of this kind is important in a world where finances are limited and all other resources are finite.

While I would strongly support the view that the total scale of inner urban revival is so great as to demand national priority, I do not believe that these areas can be dealt with by sweeping large-scale proposals. With the greater freedom I have already called for must go greater responsibility and sensitivity, and here the authorities must take the lead. They must show that they care for the physical environment of inner areas even more than for that of the suburbs. This attitude will have to be apparent in street cleaning as much as in development. In schemes for derelict land reclamation and building conservation adequate provision must be made for the future maintenance. At the same time we could have a series of local task forces which would move in to perform particular tasks, such as fencing an open site or clearing small areas of dereliction and then move on. This could be linked to an "operation eyesore" which would attempt to mobilise a wide range of local groups with a minimal involvement of officialdom. In all this the emphasis should be on the active participation of the local community. Self-help can be one of the most effective ways of returning to good urban housekeeping.

There will of course always be cases where the local authority will be developing land in its own right, either in the form of new buildings or improvements to existing buildings. Housing improvement has a central role, but the evidence so far is that homes are still deteriorating faster than they are being improved. Both central and local government have to make sure that the level of grants or other financial incentives keep pace with building costs and that people are encouraged to use them. The systems of general improvement areas and housing action areas employed in Britain could be of interest to other countries. Improvement of the external surroundings in inner city areas on a street-by-street basis is also an important way of enhancing the quality of life. There is room, too, for imaginative experiments with public transport. Orbital routes, fixed-fare minibuses on fixed routes, variations on the dial-a-ride systems modified for inner areas are examples of some of the approaches which may be tried.

There is also the opportunity to carry out environmental improvements in inner city zones which are predominantly industrial, but we should not underestimate the time and efforts such improvements require if they are to make a significant contribution. It is essential that local industrialists be drawn into preliminary discussion before specific proposals are set out. Industrial improvement schemes should not only provide cosmetic improvements, important though these are, but should also help to make industry operate more efficiently in inner areas. One key constraint at present is traffic congestion. Inner areas are in general easy to get to, but it is very difficult to move around within them, particularly if you are driving a heavy lorry. We must therefore concentrate on improving local traffic conditions within industrial areas, minimising on-street parking, providing alternative car parks for business callers and encouraging industrialists to provide off-street loading facilities.

There is probably little need for authorities to compete with the private sector in providing large or even medium-sized factories, but, as I have already pointed out, they could help in assembling suitable sites. At the moment there does seem to be a need for local authorities to provide low-cost small units, however. This can often be done by refurbishing existing empty factores and converting them to flatted workshops suited to craft skills, a growing need as conventional industrial manpower demands continue to decline.

The desire to help small firms is widespread among planners, and is probably justified. We should remember, however, that the cost of such conversions and improvements is high in terms of time and money. At the same time the net gain in jobs is likely to be very small and can be completely wiped out by the decision of one large employer to discontinue one shift. In our enthusiams for David we should not ignore the needs of Goliath.

Of course, there have always been poor areas in cities and I do not expect that disparities will disappear. Pepys, Boswell, Victor Hugo and Dickens have all written sensitively of the brutality, poverty and hopelessness of inner areas, as well as their companionability. But for far too long inner areas have had to be home for those who could not afford to live elsewhere.

There are many advantages in living close to the town centre and homesteading would open one new market. There is also a market, I believe, for new private housing in inner areas: this is reflected in increasing interest by private house-builders. In some cases the emphasis is likely to be on low-cost housing for sale but, given the right circumstances, we should also be able to attract higher quality housing. This might be part of a total scheme, the stimulus for which could be development by the public sector of a new urban park of very high quality. Few new parks of this kind have been developed since the nineteenth century and such development could make the adjacent land very attractive to builders. The restoration of the Tiergarten in West Berlin is an example of this kind of approach.

As for promoting house-building in inner areas, we should remember not only the positive advantages I have already mentioned, but also that rising petrol costs may well bring a reaction against commuting and a resurgence of interest in urban life. Most inner cities have features on which interesting and civilised surroundings can be built to stimulate a return to city living. For example, several have a network of canals, but in many cases these lie desolate and disused, though they have immense potential not only for recreation but as the focal point for new development. A number of British local authorities have already started to capitalise on their canal assets: Birmingham, Wolverhampton, Rochdale, but the surface has hardly been scratched as yet.

One of the saddest things about some inhabitants of the great industrial cities is their often scant regard for their inherited surroundings. Either there is the apologetic view that there is nothing worth saving (rarely true), or a downright philistine attitude which holds that progress is made when an old building is pulled down. The plain fact is that there is much to conserve creatively and improve in our industrial cities - and not just the major nineteenth century buildings of the railway kings, the coal dukes or the textile barons. Many people recognise the value of the minor classics in our streets, the pub carefully designed to follow the curve of a corner (rarely done today), the clock in the market place to mark perhaps the relief of Mafeking, or the thousand amiable eccentricities which make our towns different from all others. Conservation is not just the province of the special interest group. It is also good commonsense management of our surroundings to ensure that we make the best use of what we have and retain individuality in our surroundings at a time when standard buildings are making all our cities look much the same. Conservation has a considerable role to play in our inner areas - in particular to retain, improve and re-use the many solid nineteenth century buildings. We are now beginning to value Victorian architecture more highly. I am not so much concerned with grand architecture but with the style and form of ordinary housing and local buildings - the minor classics of our cities. These provide a domestic scale and a richness of design which have been missing from much of the architectural dandruff that we have suffered since 1945.

In some ways, town planners have contributed directly to the present state of the inner cities by imposing the dead hand of restriction. Whatever positive action we may take and encourage others to take in the inner city will be wasted while easier and more profitable opportunities are freely available elsewhere. The inner areas need time and assistance before they can compete freely with green-field sites outside our cities.

Opportunities for development on such sites must therefore be restricted to a minimal level. This requires sympathetic action by authorities which are often not responsible for inner areas themselves. Altruism is not a common local authority virtue, but it is certainly needed now.

Finally, I must acknowledge that the role of the planner is concentrated on the physical fabric of inner areas, and while we all hope to be able to influence economic and social events through physical action, I do not pretend that the approach I have outlined will in itself solve all the wider social problems of our cities. Action by other agencies is also essential, but, given this, I believe that our inner areas do contain the seeds of their own regeneration. It is our task to see that our cities are revived. We must provide the opportunities for others to carry out their work to ensure that we can make all parts of our cities decent places in which to live. In a world which has changed radically in the past few years, "growth" is no longer the factor that it was. We must, I believe, develop a sensitive, intricate, street-by-street entrepreneurial approach to the regeneration of our run-down areas, recognising that while there may be very little new growth, that is no excuse for bad husbandry of our inner cities. All of us were perhaps irritated by our parents when once they told us that "a stitch in time saves nine" or "waste not want not". The plain fact is that our parents were right: let us demonstrate by our actions that we can hand on to our children cities which have been carefully tended by good housekeepers.

Planning considerations in the renewal of the Old City of Ramla

24

Arie Rahamimoff and others   Israel

INTRODUCTION

Ramla, one of the historical cities of Israel, was established in the eighth century as a resting station for the journey between the cities of Jaffa and Jerusalem. The city has been populated since its inception and today is comprised of three religious denominations, Jews, Moslems and Christians. Following the establishment of the State of Israel, the population of the city increased through building around the old area, in which the pre-1948 urban fabric was left virtually unchanged. Deterioration in the physical and social condition of the Old City of Ramla led to the decision to renew the area. Shortly thereafter, in 1978, the area was included among the first renewal areas in the national Project Renewal for Distressed Neighbourhoods. This project constitutes a concentrated effort spread over sixty-five distressed neighbourhoods in Israel to improve the physical, social and economic conditions of the neighbourhood. Participating in this project are the national authorities (various government agencies), the local authorities (municipalities and local councils), the inhabitants and the Jews of the diaspora who are actively involved in the renewal process and in part of the financing. The project is being implemented by a renewal authority whose purpose is to promote and coordinate the renewal plan. A comprehensive planning system was established and the physical urban renewal plan is currently in the final stages of consolidation. Up to now, renovations, extensions and environmental improvements have been carried out with the marshalling of the required infrastructure. New building will start during 1981.

THE PLANNING BACKGROUND

Historical background. Ramla was established by Khalif Ben Abd-al-Malik for the House of Umayyad in the year 716. Its location at the important international crossroads connecting Cairo and Damascus and on the national transverse road connecting Jaffa and Jerusalem naturally led to the development of the city as a transit station providing commercial services and accommodation. At this time, the city extended over an area of 2500 hectares and was surrounded by a wall. There are no remains or findings from this period. During the Crusades, the city constituted a link in the defence network surrounding Ashkelon as well as a transit station on the road to Jerusalem. Magnificent remains exist from this period such as the Great Tower of Ramla. With the conquest by Saladin in 1260, the city was devastated. For a short period in the nineteenth century, the city was once again used by religious pilgrims and a large religious complex including a church and hostel were established, and on these remains the Franciscan

Church stands today. So too, many religious institutions and places of accommodation were erected in the Mameluke Period and the beginning of the Ottoman Period. Only at the end of the Ottoman Period did the assets of the city and its importance decline. Cheap residential buildings were erected, reflecting a poorer era, and the population declined. During the British occupation, the regional importance of Ramla again became evident, and it found expression in commercial development and in the erection of residential and public buildings.

Today, the following components comprise the built-up area of the renewal site (see Figures 3-6):

□ Single buildings or the remains of traditional monumental Moslem structures, the majority having been built between the fourteenth and eighteenth centuries. Historically, the Christian religious building complexes and residential buildings owned by the church have sustained the least damage.

□ Non-monumental structures from the late Ottoman Period, including large stone buildings such as the area of the market and the adjacent residential areas. Many of these buildings have been destroyed over the years.

□ Structures built during the British Mandate Period including public and residential buildings in the western area.

□ Buildings erected after the establishment of the State of Israel, especially housing projects.

Social and demographic background. Jewish settlement in the city of Ramla was begun in 1948. New immigrants arriving at this time were housed in the Old City in homes abandoned by the Arab population. By 1978, the total population of the renewal area including Jews and minority groups numbered 8000 persons as opposed to the 11,000 who had lived there in 1965. An examination of population movements on the site reveals two contradictory tendencies. The Jewish population declined from about 9000 in 1961 to 5000 in 1975. This trend has resulted from outmigration accompanied by a process of negative selection; that is to say, families with a relatively high socio-economic status have left the neighbourhood, leaving behind older families or large families with limited mobility. In opposition to this, the minority population grew by 60 per cent from about 1800 in 1961 to about 3000 in 1978. During the same period, the growth in the general Ramla population was even greater, being in the vicinity of 150 per cent, reaching 38,700 by the end of 1978. Generally it can be observed that the Jewish population of the site exhibits characteristics similar to population groups in other distressed neighbourhoods; on the other hand, the minority population enjoys a socio-economic status higher than the national minority average.

The demographic and social structure of the population. The demographic structure of the Jewish population is essentially homogeneous with respect to origin; about 80 per cent of all heads of households originate in Asian-African countries. Families are essentially large, the average household size being 4-6 persons (national average 3.5). The population is comprised of a large proportion of elderly people (7.1 per cent as opposed to the national average of 5.5 per cent). There is also a relatively low proportion of young people. The population has a relatively low level of education. Illiteracy among heads of households is high at 27 per cent and higher education is low at 3 per cent. There is a low level of participation in the labour force; about 25 per cent as opposed to 31 per cent in new urban settlements. Most of the working population is employed in the building trade, industry and transportation. The standard of housing is low with a large percentage of small apartments; 25 per cent of these do not possess toilet facilities and about 20 per cent do not have washing facilities. About 20 per cent of families live in densities of more than three persons per room as opposed to the 4 per cent national average.

The Moslem population has a low proportion of elderly people (4 per cent). Average household size is 6.3 persons which is similar to the national minorities average. Education levels are above average. Participation in the labour force is well above average, but housing conditions are poor. The Moslem population densities are higher than those of the Jews and the lack of toilet facilities in their apartments is greater.

The area of the Old City has a large proportion of welfare recipients, 1300 families, constituting 14 per cent of all families. Crime levels in the renewal area are similar to those found in other cities, but trade in drugs is more pronounced. Due to their relative isolation and low income levels the problems of the many elderly people are accentuated among those characteristic of this population.

A large number of public institutions are located within the renewal area serving the population of the site and of the city as a whole. The physical condition of most of the structures is deficient with regard to dampness and peeling walls.

The physical background and the development of the built-up area. The renewal site is located along the eastern and southern boundary of the city, south of the main road and adjacent to the new part of the city on its western side (see Figure 1).

The following constitute the major urban characteristics of the site:

□ The site proposed for renewal is located in the historical area of the city.
□ The centre of the site is the commercial and business centre of Ramla.
□ Within the site are located most of the administrative, governmental, and social functions of the central region of the country and of the city itself.
□ Densities on the site are low and the many unbuilt sites constitute a large part of the land reserves of the city.
□ Among the significant urban elements on the site the following can be mentioned:
  - Herzl Boulevard
  - The Old City of Ramla with its churches, mosques and alleys
  - The market and "President's Park"
  - The city park, civic centre, public institutions and the sports centre
  - Regional offices of public institutions
  - Tourism and recreation sites
  - Workshops and trades area
  - The central bus station
  - Three cemeteries
  - The railway station
□ The renewal area covers some 150 hectares, or 30 per cent of the urban area. The population of the renewal area is 6500, which is 20 per cent of the total population of the city.

□ The Old City is the central focus of Arab Ramla and is characterised by Mediterranean architecture; stacked-building around courtyards, interwoven with narrow, winding alleys. Building during the British Mandate period in the western and southern parts of the Old City is characterised by structures of one or two storeys on parcelled plots.

Towards the end of the 1950s and the beginning of the 1960s vacant areas were used for public housing projects of two to four storeys. Generally the standard of construction and infrastructure development of these housing projects was low. There are at present 1400 structures in the area including 1520 housing units and about 800 additional units which are mainly for commercial use. The number of familites in the area is 1520, 30 per cent of whom live in public housing projects while 70 per cent live in old buildings. The physical condition of the apartments has been surveyed structurally with the following results: 2 per cent of the housing units were classified as dangerous (twenty-five units); 15 per cent were classified as being in bad condition (180 units); 40 per cent of the units lack toilet facilities in the apartment; 56 per cent of the units were classified as being in good condition. Most of the public areas on the site are neglected or poorly maintained. The physical distribution of public areas is unplanned and is based on the development of vacant plots wherever they happen to be. With the exception of the main roads, most of the roads on the site are neither paved nor drained. Sidewalks are uncompleted and there is no overall pedestrian system. The underground and overhead infrastructure is insufficient and defective.

Ownership of land. Most land is government-owned with the exception of the Christian and Moslem religious areas. Only a few small plots are privately owned. The apartments in the public housing projects are privately owned, while the ownership of the structures of the Old City is vested in Amidar, the government agency for the administration of assets.

THE GOALS OF THE PLAN
The plan comprises a statement of intent and a series of guidelines for its achievement.
□ The development of the Old City of Ramla and its environs, and integrating it with the urban fabric of Ramla-Lod.
□ Realisation of the potential of the site through urban development.
□ Transformation of the negative image of the area by changing the appearance and the environmental quality of the site.
□ Raising living-standards and attracting additional population through improvements in the housing conditions and the level of services offered to the population.
□ Reducing the socio-economic gap and improving the housing conditions of the minority populations in relation to the general population.
□ Renewal without forced relocation outside the site.
□ Clear articulation of the urban circulation system through appropriate connections with the regional and national transportation axis, together with the development of internal movements systems - buses, cars, parking, pedestrians.
□ Ordering of the urban infrastructure system, based on development plans.
□ Preservation of historical sites and development, parallel to intensification and realisation of the tourist potential of the site.
□ Improving the social links between the Old City and the new.

THE PLANNING PROCESS AND THE BODIES INVOLVED IN THE AREA

The renewal site of Ramla is part of the regional planning system of the cities of Ramla and Lod, and both are influencing and responding to the renewal programme. The planning process can be distinguished by five major stages:

- Formulation of an initial planning approach. During this stage planning goals were consolidated in relation to the proposed changes in character of the neighbourhood and with regard to the urban system.
- Physical and social surveys including those of families, physical structures, buildings to be preserved, state of existing plans, transportation, and public institutions.
- Analysis of the survey material as a basis for preparing the programme. This analysis focused on the building potential of the site as well as its limitations and planning options.
- Preparation of an overall renewal programme to include housing, public institutions and transport.
- Detailing the programme and developing a planning system in which the area was divided into precincts relating to components of time and place. At this stage the implementation of the essential activities were determined and planned.

It was further determined that the decisions in each of the renewal neighbourhoods would be made on the local level through the establishment of a local steering committee chaired by the mayor and with the participation of the inhabitants, the local authority and the national institutions. The committee's tasks are to define needs, establish priorities, instigate plans, and approve budgets. The local steering committee represents the inhabitants on issues of social and physical planning. Working with the committee is the renewal authority, which administers the implementation of the plan. It should be mentioned that the planning system in Ramla began operating prior to the declaration of Project Renewal.

SITE PLANNING PRINCIPLES

The relationship of the existing physical fabric to the population structure is a guiding renewal principle. It avoids large-scale demolition of structures and forced relocation of population. In areas where the existing fabric permits building extensions, this can be done in various ways; building on roofs and around courtyards and new buildings on vacant plots in groupings of 50-100 housing units. Larger vacant spaces will be developed as new precincts. The goal is to attract a population of higher socio-economic status who require a higher level of services (see Figure 2). The character of the new building is derived from the existing pattern. The emphasis is to be placed on single-storey homes and duplexes. The type of building facilitates the idea of the growing house, of improving and extending the living area of the house over time (see Figure 11).

The existing road network will constitute the framework of the future system. This is based on financial considerations and the convenience of the inhabitants who will use the system during the renewal and building phases. The hierarchy of roads will be articulated in decreasing order from the national highway network tangential to the site, through the city and down to the residential streets approaching the houses. Landscape planning and the use of special vegetation will emphasise the different parts of the neighbourhood. Parallel to this, a continuous open space system will be created from the entrance to the home up to the urban park, while at the neighbourhood level, integration will be achieved between roads, pedestrians, institutions and parking areas. In view of the short distances between the different parts of the site and the easy topography, a bicycle network is planned. New urban boulevards will connect the old and new city (see Figure 12).

The social aspects of the renewal process will include the provision of services, leading to improvements in the standards of living and of housing. Current policy lies in the direction of revitalising and strengthening the existing system of services. The first stage will concentrate on the improvement of the housing conditions of the population of the area, which will facilitate the advancement of the renewal process. In the second stage, part of the new building will be designated for a strong population from outside the neighbourhood and the city. The creation of appropriate housing facilities for young couples will be stressed as well, so as to prevent their leaving the neighbourhood, thereby maintaining an appropriate age structure of the population.

A staging plan has been formulated for the area with the aim of dispersing the activity and the budget over the neighbourhood so as to allow the simultaneous improvement of all parts. The renewal will be done in development portions wich each portion including building additions, renovation of structures, environment and infrastructure improvements. Parts of the renewal site will undergo a process of transformation with the addition of new residential buildings, environmental improvements and revitalisation through the provision of additional urban functions.

BUILDING PRINCIPLES

The planning of the site and the planning precincts will be undertaken by different planners in order to encourage architectural variety. The overall plan will be directed by a site planner whose function will be to define principles, supervise detailed planning and coordinate building and infrastructure planning. An inventory of building forms and components will be developed including ground-related structures, balconies, roofs, pergolas, stairways and windows.

CONCLUSIONS

The Ramla renewal plan constitutes part of an overall national plan. At this juncture, the renewal depends on public investments to advance the plans. A major goal is to develop the personal initiative of the inhabitants of the neighbourhood so as to improve their social and physical conditions and to become involved enough to maintain the neighbourhoods. A further objective is to attract private investment to the neighbourhood and to encourage the participation of promoters from outside in an effort to change the image of the neighbourhood. Failure to attain these goals will result in a reversal of the condition of the neighbourhood which will necessitate repeated renewal activities. The choice and delineation of renewal neighbourhoods is often done in an arbitrary manner and thus the process should be seen as one extending over a number of years and encompassing new areas for renewal, which should, in the meantime, be maintained to prevent deterioration. The index of the success of the renewal activities should be the reduction of dependence of the neighbourhood on the renewal agency. Gradual withdrawal of the renewal authority from the neighbourhood requires the acceptance of responsibility for taking care of the neighbourhood by its inhabitants, the local authority and government agencies. Continuing dependence of the neighbourhood on public bodies endangers the prospects of the neighbourhood for independent advancement. In the national context, this dependence is liable to create a burden on the public sector which will not be able to be maintained over a long period.

ACKNOWLEDGMENTS

This paper was revised for publication in August 1980. The project was commissioned by the Ministry of Housing and Construction, and by the Company for the Development of the Lod-Ramla Region. The project was planned by Rahamimoff, Architects and Urbanists: Arie Rahamimoff, David Guggenheim, in collaboration with Maya Halevy and Geoffrey Sifrin. During the planning process the following architects participated in the detailed planning: Bracha-Chakim, Yaar, Ben-Ari, Hersman, Safdie, Spector-Amisar, Fischer, Mandl-Kertesz. The traffic consultant was Zelinger and the landscape artist was Sarig.

Figure 1
Existing urban structure

Figure 2
Comprehensive renewal plan

Figure 3
General panorama of the Old City of Ramla

Figure 4
A typical alleyway in the Old City

Figure 5
A religious institution in the Old City

Figure 6
Bialik Street: a typical street façade

Figure 8
Before proposed renovation

Figure 7
A typical alleyway in the Old City

Figure 9
After renovation

Figure 10
Model of two- and three-storey ground-related structures

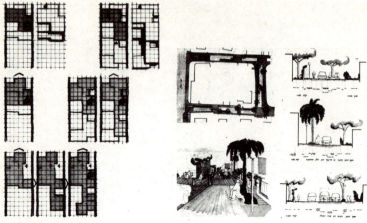

Figure 11
A "growing" home

Figure 12
An integrated urban street

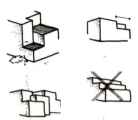

Figures 13 and 14
A residential section of the Old City before
and after proposed renovation

Figure 15
Examples of
building mass

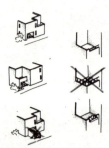

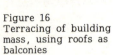

Figure 16
Terracing of building
mass, using roofs as
balconies

Figure 17
Use of roofs

Figure 18
Integration of auxiliary
structures in the building
mass

IX: SMALL-SCALE RENEWAL PROJECTS

Neighbourhood preservation and revitalisation   25

John McNamara   United States

INTRODUCTION

In the United States we have experienced a major shift from the large-scale publicly sponsored urban renewal efforts of the 1950s and 1960s to smaller scale, neighbourhood based revitalisation efforts. This shift includes a major change in the renewal approach which emphasises rehabilitation and preservation as the basis for project activities, as opposed to total clearance and redevelopment. As a result of these changes in project scale and emphasis, neighbourhood planning and urban design efforts have become a key component to guide the preservation and revitalisation of our cities, particularly their inner-city communities.

Neighbourhood-level urban planning design efforts basically fall into three categories or scales of projects. These are neighbourhood-wide urban design framework development, or community planning efforts with a major urban design emphasis (such as the Whittier Urban Design Framework which received a national urban design award in 1978); commercial area or district level revitalisation projects; and site-specific urban design and planning projects (e.g. neighbourhood pedestrian-ways, infill housing development criteria) which, in many cases, are a stage in the implementation of larger urban design frameworks on a neighbourhood scale.

In Minneapolis, the city is divided into eighty-two neighbourhoods within eleven communities or planning districts. Of these eighty-two neighbourhoods, seventy-seven have highly active neighbourhood associations and business organisations. Within the inner city (the first two rings of neighbourhood surrounding the CBD) there are eighteen neighbourhoods. Within the past four years, eleven of these have conducted a community planning/urban design study.

A number of other major core cities in the United States also have highly active neighbourhood preservation/revitalisation programmes, including Baltimore, San Francisco, Kansas City and Dallas. In the United States, funding for urban planning and design and the subsequent implementation activities has come primarily from two sources.

The first is the federal Community Development Block Grant programme. In Minneapolis, for instance, non-profit neighbourhood organisations apply for and directly receive Community Development Block Grant funds and, in turn retain private consultants or use the services of the Municipal Planning and Development Department to conduct urban design studies.

The second source is private foundation or corporation grants, e.g. the Dayton Hudson Foundation, Honeywell and the Minneapolis Star and Tribune.

My firm, BRW, is currently involved in a number of projects on each of these scales and they are funded from a variety of sources. I will use a project I have been involved in for a number of years as illustration: the Whittier Urban Design Framework and its subsequent implementation which is currently in its third year. The Whittier neighbourhood is one of the largest in Minneapolis. Located two kilometres from the CBD it is approximately thirty-six hectares in area and has a population of approximately 10,000.

NEIGHBOURHOOD URBAN DESIGN PROCESS

Before we initiate any neighbourhood-level urban design effort we approach the client group, usually a neighbourhood association, and other participants in the project and publicly discuss with them the question of what we mean by urban design, particularly at the neighbourhood level. It is very important for all those involved to have a clear understanding of the design and planning process so that they feel a part of it, actively participate in it and, most importantly, seek and pursue immediate project implementation.

The general consensus, reached more times than not, would read something like this. We need a design for a functional and secure urban environment which provides convenient goods and services to its residents and promotes healthy interaction among its members, building a strong sense of "community". This definition makes it plain that we as urban designers and planners are not simply dealing with the physical elements of the urban environment, e.g. buildings and physical infrastructure but also, and just as importantly, the socio-economic factors, e.g. the community's economic health, that of its local business district, the community's social and human services, and the residents themselves, their problems, needs, desires and aspirations.

The Whittier Urban Design Framework was a four-step neighbourhood design/planning process which included the following stages: an inventory and analysis of existing physical, social and economic conditions; a formulation of community design/planning policy; urban design framework development; and implementation strategy development for project programming and staging.

PHASES

The first phase, inventory and analysis of existing conditions, included a number of traditional planning inventory items as well as a number of inventory tasks with a specific urban design emphasis: urban context analysis, land use, property values, ownership, vehicular circulation, pedestrian circulation, visual image assessment, building conditions analysis, resident and business surveys, public space behaviour observations, and crime location analysis.

The second phase, the formulation of community design planning policy, makes use of the results of the inventory items to generate community-based urban design policy. An initial series of community meetings is held to identify major design/planning issues, to formulate community-based criteria on which to resolve the issues, and to determine priorities.

A second series of community meetings is held to review and assess design/planning concepts against established criteria and to formulate community-based design/planning policy based on the conceputal alternatives presented.

The third phase, urban design framework development, makes use of the conceptual design/planning and policies formulated in the second phase to establish detailed urban design framework elements for the neighbourhood. In the Whittier project five framework elements were developed: a housing improvement plan; a commercial redevelopment staging plan; a pedestrian improvements plan; an open space development plan; and a vehicular ciruclation parking improvement plan.

The fourth and final project phase outlines the precedures to initiate the implementation of the project.

In the case of the Whittier project, an extensive organisational framework was established with a coordinating private community development corporation to oversee fund-raising and project implementation. The Whittier Alliance, the non-profit community development corporation, receives annual grants from the Dayton Hudson Foundation, the charitable contributions arm of a major local retail corporation, and regularly applies for federal Community Development Block Grants and capital improvement grants from the city of Minneapolis. The Whittier Alliance board of directors hold annual workshops to review the past year's progress, set the next year's implementation objectives, based on the initial urban design framework, and identify target areas for special attention in the implementation programme. Within a five-year period the entire 90-block neighbourhood should receive priority improvements.

The following are examples of projects implemented to date in terms of the Whittier neighbourhood and related community-based urban design projects: housing improvement (rehabilitation programmes, multi-family acquisition and rehabilitation progrmmes, and new development programmes); open space and pedestrian improvements (boulevard street tree planting, and street furniture system development and installation); and commercial area improvements (storefront rehabilitation programmes, new development programmes, and parking and vehicular circulation system improvements).

CONCLUSIONS

In contrast to the larger urban design efforts of the 1960s, which seldom included community participation at an in-depth level, the neighbourhood-scale efforts of the 1970s and 1980s provide a new focus and scale for urban design. In many cases we have the same actors, i.e. neighbourhood residents and public agencies, but they now play different roles.

The neighbourhood (association) is now the client, i.e. it has control over the project budget and in most cases the public agencies serve as implementation agents. The client and the user are now one and the same, and intimately familiar with their neighbourhood, the project area.

The urban design/community planning project is just a beginning in the process of neighbourhood revitalisation. It is the basis, a tool, from which the neighbourhood pursues further federal grants, e.g. Community Development Block Grants, Urban Development Action Grants, Neighbourhood Self-Help Grants, and other types of state and local funding for project implementation.

In contrast to the 1960s we now have greater emphasis on the neighbourhood. With this emphasis, and political awareness, comes control at the neighbourhood level, funding directly to the neighbourhood and, perhaps most importantly, the responsibility to see a project through implementation rests with the neighbourhood, the ultimate users of that project.

New uses for existing buildings 26

Louis Karol   South Africa

INTRODUCTION

It is important to define the difference between adaptive use and recycled buildings when applied in the context of property development. Adaptive use, in essence, is the conversion of a building originally designed for one purpose to a different and contemporary use and should not be confused with the so-called recycling of a building. To recycle a building is to renew the life of that building for the same use or purpose for which it was originally designed. In the recycling process, all the existing technical services and other aspects of the building are reassessed and either renewed entirely or upgraded and modernised or altered completely, but the building is still used for the same purpose.

The term adaptive use implies adapting or changing the use of a particular building or development for any one of many reasons, usually determined by market research studies. The development would then be replanned within the confines of what exists with minimal alterations to the existing structures to suit the new needs and other requirements. For example, the conversion of a large warehouse to office space would probably require a large light-well or atrium in the middle of the warehouse in order to reduce the unusually deep office depths which would otherwise result. Adaptive use is not necessarily restricted to single-building projects. Entire groups of buildings and their surrounding environment can also be adapted, sometimes with startling benefits.

Like consumer goods, the stock and quality of commercial buildings in a town reflect the needs and desires of the market-place. The various pressures and changes in the market-place are of grave concern to the property developer. Very often success in property ventures is in direct relation to the ability of the development team to be sensitive to the shifts in the market. I think it is reasonable to state that in virtually the whole western world we are at present in a situation of change in the market place. The causes are well known: the high cost of money and building; the escalation in costs which occurs during long building programmes; the escalation in the cost of maintenance and in operational expenditure; and the growing realisation that perhaps we have been too eager to demolish existing buildings which either may have had historical value or were perfectly good buildings of which the technical services had run down.

These factors have led to growing awareness of our old stock of buildings and the need to consider adaptive use development. Today we also have the worsening energy crisis which brings with it a new challenge: let us adapt our old and disused factories and warehouses to apartment buildings and let us bring back the people to the city. Let us bring them near to where they work.

EXAMPLES

There is of course nothing new in the concept of adaptive use buildings or developments. Although the adaptation of existing buildings to house new functions may seem a recent innovation, given the attention the subject has received of late, it is in fact a very ancient practice. Often it has been a matter of improvisation according to prevailing circumstances, but rarely has it produced much theorising.

Conversion may be a last resort for state and local authorities in terms of architecture and city planning. There are many examples of adaptive use in history but let us start with the conversion of Diocletian's Baths in Rome, the last public edifices to be built before the fall of Rome. In the sixteenth century Michelangelo began to transform the middle chambers into a church, Saint Mary of the Angels, but he retained much of the decoration and arrangement of the chambers themselves. Another fragment of the original development was included in the central railway station, and still other sections have been transformed into a school, a monastery, a cloister (later re-adapted into the Roman National Museum), a prison and even apartment dwellings. This is an example of a perfectly ordered architectural composition which became, by additions, subtractions and conversions, a neighbourhood quarter of Rome. Through the preservation of architectural fragments and the general arrangement of streets and buildings which has emerged, the various functions housed in the baths have avoided the habitual urban confusion which inevitably occurs in many cases.

Other examples of adaptive use development are the following.

☐ The Cannery, San Francisco. The Del Monte Fruit Cannery was developed into a complex of shops and restaurants. The original exterior was retained but the interior was remodelled with an interesting system of walks, corridors, steps, escalators and balcony decks.

☐ Ghirandelli Square, San Francisco. A number of nineteenth and early twentieth century buildings, containing a chocolate factory, were developed into a complex of shops, restaurants and theatres. Its special charm is the mixture of buildings, outdoor spaces, object d'art and colourful wares.

☐ Gas Town, Vancouver. An old warehouse area adjacent to the docks was developed into speciality shops, restaurants and boutiques. Special features include repaved streeets with no kerbs but chains and bollards to separate pedestrians from vehicles.

☐ Faneuil Hall, Boston. Three 150-year old block-long warehouses were developed into a complex of food markets, restaurants, offices and retail shops. The mixture of activities attempts to create a festival spirit.

☐ Trolley Square, Salt Lake City. Five 120-m long trolley barns were developed into a complex of theatres, restaurants, cafes, speciality shops and a farmers' market. The salvaged components of demolished Salt Lake City mansions give a turn-of-the-century atmosphere.

☐ The Rocks, Sydney. Several blocks of slums on the waterfront were developed into a complex of restaurants, boutiques, craft shops and the like. Buildings and streets were carefully restored to create an Olde Worlde atmosphere.

BACK TO THE CITIES

The reasons why adaptive use development has become such a popular theme in planning circles today can probably be found in development in the United States. I mention the

United States because like so many other countries South Africa has often followed American precedent far too closely. We remember the 1950s as mainly devoted to enlarging the inventory of buildings which had become very low owing to the lack of building activity during the second world war. This was followed in the 1960s by the surge towards the suburbs. So the suburban sprawl continued and following the many housing estates came all the necessary additional back-up facilities, such as neighbourhood shopping centres, and regional shopping centres. In the 1970s came the depression in building activity together with the fuel crisis starting in 1973, and suddenly the realisation dawned that our cities were in fact decaying. Many downtown areas began to present pathetic scenes of boarded-up shop-fronts and slums.

It was possibly at this time that a change in attitude became apparent. Up to that point progress meant the wholesale demolition and destruction of vast city areas to make way for new super-highways and new megastructures and buildings of concrete and glass. While all this was perfectly understandable and even justifiable, it was realised that there might soon be nothing left of our heritage, certainly very little of our worth while heritage. Similarly, it was glaringly evident that the new urban developments were not necessarily all places of character, fun or interest. They simply never evoked any emotions from the users themselves. We began to realise that our cities should be as diversified as is a normal balanced society which comprises babies, teenagers, middle-aged and old people, mothers and fathers, grandmothers, grandfathers, uncles and aunts, and nieces and cousins. The contemporary all-glass building in fact needs the old articulated and moulded building next door to complement it. During these times it was also shown what innovation, inventiveness and imagination could do to revitalise one or two tired and forgotten old buildings. They were given a new lease on life and received with loving care by the community at large.

In view of the energy crisis, we talk today of the necessity of buildings that use less energy. Consultants tell us about "thermal storage" and say that our buildings need "thermal insulation" to minimise both heat loss and solar heat gain. The thick walls and the small windows of the old buildings certainly possess both these qualities. And so, with the awakening of all these concerns in people - the fuel shortages, the realisation that it would be far better to live closer to work, and the awareness of a quality of life - we today have a desire to go back to the city. Coupled with this is a desire to turn the city into an environment to live, work and play in, and above all to enjoy. In this context adaptive use development makes much sense.

Man is of course ruled by fashion. This applies as much to architecture and development as it does to everything else. However loose the word "fashion" may be in architectural terms, our experience has been that when fashions change they are usually accompanied by countless problems and mistakes. Most of the latter are made in ignorance, not only by the professions, but by clients and developers alike, more often than not through ignorance and inexperience. Thus, both developer and the professions as a team must not only know when change is needed, but should also ensure that when there is a change adequate time and resources are spent on researching the new trend and directions to be taken.

TECHNIQUES

What problems do we face as far as adaptive use buildings are concerned? The adaptive use development process has far more in common with a normal real estate development than a recycling project.

There are usually four basic steps (see Figure 1): project initiation, project feasibility, project planning and financing, and project implementation. While these phases are common to any new development, there are variations which are extremely important in successfully adapting an old structure to a new use. The first is the technical evaluation of the project. Understanding the structure is a prerequisite for designing a natural conversion that is relatively easy to construct.

Many companies have considerable experience in site evaluation and negotiations relating to new developments, but few have the expertise to evaluate opportunities offered by existing buildings and their re-use. Architects and engineers with the required skills and knowledge therefore need to become involved in the development at an early stage. Very often, a greater representation of skills is needed than in a new development.

Another consideration relates to the objectives of the various parties with an interest in the project. The primary interest of the owner of a building would be to protect or liquidate his investment; a developer would be looking for a good investment opportunity; a conservation group would be concerned with saving the integrity of a building or the environment; and a local authority or government would want to upgrade an area in order to increase its tax base. The most fundamental question is whether there are likely to be uses of the converted building. More particularly what needs to be known is whether people would require space in that area and be willing to pay rentals high enough to exceed the cost of acquiring and adapting a building to meet their needs. Problems often arise because a proper assessment of the comparative economics of alternative schemes is not done. There should be a partnership between the development team and the local authority or government so that the product can be an integral part of the city planning policy. At the same time, this makes it possible for the authority to implement its policy by using the entrepreneur, giving him encouragement and concessions, which is most probably the easiest way for a city to solve its many problems in its depressed areas.

A few additional points need to be made. The market and economic evaluation is a critical factor in the project's success. It is important to identify unusual market opportunities. The location is especially important since the developer is tied to a fixed structure. The availability of parking may be an important factor. Considerations of site and location are especially important in planning the re-use of public buildings, e.g. city halls and schools which may still be symbols of the community.

Structural and physical characteristics also need to be thoroughly investigated in relation to both suitability and building regulations introduced after the building was completed. The cost of upgrading building materials and structural and support systems must be carefully examined, e.g. lifts, toilets, fire-escapes and floor-to-ceiling heights. (Adaptive use is not a "little bit of paint".)

The architectural potential of a structure is a primary consideration. Use of space, interior circulation, architectural graphics and lighting as well as imaginative use of materials and colours can be combined to impart a unique character. The character of a building is also a marketable commodity, and the way the aesthetic problem is tackled is therefore important. The alterations should enhance the character of the building, not destroy it.

Adaptive use projects are always a tremendous challenge to the professions, developers, and city planners. These projects usually provide the opportunity to upgrade an environment on a large scale on a self-generating basis. An important factor is that city planners must always work in close liaison and partnership with the developer and his professional team.

It is also important to understand that with these projects an urban renewal scheme can be carried out piecemeal, as distinct from the total site occupation which is required to construct a large new development. In retrospect, there appear to be many instances where the continued demolition of existing buildings can be avoided, particularly where the existing fabric is perfectly sound. Similarly, with the cost escalations of today, adaptive use developments have many inherent benefits for the community as a whole.

As far as the development team is concerned, it is essential that they acquire skills additional to those usually required for a new development. The research leading to the assembly of the professional team is critical. Each project is a special case and many of the projects require above average skills. The more ingenious the architect can be in his approach to the design problem, the greater the success of the final product. It is important that the architect has a feeling for history so that he can draw on historical precedents in his designs. A structural engineer, however able he might be to work out the stresses and strains and wind loadings of a high-rise building, certainly requires completely different skills in adaptive use buildings. He must have an understanding of old structures and what the result of tampering with these structures would be. For example, a large warehouse is to be converted into an office block and the architect requires an atrium in the middle of the building. This calls for the removal of part of the structure and the stresses which may be released can be quite a problem. The professional team may include a historian because the building concerned may well be important historically. Similarly, the team could well require the services of a traffic engineer because in the case of adaptive use buildings the nature of traffic patterns is already dictated. It can thus be very important to determine in advance whether the existing infrastructure can take the changes generated by the changes in usage. The project may be designed with the utmost skill, but if the traffic flows are not adequate or suitable, the repercussions in terms of commercial viability could be serious.

As far as costs are concerned, there is nothing magical about such a venture. In many instances, the costs can be the same as those of a new development. At best it is usually not possible to save more than about 25 per cent of the cost of the building work, but there are other hidden benefits. For instance, the interest on capital can be drastically reduced because construction time is usually substantially less than for a new building. The inherent quality and charm of an old building can often be used to produce an effect which would be impossible to create in a new development. In certain countries there can also be a substantial tax benefit.

OUTLINE CASE STUDY

The Commonwealth Building in Cape Town originally housed the Colosseum Theatre and was built in the 1930s by the Schlesinger family which owned African Theatres. It occupied half a city block and the site area was bounded by three streets, St George's Street, Riebeeck Street and Adderley Street.

Originally, the city council town planners decided that Riebeeck Street should be widened to a main arterial road. When the announcement was made that the Colosseum had been bought by a consortium, the city engineer immediately announced that Riebeeck Street would be widened by three metres. With the advent of television and the decline in popularity of large cinemas, the owners considered redevelopment. However, two important difficulties manifested themselves. The three-metre widening of the road was a serious obstacle as the depth of the site was only twenty-five metres. The upper floors were rent-controlled apartments and an application for a demolition permit would be strenuously resisted by the Department of Community Development.

Following investigations of the problem from all angles, it became clear that demolition was not the only solution to the problem. The building consisted of a very large cinema on the ground floor, with some offices and apartments on the upper floors. The superstructure was carried on enormous concrete girders and the columns supporting the structure were taken down to bed-rock in the form of large concrete column bases. It became apparent that we were dealing with an enormous shell, and further investigation revealed that it would be possible to excavate below street level without endangering the structure.

After a final evaluation it was decided that, with a certain amount of excavation, we could construct a six-storey building within the space previously occupied by the cinema. It was agreed that three of the floors were to be for shops and the three upper floors for offices. Both the basement and first floor were linked to the ground floor.

The reconstruction of Commonwealth Building turned out to be a success story, both in construction and leasing. The cinema was vacated on 1 February 1973. A discount store occupying part of the ground floor and half the basement was trading by November of the same year. The remaining shops were trading in April of the following year, and all the offices were completed and occupied by September of the same year. All available space in the six storeys was leased long before completion of the building, which made it possible to cater for the special requirements of the tenants.

Let us now consider all the points that had to be taken into account.

Structure. Commonwealth Building is a reinforced concrete-framed building. For speed and ease of erection, the new floors within the shell are of steel form construction with Q-decking and a thin concrete slab. The structural steelwork was then sprayed with asbestos for fire protection. In an unfortunate compromise, the old liftshafts were used for the new building. New and larger lift should have been installed, but it was considered too great a disruption to the building to demolish the existing lift-shafts. A point to consider is that throughout these extensive demolitions and renovations all the tenants in the apartments remained in occupation. This was achieved by maintaining one bank of lifts while the second was being renewed, and by erecting temporary steel fire-escapes down to pavement level so that the existing escapes could be demolished and replaced with new ones in the desired positions and to the correct width prescribed by the new by-laws.

Services. A survey had to be made of all the existing services in the building, and much work went into diverting services below the level of the apartments into new ducts which passed down through the "new building".

Quality of internal accommodation and finishes. The space which was previously the cinema was completely gutted in order to provide for the new six storeys. We felt that as all the space was new it should be used to the best standards prevailing at the time. The shopping and office space, which is fully air-conditioned, has finishes similar in quality to those in any new shopping and office building built in the past three to four years in South Africa.

External façade. Commonwealth Building was designed in classical style, complete with heavy mouldings and ornamentation. It was considered inappropriate to disturb the character of the building or to introduce foreign elements into the elevations. Thus, a painted stone facing panel was used on the steel canopy so that the latter would fit in with the character of the building. The large columns and beams at street level were faced with travertine marble. The windows of the new office floor have aluminium frames and tinted glass but they were made to harmonise with the existing windows and have the same width of frame. The windows are quite contemporary in design but still sympathetic to the overall façade. Certain mouldings had to be removed, but additional mouldings were introduced to balance the design.

Role of the professional team. The difficulties encountered in the reconstruction of Commonwealth Building taxed the expertise of the professional team to the utmost. There were all the classic difficulties that have to be considered before an owner can take a decision to demolish or reconstruct. The team had to go through a very complicated check-list of municipal by-laws, services, structural stability, light and air problems, logistics for building operations, as well as delivery of all the heavy equipment involved.

Was it all worth it? Yes!

The project cost $2½ million and was executed in approximately twenty months. It would have been impossible to demolish the complete structure and rebuild in under thirty-six months. In addition, the owners had revenue from the apartments during the entire period of reconstruction and, as mentioned previously, income from the shops began to accrue nine months after demolition started. The remaining shops produced revenue some five or six months later. Income from the shopping element, always the largest in any project, therefore became available in half the time that it would normally have taken to rebuild.

While the building is not of any particular architectural merit, it nevertheless is a solid and dignified structure. It contrasts well with an all-glass high-rise building immediately opposite and the city-scape is probably the richer for the decision to retain the original building.

Figure 1

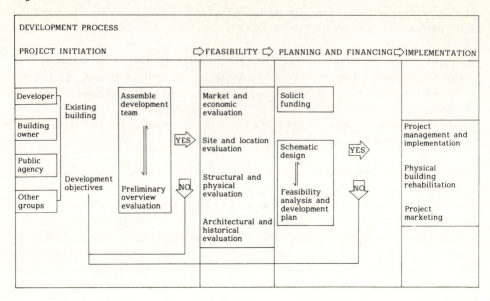

Urban renewal in Perth

27

Michael Hugo-Brunt   Australia

A REVIEW IN THE AUSTRALIAN CONTEXT

Urban renewal in Australia is less obvious than it is in other communities. As Australian towns were colonial settlements, many early buildings, particularly those built between 1840 and 1870 in Western Australia, tended to be small, somewhat mean and unimaginative. They used a great deal of timber and other local materials and were often destroyed by extremes of weather and fire or tended to be transitory, lasting for no more than forty years. Significant government establishments, warehouses, fortifications, transportation centres, railway stations, marine terminals, penological establishments, hospitals, eleemosynary and education institutions were more permanent.

After 1890 things changed. With greater prosperity in the major centres, such as Perth, Guildford, Bunbury and Albany, central areas and waterfronts developed. Society became more affluent and successful, multi-storey Victorian constructions appeared, such as hotels, taverns, then city halls, insurance and office blocks, railway stations, scientific or maritime installations, schools, hospitals and, eventually, factories and warehouses. These important examples of status and advertisement were designed by a small cadre of professionals, usually architects, surveyors and engineers, who were introduced by the British administration from the early days of colonial settlement. They were not merely pretentious, but typically represented neo-classic or other revival architectures, frequently incorporating elements from the unique Cape of Good Hope or Indian vernaculars.

There were planning experiments which reflected the ideas of the radicals and utilitarian penologists and philosophers in England, e.g. Rottnest or Toodyay. While all this was occurring, the polite harmonics of the squirearchial societies were being picked up by expatriate officers, the squatters and agriculturists, particularly those who had pretensions to gentility or office. On occasion there were direct importations of European style, as may be seen in the Benedictine Monastery of New Norcia or the Drysdale Mission in the north-west. Wherever there were groups of agricultural and rural buildings one usually found the nucleus of a small township.

However, it is in the larger communities that obsolescence may be seen. It became demonstrably apparent after the first world war when many of the returned servicemen moved to urban areas after failure of the farm grants. The increased migration from overseas, business expansion and improved mobility, heralded by the automobile, stimulated this move. As central area costs per square foot increased, multi-storeyed constructions slowly appeared and the early Victoriana was replaced with neo-classic office buildings, occasional apartments and more comprehensive restrictions. This renewal started in 1870 with self-government, but was not immediately apparent since the local bureaucracy expanded slowly.

Nevertheless, there was early respect and affection for the first cathedrals, churches, offices, town halls, insurance houses, banks and other institutions and, unlike their European or American counterparts, Australians clung tenaciously to good and older buildings as symbols of their society. Even after the first world war they tended to remodel, extend and expand them rather than demolish them and start again. Consequently, without publicity and fanfare, architects and other professionals tended to be more sensitive to the preservation of Western Australia's past. This was, of course, frequently an expedient. Investment monies were simply unavailable on a large scale.

Civic improvement tended to be individual. Usually, a businessman, often not an Anglo-Saxon, would assemble several parcels of land, mostly occupied by less resplendent residences. Some of the land might have been subdivided some thirty years before 1900 and the houses replaced with semi-detached terrace housing or occasional apartments. He would demolish and replace these with an office block or a shop, sometimes with living accommodation on the top floor. These three to four-storeyed buildings were garbed with neo-classic, Etruscan, Renaissance or Gothic frontages, frequently of masonry or solid load-bearing brickwork. On occasion, steel frames with panels and glass were introduced. Some still survive, dating from between 1902 and 1933-4. Between 1933 and 1938 early functionalism began to have an impact. Stores also adopted Ritz cinema "modern" the same poor expressionistic interpretations of their counterparts in the United States and England. Eventually this gave way to more sophisticated buildings, usually with solid load-bearing disguising their frames. Others expressed the frames boldly, subordinating their glass and panels. Planning was good, but it has always been strong and generous in Australia.

Colin Rowe has described the American city as a pastiche. This could apply to the Australian city, too, since the old colonial three-storeyed métier gradually began to change in silhouette as it expanded into the side lanes. New structures now shared party walls, but managed to preserve rear space of some sort.

Urban renewal in Perth is absorbed in overall planning. The cultural precinct, the cathedral precinct, the Queen Elizabeth II hospital complex, the concert hall complex, the entertainment centre, the parliamentary precinct, the various city centres, the major shopping centres and the institutional complexes all represent aspects of urban renewal in whole or in part. By North American criteria, many subdivisions could be taken to represent aspects of renewal, especially in the provision of amenity spaces and better housing (such as the Somerville complex of the University of Western Australia), but it is more frequently seen in new subdivisions which incorporate part or a "corner" of an older nucleus.

The rehabilitation of existing housing, particularly those buildings with the connotations of conservation and preservation, is the more obvious manifestation of urban renewal. Numerous older houses are incorporated into the new subdivisions or, better still, isolated in new subdivisions, such as Shenton House or Tranby-on-Swan. In many cases their uses have changed, in that they have become museums, health centres, nursery schools, etc.

Another aspect of residential replacement is the extensive development of high-density apartment blocks (six to eight storeys and more) on lots which formerly accommodated prestige dwellings. Within the past fifteen years the cluster house has also made its appearance. Here, two or three former residential sites are assembled and laid out with maisonettes and, in the better examples, individual houses. This has increased densities and tends to occur in the central fringes and in the inner ring or, occasionally, near the industrial estates. It has not only increased the density of accommodation but also shortened distances to work. There have been one or two isolated experiments with Radburn concepts, some of which were pre-war (as at Cottesloe), but the most obvious example is Crestwood by Paul Ritter.

Changes in density by soaking up population in the regional centres or around institutional complexes, such as universities, hospitals, or in the suburbs, is having an effect on transportation. There have been several transportation studies for Perth and the region. These have been reappraised since the energy crisis. The elimination of railways has also evoked controversy. Their replacement with high-speed bus routes (as in Jerusalem and Tel Aviv) as opposed to lanes in existing throughway systems has encountered oppostion from the exponents of a Tokyo-Kobe type high-speed system. Others would like to see an upgrading of railways, not only across the continent, but locally to regional centres; while others are advocating an underground-surface combination as in Montreal or Lisbon. None appear feasible or possible, since the metropolitan plans have allocated the existing railway concessions for high-speed bus routes in assocation with the introduction and elaboration of the existing public transport system. A bus system with a fast non-paying clipper service around the central area as well as reduced fares might accompany the introduction of more luxurious vehicles penetrating to the suburbs. At the moment these converge on suburban stations and run through local routes. Unfortunately, no matter how careful an analysis has been made, the issue is so awkward in political terms that the transportation problems can only be described as partially resolved and subject to further debate and criticism by the main political parties. Nobody wants to face the realities of a growing city approaching metropolitan scale or the implications of financial investment to meet that scale of growth.

The issue is also associated with the recognition that the central area "dies" over the weekend and a particularly romantic concept, much championed by architects and others, that residential accommodation be reintroduced into the core, particularly for pensioners and young people. This idea, too, has its opponents among the "law and order" school who consider that central and regional centres have, in fact, stimulated the rise in vagrancy, delinquency and crime. Perhaps it should be pointed out that some of these people also believe that park systems should be preserved as amenities but not used by the public!

Politicians and others also advocate more extensive recreational facilities in the form of national parks, zoos, marinas, the preservation of the present lakes, bird sanctuaries, beaches and mountain areas. This, too, has been criticised by environmentalists who claim that such public amenities are desecrated, particularly in the exploitation of resources by private enterprise, various government departments, the timber industry and others. Some mistakes have been made with unfortunate results, but it is true that the most ferocious of these critics are specialists outside the field.

The great Western Australian public, particularly the citizens of Perth, recognise that some of the great deracinators of the environment are the agents of the government and its departments, respected institutions (such as religious bodies), pressure groups of the more prestigious sporting organisations, and the entrepreneurs in pollution-producing industries such as those in the Kwinana area. They acknowledge the ever-increasing social dislocation manifested by juvenile and adult delinquents - often a direct reflection of the lack of amenities, racial prejudice or an insensitive, uneducated and unconcerned bureaucracy.

Perhaps the worst manifestation of failure in Australia is governmental. Authorities often exercise their office without intelligence or imagination, often through a specialist elite drawn from the most unimaginative, least qualified and totally unambitious trainees. Fortunately, there are shining exceptions, frequently women, but the political direction offered to society by its elected representatives is hopelessly split in a struggle between conservatism and labour, the former euphemistically described as "liberal", the latter purporting to represent the interests of artisan and labourer. Both try to operate within rigid class interests, which implies family compacts, racial bias, group gatherings in club and public house, status and sex. This society tends to be outdoor, anti-intellectual, indifferent to environment, and believes itself to be composed of "laisser faire" democratic individualists.

It is true that the media frequently highlight these problems, but it is also equally true that Australian men are singularly inactive on the more frightening long-term implications of such policies. One finds that all media tend to create a Utopian euphoria, ostensibly modelled on the American way of life, but with "decent British overtones" which do not help. The term "urban renewal" evokes mixed response. On the one hand it is seen as "planners' jargon", and on the other it is perceived as an attempt by authorities to usurp the individual's prerogative. Nevertheless, many would like to see an established procedure for urban renewal.

X: SOCIAL PLANNING

Social impact planning 28

Leon Kumove   Canada

A WAY TO MEET THE FUTURE

Social impact planning is the effort to provide goals, objectives, policies and programmes which will enable a social unit to cope with the effects of major social, economic or technological or physical changes on its structure and functioning. Social impact planning should be distinguished from the more familiar term social impact analysis, which is the evaluation of the expected effects of specific policies and programmes on a social unit. Social impact analysis can be considered a part of any social impact planning process.

Social impact planning is concerned with effects which are sometimes described as second-order consequences[1] or potential secondary effects.[2] In traditional types of social impact planning, these consequences or effects are treated in two ways. One is to disregard them and go full steam ahead with mechanistic planning formulae for economic or technological development, on the assumption that too great a concern for second-order consequences of one's actions inhibits one's ability to pursue primary goals. When these secondary effects become difficult to the point of halting or diverting the primary efforts, coercion is exercised. Stalinist industrialisation is an extreme example of this kind of planning and development. However, in the democratic countries too, there have been numerous examples of the use of coercive powers to achieve specific goals. To this day, American folklore retains bitter memories of the railway building era of the nineteenth century. Attempts to rebuild parts of North American and European cities have left some harsh memories as well.

The second way, a more humane one, is a residual approach. Extensive planning for social consequences is avoided and problems are met as they arise. This is the doctrine of muddling through. Bauer states that this approach is based on an elaborate concern for second-order consequences of actions. "It assumes that social systems and processes are very complex phenomena and that it is impossible to determine in advance exactly what results will be created by one's actions or what difficulties will be encountered."[3]

Because of the tremendous efforts required in most parts of the world to meet human needs, neither of these approaches is satisfactory. Many large-scale decisions need to be made, committing huge amounts of resources. This requires a sensitivity to these consequences if we are to avoid the build-up of long-term tensions and breakdowns as the social incentives and controls disintegrate. Our concerns may be related to large societies or the interests of an urban neighbourhood or a small band of indigenous people in remote regions.

PRIMARY IMPACTING FORCES

The primary impacting forces under discussion may include the entire range of policies and programmes that may be brought into play. These include some of the following: redevelopment of cities or parts of them, rural development, resource development, transportation projects, economic development, new technologies and social development programmes. These are only a few of the types of primary impacting forces.

Fundamentally, social impact planning asks these questions: What effects will the primary mission have on the social unit? What influence will the expected effects have on the primary mission? What opportunities does the impacting force create for the social unit to develop, meet its needs and deal with its long-standing problems? What policies and programmes will be required to meet the problems created and assist the social unit in meeting its long-term goals and values? When all the opportunities and social and physical costs have been considered, should the primary mission be modified or reconsidered?

SOCIAL CONCERNS

The social concerns in this discussion relate to the following: social organisation by which the unit exists as an enduring entity; social relationships (the actions and interactions among people); and values, i.e. the expression of ultimate ends, goals and purposes of social structure and function.

From a more institutional view we are concerned with the following: individuals and their physical health, personalities and roles in the social structure; families, as the basic units of society for bearing and rearing children and transmitting social values; and other social institutions in which roles are organised around certain activities or needs.

Subjects of concern might be described as "non-market goods and services".[4]

TYPES OF SOCIAL CHANGE

There are three kinds of social change: organic, planned and overwhelming change. Organic change is produced by a series of events over time. Most changes have been over time. In recent history, as Toffler points out in Future shock, the rate of increment has accelerated significantly and the time span has been telescoped. Planned or induced change results from conscious social or political decisions to apply policies or programmes to meet specific goals. Overwhelming change occurs when some powerful event or series of events takes place in a short space of time and produces major change rapidly. These events might be earthquakes, war, discovery of significant natural resources, political revolution or major technological changes which could set a series of events into rapid motion to transform a society. Some of this overwhelming change occurs naturally but most is the product of human endeavour.

All of these processes for change exist together. However, important aspects of our society are increasingly subjected to planned, conscious decisions of governments and international corporations. The size and scale of some projects become overwhelming events in relation to the people affected and set major change processes in motion.

Social impact planning is the attempt to widen the scope of planned change, deal with all the effects that can be anticipated and reduce all the accidental spin-offs which can be foreseen. We as planners, engineers, architects, economists and social scientists are part of a larger historical process known as modernisation. It is a complex process, just beginning among some peoples and an ever continuing one for the "modern" peoples.

The following are a few of the characteristics of modernisation:

☐ Social mobilisation in which "old social, economic and psychological elements are broken and eroded and people become available for new patterns of socialisation and behaviour",[5] freeing large numbers of people from the need to provide food and basic goods for themselves; movements of population, urbanisation, weakening and breaking of kinship systems, tribal and local ties.

☐ Increasing separation and continuing differentiation of social roles of individuals, groups and institutions.

☐ Growth of technology and use of rational techniques.

☐ Development of symbols for identification with social entities beyond the tribal, kinship and local groups.

☐ Growing central administrative organisations and complex systems of coordination.

☐ Growing scope and complexity of markets for the exchange of goods and services.[6]

☐ Post-industrialism - growth of the service rather than goods sector of the economy.[7]

☐ Political extension, i.e. democratic or populist government in which the sources of power are deemed to derive from "the people", not from external sources, e.g. divine election, ascription, magical omens, fate or "history". (Even in modern authoritarian states subjects are considered the source of legitimate authority and the objects or beneficiaries of the exercise of authority.)

☐ Growing differentiation of major value orientations; elaboration of intellectual disciplines, the arts, culture, religious beliefs; emphasis upon "happiness", i.e. human satisfaction as the basis of ethics; expression of individual ability, personality and feelings.[8]

The processes of modernisation are virtually universal. Rarely has there been a balanced or harmonious situation. In the modernised countries elements of traditional belief and practice continue to exist. There are people who resist the continuing differentation and complexity and new ideas. This resistance is active and passive and may be reflected in apathy, outbreaks of senseless violence, group and personal disorganisation. Organised violence or terrorism appears and the imbalances produce poverty, unemployment and alienation.

There are other societies at different stages of modernisation in which strong traditional elements remain. Some peoples at the early stages of modernisation use the tools of modern technology but still believe in magic. It could be that they will do no worse with modern arms than anyone else has done thus far. Elite elements of some societies have learned modern value systems, rational and centralised administrative techniques and have attempted to impose them upon people who retain more trust in traditional ways of doing things. The outcome is tribalism, nepotism and corruption.

Major developments in modern and modernising nations have much potential for disturbing and disorganising social systems and accelerating imbalances in the process of modernisation. Each project potentially increases the rate of differentiation and complexity. A fairly typical example of this is the situation of native Indians in the remote areas of Canada. At one state, entrepeneurs provided them with rifles and modern traps so that they could participate in the fur trade which was the mainstay of Canada's nineteenth century economy. They traded furs for the industrial goods of the era (blankets, milled flour and clothing) and gave up many of their traditional skills. The use of rifles quickly depleted the stock of fur-bearing animals and sources of meat. High rates of infant and maternal mortality, starvation and disease reduced the native population. (There were few Indian wars in Canada.) In due course, health and social services were introduced and the native population began to rise. The needs and social organisation of this increased native population were such that they could no longer continue their nomadic life in pursuit of game and fish. They have become townspeople in settlements in which an important economic activity is the very health and social services system which has grown to meet the problems of poverty, education, alcoholism and other needs.[9] The urgency of energy exploration and exploitation will bring these indigenous peoples into new confrontations with modernisation. The situation of the Canadian native probably has parallels in many parts of the world where the consequences of particular actions, however well intended, can lead to social pathologies.

This example illustrates some of the problems which arise when particular actions are undertaken without regard for the whole environment. Toffler states "...as the number of social components grow and change, the system becomes less stable. It becomes less and less possible to ignore the demands of political minorities...any minority can, by sabotage, strike or a thousand other means disrupt the entire system. As interdependence grows smaller and smaller, groups within the society achieve greater and greater power of critical disruption."[10]

The Canadian Indians are relatively few in number but some are critically located for future major capital developments. They have learned to act politically and to use publicity, demonstrations and legal action to place some serious problems before those who wish to explore and exploit new and urgently needed energy resources. In other parts of the world, situations similar to this have produced violence and repression.

Some type of social impact planning has always existed in the past. Usually it depended upon the actions of interest groups and concerned citizens who called to attention problems arising from development projects. These groups acted politically and sometimes subversively.

Interest groups will continue to be useful in social development planning because decision-making elites would otherwise settle for satisfying solutions. Etzioni suggests that one group, the intellectuals, act as critical examiners of tabooed assumptions.[11] Too often, however, these groups act on the basis of limited information and objectives and at too late a stage, when the dynamics of the situation have moved past them. They tend to focus on limited aspects of a situation, realising the narrow objective but creating more problems in the broader scheme of things.

BASIS FOR SOCIAL IMPACT PLANNING

The basis for social impact planning lies in the fact that large development decisions have to be made over a long term, involving or affecting large numbers of people. Some other approach is required which relates to the change and modernisation processes that are in motion and will be affected.[12]

There are many problems inherent in social impact planning. These are related to fundamental questions of social science and planning. How much do we really know about human behaviour and about social change in order to make predictions? Are there not too many irrational and irregular aspects to human behaviour?

Proper scientific scepticism and modesty prompt many social scientists to point out the lack of theory and knowledge on social structure. More significantly, even less is known about social change.[13] However, a body of knowledge has been accumulated.[14] Many other disciplines have proceeded even in the absence of a full development theory. Most notably, medicine has developed along with the biological sciences with no general theory of the life cycle.[15] Planning is an applied art.

Planning is "the search for alternative policies...definition of goals on the basis of measured needs among (and between) populations and the development of rational strategy and appropriate means to fulfil those objectives most quickly". The ultimate choice of goals, policies and definitions of the "rational" is what decision-makers do.[16]

They use a mix of scientific measures, rational techniques and intuition. Millikan has written: "Any decision to act must be based upon a judgment that the net consequences of the preferred course of action will be more favourable than those of some alternative...such a judgment can seldom be effectively made by 'scientific procedures'. One of the functions of science is to make these concepts and assumptions explicit, to test their generality and to set forth some of the circumstances in which they are valid...[Such a judgment] can illuminate the variety of forces at work, can place limits on the range of possible outcomes...can explore the variety and the internal consistency of a variety of intuitive expectations."[17]

Planning has a mixture of normative and positive elements. There is a desire to achieve certain ends and to relate the achieving processes as well as the ends to human behaviour.

THE SOCIAL IMPACT PROCESS

Social impact planning depends on the skill and thoroughness with which we do the following:

□ Describe and analyse the social unit in question before the primary impacting force comes into play.

□ Analyse the "natural" trends and forces for change, internally and externally, and the potential directions these changes may take regardless of the primary impacting policy or programme.

□ Forecast how the existing social unit and the forces for change present will be affected by the primary impact (social impact analysis).

□ Formulate the range of plans, goals, objectives, policies and programmes; ways of meeting the opportunities and problems created by the primary impacting force.

□ Select a social impact plan and programme and monitor procedures to make assessments of the state of the social unit as conditions change (social accounting).

□ Review and adjust the social impact plans continuously to meet changing situations.

□ Monitor, review and revise, also on a continuous basis

The social impact process might be described by the following diagram:

$$D \longrightarrow \begin{bmatrix} C_1 \\ C_2 \end{bmatrix} \longrightarrow \begin{bmatrix} C_1 I_1 \\ C_1 I_n \\ C_n I_n \end{bmatrix} \longrightarrow \begin{bmatrix} C_1 I_1 P_1 \\ C_1 I_1 P_n \\ C_1 I_n P_n \\ C_n I_n P_n \end{bmatrix} \longrightarrow S \longrightarrow M \longrightarrow A$$

D: Describing and analysing the existing social situation

C: Changing tendencies

I: Social impact analysis

P: Plans, policies and programmes

S: Selection of plan

M: Monitoring and social accounting

A: Adjustment and review

Describing the existing social situation. An analysis of the existing situation will provide all information required for plan formulation. The precise detail will depend on the primary mission and conditions surrounding it. The following groups of elements will be considered.

☐ The first group comprises structures and functional elements; patterns of cooperation and conflict; major institutions and subgroups; human rights and civic responsibilities; ethnic, cultural, religious, linguistic elements; socio-economic factors; major social values; distribution of power and status; levels of social participation; family and household patterns.

☐ The physio-social environment includes the man-made or humanly regulated elements which play a part in the social life of the community. These include housing, parks, public utilities, natural features and environment; attitudes and conflicts on the physio-social environment.

☐ Major institutions, generally and universally available or used by most people at least some of the time, are also considered. These include health care, education, social security, safety and security, recreation, cultural services and religious institutions.

☐ Economic development includes the systems of exchange and livelihood, basic economic rights, employment, labour-management relations, the character of the labour supply, cooperative, communal and individual enterprises.

Most of the elements will be found in most social units. The degree, intensity and importance will vary. In this examination the history, background and interrelations are to be identified. The capacities of the institutions to meet their goals and to change are significant. Etzioni distinguishes between the investment in collecting and that in processing information: "A societal unit that emphasises the collection of information disproportionately will, we expect, have a fragmented view of itself and its environment...Such inadequate processing will tend to be associated with drifting (or passiviity), because information that is not sufficiently processed is, in effect, not available for societal guidance...On the other hand, a unit that overemphasises processing is expected to have an 'unempirical' view of itself and its environment, because it will tend to draw more conclusions from the available information than are warranted..."[18]

Changing tendencies and trends of change. These require description and analysis. Social science theory has been limited in the area of social change. Millikan has said: "Dynamics is always more complicated than statics; rates of change are harder to measure and analyse than states of affairs...from a policy point of view the most important characteristic of our time is that societies are changing in almost all their fundamental dimensions at a rate unprecedented in history. All our policy problems require an appraisal not of states of affairs but of patterns of evolution."[19]

One examines processes of change in order to predict and anticipate. Despite all the difficulties, it has been pointed out that "considerable accuracy could be achieved by well-informed persons in predicting technological and social events".[20] There are many events which cannot be foreseen, however. In this discussion, it is a matter of anticipating whatever is possible and reducing the unpredictable to the minimum. An analysis of change trends should include a number of methods and approaches. It should use imaginative and speculative techniques to elaborate the largest possible number of courses based on historical analogies, comparative social studies, statistical possibilities and dynamic systems models. Any number should be used to develop the levels of anticipation of events and the conditions under which each of these directions of change might occur. It should be possible to eliminate those anticipated courses that are least probable. The description of the existing social situation and the potential courses of change will provide information which will be useful in developing social impact plans.

Development of social impact plans. These plans should aim at providing adequate policies and programmes to deal with concrete situations and real needs. They should be flexible enough to deal with changing situations and should take into account not only the substance of human needs as determined by rational and scientific methods but also the processes by which decisions will be made so that consensus can be achieved and renewed.

A social impact plan should be based on what is politically and administratively realistic; interaction between "the knowledge-producing planners and decision-making units";[21] and consensus produced by interaction between sub-groups. The social impact plan will provide goals and rational strategy and means to achieve certain objectives. Basically, policy is a social choice. Townsend states: "Social policy is the rationale by which societies are steered toward social ends. Policy depends on a definition of needs that are perceived rather than measured...It also depends on a concept of social change as it is perceived within a society rather than as something absolute or 'objective'."[22]

The role of the social planner is to elaborate all possible plans and policies, make explicit the consequences of various courses of action and collect and process information for use in decision-making and consensus formation. Any social impact plan put into operation will be based on a number of assumptions and hypotheses on behaviour and the likely effects of the primary impact. Wiener has pointed out that "...error is an inherent aspect of natural, physical and social systems".[23] A rigorous monitoring system is therefore required to measure the discrepancies and the consequences of a system.

Social science and social planning deal with the known, the knowable, the predictable and the rational. There should be processes to take the unpredictable and the irrational elements into consideration as they occur. There is a dialectic to planning. To paraphrase Mannheim: planning is a function of reality; it leads to certain kinds of action; action changes the reality or, in the case of failure, forces us to revise the planning.[24]

The system of monitoring requires two main elements. The first is social accounting, i.e. the collection and processing of information so that the social unit as a whole and the participants in it can have as integrated and complete a knowledge as possible of themselves and consider the discrepancies and new elements in their plans, goals and policies. Also required is the effective distribution of information on a fair and equitable basis among all elements, including planners, decision-makers and sub-units of society, together with the sharing of the conceptions of the situation and development to the highest possible levels of shared definitions. Monitoring procedures should include ways and means of social accounting, distribution and interaction among interests and sub-groups.

Adjustment and revision of the social impact plan is a continuous process by which decisions are made by the sharing, exchange and confrontation of interests among planners, decision-makers and sub-groups. It is a process "...in which given preferences and guided efforts affect each other, the outcome of which tends to be continuous flux".[25]

The process of monitoring, adjustment and revision is a continuous loop.

As planners, architects, engineers and social scientists, we are part of this larger scheme of modernisation which brings complexity, differentiation and rapid change. There is little point in evaluating this process since it has achieved mixed results throughout the world. We are participants in this process. Social impact planning should be an effort make good use of opportunities presented while minimising the ill-effects of development.

Eisenstaedt has indicated the following criteria for successful modernisation: the integration of different types of interest groups in a wider framework; the ways in which the various concrete issues are dealt with; and the crystallisation and implementation of policies that can, at least to some extent, meet the demands of different groups and deal with the problems from which these demands arise. He goes on to state: "The crucial test of relatively successful absorption of change and of dealing with continually emerging problems has been...the extent to which such policies were implemented in such a way that even those losing groups were not entirely deprived of some of their positions and their feelings of belonging to the society were not entirely alienated from it and could still maintain some positive orientation to its central institutions and symbols."[26]

The ultimate goal of social impact planning is to maintain and renew the integrity of social relationships in the face of continuing challenges.

REFERENCES

[1] Bauer, R., Social Indicators (1966), MIT Press, page 6.
[2] Ibid, page 3.
[3] Ibid, page 7.
[4] Bell, D., "The idea of a social report", Public Interest (1969), Vol 15, page 72.
[5] Deutsch, K.W., "Social mobilisation and political development", American Political Science Review (1961), No 55, pages 494-5.
[6] Eisenstaedt, S.M., Modernisation: protest and change (1966), Prentice-Hall, pages 2-5.
[7] Bell, D., Cultural contradictions of apitalism (1976), Basic Books, page 490.
[8] Eisenstaedt, S.M., Modernisation: protest and change (1966), Prentice-Hall, pages 6-7.
[9] Robertson, Heather, Reservations are for Indians (1968), Lorimer, Lewis & Samuel, page 64.
[10] Toffler, A., Future shock (1970), Random House, page 22.
[11] Etzioni, A., "Toward a theory of societal guidance", Social Change (1973), Basic Books, page 149.
[12] Mannheum, K., Man and society (1948), Harcourt, Brace & Co.
[13] Parsons, T., The social system (1951), The Free Press, pages 481-90.
[14] Berlson, B., and Steiner, G., Human behaviour - an inventory of findings, Harcourt Brace & World, page 164.
[15] Parsons, T., The social system (1951), The Free Press, page 484.

[16] Townsend, P., Sociology and social policy (1975), Penguin Books, pages 6-7.
[17] Millikan, M., "Inquiry and policy: the relation of policy to action", Daniel Learner (ed), The human meaning of the social sciences (1959), World Publishing, pages 165-6.
[18] Etzioni, A., "Toward a theory of societal guidance", Social Change (1973), Basic Books, page 147.
[19] Millikan, M., "Inquiry and policy: the relation of policy to action", Daniel Learner (ed), The human meaning of the social sciences (1959), World Publishing, pages 173-4.
[20] Kaplan, A., Skogatad, A.L., and Girshick, M.A., "The prediction of sociological and technological events", The Public Opinion Quarterly (1959), pages 93-110.
[21] Etzioni, A., "Toward a theory of societal guidance", Social Change (1973), Basic Books, page 147.
[22] Townsend, P., Sociology and social policy (1975), Penguin Books, page 7.
[23] Bauer, R., Social Indicators (1966), MIT Press, pages 6 and 58.
[24] Mannheim, K., Ideology and Utopia (1936), Harcourt, Brace & Co, page 127-8.
[25] Etzioni, A., "Toward a theory of societal guidance", Social Change (1973), Basic Books, page 154.
[26] Eisenstaedt, S.M., Modernisation: protest and change (1966), Prentice-Hall, pages 142-3.

Planning, implementation and evaluation of social programmes

29

Hans Esping   Sweden

INTRODUCTION

Throughout virtually the whole of this century, economic growth has been rapid in the industrialised world, both in the free Western economies and in the controlled economic systems of the East. For a long time, however, it has become progressively more difficult to balance demands and resources. To no mean extent, this has been attributed to the economic activities which we sometimes term the "common sector", i.e. the part of the economy in which the volume and focus of supply are determined politically. This part of the economy has grown much faster than the economy as a whole, and has therefore increased its share of the available resources.

In Sweden, both Social Democrats and non-socialists have for a long time regarded this as a problem and varied solutions have been attempted. A long succession of government commissions has endeavoured to reduce the public sector to cover the most pressing needs, or has tried by various means to streamline the public consumption of resources. Most of these attempts have been signal failures. Political, administrative and organisational barriers have proved too strong to be shifted by even the most dynamic ministers of finance. It would seem as though the administration itself incorporates vested interests of such magnitude as to circumscribe all opportunities of reform. It has been compared to a gear wheel with a ratchet allowing movement in one direction only.

But the economic claims of the public sector are only part of the story. As a result of technological progress, environmental problems, considerations of social equality and the demand for the coordination of progressively more complex processes, the state has felt obliged to circumscribe the freedom of action enjoyed by citizens and enterprise in many areas. Efforts to secure justice and security have resulted in an intricate network of laws, regulations and administrative decrees which are as difficult to change as they are complicated.

Today we are faced with a situation in which political freedom of action is heavily constricted. It is no longer possible to change the administration by adding new authorities or new resources. It is difficult to pass new legislation that does not clash with legislation passed before. Every new government is liable to get into a position where it can do little more than administer previous reforms.

Various efforts have been made to tackle the dual problem of the public administration, which is considered to be both too large and excessively rigid and complicated. Ever since the 1920s, general measures of "disarmament" and retrenchment have been resorted to in Sweden in a bid to bring down costs. Most such attempts have failed. New administrative systems, such as improved planning, programme budgeting and effectiveness auditing, have been thrown into the breach, but after an initial burst of enthusiasm they have all become fossil remains in the decision system. Efforts have been made to achieve coordination and simplicity by amalgamating public authorities (and enactments) or setting up special "integration authorities". These have, however, rapidly petrified, making things more complicated than ever. The true life-span of a public authority seems to be a good deal shorter than its formal existence.

REFORM IN A COMPLEX SOCIAL ENVIRONMENT

There are many reasons why a critical review ought to provide good grounds for reorganisation and simplification. And yet we fail, time and time again. One reason is that we have not studied and observed the complex social and organisational environment in which the concepts of reform are to be worked out and applied. Instead, we have used frameworks based on notions derived from planning theories and administrative law. These normative and "rationalistic" ideas have proved inadequate when applied to various obstacles to reconsideration and implementation.

Failures appear to have elicited two distinct reactions. One of these is to adhere obstinately to the normative models and to place more emphasis on formalised planning systems and mechanised follow-up. The other implies something of an abdication by national bodies in favour, for example, of local authorities, workers' co-determination and "tenant democracy". Both reactions would seem both unnecessary and inappropriate.

It is true that the rationalistic models possibly tell us something about what things ought to be (in the best of all possible worlds) but not much about how they actually are (in this vale of tears). On the other hand, the general criticism of rationalistic methods of analysing official policy and administration has remarkably little to offer in the way of constructive alternatives. The realistic models launched in recent years by, for example, March (with his "garbage-can model") or Emery yield greater understanding but hardly provide us with simple guidance. Both reactions - isolating ourselves from reality and refusing to control it - seem to be exaggerated. It is surely unnecessary to throw out all the rationalistic babies with the bath water.

The problem of increasing freedom of action in the establishment of official policy can be divided into at least three parts. In the first place, it is naturally a matter of understanding the context - the relationships involved. The mass of authorities and legislation in many fields is far from easy to comprehend. Relations between various problems and measures are far from obvious and closer analysis often reveals surprising connections. In the main, public administration no longer permits itself to be seen through on the basis of mere commonsense or grass-root political discussions.

In the second place we have to implement the changes decided on; fresh ideas and new methods. This is no easy task either. In our society there is a naive belief that people and organisations loyally act in compliance with instructions transmitted by formal authorities in the form of laws, ordinances and administrative regulations. Naturally, this is a serious underestimation of the ability of administration to adapt itself to "threat images" and conflicting claims. Spontaneous counteractions and structural changes which work against or completely thwart the intentions of the policy-makers are not uncommon in the administrative system.

Finally, of course, there is the difficulty of reaching agreement (consensus) on a particular line of action. This applies especially to the Western industrialised countries with their strongly pluralistic power structure, but possibly to a lesser extent to the countries of Eastern Europe. These difficulties, however, may possibly be exaggerated, both in the political debate and in traditional social science. A review of the resolutions passed by the Swedish parliament in 1978 showed that only about 10 per cent represented party issues. Not all of them were of primary importance from the point of view of the national economy. Thus, there is reason to believe that the greater part of public policy is uncontroversial in the party political sense. The common scale of values and insight into problems outweigh ideological differences. Obviously, this does not mean that there are no conflicting interests in society, differences which indirectly find expression in the work of Parliament, the composition of committees, answers to political questions and informal contacts of a general nature.

THINKING OUT PUBLIC POLICY

Of the problems stated above, this paper deals with the first and second. The third lies outside the scope of this account, the object of which is to present views on how we ought to think when working out public policy, rather than how we ought to act in order to obtain sufficient parliamentary and other support for a particular course of action. We propose that when we consider the first two problems we, as an intellectual model, should conceive of public administration as a complex fabric of interrelated social programmes, each corresponding to a particular social or communal problem.

A social programme of this kind consists of three sub-systems in dynamic interaction, namely a collective undertaking to solve the problem or relieve the tension, an organisation with the appropriate economic and physical resources, and finally a series of rules governing the way authorities, civic bodies and citizens should conduct themselves in relation to each other and to the original problem. The expression "social programme" does not refer only to social policy in the restricted sense. "Social" stands for what is common and decided upon by the state. "Programme" means, in part, the direction of intention, as in party programmes, and in part the organisational structure and resources, as in programme budgeting. A social programme can cover all possible variants of community problems, from child care and the supply of energy to consumer policy and traffic safety.

It should also be emphasised that the term social programme is used here mainly to indicate a support for thinking: an analytical aid. We have no intention of claiming that public policy is actually formulated in terms which would merit the designation "programme". In practice, public policy is created under much more haphazard conditions and in response to a mass of minor and major factors which scarcely permit adaptation in a simple chain "from problem to solution". Nevertheless, we believe that a notion of this kind can be a useful intellectual aid which can reveal some of the errors liable to creep into policital processes.

The concept can also provide points of departure for establishing whether the programme structure is tenable in a rational perspective, or whether other political motivations have to be sought to justify the measures taken. We thus wish to claim that whereas policy (i.e. the shaping of social programmes) is a multiple process which cannot really be understood without the aid of complex socio-economic and socio-psychological models (and perhaps not even with them), the results of policy-making, its rationality, can in certain circumstances be systematically evaluated and assayed against the criterion of vague and generally perceived social benefits.

The idea is that it is possible to analyse public policy, a specific programme, in relation to social problems or tensions without being obliged on that account to be submerged in the intellectual morass of political goal formulations and consensus-generating processes. The notion is somewhat élitist, in that it is based in the idea that there should be some kind of analytical truth beyond or above the power game which finds expression in the democratic processes. It derives from the thought that society is now so complicated that the parties involved in the political "game" are not always conscious of what action is best for themselves or for society. The politician is easily duped if and when he believes that party meetings or mass media discussions will reveal abuses and waste. This may possibly work when the problem is to repair cracks in the welfare landscape or to meet obvious and isolated needs, but not when the problems are structural - when it is not so much "rigorous action" that is required but rather precision and finesse in the application of social resources. In a complicated world it can easily happen that the links become such that the intuitively correct solution - the one launched on grass-roots contacts and "commonsense" - will be demonstrably disastrous.

AN EXAMPLE: SOCIETY AND THE ELDERLY
In order to determine how a social programme really comes into existence, is implemented and evaluated, we have examined in some detail "Society and the elderly". Admittedly, this has never been regarded as a distinct programme, as distinct from 1 000 000 flats or 100 000 places in day nurseries, but it is easy to regard it from that point of view. A historical review shows that the programme was first given shape during the sowing period of the Social Democrats in the mid-1940s. However, since that time it has been subjected to a series of evaluations and reconstructions, of which the most recent and important was that of the late 1970s.

In recent years "Society and the elderly" has proved to be a programme with more than its fair share of problems. The measures and methods applied have led to economically and socially unacceptable consequences. At least in some aspects, the programme has turned out to be a serious failure, but this fact is scarcely revealed or acknowledged in the official reports on the subject, in any case not by the government. What is to be learned from "Society and the elderly" is, above all, how organisation and legislation gradually limit the available technological alternatives. Even when various evaluations show that a radical reconsideration or a new start would be justified, institutional circumstances constitute an almost impenetrable barrier. Also, proposals clearly embedded in the political will of the government become notes in the margin of a budget resolution, hardly more.

Another development is that the growing organisation gradually ceases to discuss the problems of the elderly and instead takes up those of the organisation itself. This also applies to the various committees on the care of old people, and their relations to the organisation. Finally, discussion is centred exclusively on the problems of municipalities, county councils and social workers, the problems of the clients and the elderly being taken as read. In programme formulations, more gradually comes to mean better, while there is a tendency to overlook "coordination" of the satisfaction of needs, i.e. the quality of life as a composite value as well as the synergetic of different measures. To a great extent, the deviations are dysfunctional in the sense that they result either in inferior care, in terms of gerontological science and tested experience, or unnecessary costs. The positive deviations are mainly those caused by untrained and isolated home-helps doing a better job than they were expected to or had been instructed to do. The loyalty and intelligence of low-level field workers often hide top-level clumsiness and lack of creative ability.

Of course, there is disagreement on the causes of this state of affairs. In the report on field studies we have discussed some explanatory models. In general, however, it appears that the explanation is to be sought in the over-emphasis on security and precision, which flows from the strictly hierarchical and relatively central organisation of the system. In one of the municipalities studied, eight hierarchical levels were identified between the social welfare board and the elderly person in need of care. The information was markedly standardised, with the result that wrong notions about the meaning of "bed-day" or an "hour of home help" were perpetuated. This, more than bad intentions, seems to be the principal reason why the decision-maker was unable to take structural measures to make the system "reflect" the problems of the elderly. At the same time, of course, there is considerable inertia in systems as big as "Society and the elderly".

"Society and the elderly" has never really been regarded as an integrated social programme. However, our studies have demonstrated that it can be considered such a programme. In its gradual development we can distinguish between a number of phases which are repeated at certain intervals like continuous chains. This gives us a theoretical diagram with the following structure:

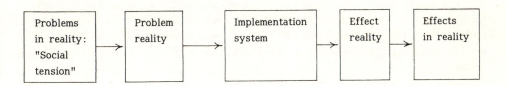

A primary stage in the process is the political experience of social tension - of <u>problems in reality</u>. The tension may assume many different forms, but essentially it represents the difference between the expectations of people with regard to security, justice and standard of living, and their experience or image of the actual state of affairs. During the period of, industrialisation expectations greatly increased with respect to communal care of the elderly and gave rise to political action. In the 1970s large groups of people feel a corresponding tension between anticipated and surmised security in the nuclear power society. In general, consciousness of social tension of this kind results in political action. In Sweden a public commission is often set up to formulate a solution to the problem.

In order to do so, we must distinguish a <u>problem reality</u> - a "figure" sufficiently sturdy for solutions to be drawn up. The chosen problem reality is often only one of numerous possible ways to confine it and describe a given problem in reality. The choice is influenced consciously and unconsciously by "political", institutional (legal and organisational) and intellectual (e.g. choice of method of study) factors.

The design is an <u>implementation system</u> which is assumed to "reflect" the problem reality. When we examine "Society and the elderly" from 1945 to 1975 we find that this system has for the greater part brought about relatively marginal changes in the measures, organisations and rules which make up the programme. Only the decisions of 1946 can be described as a new departure. The phenomenon of successive but marginal changes during a lengthy period is characteristic of the reform traditions of a number of Western European countries but, according to Levine, not that of the United States. We may assume that this is related to the dissimilar administrative structures.

Once the system of implementation has come into being through legislation, new resources, etc, there arises an effect reality. This can be measured in the same terms as the problem reality. If the problem reality is formulated to express a shortage of places in old-age homes or to state that many elderly people are accommodated in poor quality housing, the effect reality is concerned with the number of new places provided in homes of the number of improved and new houses for old people.

We are now confronted with a number of problems. As soon as it becomes necessary to express the problem reality in somewhat more complicated terms than the number of places, etc, it becomes difficult to understand the effect reality. In the care of the aged, it was understood at an early stage that one problem was the authoritarian structure of old people's homes and the mixed clientèle. To abolish these unsatisfactory features, new legislation was enacted and radical changes were made in the way responsibility was shared between social and medical authorities. Field studies revealed, however, that the organisation protected its interests by means of various kinds of counter-measures. Denied the possibility of police assistance, the organisation resorted to psycho-drugs and compulsory meals. The legislator succeeded in abolishing some of the more obvious aspects of compulsion against old people, but basically it was necessary for personnel to have means of compulsion at their disposal. The authorities did not realise this, partly because they did not understand the social mechanisms of old people's homes and partly because no steps were taken to create an adequate information system.

However, the effect in reality is another matter. We can identify at least three occasions when the social programme receives effects in reality which are not covered by the effect reality. It is obvious that a given programme not only has intended or expected effects but quite frequently others, not intended and possibly undesired. At the same time, the effects of a particular programme can seldom be distinguished from the general "background noises" of social life as a whole. This is particularly so because, for institutional and professional reasons, the scanning system is markedly selective in what it does or does not record. Thus, a social programme can easily have negative effects which are not intended or perhaps even noticed.

It may also happen that the clients react in a way which reinforces or sometimes dilutes the nature or magnitude of the original problem. An ambitious programme for the care of the elderly launched under official auspices may eventually lead to the undermining of family or neighbour loyalties, thereby making the problem still worse. When society declares its willingness to take over, the will of elderly people and their relatives to manage on their own is reduced. In the same way, ambitious child-care programmes possibly may have resulted in a reduced birthrate. Such changes in social behaviour are often irrevocable. In a third situation, an ambitious programme addresses a social situation after enough time has elapsed for peripheral and decisive conditions to change. This is a not uncommon state of affairs. The period of time between the discovery of a problem and the beginning of its solution (between diagnosis and therapy) is often rather long. This is particularly true in politically emotive questions such as energy policy.

These three circumstances (and others) can therefore result in the launching of a programme which actually creates new social tensions rather than solves old ones. This state of affairs can be especially clear in a situation where the public economy is strained. This can then lead to a willingness to reconsider the decision, provided the decision-maker has seen through the problem and admitted to himself the gap between a well-intentioned programme decision and the by-no-means equally satisfactory consequences.

"Society and the elderly" reveals some cases of this kind. If nothing fresh is added, the chain of thought from problems in reality to a registered effect in reality will be repeated. Ideas on problems will be stacked on top of one another, constituting a "paradigmatic" legacy, a straitjacket which will halt our imagination and powers of discovery for many years to come.

In the successive development of problem/solutions the degrees of institutional freedom are gradually reduced. The Commission on Social Care (1942-46) was able to formulate its recommendations and the state was able to accept them more or less independently of previous measures and an existing organisation. Ten years later the Commission on the Care of Elderly People was obliged to recognise the division of labour between county council and primary communities, while the already defined hierarchy of authorities and laws had a markedly restrictive effect on the scope for independent action. In 1962 the Committee on Social Policy was actually forced to adapt its investigatory logic to existing organisational and legal structures and to conduct interviews on the problems of the organisations rather than those of the elderly.

Thus the position of old people and their relatives is relegated to the background while the difficulties of the organisations come to the fore. The fact that the elderly suffer is of less consequence than the problems of the organisation. Queues for wards for long-term patients, drawing lines of demarcation for cooperation between social and medical authorities, and extensions to nursing homes and old people's homes are presented as the forces which will bring about action. The organisation and production conditions become the decisive reasons for bringing about social action.

While the "Society and the elderly" programme has gradually advanced, it has, of course, been subjected to a kind of political and administrative surveillance. But this surveillance has certain weaknesses in the information received, the analyses that can be made and the measures that can be taken. Above all, it is a kind of supervision which takes account of unsatisfied needs but hardly of wasted resources. Nor is it really constructive in the sense of leading to fresh structural technologies or systems designs.

A closer study of the various stages from the problem in reality to effects reveals that there are situations in which there is genuine uncertainly about which causal relationships and retro-actions are in fact involved. This should persuade any intelligent politician that a critical study and reconsideration is necessary.

THE DEMOCRATIC PARADOX
The matter is, however, complicated by what we may call the democratic paradox. Certain kinds of uncertainty cannot be admitted because they lead to problems of

political legitimacy. The politicians claim - and must claim - that they represent the right decision, while the scientists and analysts insist that their role is to contribute to finding what is right. Hence, serious scientific studies of the effects of a social programme can start only when there is a recognised political doubt and a serious wish for reappraisal. But in many cases this situation will only arise when systematic evaluation in institutionalised forms has revealed new knowledge, which, in turn, can only be started when the political will is there.

The current debate throughout the industrialised world on the risks and necessity of nuclear power affords a clear example of how, for political reasons, we are obliged to take a position in an assured manner on uncertain grounds and then find ourselves in a psychological field of force in which readiness to take account of new facts is minimal. Most independent judges will certainly agree that neither the hazards of nuclear power nor its necessity for economic or other reasons have so far been established. Geologists, physicists, economists and sociologists, i.e. "the experts", are sharply divided on the issue. It would not be difficult to counter every negative opinion of distinguished experts with an affirmative one of equally distinguished colleagues.

The democratic paradox declares that official evaluation must be legitimated by political volition for reconsideration. With "The society and the elderly" programme in mind, we have tested a number of situations in which legitimation of this kind would appear to be politically reasonable. Such situations, naturally, are not independent of the political climate for the individual programme. If the question is of a highly controversial nature, by reason of ideological differences, for instance, evaluation will lack legitimacy and no attention will be paid to it in any case. In cases of this kind, reconsideration can only come about by means of parliamentary political processes. Politicians alone have the absolute democratic right to challenge politically controversial decisions. But in the great majority of programmes based on common Swedish values it should prove possible to identify the uncertainty, and the evaluation should be legitimated without setting democratic values aside. (We may note that "Security for elderly people" was favoured by all the parties in the 1979 election.)

When we go through empirical material we come across two typical situations in which it is generally admitted that we have political legitimation for future evaluation and research. One of these situations arises when the programme is so "badly" prepared that the uncertainty becomes evident during the political preparation, but not so controversial as to require a precisely formulated political solution. Thus, the authorities have expressed uncertainty at the very time of the resolution, and thereby admitted that corrective measures may prove necessary. The problem may be dealt with by calling the programme "experimental", thus by definition implying the need for evaluation. However, this rarely leads to anything other than the experimental activity being made permanent in a somewhat modified form.

It is not always possible, however - for example, for reasons of justice - to conduct "experimental activities". A programme may be of such a nature that a possible reversion would seem unreasonable. Yet, the uncertainty can still be admitted if the authorities give their resolution an imprecise character (framework legislation) and leave to subordinate authorities and law courts the task of giving the programme a more precise nature and making the necessary amendments. This way of legitimating evaluations and amendments has become increasingly common during the past decade.

The other kind of uncertainty situation is the one that arises at government level when negative information on a programme reaches the government authorities with sufficient force from a public debate, the political system, independent research or the executive bodies (agencies and municipalities). In certain circumstances this may justify systematic evaluation which often takes the form of directives addressed to an official committee, or a major departmental commission of enquiry, which is instructed to ascertain whether the conditions which led to the original programme are still applicable. Usually, the committee or commission is free to determine its own "scientific" policy, while the directives on the other hand, often exclude certain types of proposed measures as unacceptable. It sometimes happens that the task is referred directly to a research institute.

This second type of uncertainty can be acknowledged only when the programme in question is more or less neutral in terms of party politics. In other cases, the problem gives rise to argument and propaganda rather than evaluation. It is also obvious that only certain types of information can be obtained in this way. In view of the rapid growth and institutionalisation of a programme the authorities cease to provide a functional feedback. Municipalities can function somewhat longer, at least if they have difficulties in implementing or financing the programme. Official discussion and party organisations (with few exceptions) are more interested in launching new programmes than scrutinising existing ones.

These two legitimated evaluation situations are found in the empirical material, though they occur rather infrequently. Their origin is to be sought in the structure of the politico-administrative system rather than any conscious scanning of genuine uncertainties.

With the aid of the diagram model discussed earlier, we can see that at least three additional types of situations of genuine uncertainty may arise because our society is complex and our commonsense understanding limited. In such situations it ought to be possible to admit uncertainty without shame and to legitimate an evaluation without political embarrassment. Only by means of a system of this kind can "changes as a result of reconsideration" be claimed to be a functional working method.

The first of these situations is concerned with the "problem reality - effect reality" part of the model. In discussions on policy and administration we generally assume that political resolutions will be religiously implemented in the form and with the general intentions laid down. In our studies of society and the elderly we have seen that this is not necessarily the case. We may assume that formal directives in the form of regulations, standards, administrative instructions, job descriptions and manuals on methods are followed only to the extent permitted by the social situation. The superintendent of an old people's home, faced with the contradictory demands of the safety of the old people and their integrity, must determine her priorities. If the legislator and the administrative management have not foreseen this, she is going to choose the one with the means she can mobilise. If she is denied police assistance, she will make do with psycho-drugs! There is always a considerable element of uncertainty in the implementation of a social programme. The political commitment alone is no guarantee that the problem will be solved.

Another kind of problem is due to the fact that the link "implementation - effect reality" consciously or unconsciously exerts influence on the same social sub-systems so that different social programmes are in reality like communicating vessels: if we raise the ambitions in one part we also influence the effects and needs in another part. There is reason to suppose, for example, that increased education as a consequence of more schools and adult education should reduce the need for consumer information. Is it possible that the debate on environmental control has reduced the need for the control itself? Such links between programmes can be difficult to locate because the administrative and political supervision is exercised sector by sector in the channels laid down by the organisation. It is not often than we come across an official study limited to an entire social system.

A third potential evaluation situation affects the entire chain from "problems in reality" to "effects in reality" and deals essentially with aims and the question whether these are formulated in relevant terms. It is obvious that the programme can contain elements and intentions which are not openly reported. But if we make allowance for this, there still remains two problems, one of which is concerned with our ability to understand a complicated social reality, and the other with our willingness to deal with it.

The more epistemologically aligned difficulties are linked to our ability to see "images" in systems of causes and effects. A Bill which has been passed or an organisation which has been established also means something in the way we are to comprehend reality. When we resolve to make a social assistance Bill cover parts of the needs of the elderly, rather than introduce a special Bill for the care of old people, we have also decided to comprehend the problem in a special reference framework. If we give the municipalities and county councils shared responsibility for the care of the old, this also means a decisive resolution on which paradigm is to govern future action.

In part, this is dependent on socio-psychological conditions within the framework of the organisation. It is well known that organisations tend to look to their security and defend their territory. But in modern society we must also use authorities as bodies to acquire information, as the instruments we need to study society. If these instruments are tendentiously bound to a particular view of society, then the highest bodies will also be half-blind. The "Society and the elderly" programme has shown that organisational structures (above all, at executive levels in municipalities and county councils) have done much to prevent the reconsideration of strategies.

The three situations mentioned are of interest if we wish to enlarge political freedom of action and scope to discontinue out-of-date measures and costs. Ultimately, this means increasing the sphere of possible new reforms. They should therefore be regarded as justifiable for evaluation and systematic analysis, which is hardly the case at present. But formal legitimation is not enough. Organisational arrangements and resources are required if reconsideration designed to establish freedom of action is to become a reality. How these should be designed is somewhat uncertain. It seems, however, that some kind of dynamic cooperation is required between the political and scientific social system.